THE CHILDREN OF
CAPTAIN GRANT

Jules Verne

Harry Grant

Alexis ✦ Nesme

SUPER GENIUS

New York

To Faustine and Nadia for their love and their (invaluable) encouragement.

Thanks to Julie, Virginie, Arnaud, Thomas, Alex, and Nico for their (uncompromising) critical gaze.

And to my dear Violette.

—Alexis Nesme

THE CHILDREN OF
CAPTAIN GRANT

Les Enfants du capitaine Grant by Jules Verne, volumes 1 to 3,
adapted by Alexis Nesme.
© Éditions Delcourt — 2009/2014
Les Enfants du Capitaine Grant de Jules Verne and related indicia are
copyright, trademark and exclusive license of Guy Delcourt Productions.
All other editorial material © 2016 by Super Genius.
All rights reserved.

Adaptation and art by Alexis Nesme
From a novel by Jules Verne
Translation by Joe Johnson
Lettering by Wilson Ramos Jr.

Groupe Delcourt
8, rue Léon Jouhaux
75010 Paris, France
http://www.editions-delcourt.fr/

Super Genius books may be purchased for business or promotional use.
For information on bulk purchases please contact Macmillan Corporate
and Premium Sales Department at (800) 221-7945 x5442.

Production – Dawn Guzzo
Production Coordinator – Jeff Whitman
Editor – C. Burrell
Associate Editor – Bethany Bryan
Jim Salicrup
Editor-in-Chief

HC ISBN: 978-1-62991-467-1
PB ISBN: 978-1-62991-466-4

Printed in China
July 2016 by Toppan Leefung Printing Limited
Jin Ju Guan Li Qu,
Da Ling Shan Town,
Dongguan, PRC
China

Distributed by Macmillan
First Super Genius Printing

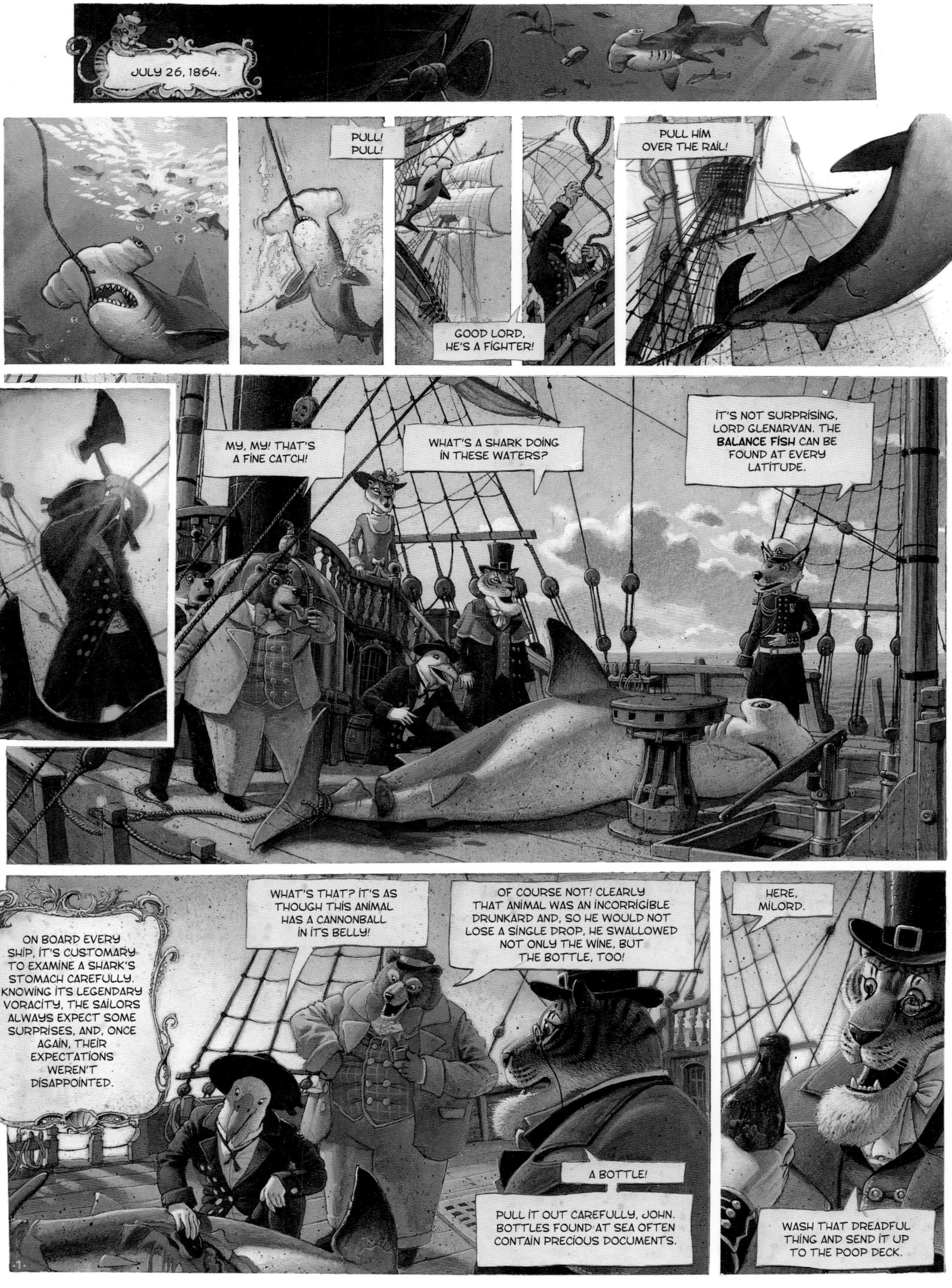
JULY 26, 1864.
PULL! PULL!
GOOD LORD, HE'S A FIGHTER!
PULL HIM OVER THE RAIL!
MY, MY! THAT'S A FINE CATCH!
WHAT'S A SHARK DOING IN THESE WATERS?
IT'S NOT SURPRISING, LORD GLENARVAN. THE **BALANCE FISH** CAN BE FOUND AT EVERY LATITUDE.
ON BOARD EVERY SHIP, IT'S CUSTOMARY TO EXAMINE A SHARK'S STOMACH CAREFULLY. KNOWING ITS LEGENDARY VORACITY, THE SAILORS ALWAYS EXPECT SOME SURPRISES, AND, ONCE AGAIN, THEIR EXPECTATIONS WEREN'T DISAPPOINTED.
WHAT'S THAT? IT'S AS THOUGH THIS ANIMAL HAS A CANNONBALL IN ITS BELLY!
OF COURSE NOT! CLEARLY THAT ANIMAL WAS AN INCORRIGIBLE DRUNKARD AND, SO HE WOULD NOT LOSE A SINGLE DROP, HE SWALLOWED NOT ONLY THE WINE, BUT THE BOTTLE, TOO!
A BOTTLE!
PULL IT OUT CAREFULLY, JOHN. BOTTLES FOUND AT SEA OFTEN CONTAIN PRECIOUS DOCUMENTS.
HERE, MILORD.
WASH THAT DREADFUL THING AND SEND IT UP TO THE POOP DECK.

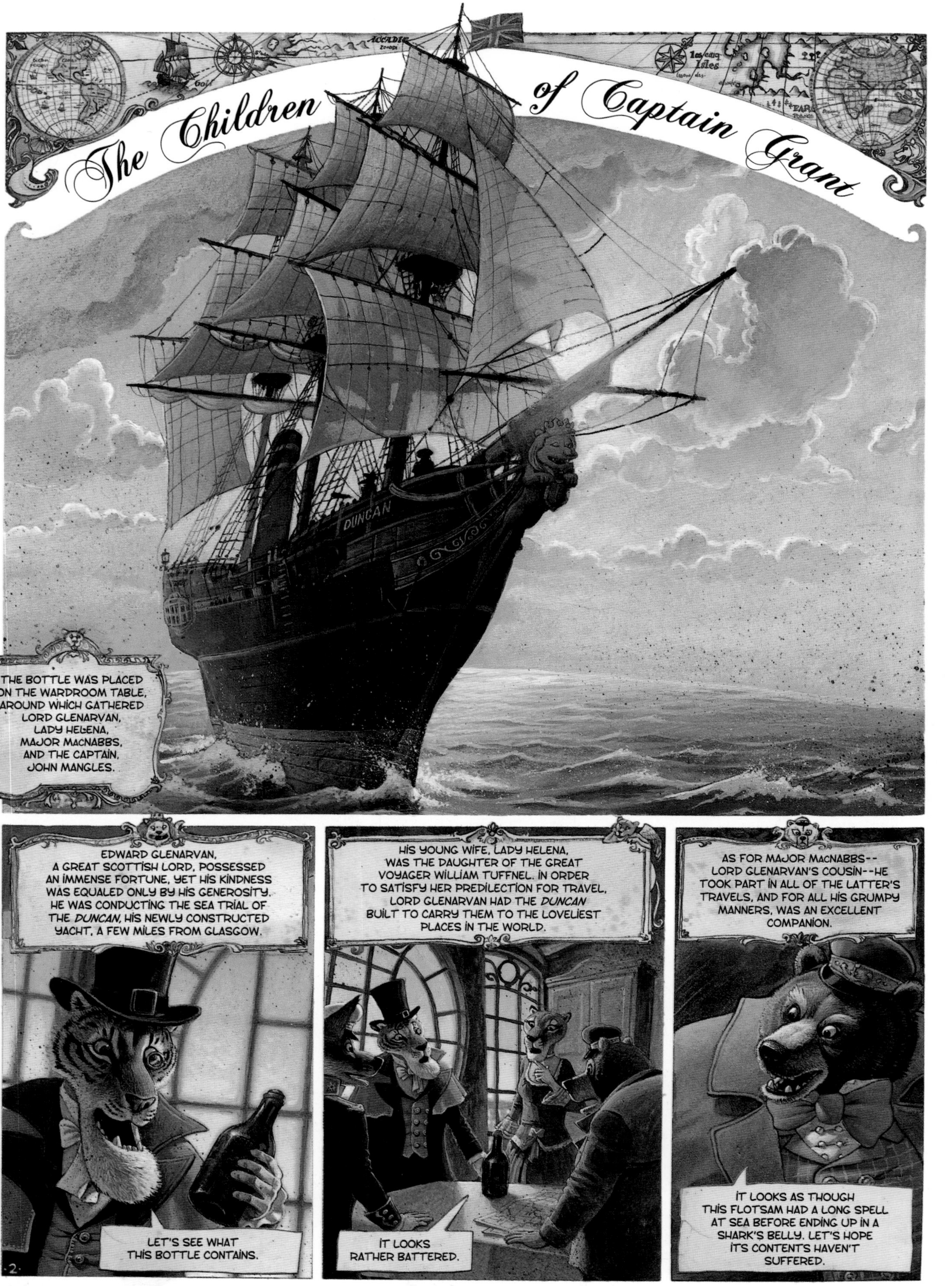
The Children of Captain Grant
DUNCAN
THE BOTTLE WAS PLACED ON THE WARDROOM TABLE, AROUND WHICH GATHERED LORD GLENARVAN, LADY HELENA, MAJOR MACNABBS, AND THE CAPTAIN, JOHN MANGLES.
EDWARD GLENARVAN, A GREAT SCOTTISH LORD, POSSESSED AN IMMENSE FORTUNE, YET HIS KINDNESS WAS EQUALED ONLY BY HIS GENEROSITY. HE WAS CONDUCTING THE SEA TRIAL OF THE *DUNCAN*, HIS NEWLY CONSTRUCTED YACHT, A FEW MILES FROM GLASGOW.
LET'S SEE WHAT THIS BOTTLE CONTAINS.
HIS YOUNG WIFE, LADY HELENA, WAS THE DAUGHTER OF THE GREAT VOYAGER WILLIAM TUFFNEL. IN ORDER TO SATISFY HER PREDILECTION FOR TRAVEL, LORD GLENARVAN HAD THE *DUNCAN* BUILT TO CARRY THEM TO THE LOVELIEST PLACES IN THE WORLD.
IT LOOKS RATHER BATTERED.
AS FOR MAJOR MACNABBS--LORD GLENARVAN'S COUSIN--HE TOOK PART IN ALL OF THE LATTER'S TRAVELS, AND FOR ALL HIS GRUMPY MANNERS, WAS AN EXCELLENT COMPANION.
IT LOOKS AS THOUGH THIS FLOTSAM HAD A LONG SPELL AT SEA BEFORE ENDING UP IN A SHARK'S BELLY. LET'S HOPE ITS CONTENTS HAVEN'T SUFFERED.

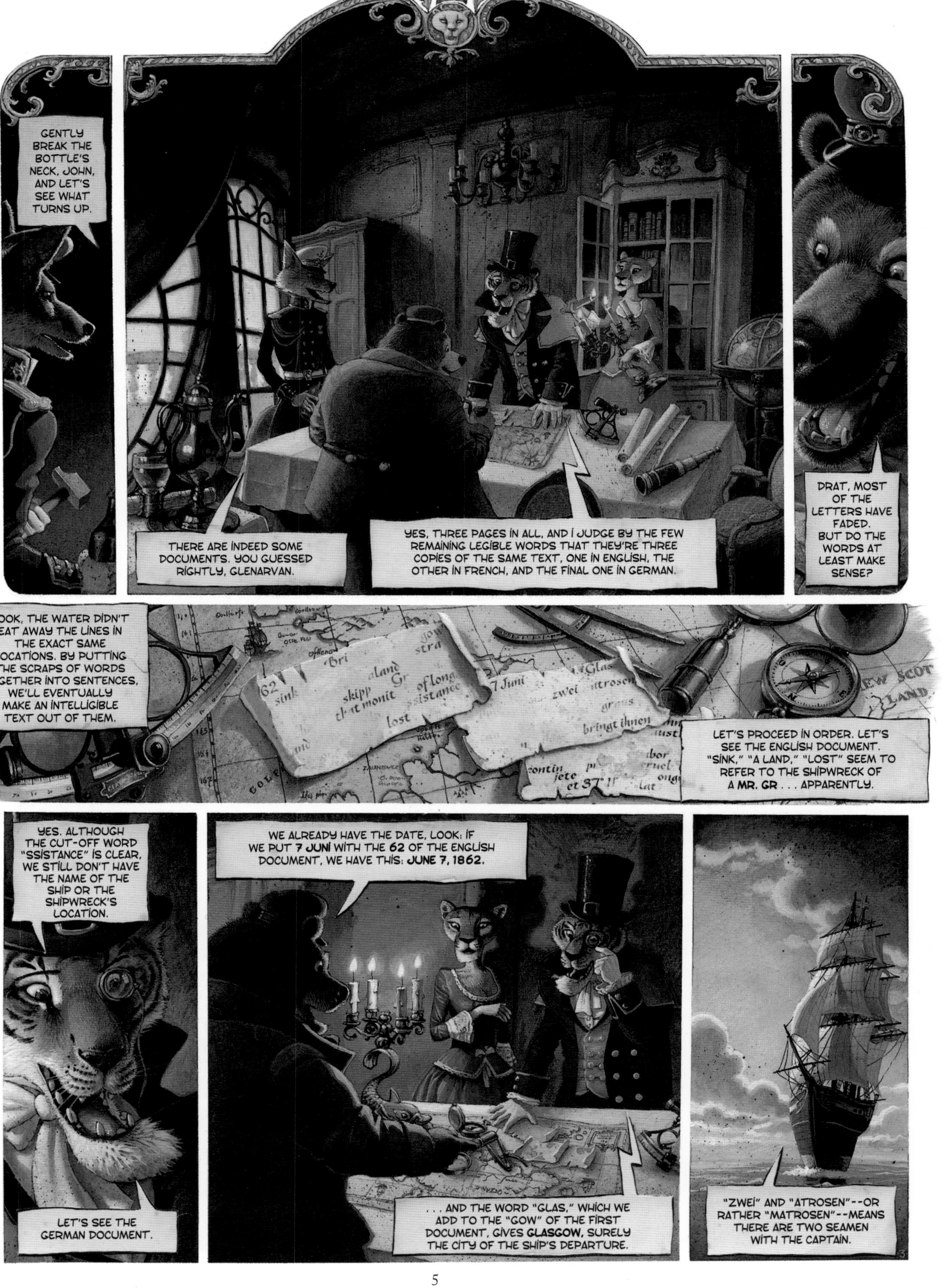
GENTLY BREAK THE BOTTLE'S NECK, JOHN, AND LET'S SEE WHAT TURNS UP.
THERE ARE INDEED SOME DOCUMENTS. YOU GUESSED RIGHTLY, GLENARVAN.
YES, THREE PAGES IN ALL, AND I JUDGE BY THE FEW REMAINING LEGIBLE WORDS THAT THEY'RE THREE COPIES OF THE SAME TEXT, ONE IN ENGLISH, THE OTHER IN FRENCH, AND THE FINAL ONE IN GERMAN.
DRAT, MOST OF THE LETTERS HAVE FADED. BUT DO THE WORDS AT LEAST MAKE SENSE?
LOOK, THE WATER DIDN'T EAT AWAY THE LINES IN THE EXACT SAME LOCATIONS. BY PUTTING THE SCRAPS OF WORDS TOGETHER INTO SENTENCES, WE'LL EVENTUALLY MAKE AN INTELLIGIBLE TEXT OUT OF THEM.
62 sink Bri aland Gr skipp that monit of long ssistance lost gow stra
7 Juni Glas zwei atrosen graus bringt ihnen
contin pr jete et 37° 11 cruel ongi lat
LET'S PROCEED IN ORDER. LET'S SEE THE ENGLISH DOCUMENT. "SINK," "A LAND," "LOST" SEEM TO REFER TO THE SHIPWRECK OF A **MR. GR** . . . APPARENTLY.
YES. ALTHOUGH THE CUT-OFF WORD "SSISTANCE" IS CLEAR, WE STILL DON'T HAVE THE NAME OF THE SHIP OR THE SHIPWRECK'S LOCATION.
LET'S SEE THE GERMAN DOCUMENT.
WE ALREADY HAVE THE DATE, LOOK: IF WE PUT **7 JUNI** WITH THE **62** OF THE ENGLISH DOCUMENT, WE HAVE THIS: **JUNE 7, 1862.**
. . . AND THE WORD "GLAS," WHICH WE ADD TO THE "GOW" OF THE FIRST DOCUMENT, GIVES **GLASGOW**, SURELY THE CITY OF THE SHIP'S DEPARTURE.
"ZWEI" AND "ATROSEN"--OR RATHER "MATROSEN"--MEANS THERE ARE TWO SEAMEN WITH THE CAPTAIN.

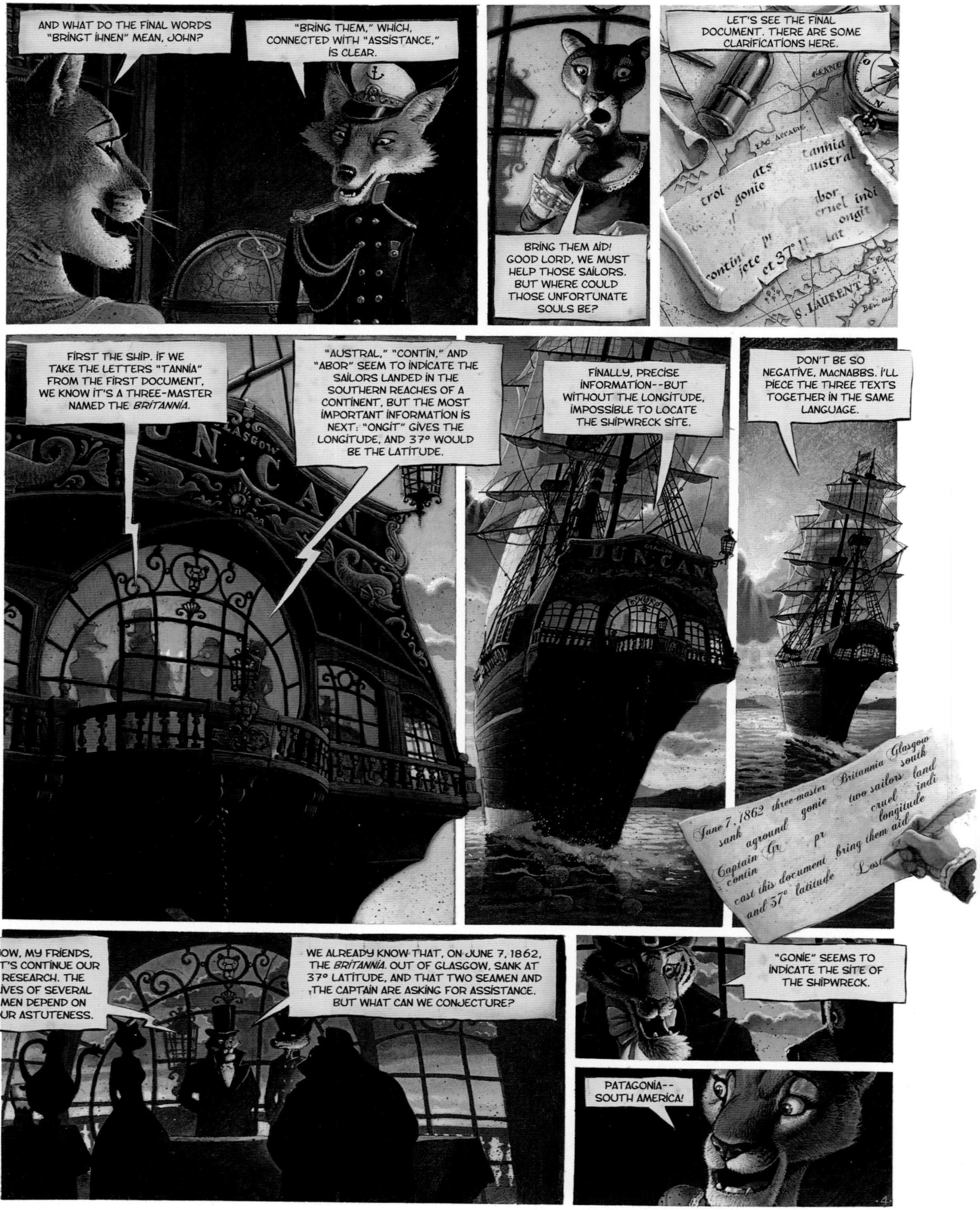

AND WHAT DO THE FINAL WORDS "BRINGT IHNEN" MEAN, JOHN?
"BRING THEM," WHICH, CONNECTED WITH "ASSISTANCE," IS CLEAR.
BRING THEM AID! GOOD LORD, WE MUST HELP THOSE SAILORS. BUT WHERE COULD THOSE UNFORTUNATE SOULS BE?
LET'S SEE THE FINAL DOCUMENT. THERE ARE SOME CLARIFICATIONS HERE.
troi ats tannia
gonie austral
abor
cruel indi
ongit
contin pr
jete et 37° lat
S. LAURENT
FIRST THE SHIP. IF WE TAKE THE LETTERS "TANNIA" FROM THE FIRST DOCUMENT, WE KNOW IT'S A THREE-MASTER NAMED THE *BRITANNIA*.
"AUSTRAL," "CONTIN," AND "ABOR" SEEM TO INDICATE THE SAILORS LANDED IN THE SOUTHERN REACHES OF A CONTINENT, BUT THE MOST IMPORTANT INFORMATION IS NEXT: "ONGIT" GIVES THE LONGITUDE, AND 37° WOULD BE THE LATITUDE.
FINALLY, PRECISE INFORMATION--BUT WITHOUT THE LONGITUDE, IMPOSSIBLE TO LOCATE THE SHIPWRECK SITE.
DON'T BE SO NEGATIVE, MACNABBS. I'LL PIECE THE THREE TEXTS TOGETHER IN THE SAME LANGUAGE.
DUNCAN
June 7, 1862 three-master Britannia Glasgow
sank aground gonie two sailors south
Captain Gr contin pr cruel land
cast this document bring them aid longitude indi
and 37° latitude Lost
NOW, MY FRIENDS, LET'S CONTINUE OUR RESEARCH. THE LIVES OF SEVERAL MEN DEPEND ON OUR ASTUTENESS.
WE ALREADY KNOW THAT, ON JUNE 7, 1862, THE *BRITANNIA*, OUT OF GLASGOW, SANK AT 37° LATITUDE, AND THAT TWO SEAMEN AND THE CAPTAIN ARE ASKING FOR ASSISTANCE. BUT WHAT CAN WE CONJECTURE?
"GONIE" SEEMS TO INDICATE THE SITE OF THE SHIPWRECK.
PATAGONIA-- SOUTH AMERICA!

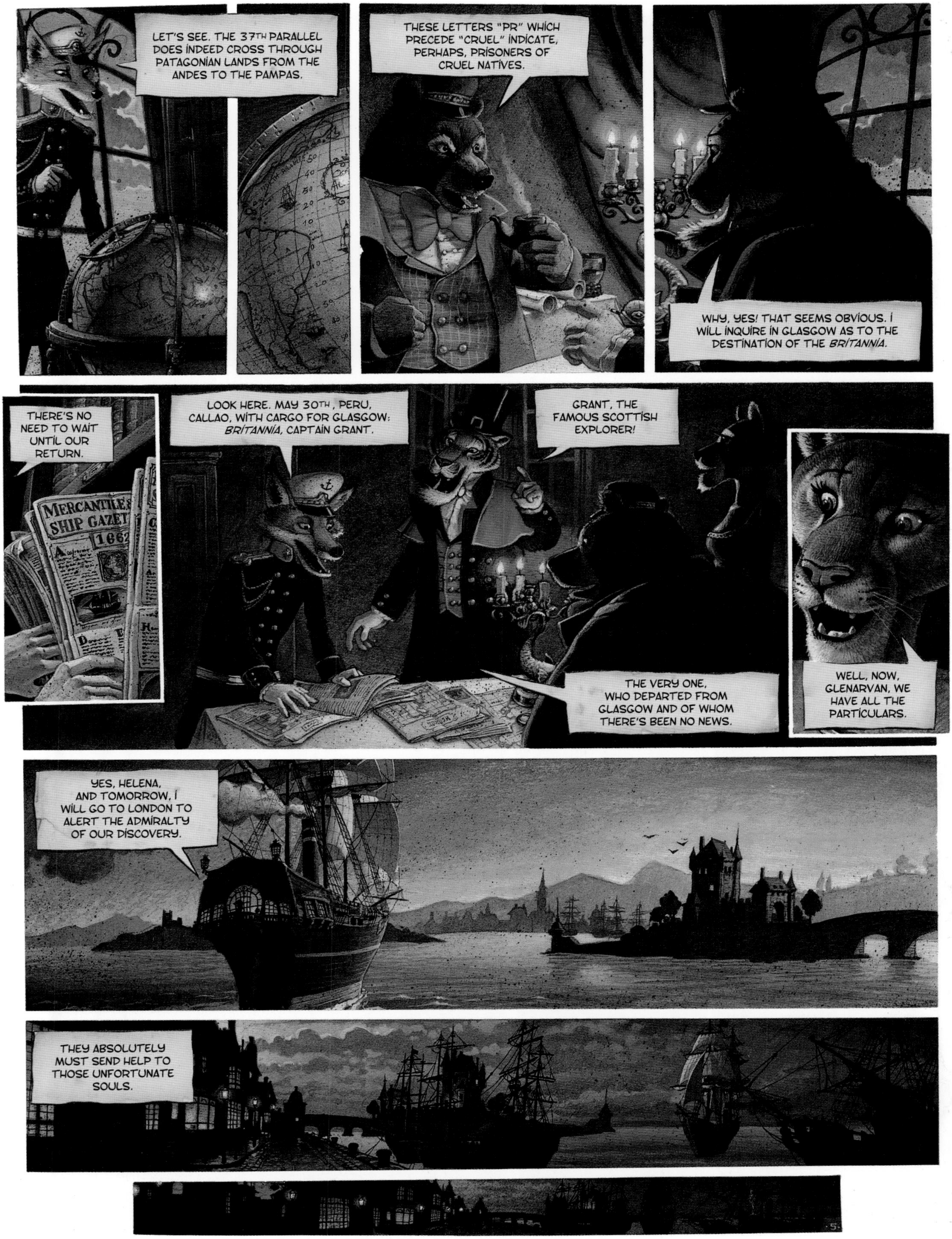
LET'S SEE. THE 37TH PARALLEL DOES INDEED CROSS THROUGH PATAGONIAN LANDS FROM THE ANDES TO THE PAMPAS.
THESE LETTERS "PR" WHICH PRECEDE "CRUEL" INDICATE, PERHAPS, PRISONERS OF CRUEL NATIVES.
WHY, YES! THAT SEEMS OBVIOUS. I WILL INQUIRE IN GLASGOW AS TO THE DESTINATION OF THE *BRITANNIA*.
THERE'S NO NEED TO WAIT UNTIL OUR RETURN.
MERCANTILE SHIP GAZET
1862
LOOK HERE. MAY 30TH, PERU, CALLAO, WITH CARGO FOR GLASGOW: *BRITANNIA*, CAPTAIN GRANT.
GRANT, THE FAMOUS SCOTTISH EXPLORER!
THE VERY ONE, WHO DEPARTED FROM GLASGOW AND OF WHOM THERE'S BEEN NO NEWS.
WELL, NOW, GLENARVAN, WE HAVE ALL THE PARTICULARS.
YES, HELENA, AND TOMORROW, I WILL GO TO LONDON TO ALERT THE ADMIRALTY OF OUR DISCOVERY.
THEY ABSOLUTELY MUST SEND HELP TO THOSE UNFORTUNATE SOULS.

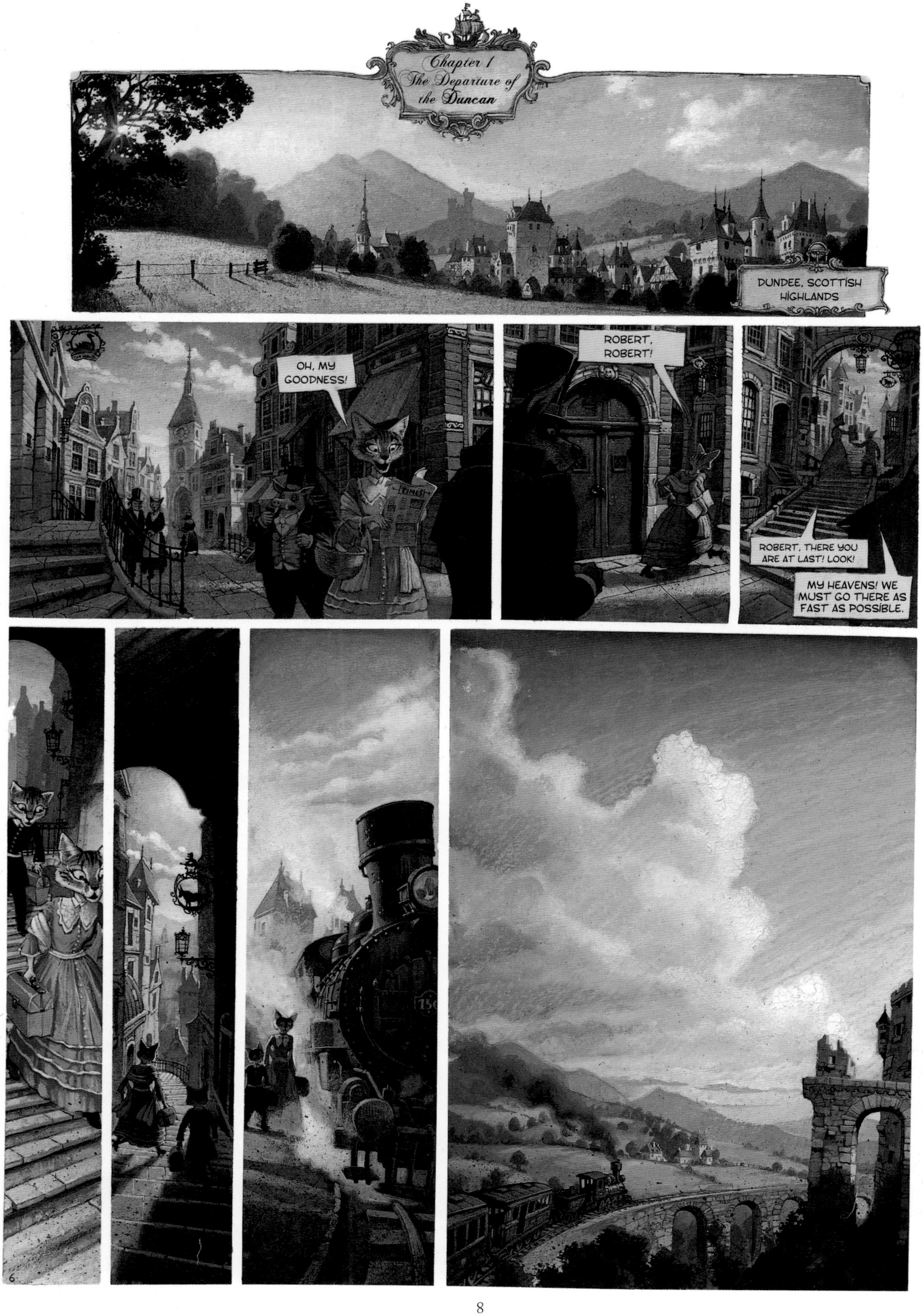
Chapter 1
The Departure of the Duncan
DUNDEE, SCOTTISH HIGHLANDS
OH, MY GOODNESS!
ROBERT, ROBERT!
ROBERT, THERE YOU ARE AT LAST! LOOK!
MY HEAVENS! WE MUST GO THERE AS FAST AS POSSIBLE.

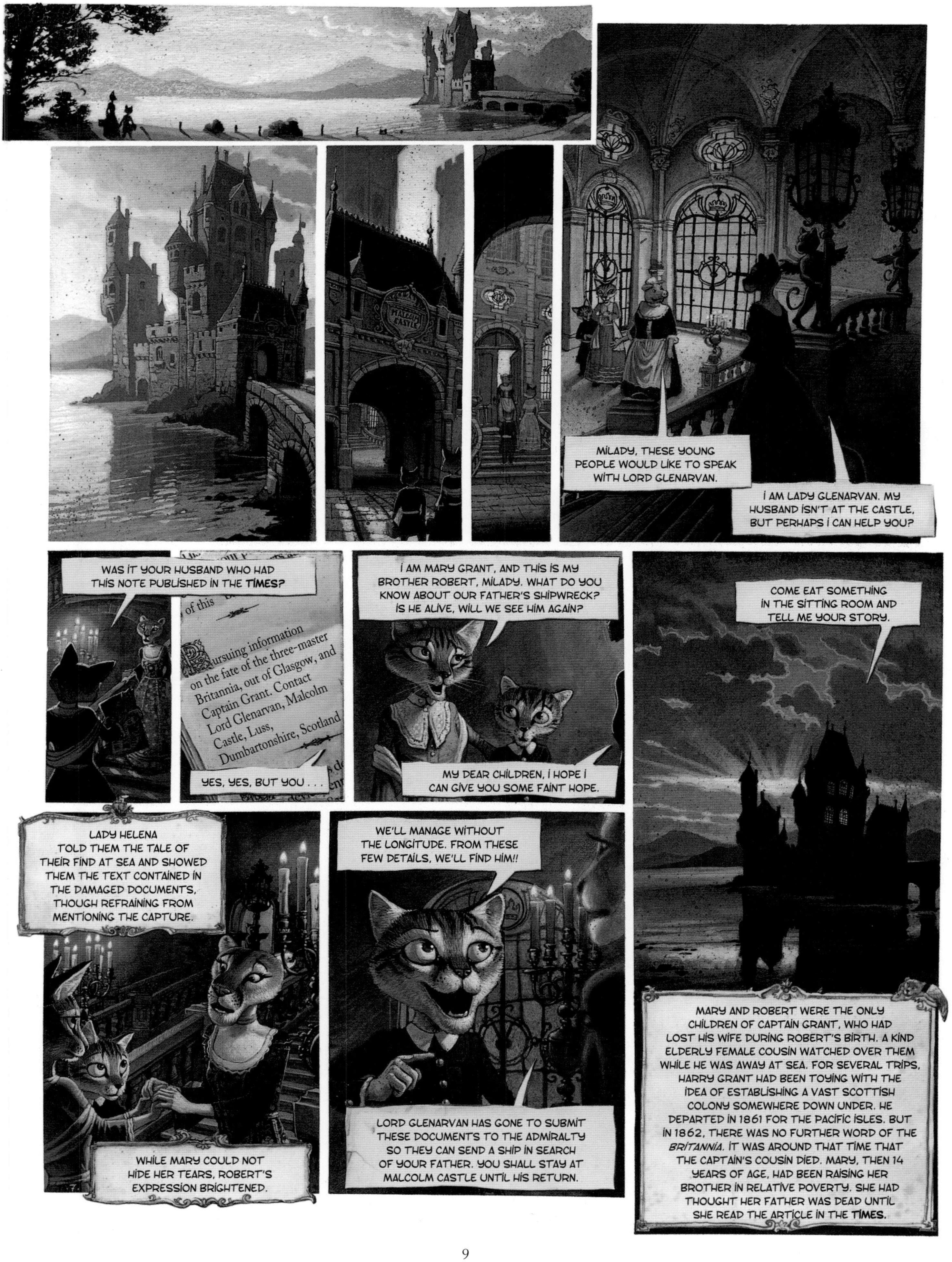
MALCOLM CASTLE
MILADY, THESE YOUNG PEOPLE WOULD LIKE TO SPEAK WITH LORD GLENARVAN.
I AM LADY GLENARVAN. MY HUSBAND ISN'T AT THE CASTLE, BUT PERHAPS I CAN HELP YOU?
WAS IT YOUR HUSBAND WHO HAD THIS NOTE PUBLISHED IN THE TIMES?
Pursuing information on the fate of the three-master Britannia, out of Glasgow, and Captain Grant. Contact Lord Glenarvan, Malcolm Castle, Luss, Dumbartonshire, Scotland
YES, YES, BUT YOU . . .
I AM MARY GRANT, AND THIS IS MY BROTHER ROBERT, MILADY. WHAT DO YOU KNOW ABOUT OUR FATHER'S SHIPWRECK? IS HE ALIVE, WILL WE SEE HIM AGAIN?
MY DEAR CHILDREN, I HOPE I CAN GIVE YOU SOME FAINT HOPE.
COME EAT SOMETHING IN THE SITTING ROOM AND TELL ME YOUR STORY.
LADY HELENA TOLD THEM THE TALE OF THEIR FIND AT SEA AND SHOWED THEM THE TEXT CONTAINED IN THE DAMAGED DOCUMENTS, THOUGH REFRAINING FROM MENTIONING THE CAPTURE.
WHILE MARY COULD NOT HIDE HER TEARS, ROBERT'S EXPRESSION BRIGHTENED.
WE'LL MANAGE WITHOUT THE LONGITUDE. FROM THESE FEW DETAILS, WE'LL FIND HIM!!
LORD GLENARVAN HAS GONE TO SUBMIT THESE DOCUMENTS TO THE ADMIRALTY SO THEY CAN SEND A SHIP IN SEARCH OF YOUR FATHER. YOU SHALL STAY AT MALCOLM CASTLE UNTIL HIS RETURN.
MARY AND ROBERT WERE THE ONLY CHILDREN OF CAPTAIN GRANT, WHO HAD LOST HIS WIFE DURING ROBERT'S BIRTH. A KIND ELDERLY FEMALE COUSIN WATCHED OVER THEM WHILE HE WAS AWAY AT SEA. FOR SEVERAL TRIPS, HARRY GRANT HAD BEEN TOYING WITH THE IDEA OF ESTABLISHING A VAST SCOTTISH COLONY SOMEWHERE DOWN UNDER. HE DEPARTED IN 1861 FOR THE PACIFIC ISLES. BUT IN 1862, THERE WAS NO FURTHER WORD OF THE BRITANNIA. IT WAS AROUND THAT TIME THAT THE CAPTAIN'S COUSIN DIED. MARY, THEN 14 YEARS OF AGE, HAD BEEN RAISING HER BROTHER IN RELATIVE POVERTY. SHE HAD THOUGHT HER FATHER WAS DEAD UNTIL SHE READ THE ARTICLE IN THE TIMES.

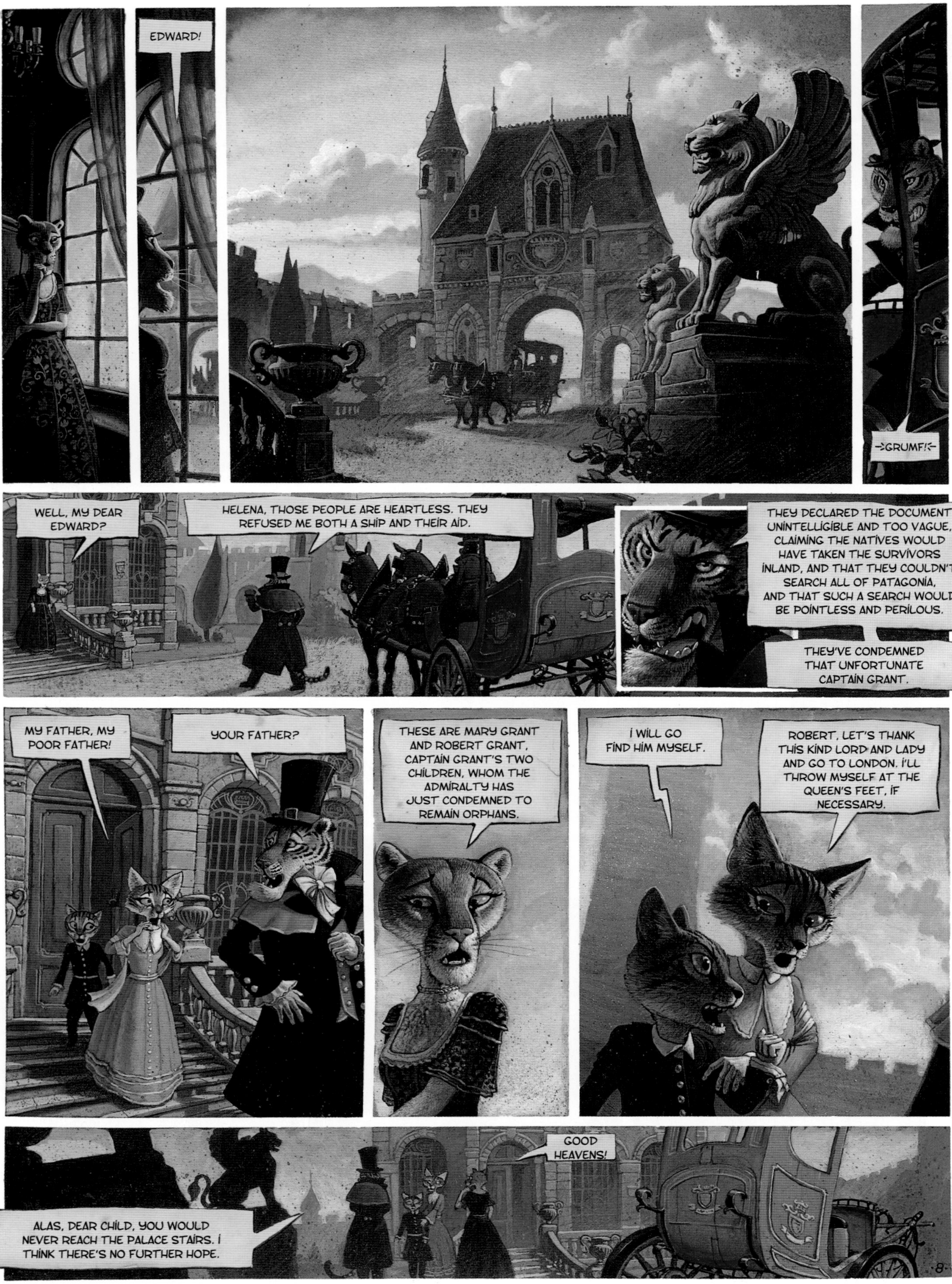
EDWARD!
-GRUMF!-
WELL, MY DEAR EDWARD?
HELENA, THOSE PEOPLE ARE HEARTLESS. THEY REFUSED ME BOTH A SHIP AND THEIR AID.
THEY DECLARED THE DOCUMENT UNINTELLIGIBLE AND TOO VAGUE, CLAIMING THE NATIVES WOULD HAVE TAKEN THE SURVIVORS INLAND, AND THAT THEY COULDN'T SEARCH ALL OF PATAGONIA, AND THAT SUCH A SEARCH WOULD BE POINTLESS AND PERILOUS.
THEY'VE CONDEMNED THAT UNFORTUNATE CAPTAIN GRANT.
MY FATHER, MY POOR FATHER!
YOUR FATHER?
THESE ARE MARY GRANT AND ROBERT GRANT, CAPTAIN GRANT'S TWO CHILDREN, WHOM THE ADMIRALTY HAS JUST CONDEMNED TO REMAIN ORPHANS.
I WILL GO FIND HIM MYSELF.
ROBERT, LET'S THANK THIS KIND LORD AND LADY AND GO TO LONDON. I'LL THROW MYSELF AT THE QUEEN'S FEET, IF NECESSARY.
GOOD HEAVENS!
ALAS, DEAR CHILD, YOU WOULD NEVER REACH THE PALACE STAIRS. I THINK THERE'S NO FURTHER HOPE.
8.

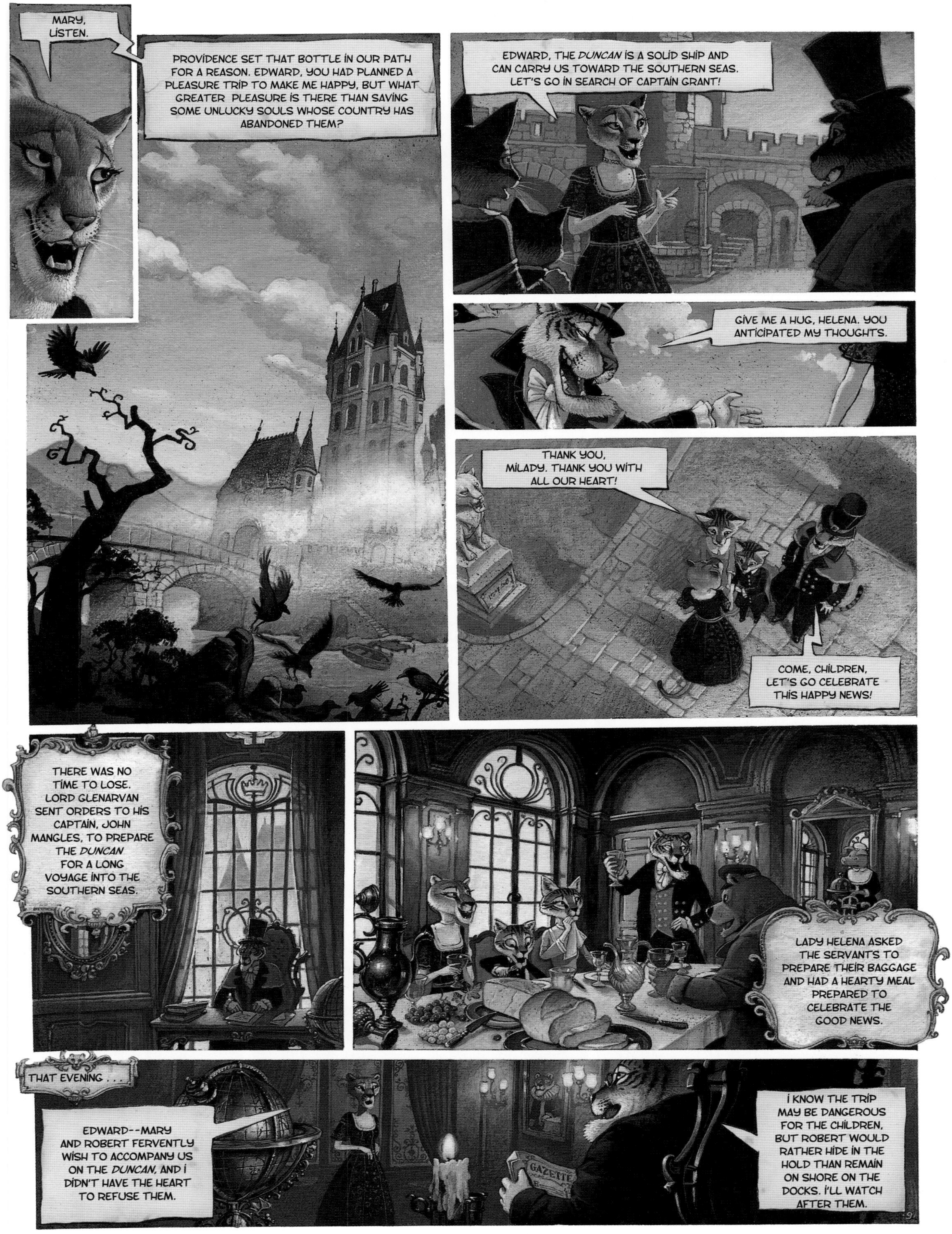
MARY, LISTEN.
PROVIDENCE SET THAT BOTTLE IN OUR PATH FOR A REASON. EDWARD, YOU HAD PLANNED A PLEASURE TRIP TO MAKE ME HAPPY, BUT WHAT GREATER PLEASURE IS THERE THAN SAVING SOME UNLUCKY SOULS WHOSE COUNTRY HAS ABANDONED THEM?
EDWARD, THE *DUNCAN* IS A SOLID SHIP AND CAN CARRY US TOWARD THE SOUTHERN SEAS. LET'S GO IN SEARCH OF CAPTAIN GRANT!
GIVE ME A HUG, HELENA. YOU ANTICIPATED MY THOUGHTS.
THANK YOU, MILADY. THANK YOU WITH ALL OUR HEART!
COME, CHILDREN, LET'S GO CELEBRATE THIS HAPPY NEWS!
THERE WAS NO TIME TO LOSE. LORD GLENARVAN SENT ORDERS TO HIS CAPTAIN, JOHN MANGLES, TO PREPARE THE *DUNCAN* FOR A LONG VOYAGE INTO THE SOUTHERN SEAS.
LADY HELENA ASKED THE SERVANTS TO PREPARE THEIR BAGGAGE AND HAD A HEARTY MEAL PREPARED TO CELEBRATE THE GOOD NEWS.
THAT EVENING . . .
EDWARD--MARY AND ROBERT FERVENTLY WISH TO ACCOMPANY US ON THE *DUNCAN*, AND I DIDN'T HAVE THE HEART TO REFUSE THEM.
GAZETTE
I KNOW THE TRIP MAY BE DANGEROUS FOR THE CHILDREN, BUT ROBERT WOULD RATHER HIDE IN THE HOLD THAN REMAIN ON SHORE ON THE DOCKS. I'LL WATCH AFTER THEM.

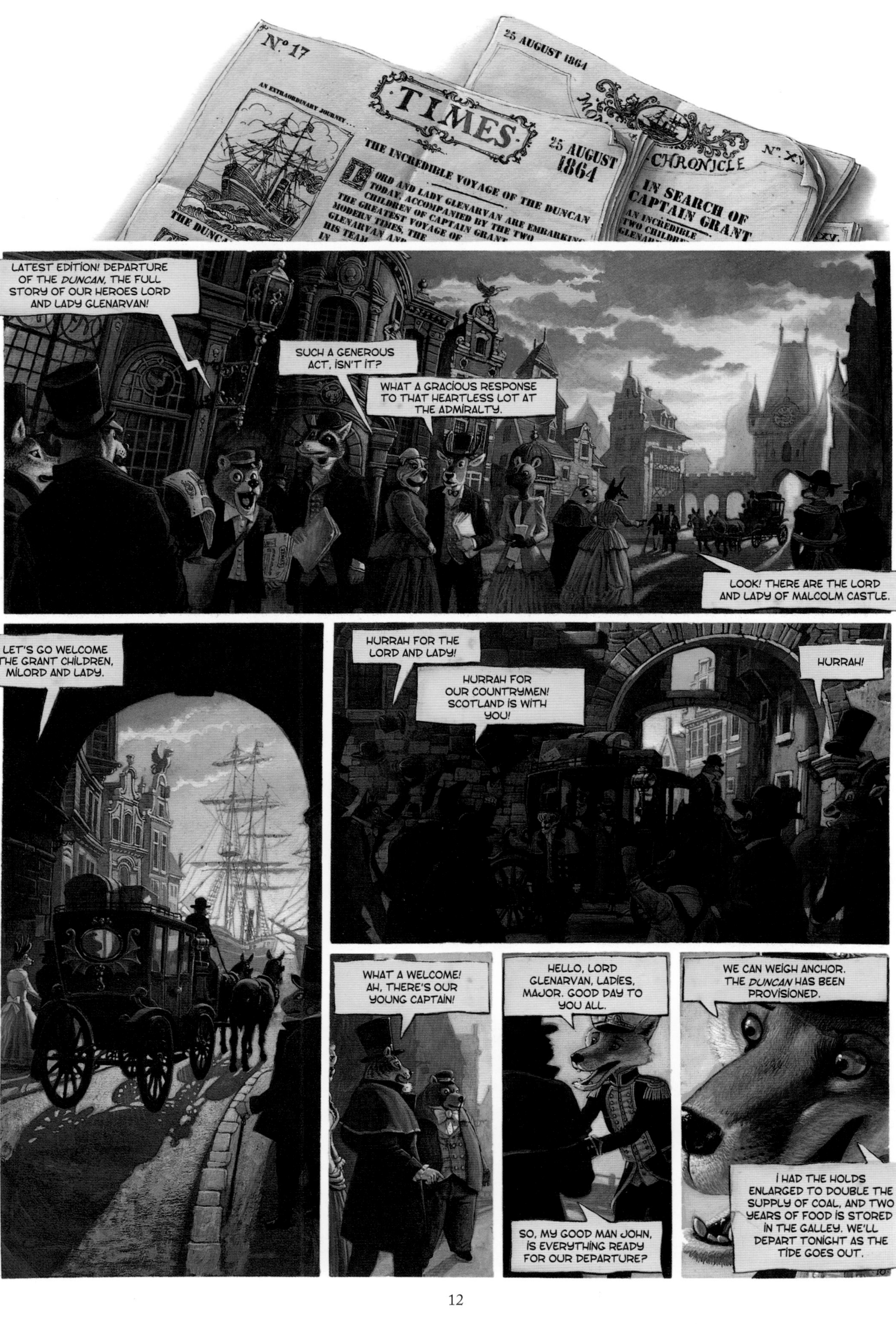
N° 17
25 AUGUST 1864
AN EXTRAORDINARY JOURNEY...
TIMES
25 AUGUST 1864
THE INCREDIBLE VOYAGE OF THE DUNCAN
CHRONICLE
IN SEARCH OF CAPTAIN GRANT
LATEST EDITION! DEPARTURE OF THE *DUNCAN*, THE FULL STORY OF OUR HEROES LORD AND LADY GLENARVAN!
SUCH A GENEROUS ACT, ISN'T IT?
WHAT A GRACIOUS RESPONSE TO THAT HEARTLESS LOT AT THE ADMIRALTY.
LOOK! THERE ARE THE LORD AND LADY OF MALCOLM CASTLE.
LET'S GO WELCOME THE GRANT CHILDREN, MILORD AND LADY.
HURRAH FOR THE LORD AND LADY!
HURRAH FOR OUR COUNTRYMEN! SCOTLAND IS WITH YOU!
HURRAH!
WHAT A WELCOME! AH, THERE'S OUR YOUNG CAPTAIN!
HELLO, LORD GLENARVAN, LADIES, MAJOR. GOOD DAY TO YOU ALL.
SO, MY GOOD MAN JOHN, IS EVERYTHING READY FOR OUR DEPARTURE?
WE CAN WEIGH ANCHOR. THE *DUNCAN* HAS BEEN PROVISIONED.
I HAD THE HOLDS ENLARGED TO DOUBLE THE SUPPLY OF COAL, AND TWO YEARS OF FOOD IS STORED IN THE GALLEY. WE'LL DEPART TONIGHT AS THE TIDE GOES OUT.

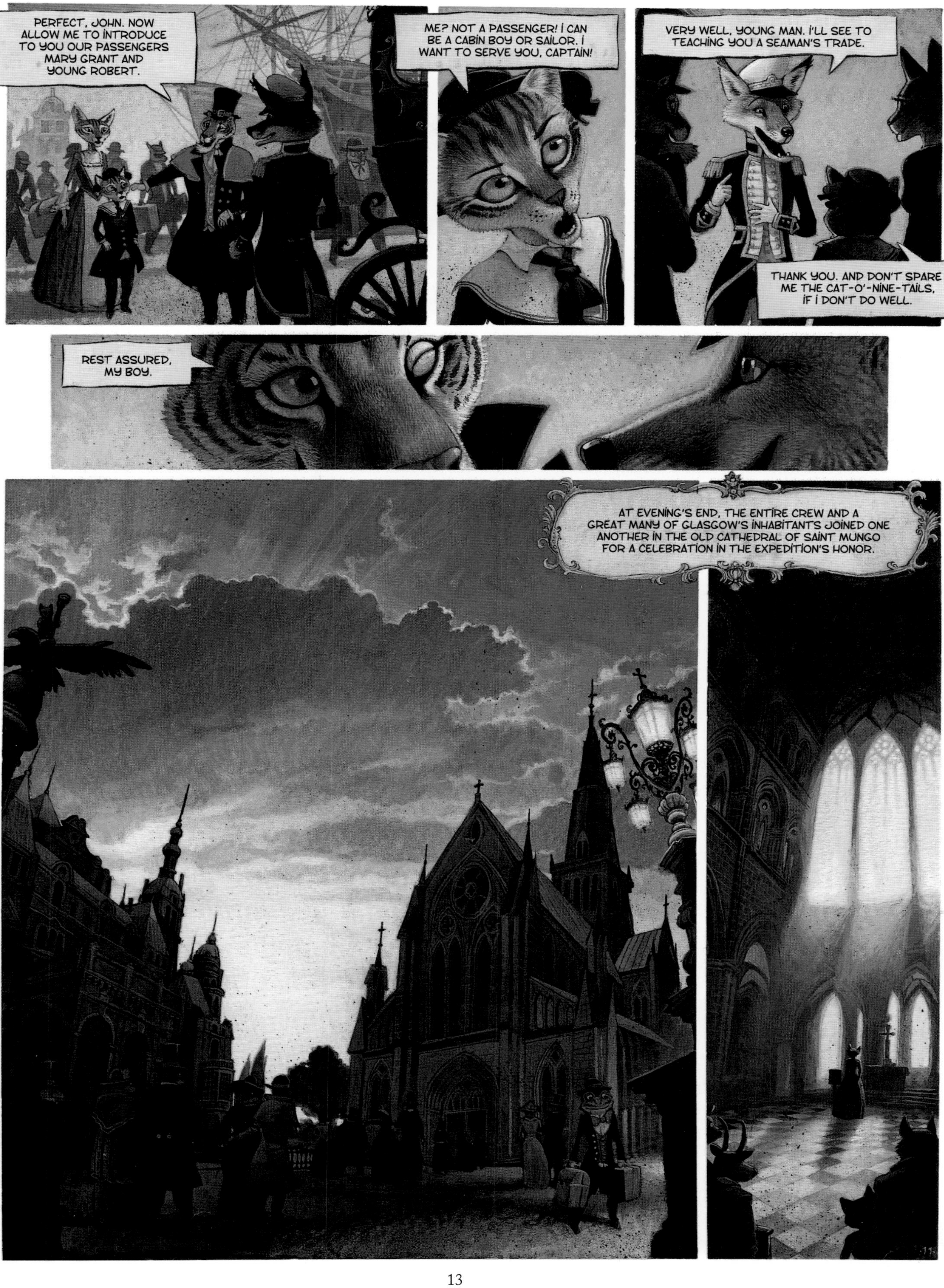
PERFECT, JOHN. NOW ALLOW ME TO INTRODUCE TO YOU OUR PASSENGERS MARY GRANT AND YOUNG ROBERT.
ME? NOT A PASSENGER! I CAN BE A CABIN BOY OR SAILOR. I WANT TO SERVE YOU, CAPTAIN!
VERY WELL, YOUNG MAN. I'LL SEE TO TEACHING YOU A SEAMAN'S TRADE.
THANK YOU. AND DON'T SPARE ME THE CAT-O'-NINE-TAILS, IF I DON'T DO WELL.
REST ASSURED, MY BOY.
AT EVENING'S END, THE ENTIRE CREW AND A GREAT MANY OF GLASGOW'S INHABITANTS JOINED ONE ANOTHER IN THE OLD CATHEDRAL OF SAINT MUNGO FOR A CELEBRATION IN THE EXPEDITION'S HONOR.

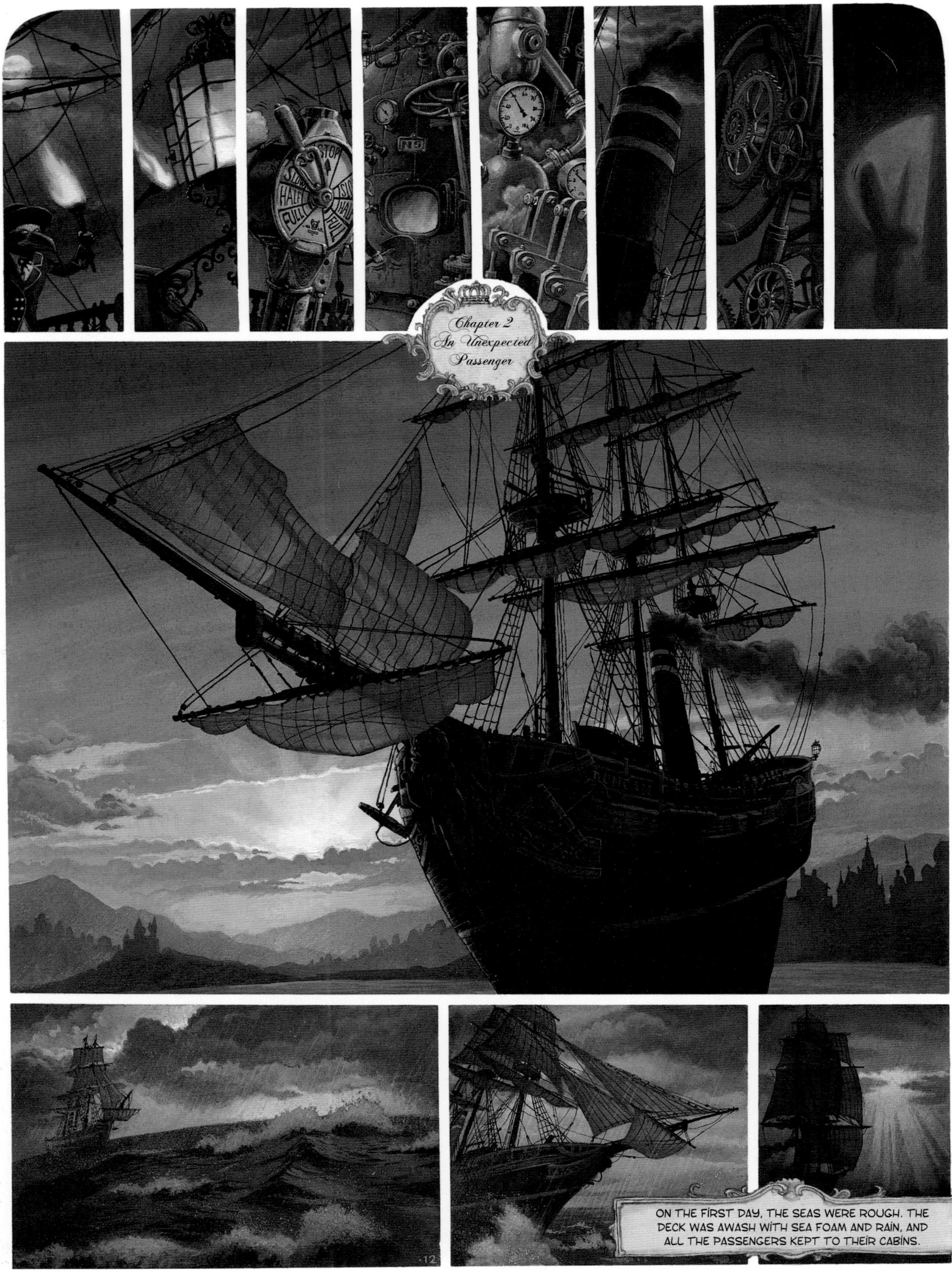
STOP
HALF
FULL
STOP
HALF
FULL
Chapter 2
An Unexpected
Passenger
ON THE FIRST DAY, THE SEAS WERE ROUGH. THE DECK WAS AWASH WITH SEA FOAM AND RAIN, AND ALL THE PASSENGERS KEPT TO THEIR CABINS.

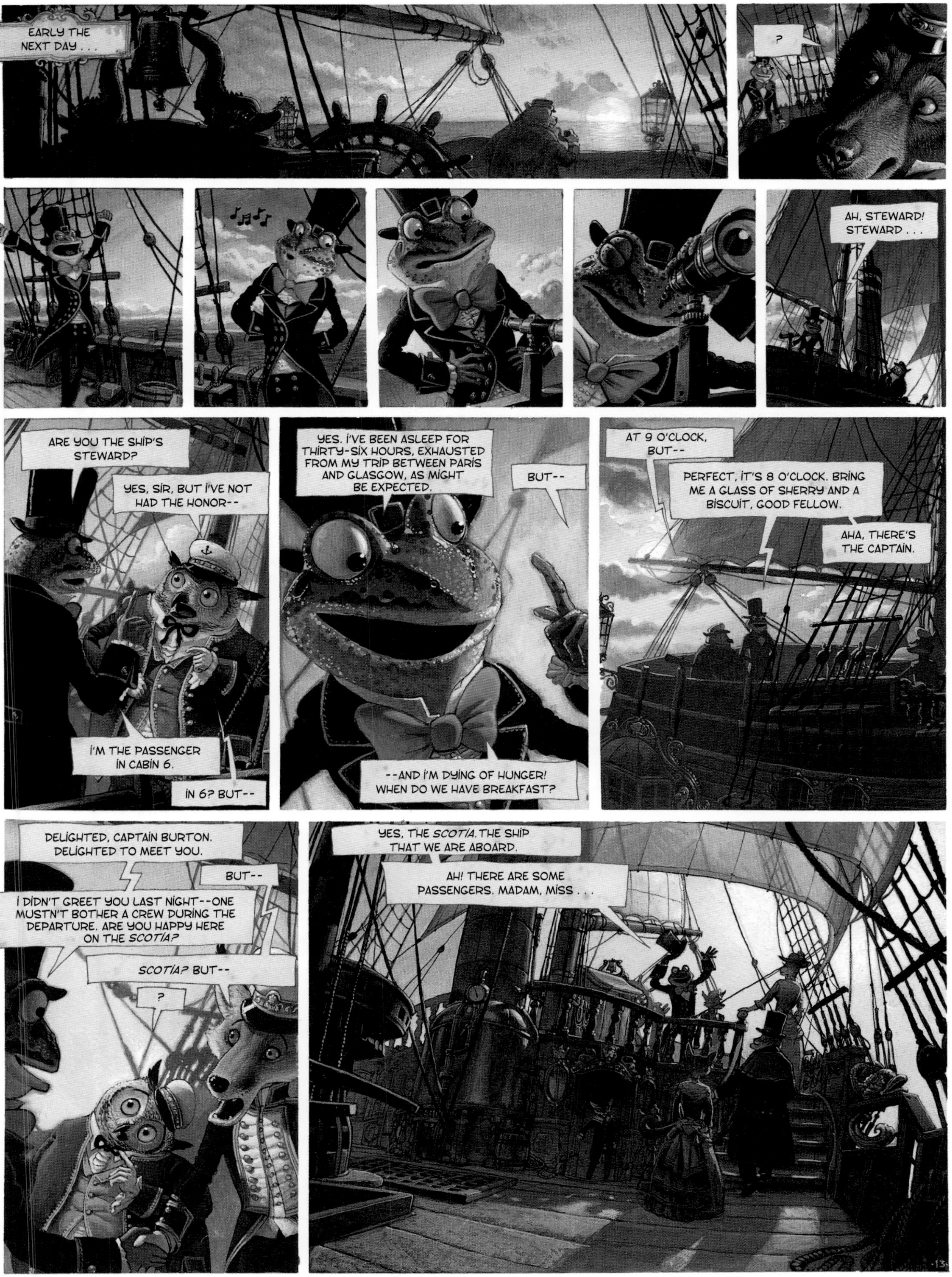

EARLY THE NEXT DAY . . .
?
AH, STEWARD! STEWARD . . .
ARE YOU THE SHIP'S STEWARD?
YES, SIR, BUT I'VE NOT HAD THE HONOR--
I'M THE PASSENGER IN CABIN 6.
IN 6? BUT--
YES. I'VE BEEN ASLEEP FOR THIRTY-SIX HOURS, EXHAUSTED FROM MY TRIP BETWEEN PARIS AND GLASGOW, AS MIGHT BE EXPECTED.
BUT--
--AND I'M DYING OF HUNGER! WHEN DO WE HAVE BREAKFAST?
AT 9 O'CLOCK, BUT--
PERFECT, IT'S 8 O'CLOCK. BRING ME A GLASS OF SHERRY AND A BISCUIT, GOOD FELLOW.
AHA, THERE'S THE CAPTAIN.
DELIGHTED, CAPTAIN BURTON. DELIGHTED TO MEET YOU.
BUT--
I DIDN'T GREET YOU LAST NIGHT--ONE MUSTN'T BOTHER A CREW DURING THE DEPARTURE. ARE YOU HAPPY HERE ON THE *SCOTIA*?
SCOTIA? BUT--
?
YES, THE *SCOTIA*. THE SHIP THAT WE ARE ABOARD.
AH! THERE ARE SOME PASSENGERS. MADAM, MISS . . .
13

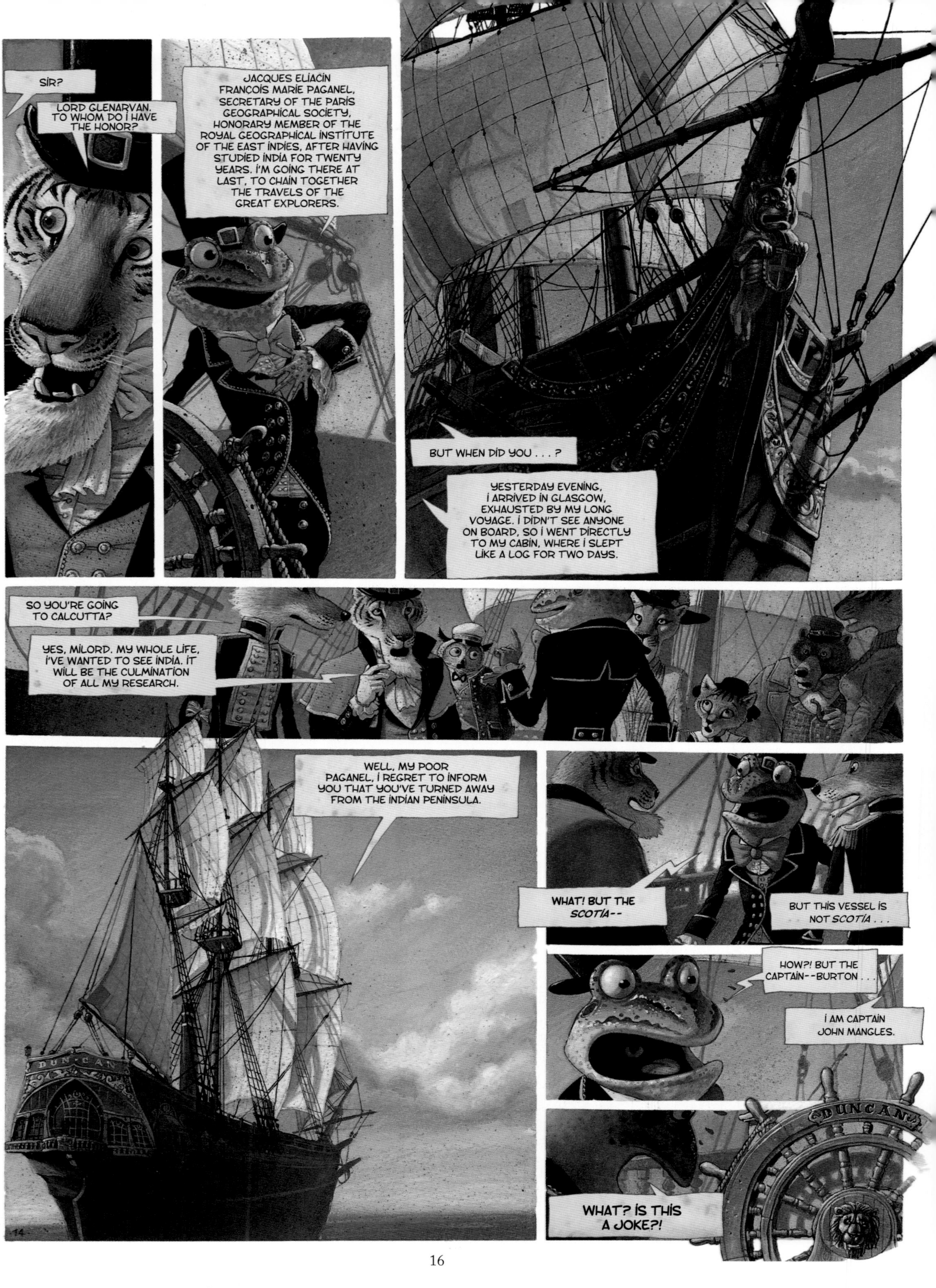
SIR?
LORD GLENARVAN. TO WHOM DO I HAVE THE HONOR?
JACQUES ELIACIN FRANCOIS MARIE PAGANEL, SECRETARY OF THE PARIS GEOGRAPHICAL SOCIETY, HONORARY MEMBER OF THE ROYAL GEOGRAPHICAL INSTITUTE OF THE EAST INDIES, AFTER HAVING STUDIED INDIA FOR TWENTY YEARS. I'M GOING THERE AT LAST, TO CHAIN TOGETHER THE TRAVELS OF THE GREAT EXPLORERS.
BUT WHEN DID YOU . . . ?
YESTERDAY EVENING, I ARRIVED IN GLASGOW, EXHAUSTED BY MY LONG VOYAGE. I DIDN'T SEE ANYONE ON BOARD, SO I WENT DIRECTLY TO MY CABIN, WHERE I SLEPT LIKE A LOG FOR TWO DAYS.
SO YOU'RE GOING TO CALCUTTA?
YES, MILORD. MY WHOLE LIFE, I'VE WANTED TO SEE INDIA. IT WILL BE THE CULMINATION OF ALL MY RESEARCH.
WELL, MY POOR PAGANEL, I REGRET TO INFORM YOU THAT YOU'VE TURNED AWAY FROM THE INDIAN PENINSULA.
DUNCAN
WHAT! BUT THE *SCOTIA*--
BUT THIS VESSEL IS NOT *SCOTIA* . . .
HOW?! BUT THE CAPTAIN--BURTON . . .
I AM CAPTAIN JOHN MANGLES.
DUNCAN
WHAT? IS THIS A JOKE?!

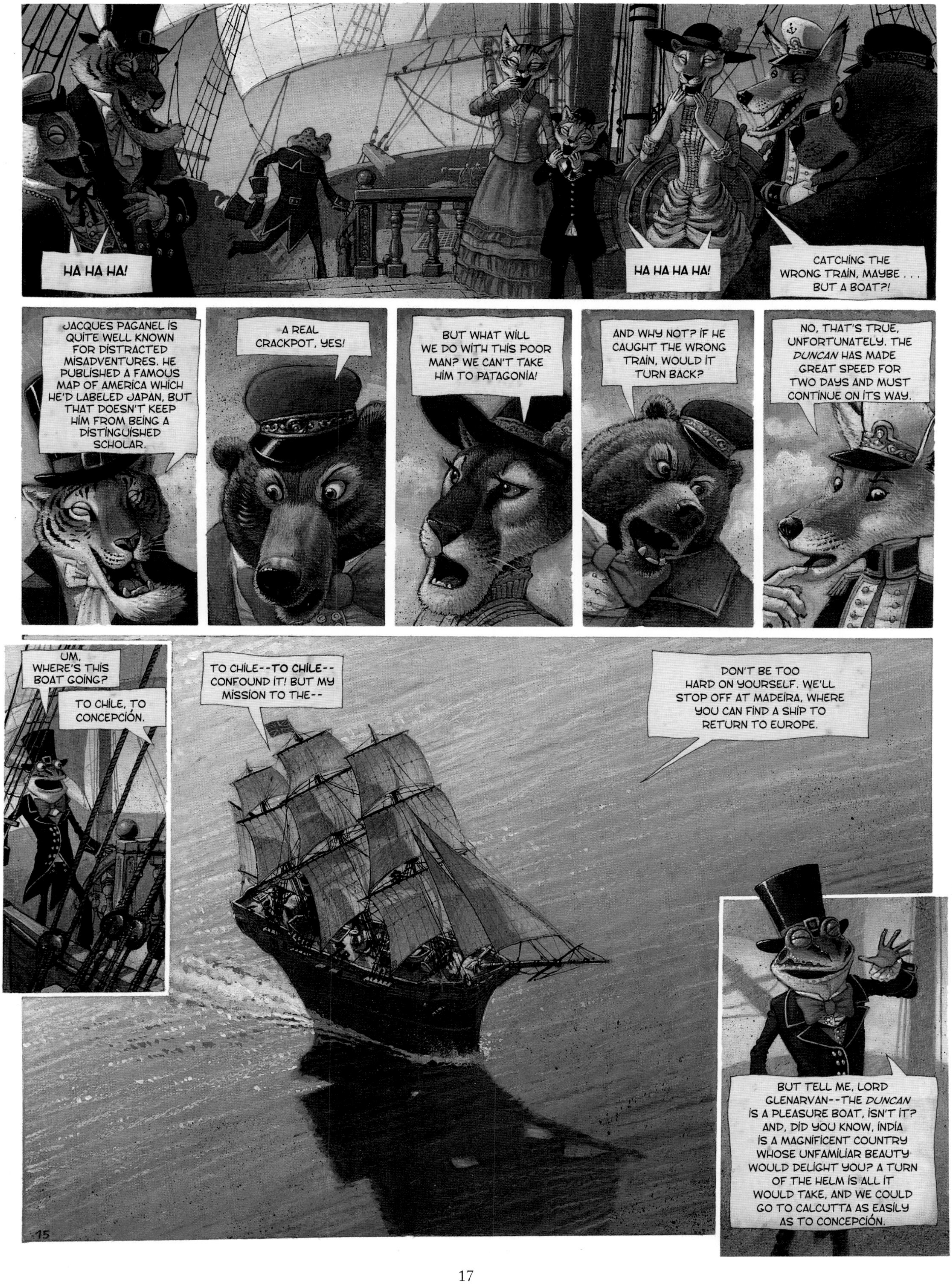
HA HA HA!
HA HA HA HA!
CATCHING THE WRONG TRAIN, MAYBE . . . BUT A BOAT?!
JACQUES PAGANEL IS QUITE WELL KNOWN FOR DISTRACTED MISADVENTURES. HE PUBLISHED A FAMOUS MAP OF AMERICA WHICH HE'D LABELED JAPAN, BUT THAT DOESN'T KEEP HIM FROM BEING A DISTINGUISHED SCHOLAR.
A REAL CRACKPOT, YES!
BUT WHAT WILL WE DO WITH THIS POOR MAN? WE CAN'T TAKE HIM TO PATAGONIA!
AND WHY NOT? IF HE CAUGHT THE WRONG TRAIN, WOULD IT TURN BACK?
NO, THAT'S TRUE, UNFORTUNATELY. THE *DUNCAN* HAS MADE GREAT SPEED FOR TWO DAYS AND MUST CONTINUE ON ITS WAY.
UM, WHERE'S THIS BOAT GOING?
TO CHILE, TO CONCEPCIÓN.
TO CHILE--TO CHILE--CONFOUND IT! BUT MY MISSION TO THE--
DON'T BE TOO HARD ON YOURSELF. WE'LL STOP OFF AT MADEIRA, WHERE YOU CAN FIND A SHIP TO RETURN TO EUROPE.
BUT TELL ME, LORD GLENARVAN--THE *DUNCAN* IS A PLEASURE BOAT, ISN'T IT? AND, DID YOU KNOW, INDIA IS A MAGNIFICENT COUNTRY WHOSE UNFAMILIAR BEAUTY WOULD DELIGHT YOU? A TURN OF THE HELM IS ALL IT WOULD TAKE, AND WE COULD GO TO CALCUTTA AS EASILY AS TO CONCEPCIÓN.
15

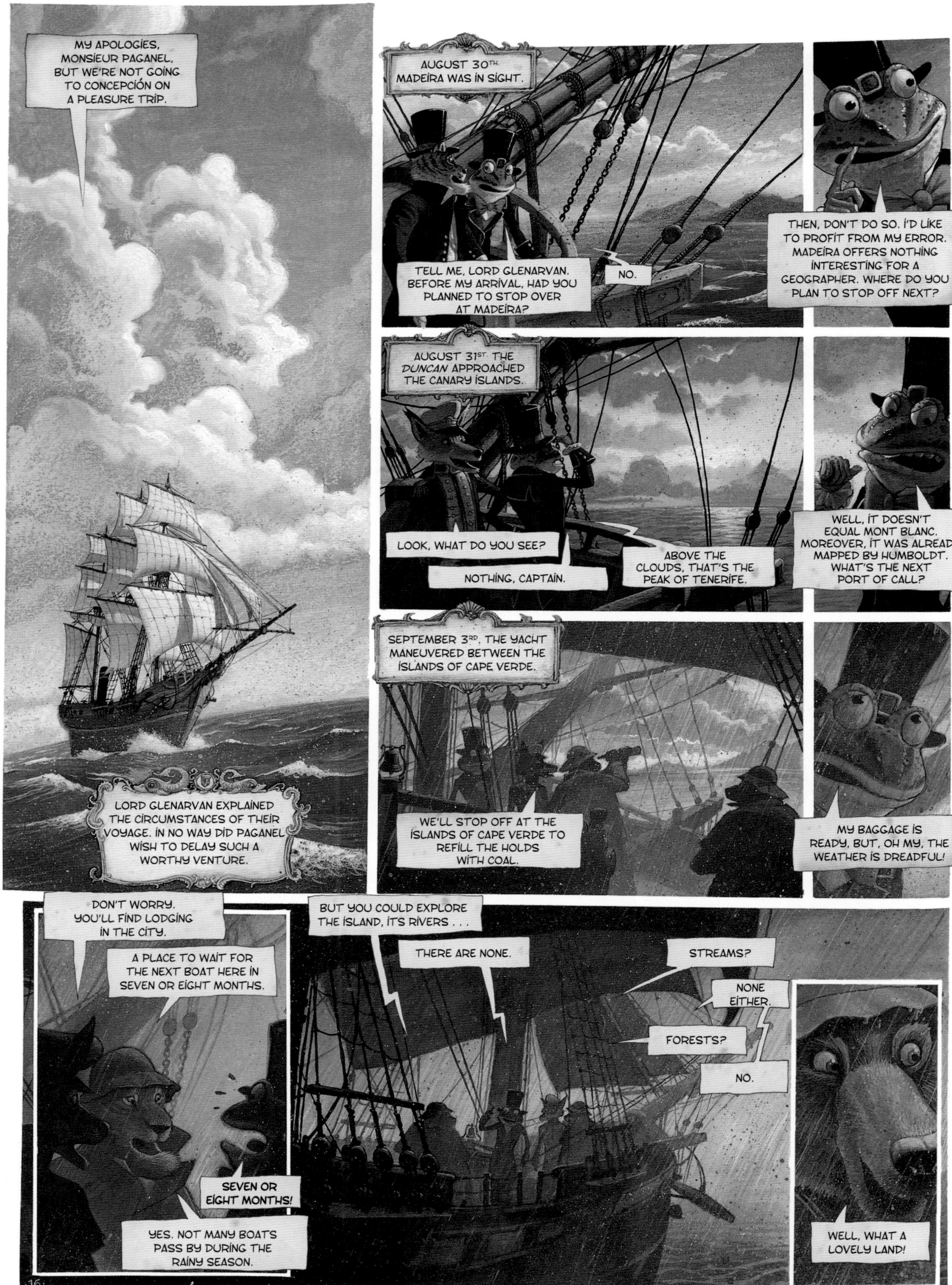

MY APOLOGIES, MONSIEUR PAGANEL, BUT WE'RE NOT GOING TO CONCEPCIÓN ON A PLEASURE TRIP.
LORD GLENARVAN EXPLAINED THE CIRCUMSTANCES OF THEIR VOYAGE. IN NO WAY DID PAGANEL WISH TO DELAY SUCH A WORTHY VENTURE.
AUGUST 30TH. MADEIRA WAS IN SIGHT.
TELL ME, LORD GLENARVAN. BEFORE MY ARRIVAL, HAD YOU PLANNED TO STOP OVER AT MADEIRA?
NO.
THEN, DON'T DO SO. I'D LIKE TO PROFIT FROM MY ERROR. MADEIRA OFFERS NOTHING INTERESTING FOR A GEOGRAPHER. WHERE DO YOU PLAN TO STOP OFF NEXT?
AUGUST 31ST. THE DUNCAN APPROACHED THE CANARY ISLANDS.
LOOK, WHAT DO YOU SEE?
NOTHING, CAPTAIN.
ABOVE THE CLOUDS, THAT'S THE PEAK OF TENERIFE.
WELL, IT DOESN'T EQUAL MONT BLANC. MOREOVER, IT WAS ALREADY MAPPED BY HUMBOLDT. WHAT'S THE NEXT PORT OF CALL?
SEPTEMBER 3RD. THE YACHT MANEUVERED BETWEEN THE ISLANDS OF CAPE VERDE.
WE'LL STOP OFF AT THE ISLANDS OF CAPE VERDE TO REFILL THE HOLDS WITH COAL.
MY BAGGAGE IS READY, BUT, OH MY, THE WEATHER IS DREADFUL!
DON'T WORRY. YOU'LL FIND LODGING IN THE CITY.
A PLACE TO WAIT FOR THE NEXT BOAT HERE IN SEVEN OR EIGHT MONTHS.
SEVEN OR EIGHT MONTHS!
YES. NOT MANY BOATS PASS BY DURING THE RAINY SEASON.
BUT YOU COULD EXPLORE THE ISLAND, ITS RIVERS . . .
THERE ARE NONE.
STREAMS?
NONE EITHER.
FORESTS?
NO.
WELL, WHAT A LOVELY LAND!
16

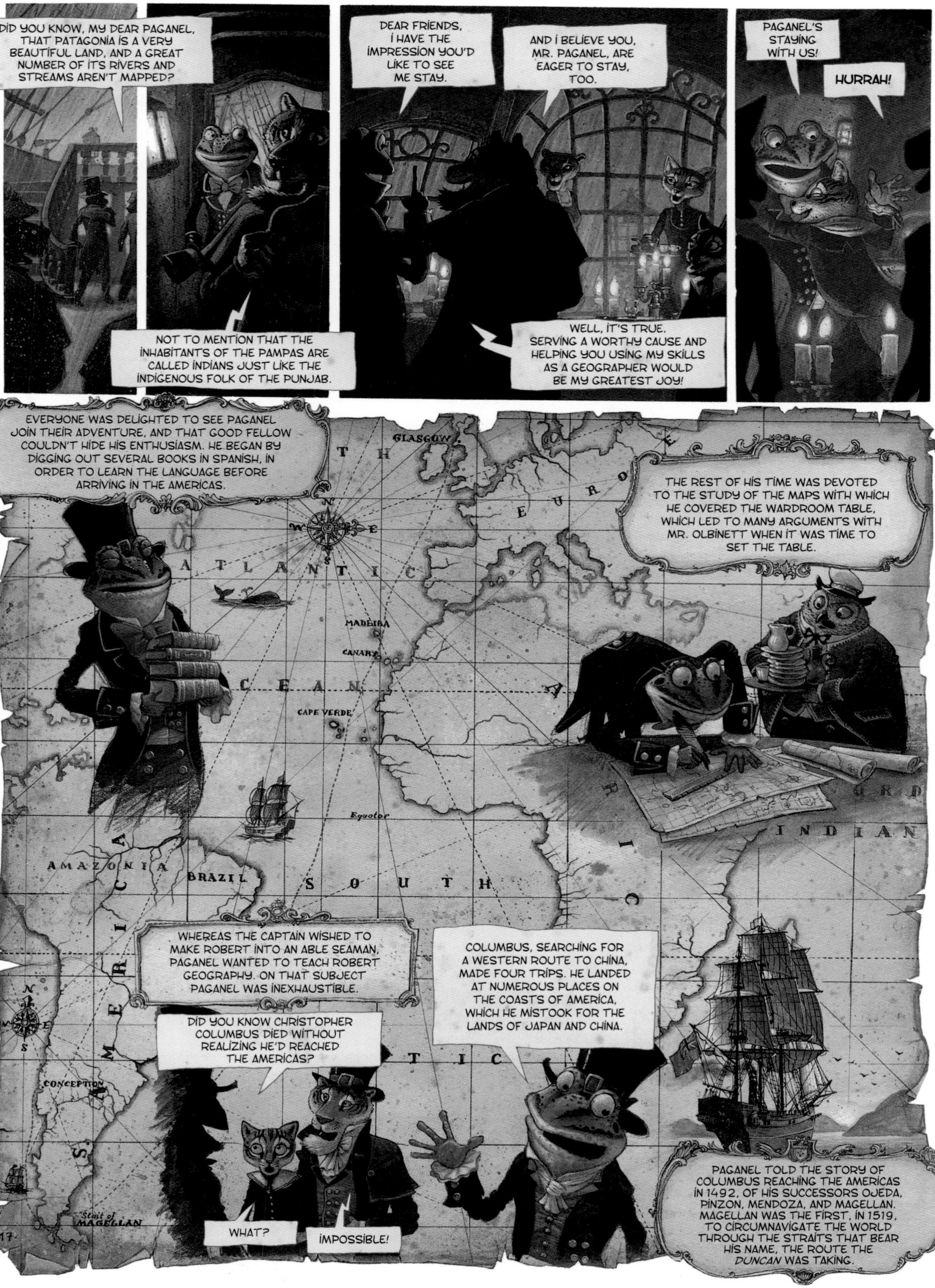
DID YOU KNOW, MY DEAR PAGANEL, THAT PATAGONIA IS A VERY BEAUTIFUL LAND, AND A GREAT NUMBER OF ITS RIVERS AND STREAMS AREN'T MAPPED?
NOT TO MENTION THAT THE INHABITANTS OF THE PAMPAS ARE CALLED INDIANS JUST LIKE THE INDIGENOUS FOLK OF THE PUNJAB.
DEAR FRIENDS, I HAVE THE IMPRESSION YOU'D LIKE TO SEE ME STAY.
AND I BELIEVE YOU, MR. PAGANEL, ARE EAGER TO STAY, TOO.
WELL, IT'S TRUE. SERVING A WORTHY CAUSE AND HELPING YOU USING MY SKILLS AS A GEOGRAPHER WOULD BE MY GREATEST JOY!
PAGANEL'S STAYING WITH US!
HURRAH!
EVERYONE WAS DELIGHTED TO SEE PAGANEL JOIN THEIR ADVENTURE, AND THAT GOOD FELLOW COULDN'T HIDE HIS ENTHUSIASM. HE BEGAN BY DIGGING OUT SEVERAL BOOKS IN SPANISH, IN ORDER TO LEARN THE LANGUAGE BEFORE ARRIVING IN THE AMERICAS.
THE REST OF HIS TIME WAS DEVOTED TO THE STUDY OF THE MAPS WITH WHICH HE COVERED THE WARDROOM TABLE, WHICH LED TO MANY ARGUMENTS WITH MR. OLBINETT WHEN IT WAS TIME TO SET THE TABLE.
GLASGOW
MADEIRA
CANARY
CAPE VERDE
Equator
AMAZONIA
BRAZIL
INDIAN
CONCEPTION
Strait of MAGELLAN
WHEREAS THE CAPTAIN WISHED TO MAKE ROBERT INTO AN ABLE SEAMAN, PAGANEL WANTED TO TEACH ROBERT GEOGRAPHY. ON THAT SUBJECT PAGANEL WAS INEXHAUSTIBLE.
DID YOU KNOW CHRISTOPHER COLUMBUS DIED WITHOUT REALIZING HE'D REACHED THE AMERICAS?
WHAT?
IMPOSSIBLE!
COLUMBUS, SEARCHING FOR A WESTERN ROUTE TO CHINA, MADE FOUR TRIPS. HE LANDED AT NUMEROUS PLACES ON THE COASTS OF AMERICA, WHICH HE MISTOOK FOR THE LANDS OF JAPAN AND CHINA.
PAGANEL TOLD THE STORY OF COLUMBUS REACHING THE AMERICAS IN 1492, OF HIS SUCCESSORS OJEDA, PINZON, MENDOZA, AND MAGELLAN. MAGELLAN WAS THE FIRST, IN 1519, TO CIRCUMNAVIGATE THE WORLD THROUGH THE STRAITS THAT BEAR HIS NAME, THE ROUTE THE *DUNCAN* WAS TAKING.

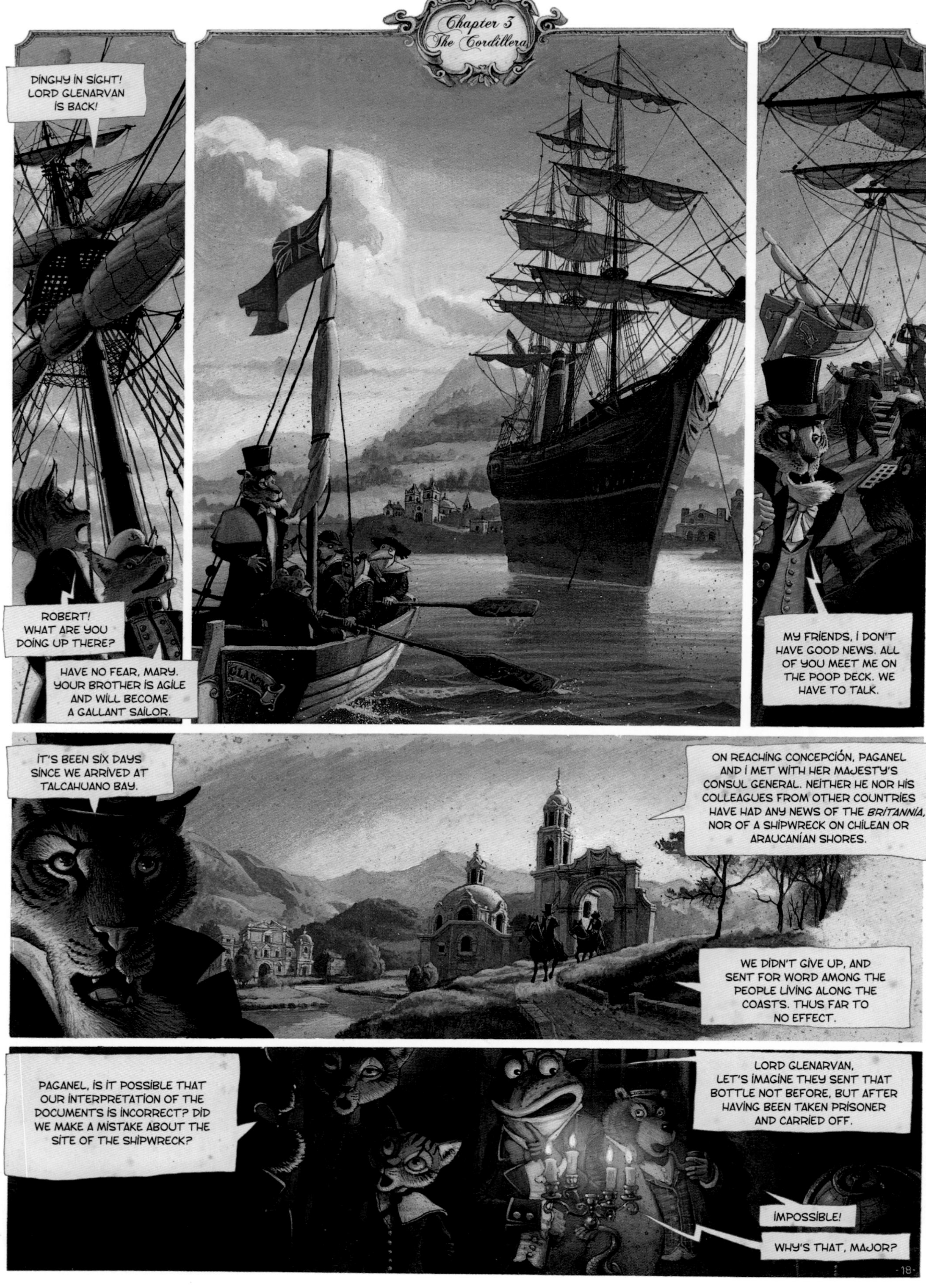
Chapter 3
The Cordillera
DINGHY IN SIGHT! LORD GLENARVAN IS BACK!
ROBERT! WHAT ARE YOU DOING UP THERE?
HAVE NO FEAR, MARY. YOUR BROTHER IS AGILE AND WILL BECOME A GALLANT SAILOR.
MY FRIENDS, I DON'T HAVE GOOD NEWS. ALL OF YOU MEET ME ON THE POOP DECK. WE HAVE TO TALK.
IT'S BEEN SIX DAYS SINCE WE ARRIVED AT TALCAHUANO BAY.
ON REACHING CONCEPCIÓN, PAGANEL AND I MET WITH HER MAJESTY'S CONSUL GENERAL. NEITHER HE NOR HIS COLLEAGUES FROM OTHER COUNTRIES HAVE HAD ANY NEWS OF THE *BRITANNIA*, NOR OF A SHIPWRECK ON CHILEAN OR ARAUCANIAN SHORES.
WE DIDN'T GIVE UP, AND SENT FOR WORD AMONG THE PEOPLE LIVING ALONG THE COASTS. THUS FAR TO NO EFFECT.
PAGANEL, IS IT POSSIBLE THAT OUR INTERPRETATION OF THE DOCUMENTS IS INCORRECT? DID WE MAKE A MISTAKE ABOUT THE SITE OF THE SHIPWRECK?
LORD GLENARVAN, LET'S IMAGINE THEY SENT THAT BOTTLE NOT BEFORE, BUT AFTER HAVING BEEN TAKEN PRISONER AND CARRIED OFF.
IMPOSSIBLE!
WHY'S THAT, MAJOR?
-18-

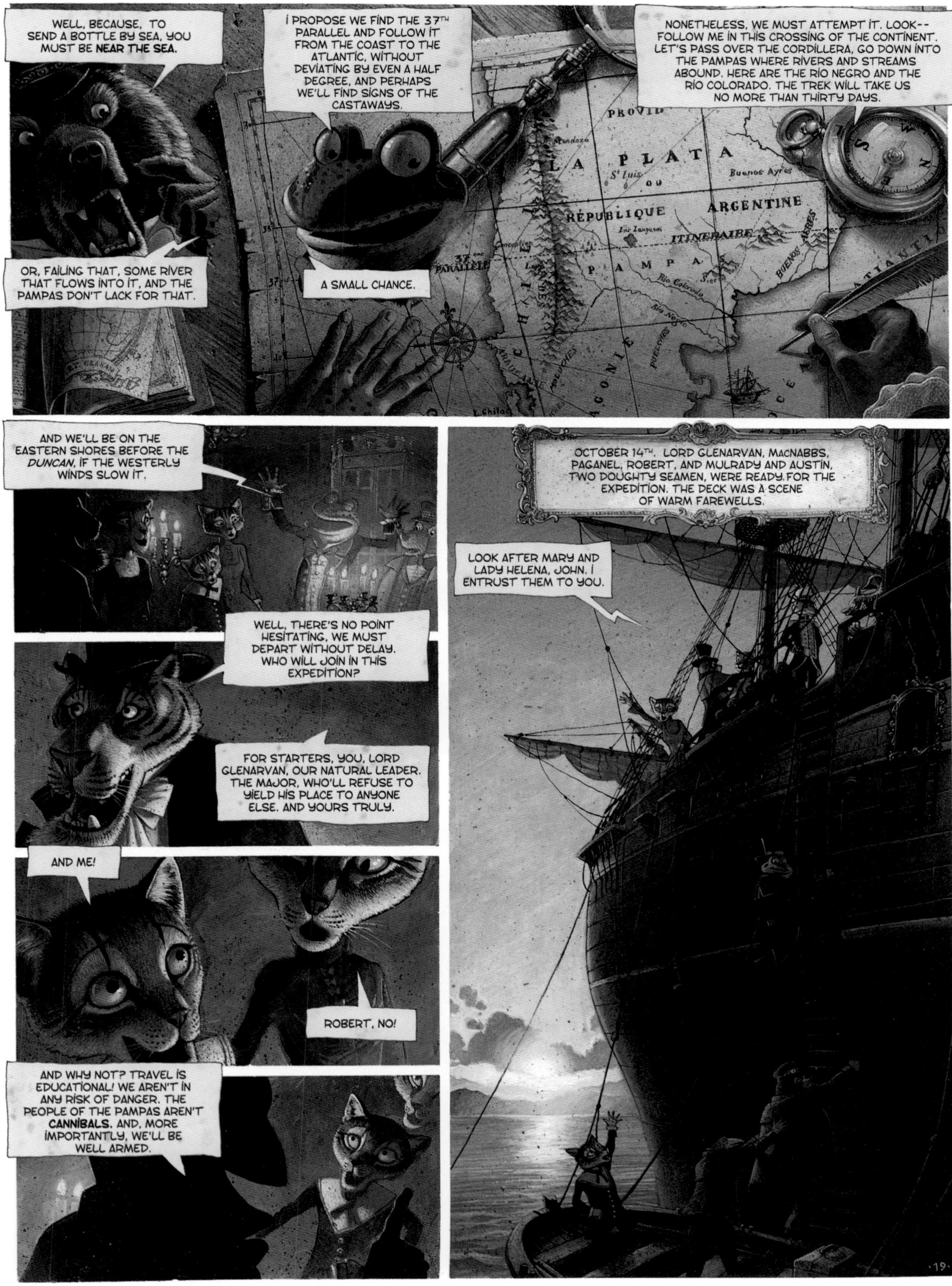
WELL, BECAUSE, TO SEND A BOTTLE BY SEA, YOU MUST BE **NEAR THE SEA.**
I PROPOSE WE FIND THE 37TH PARALLEL AND FOLLOW IT FROM THE COAST TO THE ATLANTIC, WITHOUT DEVIATING BY EVEN A HALF DEGREE, AND PERHAPS WE'LL FIND SIGNS OF THE CASTAWAYS.
NONETHELESS, WE MUST ATTEMPT IT. LOOK-- FOLLOW ME IN THIS CROSSING OF THE CONTINENT. LET'S PASS OVER THE CORDILLERA, GO DOWN INTO THE PAMPAS WHERE RIVERS AND STREAMS ABOUND. HERE ARE THE RIO NEGRO AND THE RIO COLORADO. THE TREK WILL TAKE US NO MORE THAN THIRTY DAYS.
OR, FAILING THAT, SOME RIVER THAT FLOWS INTO IT, AND THE PAMPAS DON'T LACK FOR THAT.
A SMALL CHANCE.
AND WE'LL BE ON THE EASTERN SHORES BEFORE THE *DUNCAN*, IF THE WESTERLY WINDS SLOW IT.
WELL, THERE'S NO POINT HESITATING, WE MUST DEPART WITHOUT DELAY. WHO WILL JOIN IN THIS EXPEDITION?
FOR STARTERS, YOU, LORD GLENARVAN, OUR NATURAL LEADER. THE MAJOR, WHO'LL REFUSE TO YIELD HIS PLACE TO ANYONE ELSE. AND YOURS TRULY.
AND ME!
ROBERT, NO!
AND WHY NOT? TRAVEL IS EDUCATIONAL! WE AREN'T IN ANY RISK OF DANGER. THE PEOPLE OF THE PAMPAS AREN'T **CANNIBALS.** AND, MORE IMPORTANTLY, WE'LL BE WELL ARMED.
OCTOBER 14TH. LORD GLENARVAN, MACNABBS, PAGANEL, ROBERT, AND MULRADY AND AUSTIN, TWO DOUGHTY SEAMEN, WERE READY FOR THE EXPEDITION. THE DECK WAS A SCENE OF WARM FAREWELLS.
LOOK AFTER MARY AND LADY HELENA, JOHN. I ENTRUST THEM TO YOU.

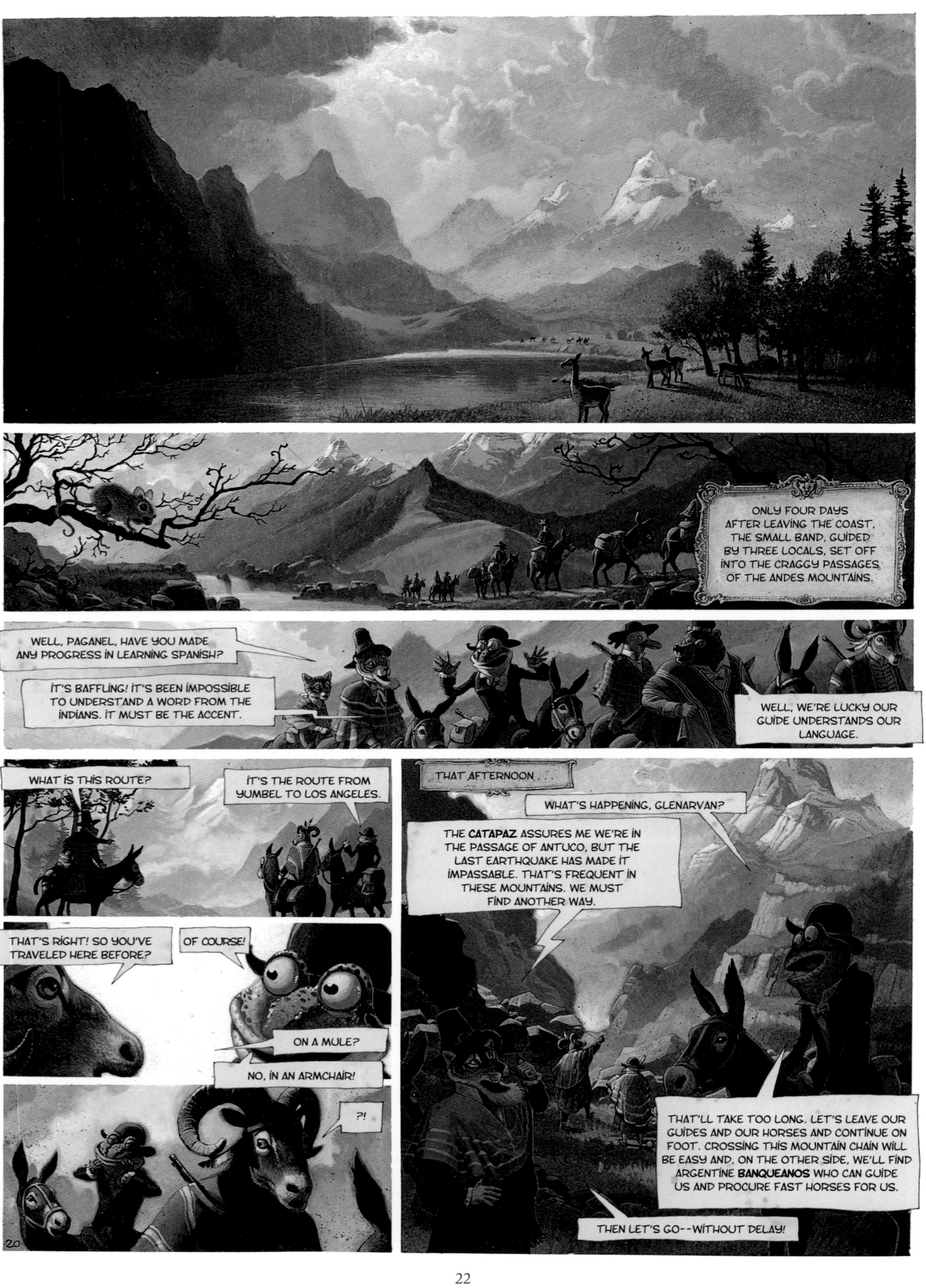
ONLY FOUR DAYS AFTER LEAVING THE COAST, THE SMALL BAND, GUIDED BY THREE LOCALS, SET OFF INTO THE CRAGGY PASSAGES OF THE ANDES MOUNTAINS.
WELL, PAGANEL, HAVE YOU MADE ANY PROGRESS IN LEARNING SPANISH?
IT'S BAFFLING! IT'S BEEN IMPOSSIBLE TO UNDERSTAND A WORD FROM THE INDIANS. IT MUST BE THE ACCENT.
WELL, WE'RE LUCKY OUR GUIDE UNDERSTANDS OUR LANGUAGE.
WHAT IS THIS ROUTE?
IT'S THE ROUTE FROM YUMBEL TO LOS ANGELES.
THAT'S RIGHT! SO YOU'VE TRAVELED HERE BEFORE?
OF COURSE!
ON A MULE?
NO, IN AN ARMCHAIR!
?!
20
THAT AFTERNOON . . .
WHAT'S HAPPENING, GLENARVAN?
THE CATAPAZ ASSURES ME WE'RE IN THE PASSAGE OF ANTUCO, BUT THE LAST EARTHQUAKE HAS MADE IT IMPASSABLE. THAT'S FREQUENT IN THESE MOUNTAINS. WE MUST FIND ANOTHER WAY.
THAT'LL TAKE TOO LONG. LET'S LEAVE OUR GUIDES AND OUR HORSES AND CONTINUE ON FOOT. CROSSING THIS MOUNTAIN CHAIN WILL BE EASY AND, ON THE OTHER SIDE, WE'LL FIND ARGENTINE BANQUEANOS WHO CAN GUIDE US AND PROCURE FAST HORSES FOR US.
THEN LET'S GO--WITHOUT DELAY!

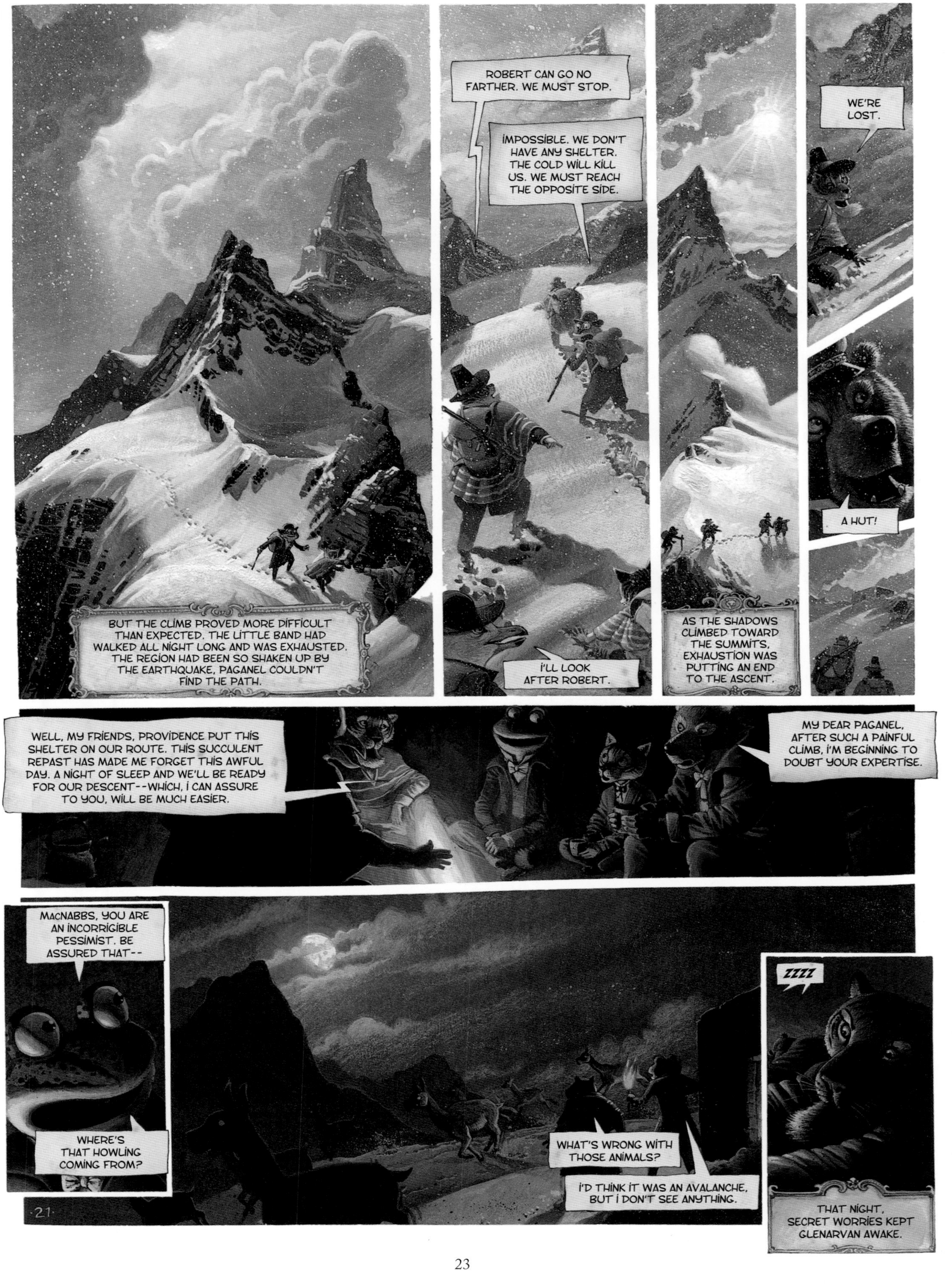

BUT THE CLIMB PROVED MORE DIFFICULT THAN EXPECTED. THE LITTLE BAND HAD WALKED ALL NIGHT LONG AND WAS EXHAUSTED. THE REGION HAD BEEN SO SHAKEN UP BY THE EARTHQUAKE, PAGANEL COULDN'T FIND THE PATH.
ROBERT CAN GO NO FARTHER. WE MUST STOP.
IMPOSSIBLE. WE DON'T HAVE ANY SHELTER. THE COLD WILL KILL US. WE MUST REACH THE OPPOSITE SIDE.
I'LL LOOK AFTER ROBERT.
AS THE SHADOWS CLIMBED TOWARD THE SUMMITS, EXHAUSTION WAS PUTTING AN END TO THE ASCENT.
WE'RE LOST.
A HUT!
WELL, MY FRIENDS, PROVIDENCE PUT THIS SHELTER ON OUR ROUTE. THIS SUCCULENT REPAST HAS MADE ME FORGET THIS AWFUL DAY. A NIGHT OF SLEEP AND WE'LL BE READY FOR OUR DESCENT--WHICH, I CAN ASSURE TO YOU, WILL BE MUCH EASIER.
MY DEAR PAGANEL, AFTER SUCH A PAINFUL CLIMB, I'M BEGINNING TO DOUBT YOUR EXPERTISE.
MACNABBS, YOU ARE AN INCORRIGIBLE PESSIMIST. BE ASSURED THAT--
WHERE'S THAT HOWLING COMING FROM?
WHAT'S WRONG WITH THOSE ANIMALS?
I'D THINK IT WAS AN AVALANCHE, BUT I DON'T SEE ANYTHING.
ZZZZ
THAT NIGHT, SECRET WORRIES KEPT GLENARVAN AWAKE.
21

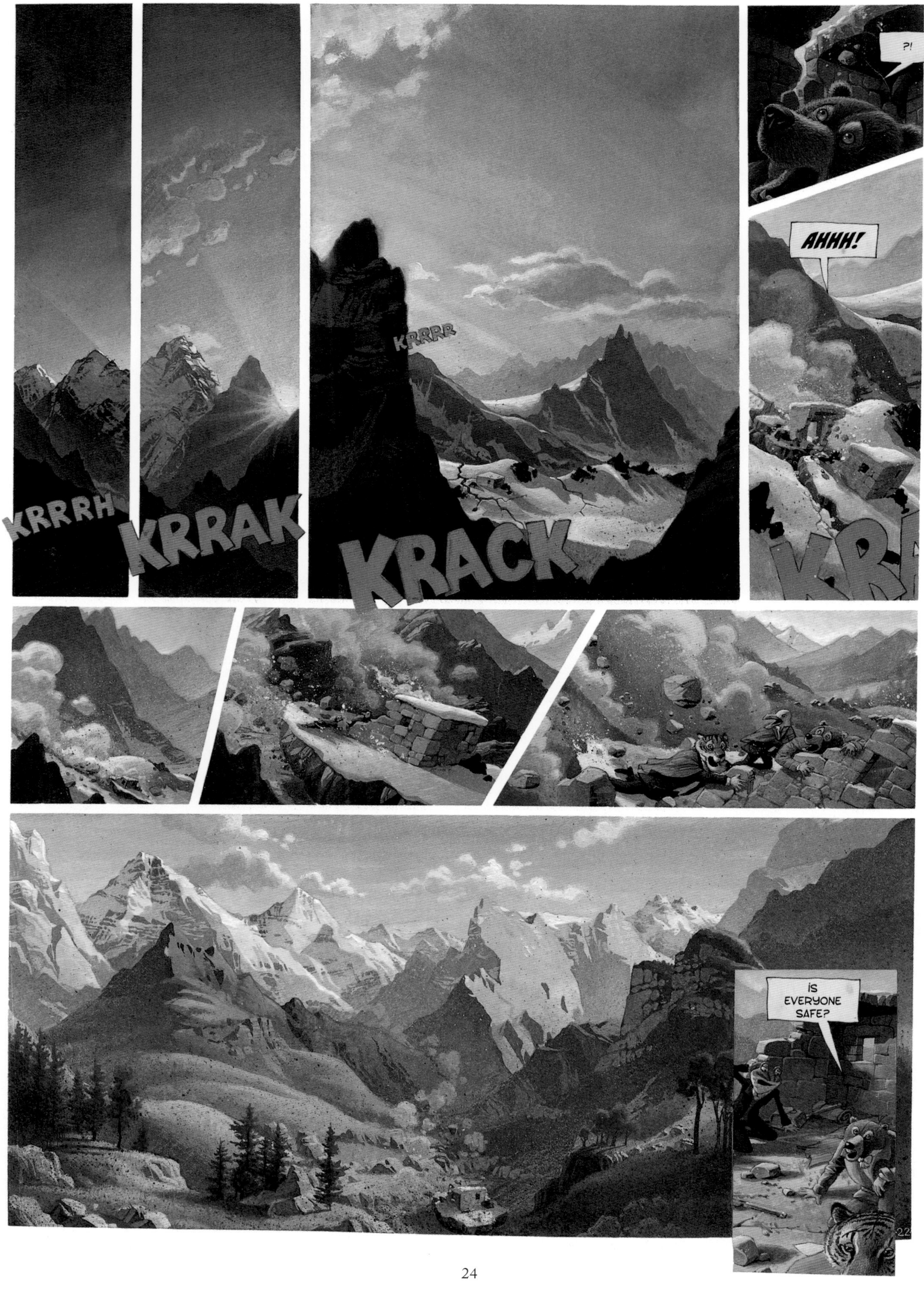
KRRRH
KRRAK
KRRRR
KRACK
?!
AHHH!
IS EVERYONE SAFE?

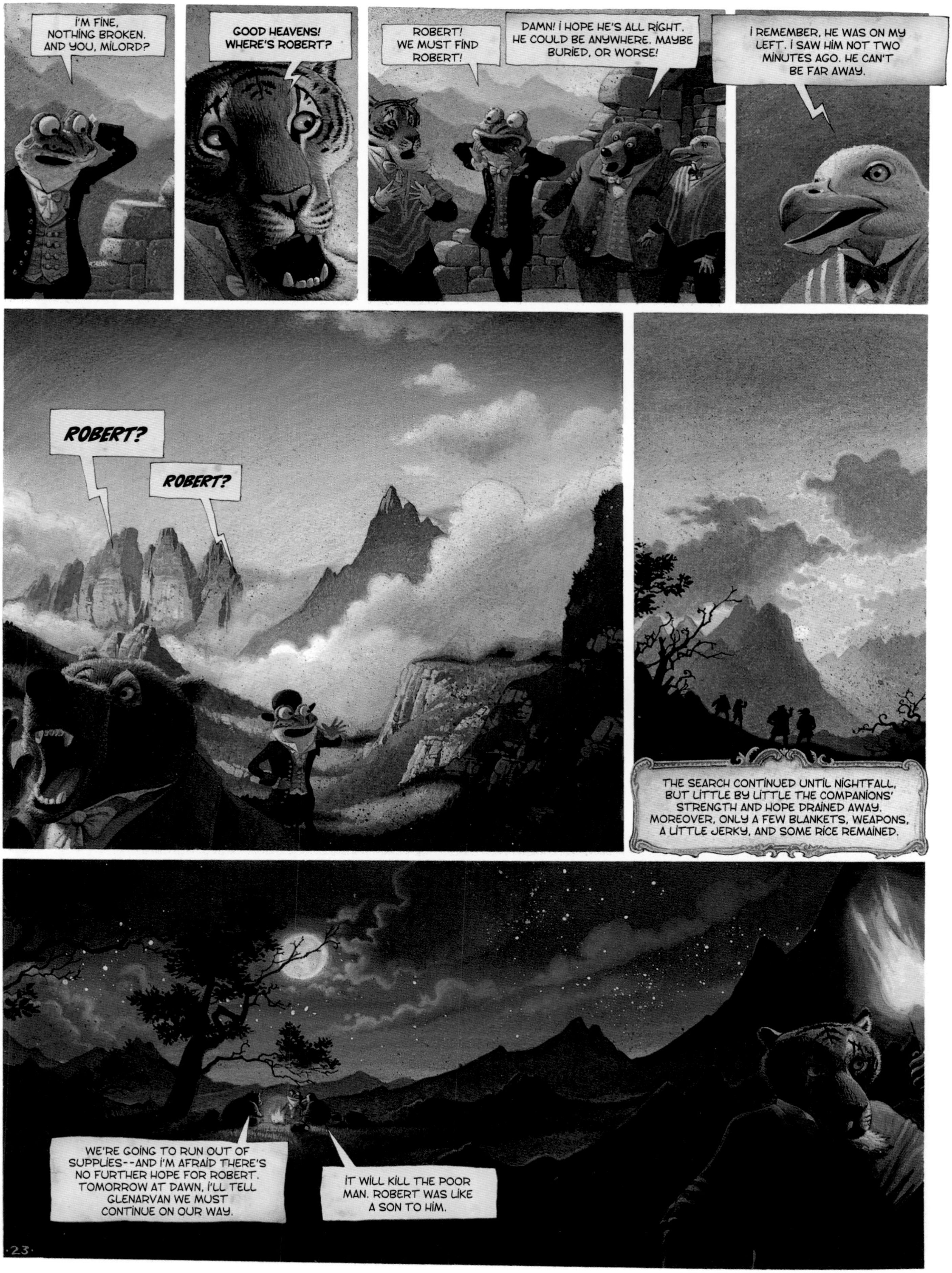
I'M FINE, NOTHING BROKEN. AND YOU, MILORD?
GOOD HEAVENS! WHERE'S ROBERT?
ROBERT! WE MUST FIND ROBERT!
DAMN! I HOPE HE'S ALL RIGHT. HE COULD BE ANYWHERE. MAYBE BURIED, OR WORSE!
I REMEMBER, HE WAS ON MY LEFT. I SAW HIM NOT TWO MINUTES AGO. HE CAN'T BE FAR AWAY.
ROBERT?
ROBERT?
THE SEARCH CONTINUED UNTIL NIGHTFALL, BUT LITTLE BY LITTLE THE COMPANIONS' STRENGTH AND HOPE DRAINED AWAY. MOREOVER, ONLY A FEW BLANKETS, WEAPONS, A LITTLE JERKY, AND SOME RICE REMAINED.
WE'RE GOING TO RUN OUT OF SUPPLIES--AND I'M AFRAID THERE'S NO FURTHER HOPE FOR ROBERT. TOMORROW AT DAWN, I'LL TELL GLENARVAN WE MUST CONTINUE ON OUR WAY.
IT WILL KILL THE POOR MAN. ROBERT WAS LIKE A SON TO HIM.
·23·

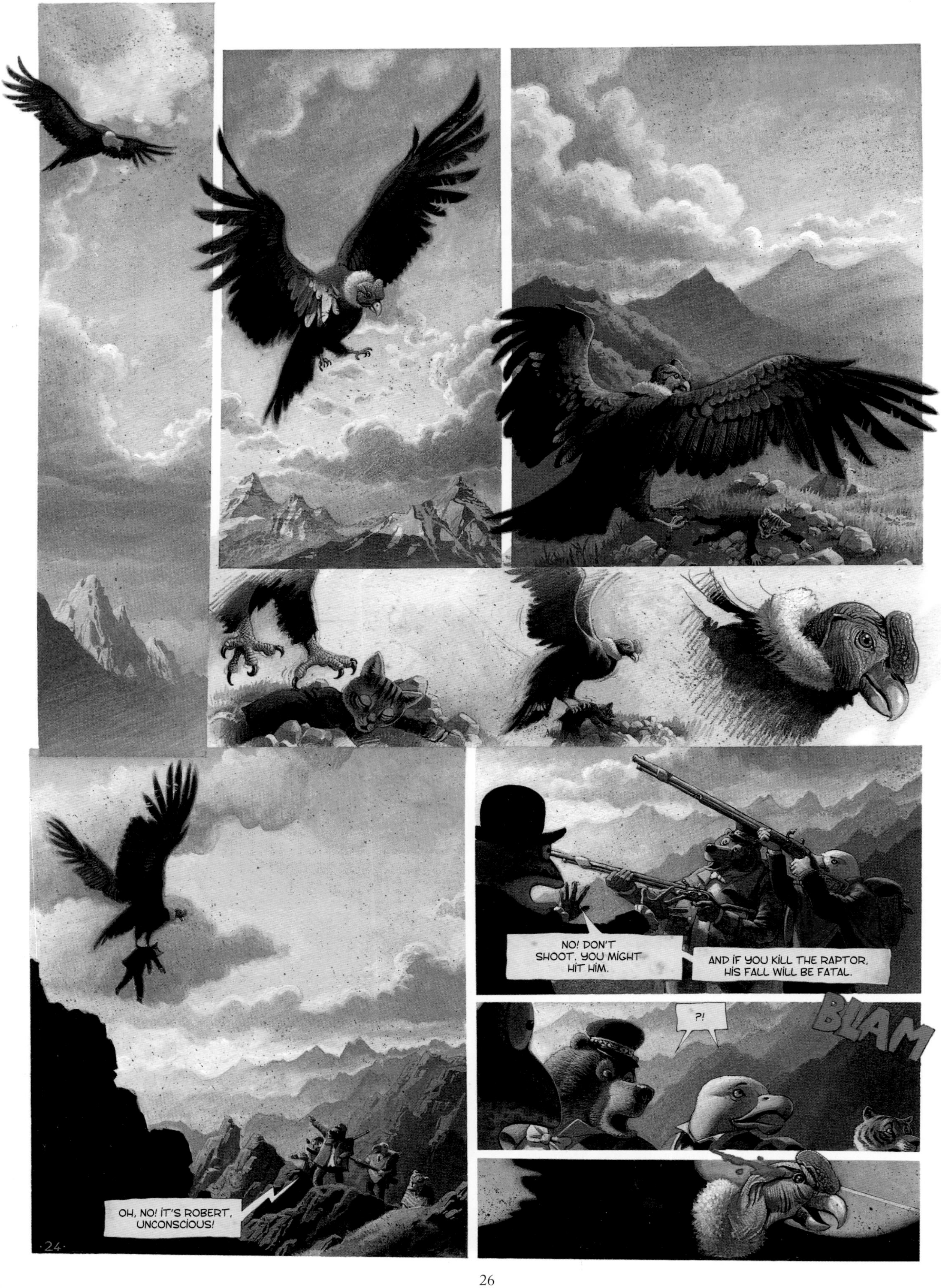
OH, NO! IT'S ROBERT, UNCONSCIOUS!
NO! DON'T SHOOT. YOU MIGHT HIT HIM.
AND IF YOU KILL THE RAPTOR, HIS FALL WILL BE FATAL.
?!
BLAM
·24·

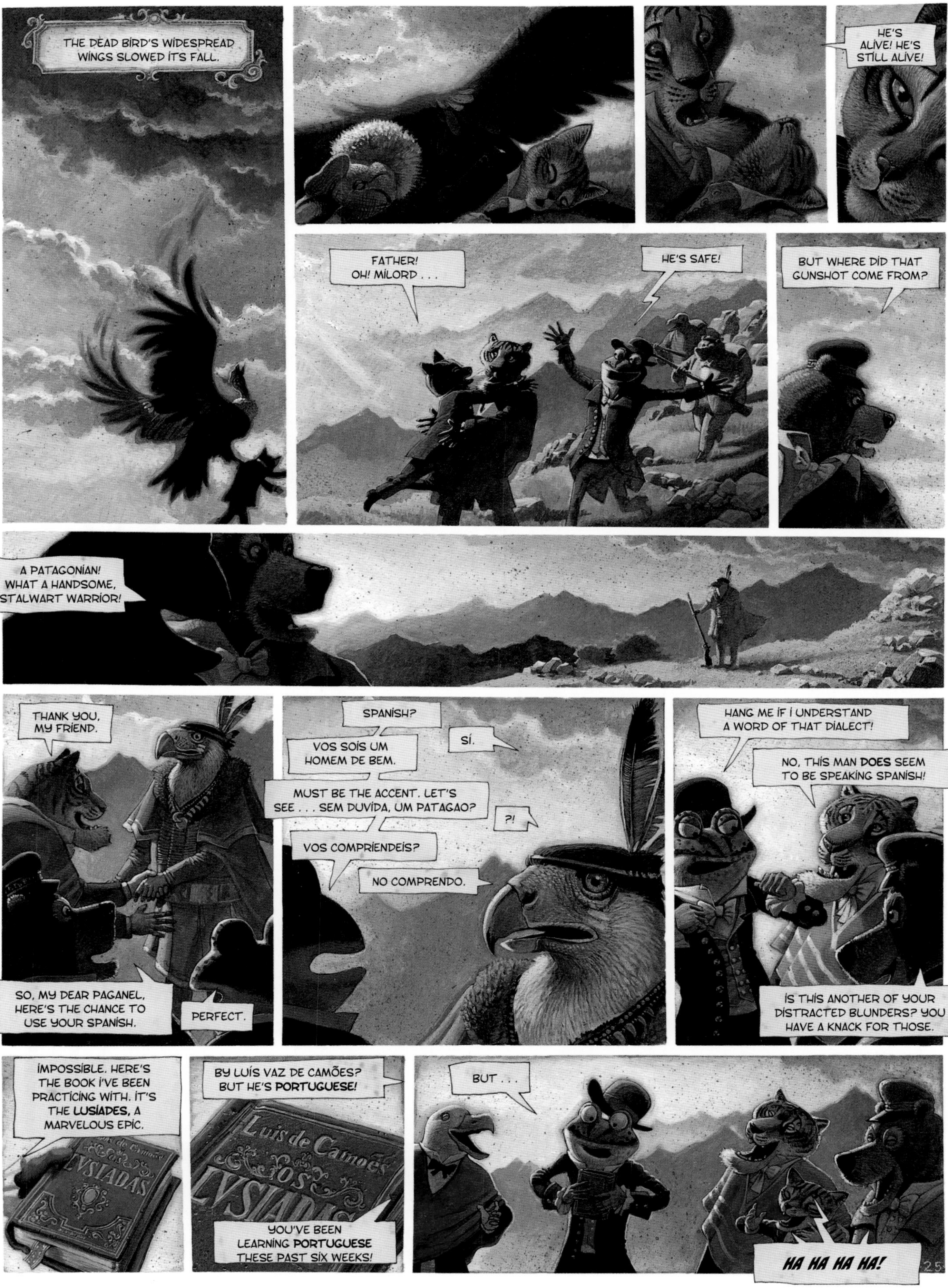
THE DEAD BIRD'S WIDESPREAD WINGS SLOWED ITS FALL.
HE'S ALIVE! HE'S STILL ALIVE!
FATHER! OH! MILORD . . .
HE'S SAFE!
BUT WHERE DID THAT GUNSHOT COME FROM?
A PATAGONIAN! WHAT A HANDSOME, STALWART WARRIOR!
THANK YOU, MY FRIEND.
SO, MY DEAR PAGANEL, HERE'S THE CHANCE TO USE YOUR SPANISH.
PERFECT.
SPANISH?
SÍ.
VOS SOIS UM HOMEM DE BEM.
MUST BE THE ACCENT. LET'S SEE . . . SEM DUVIDA, UM PATAGAO?
?!
VOS COMPRIENDEIS?
NO COMPRENDO.
HANG ME IF I UNDERSTAND A WORD OF THAT DIALECT!
NO, THIS MAN **DOES** SEEM TO BE SPEAKING SPANISH!
IS THIS ANOTHER OF YOUR DISTRACTED BLUNDERS? YOU HAVE A KNACK FOR THOSE.
IMPOSSIBLE. HERE'S THE BOOK I'VE BEEN PRACTICING WITH. IT'S THE **LUSIADES,** A MARVELOUS EPIC.
LVSIADAS
BY LUÍS VAZ DE CAMÕES? BUT HE'S **PORTUGUESE!**
Luis de Camoẽs OS LVSIADAS
YOU'VE BEEN LEARNING **PORTUGUESE** THESE PAST SIX WEEKS!
BUT . . .
HA HA HA HA!
25

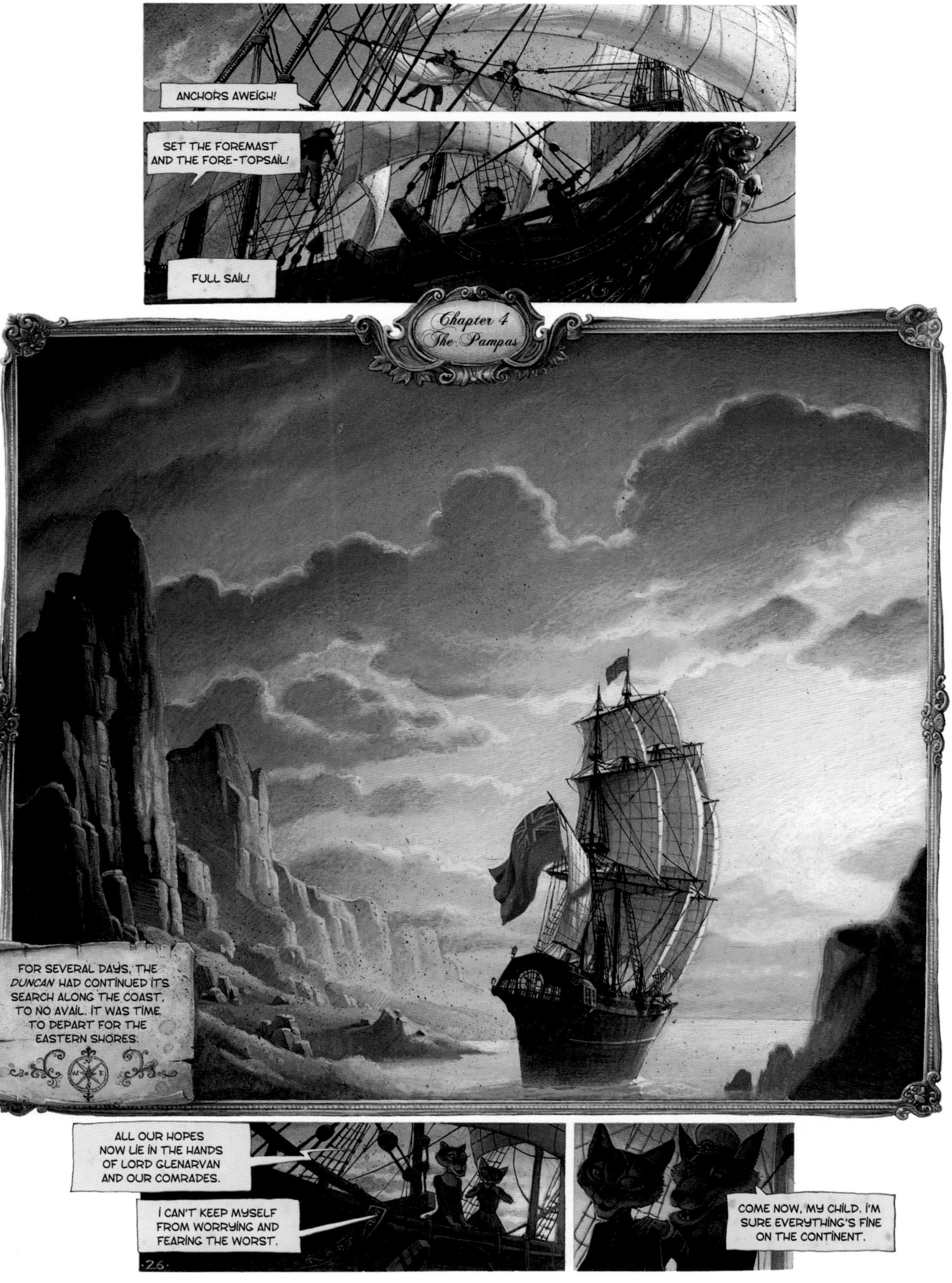
ANCHORS AWEIGH!
SET THE FOREMAST AND THE FORE-TOPSAIL!
FULL SAIL!
Chapter 4
The Pampas
FOR SEVERAL DAYS, THE *DUNCAN* HAD CONTINUED ITS SEARCH ALONG THE COAST, TO NO AVAIL. IT WAS TIME TO DEPART FOR THE EASTERN SHORES.
ALL OUR HOPES NOW LIE IN THE HANDS OF LORD GLENARVAN AND OUR COMRADES.
I CAN'T KEEP MYSELF FROM WORRYING AND FEARING THE WORST.
-26-
COME NOW, MY CHILD. I'M SURE EVERYTHING'S FINE ON THE CONTINENT.

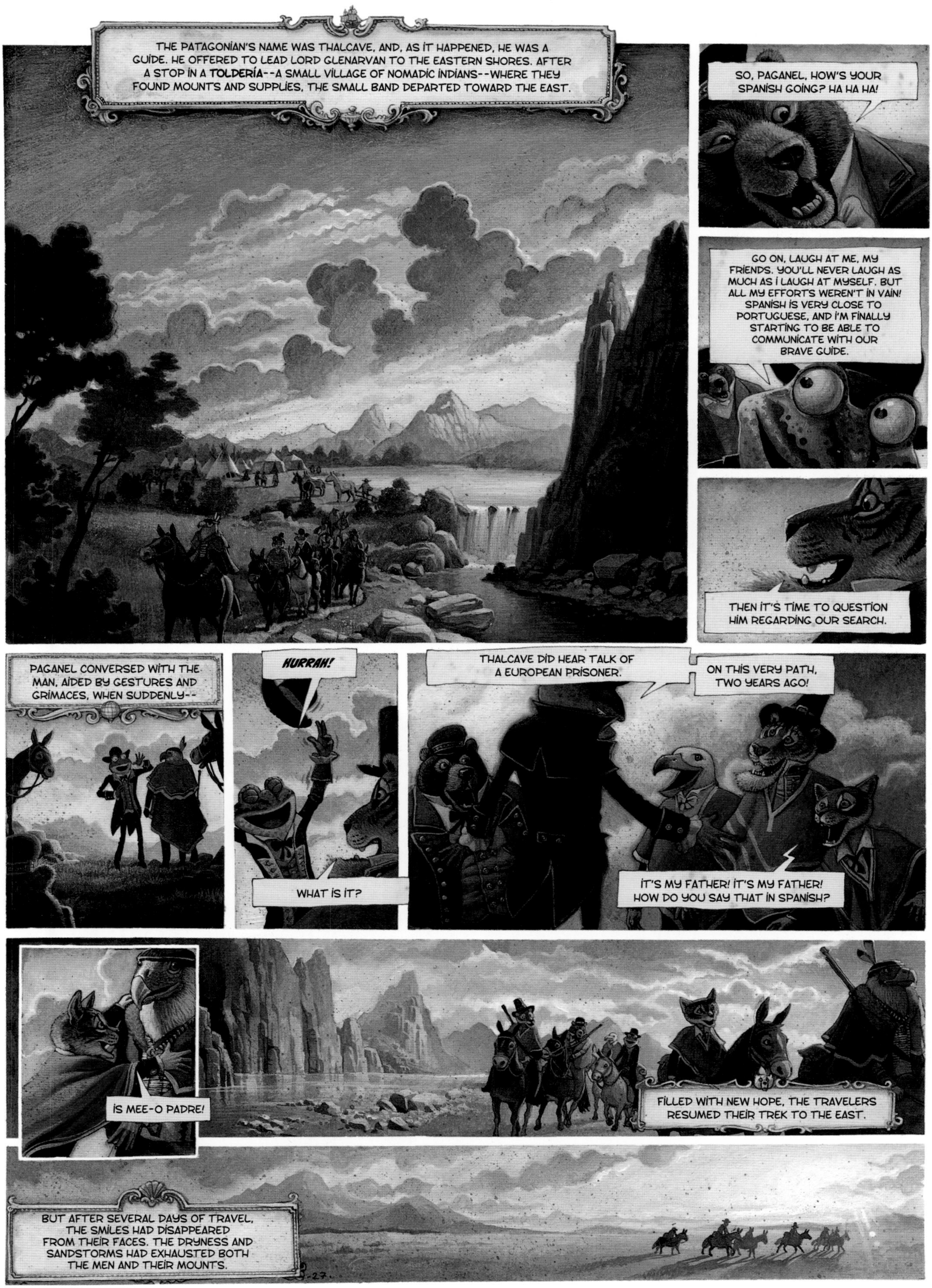
THE PATAGONIAN'S NAME WAS THALCAVE, AND, AS IT HAPPENED, HE WAS A GUIDE. HE OFFERED TO LEAD LORD GLENARVAN TO THE EASTERN SHORES. AFTER A STOP IN A TOLDERÍA--A SMALL VILLAGE OF NOMADIC INDIANS--WHERE THEY FOUND MOUNTS AND SUPPLIES, THE SMALL BAND DEPARTED TOWARD THE EAST.
SO, PAGANEL, HOW'S YOUR SPANISH GOING? HA HA HA!
GO ON, LAUGH AT ME, MY FRIENDS. YOU'LL NEVER LAUGH AS MUCH AS I LAUGH AT MYSELF. BUT ALL MY EFFORTS WEREN'T IN VAIN! SPANISH IS VERY CLOSE TO PORTUGUESE, AND I'M FINALLY STARTING TO BE ABLE TO COMMUNICATE WITH OUR BRAVE GUIDE.
THEN IT'S TIME TO QUESTION HIM REGARDING OUR SEARCH.
PAGANEL CONVERSED WITH THE MAN, AIDED BY GESTURES AND GRIMACES, WHEN SUDDENLY--
HURRAH!
WHAT IS IT?
THALCAVE DID HEAR TALK OF A EUROPEAN PRISONER.
ON THIS VERY PATH, TWO YEARS AGO!
IT'S MY FATHER! IT'S MY FATHER! HOW DO YOU SAY THAT IN SPANISH?
IS MEE-O PADRE!
FILLED WITH NEW HOPE, THE TRAVELERS RESUMED THEIR TREK TO THE EAST.
BUT AFTER SEVERAL DAYS OF TRAVEL, THE SMILES HAD DISAPPEARED FROM THEIR FACES. THE DRYNESS AND SANDSTORMS HAD EXHAUSTED BOTH THE MEN AND THEIR MOUNTS.

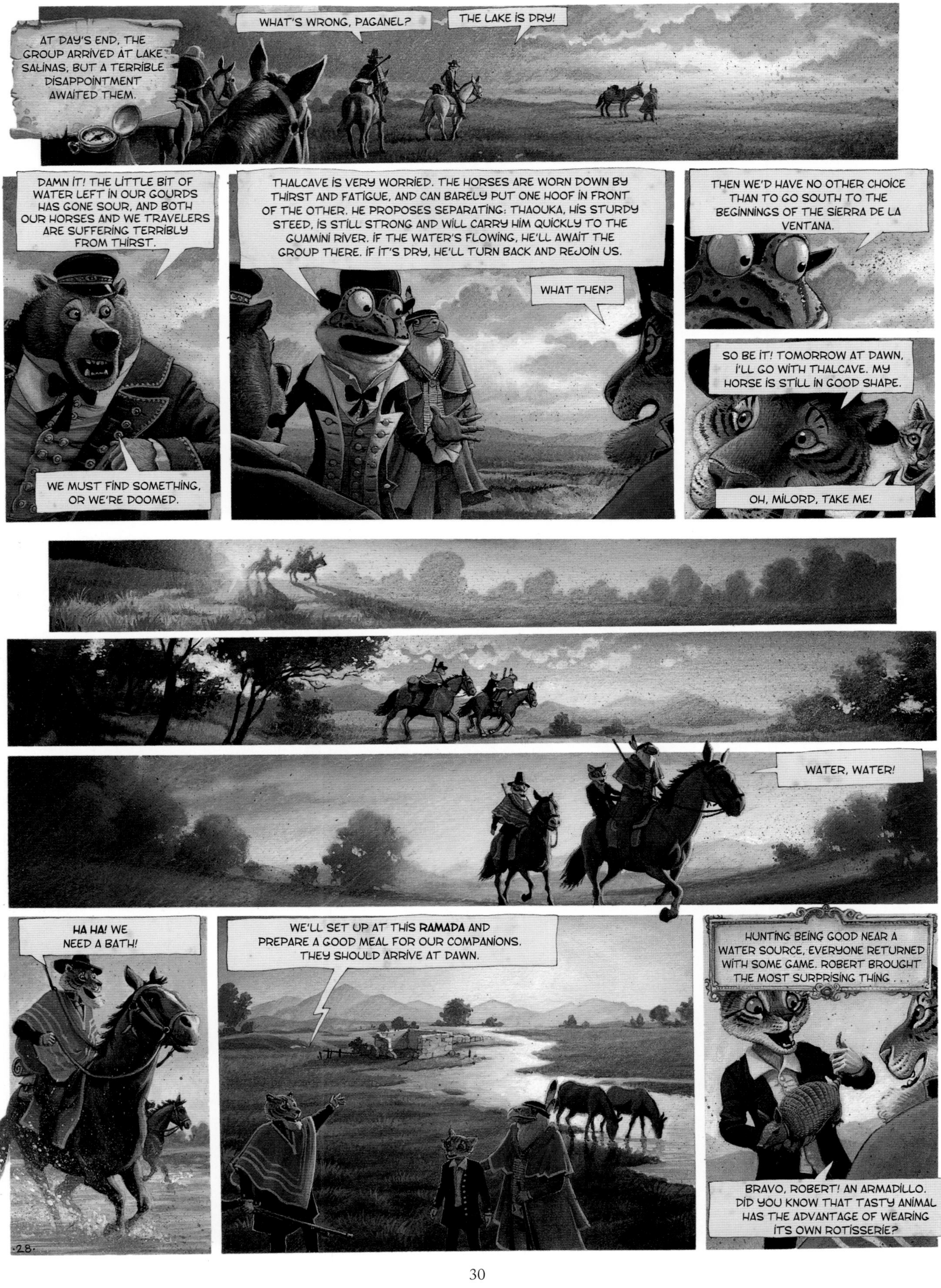
AT DAY'S END, THE GROUP ARRIVED AT LAKE SALINAS, BUT A TERRIBLE DISAPPOINTMENT AWAITED THEM.
WHAT'S WRONG, PAGANEL?
THE LAKE IS DRY!
DAMN IT! THE LITTLE BIT OF WATER LEFT IN OUR GOURDS HAS GONE SOUR, AND BOTH OUR HORSES AND WE TRAVELERS ARE SUFFERING TERRIBLY FROM THIRST.
WE MUST FIND SOMETHING, OR WE'RE DOOMED.
THALCAVE IS VERY WORRIED. THE HORSES ARE WORN DOWN BY THIRST AND FATIGUE, AND CAN BARELY PUT ONE HOOF IN FRONT OF THE OTHER. HE PROPOSES SEPARATING: THAOUKA, HIS STURDY STEED, IS STILL STRONG AND WILL CARRY HIM QUICKLY TO THE GUAMINI RIVER. IF THE WATER'S FLOWING, HE'LL AWAIT THE GROUP THERE. IF IT'S DRY, HE'LL TURN BACK AND REJOIN US.
WHAT THEN?
THEN WE'D HAVE NO OTHER CHOICE THAN TO GO SOUTH TO THE BEGINNINGS OF THE SIERRA DE LA VENTANA.
SO BE IT! TOMORROW AT DAWN, I'LL GO WITH THALCAVE. MY HORSE IS STILL IN GOOD SHAPE.
OH, MILORD, TAKE ME!
WATER, WATER!
HA HA! WE NEED A BATH!
WE'LL SET UP AT THIS **RAMADA** AND PREPARE A GOOD MEAL FOR OUR COMPANIONS. THEY SHOULD ARRIVE AT DAWN.
HUNTING BEING GOOD NEAR A WATER SOURCE, EVERYONE RETURNED WITH SOME GAME. ROBERT BROUGHT THE MOST SURPRISING THING . . .
BRAVO, ROBERT! AN ARMADILLO. DID YOU KNOW THAT TASTY ANIMAL HAS THE ADVANTAGE OF WEARING ITS OWN ROTISSERIE?
28

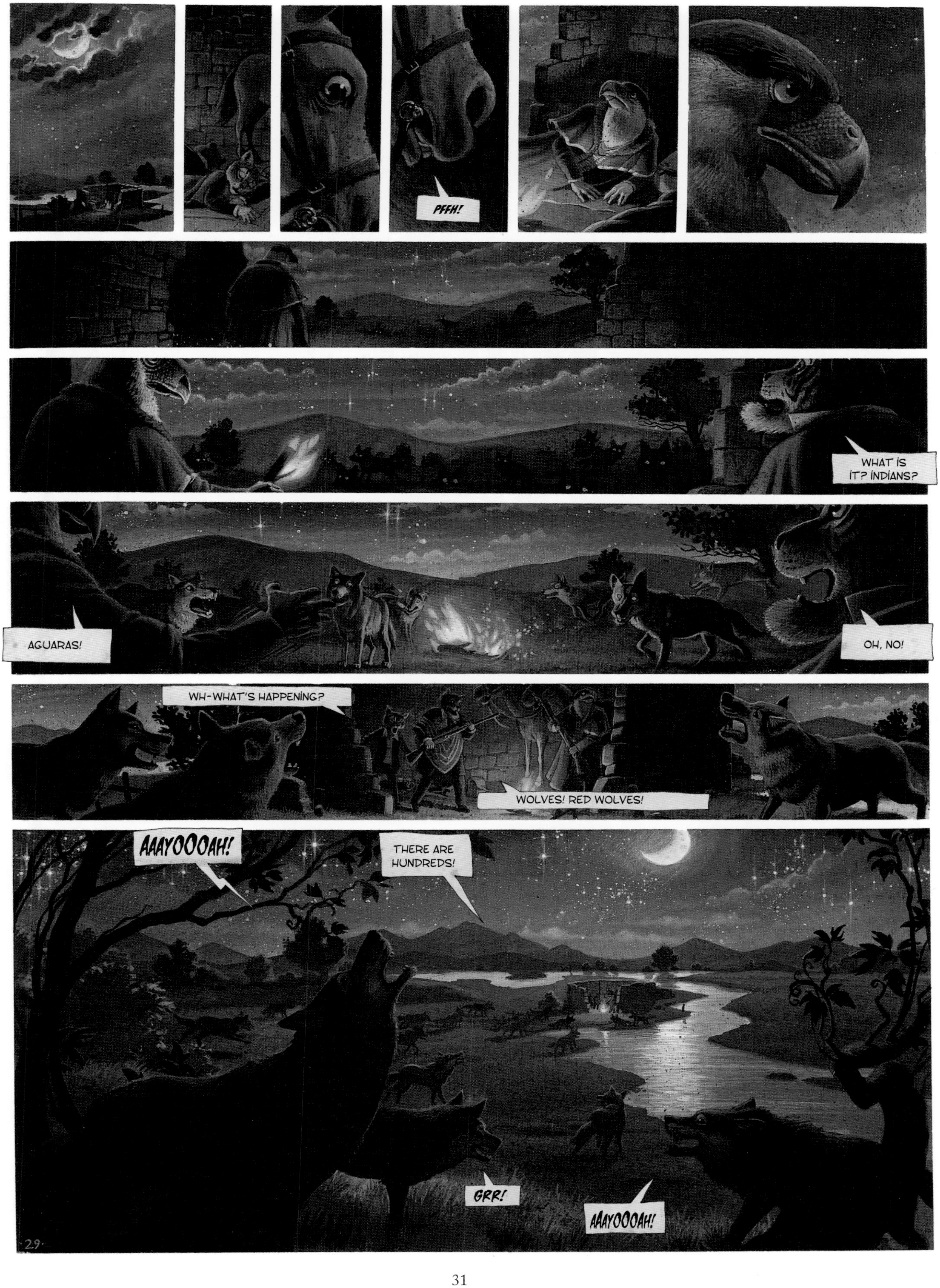
PFFH!
WHAT IS IT? INDIANS?
AGUARAS!
OH, NO!
WH-WHAT'S HAPPENING?
WOLVES! RED WOLVES!
AAAYOOOAH!
THERE ARE HUNDREDS!
GRR!
AAAYOOOAH!
29

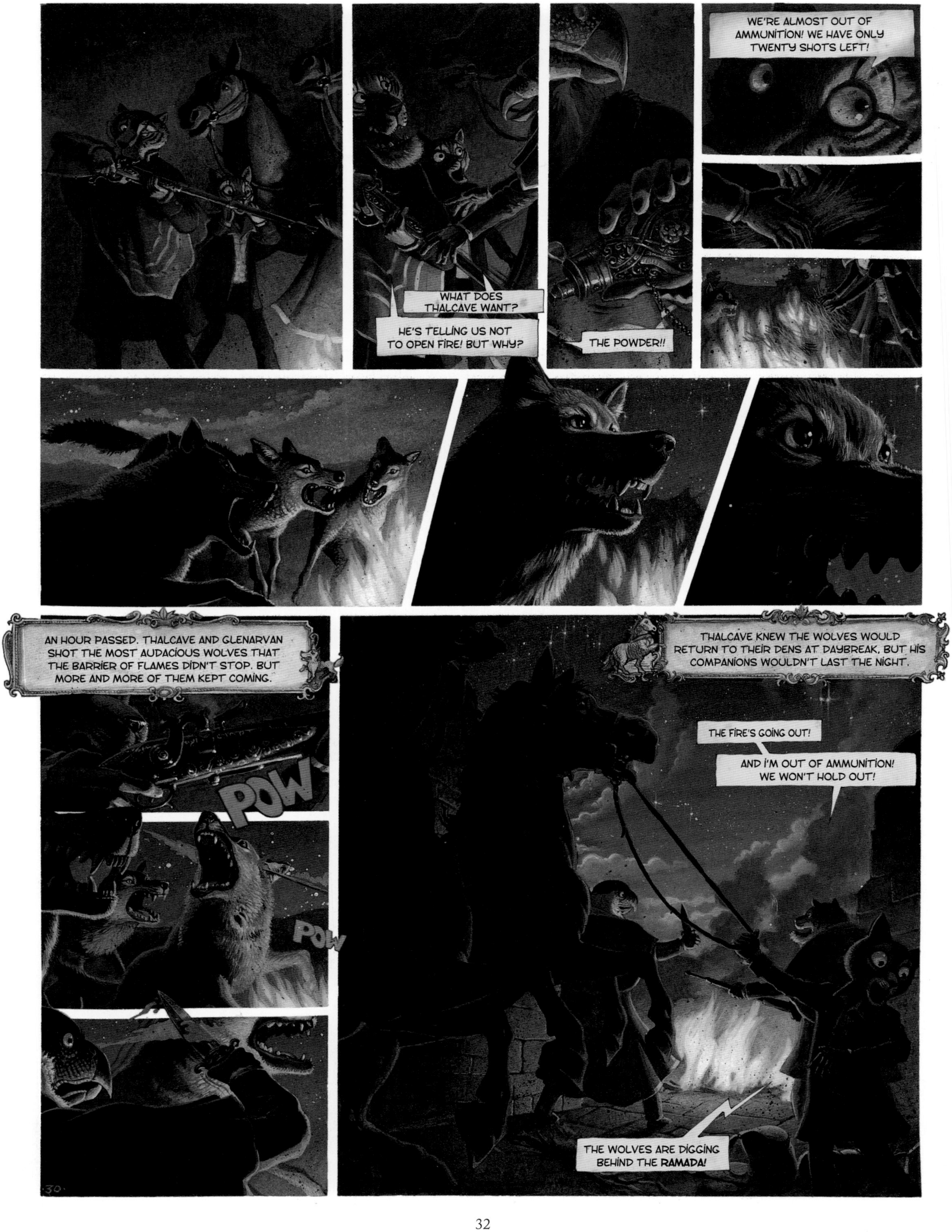
WHAT DOES THALCAVE WANT?
HE'S TELLING US NOT TO OPEN FIRE! BUT WHY?
THE POWDER!!
WE'RE ALMOST OUT OF AMMUNITION! WE HAVE ONLY TWENTY SHOTS LEFT!
AN HOUR PASSED. THALCAVE AND GLENARVAN SHOT THE MOST AUDACIOUS WOLVES THAT THE BARRIER OF FLAMES DIDN'T STOP. BUT MORE AND MORE OF THEM KEPT COMING.
POW
POW
THALCAVE KNEW THE WOLVES WOULD RETURN TO THEIR DENS AT DAYBREAK, BUT HIS COMPANIONS WOULDN'T LAST THE NIGHT.
THE FIRE'S GOING OUT!
AND I'M OUT OF AMMUNITION! WE WON'T HOLD OUT!
THE WOLVES ARE DIGGING BEHIND THE **RAMADA!**
·30·

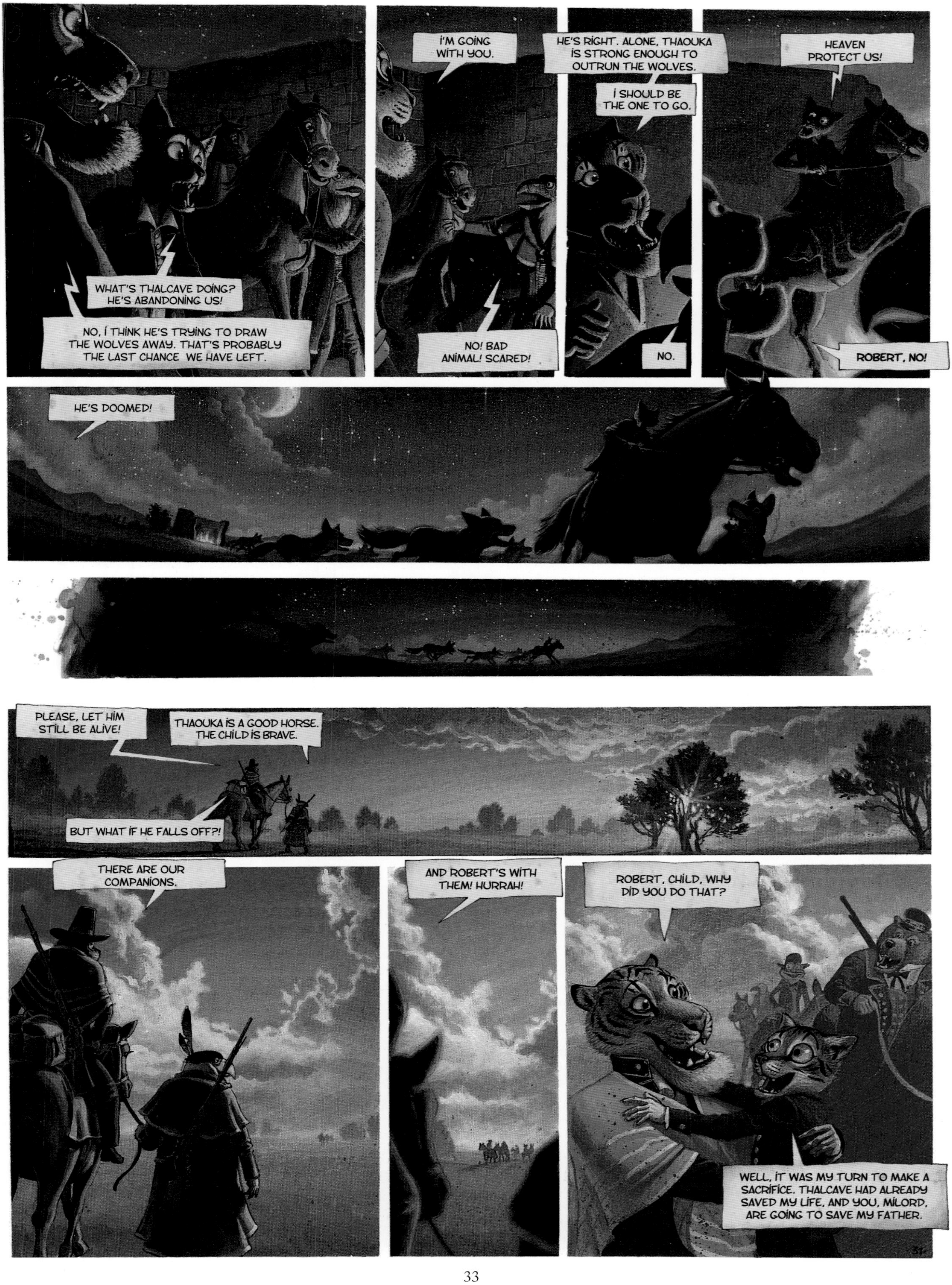
WHAT'S THALCAVE DOING? HE'S ABANDONING US!
NO, I THINK HE'S TRYING TO DRAW THE WOLVES AWAY. THAT'S PROBABLY THE LAST CHANCE WE HAVE LEFT.
I'M GOING WITH YOU.
NO! BAD ANIMAL! SCARED!
HE'S RIGHT. ALONE, THAOUKA IS STRONG ENOUGH TO OUTRUN THE WOLVES.
I SHOULD BE THE ONE TO GO.
NO.
HEAVEN PROTECT US!
ROBERT, NO!
HE'S DOOMED!
PLEASE, LET HIM STILL BE ALIVE!
THAOUKA IS A GOOD HORSE. THE CHILD IS BRAVE.
BUT WHAT IF HE FALLS OFF?!
THERE ARE OUR COMPANIONS.
AND ROBERT'S WITH THEM! HURRAH!
ROBERT, CHILD, WHY DID YOU DO THAT?
WELL, IT WAS MY TURN TO MAKE A SACRIFICE. THALCAVE HAD ALREADY SAVED MY LIFE, AND YOU, MILORD, ARE GOING TO SAVE MY FATHER.

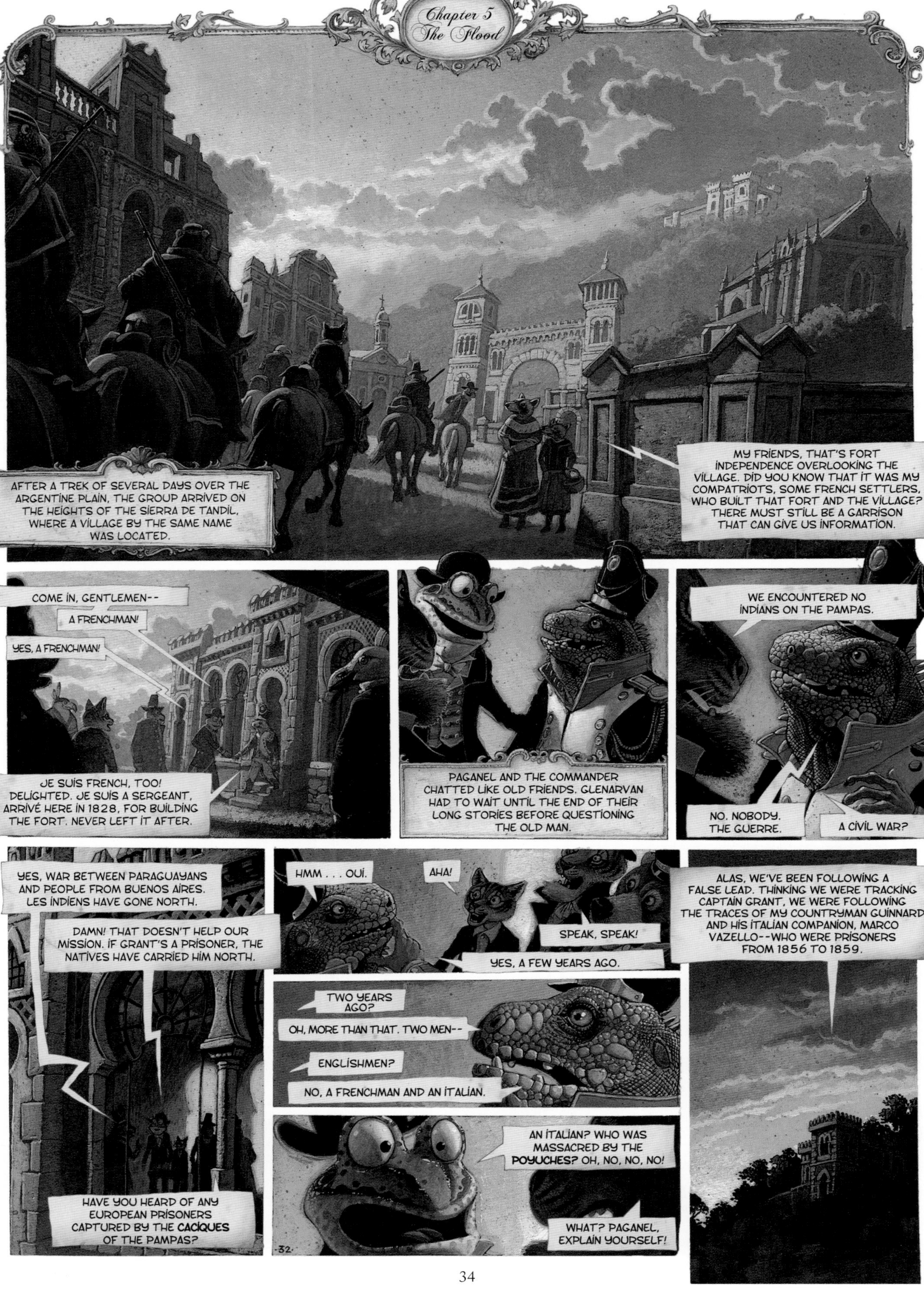
Chapter 5
The Flood
AFTER A TREK OF SEVERAL DAYS OVER THE ARGENTINE PLAIN, THE GROUP ARRIVED ON THE HEIGHTS OF THE SIERRA DE TANDIL, WHERE A VILLAGE BY THE SAME NAME WAS LOCATED.
MY FRIENDS, THAT'S FORT INDEPENDENCE OVERLOOKING THE VILLAGE. DID YOU KNOW THAT IT WAS MY COMPATRIOTS, SOME FRENCH SETTLERS, WHO BUILT THAT FORT AND THE VILLAGE? THERE MUST STILL BE A GARRISON THAT CAN GIVE US INFORMATION.
COME IN, GENTLEMEN--
A FRENCHMAN!
YES, A FRENCHMAN!
JE SUIS FRENCH, TOO! DELIGHTED. JE SUIS A SERGEANT, ARRIVÉ HERE IN 1828, FOR BUILDING THE FORT. NEVER LEFT IT AFTER.
PAGANEL AND THE COMMANDER CHATTED LIKE OLD FRIENDS. GLENARVAN HAD TO WAIT UNTIL THE END OF THEIR LONG STORIES BEFORE QUESTIONING THE OLD MAN.
WE ENCOUNTERED NO INDIANS ON THE PAMPAS.
NO. NOBODY. THE GUERRE.
A CIVIL WAR?
YES, WAR BETWEEN PARAGUAYANS AND PEOPLE FROM BUENOS AIRES. LES INDIENS HAVE GONE NORTH.
DAMN! THAT DOESN'T HELP OUR MISSION. IF GRANT'S A PRISONER, THE NATIVES HAVE CARRIED HIM NORTH.
HAVE YOU HEARD OF ANY EUROPEAN PRISONERS CAPTURED BY THE **CACIQUES** OF THE PAMPAS?
HMM . . . OUI.
AHA!
SPEAK, SPEAK!
YES, A FEW YEARS AGO.
TWO YEARS AGO?
OH, MORE THAN THAT. TWO MEN--
ENGLISHMEN?
NO, A FRENCHMAN AND AN ITALIAN.
AN ITALIAN? WHO WAS MASSACRED BY THE **POYUCHES?** OH, NO, NO, NO!
WHAT? PAGANEL, EXPLAIN YOURSELF!
ALAS, WE'VE BEEN FOLLOWING A FALSE LEAD. THINKING WE WERE TRACKING CAPTAIN GRANT, WE WERE FOLLOWING THE TRACES OF MY COUNTRYMAN GUINNARD AND HIS ITALIAN COMPANION, MARCO VAZELLO--WHO WERE PRISONERS FROM 1856 TO 1859.
-32-

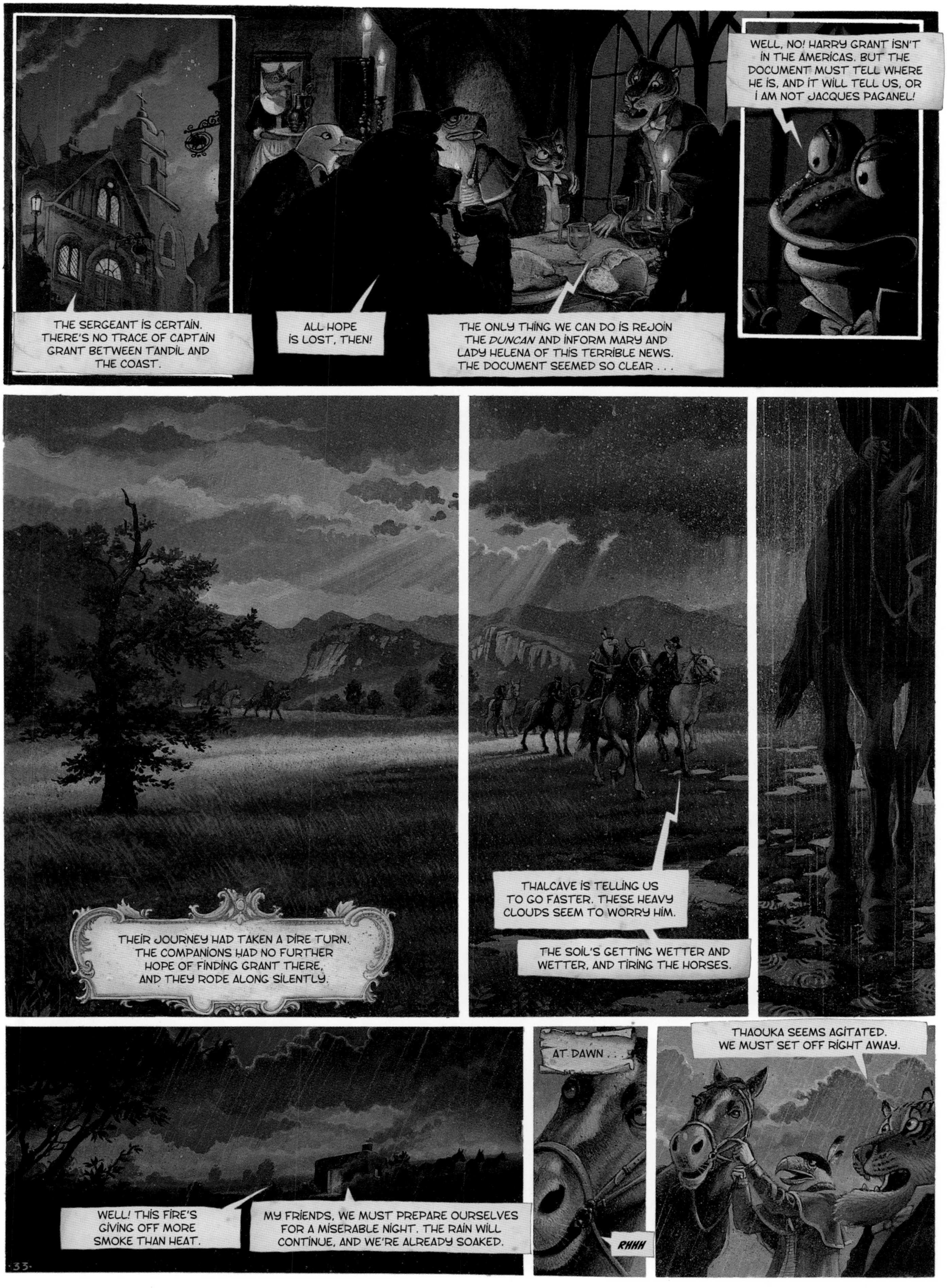
WELL, NO! HARRY GRANT ISN'T IN THE AMERICAS. BUT THE DOCUMENT MUST TELL WHERE HE IS, AND IT WILL TELL US, OR I AM NOT JACQUES PAGANEL!
THE SERGEANT IS CERTAIN. THERE'S NO TRACE OF CAPTAIN GRANT BETWEEN TANDIL AND THE COAST.
ALL HOPE IS LOST, THEN!
THE ONLY THING WE CAN DO IS REJOIN THE *DUNCAN* AND INFORM MARY AND LADY HELENA OF THIS TERRIBLE NEWS. THE DOCUMENT SEEMED SO CLEAR . . .
THEIR JOURNEY HAD TAKEN A DIRE TURN. THE COMPANIONS HAD NO FURTHER HOPE OF FINDING GRANT THERE, AND THEY RODE ALONG SILENTLY.
THALCAVE IS TELLING US TO GO FASTER. THESE HEAVY CLOUDS SEEM TO WORRY HIM.
THE SOIL'S GETTING WETTER AND WETTER, AND TIRING THE HORSES.
WELL! THIS FIRE'S GIVING OFF MORE SMOKE THAN HEAT.
MY FRIENDS, WE MUST PREPARE OURSELVES FOR A MISERABLE NIGHT. THE RAIN WILL CONTINUE, AND WE'RE ALREADY SOAKED.
AT DAWN . . .
RHHH
THAOUKA SEEMS AGITATED. WE MUST SET OFF RIGHT AWAY.
-33-

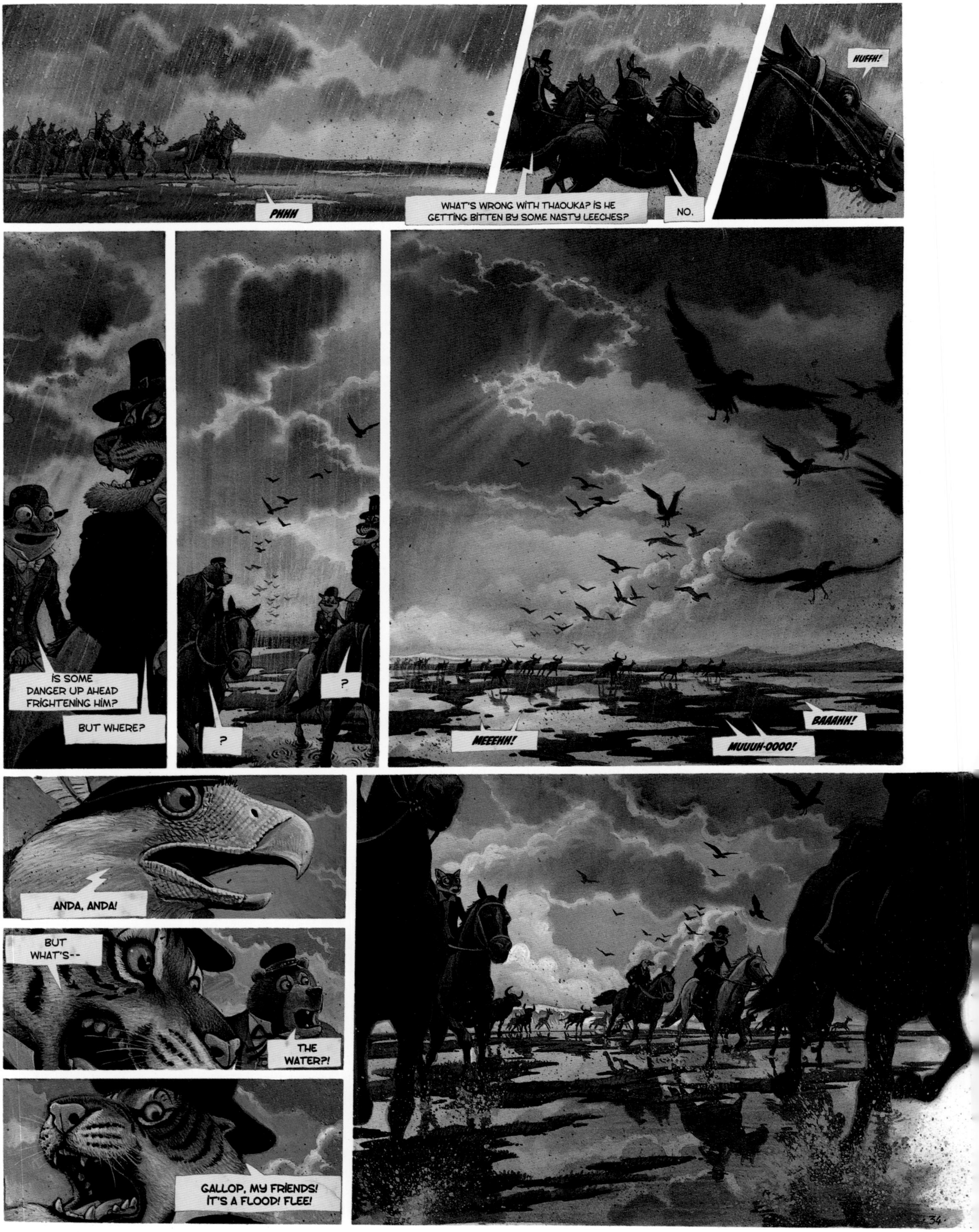
PHHH
WHAT'S WRONG WITH THAOUKA? IS HE GETTING BITTEN BY SOME NASTY LEECHES?
NO.
HUFFH!
IS SOME DANGER UP AHEAD FRIGHTENING HIM?
BUT WHERE?
?
?
MEEEHH!
MUUUH-OOOO!
BAAAHH!
ANDA, ANDA!
BUT WHAT'S--
THE WATER?!
GALLOP, MY FRIENDS! IT'S A FLOOD! FLEE!
34

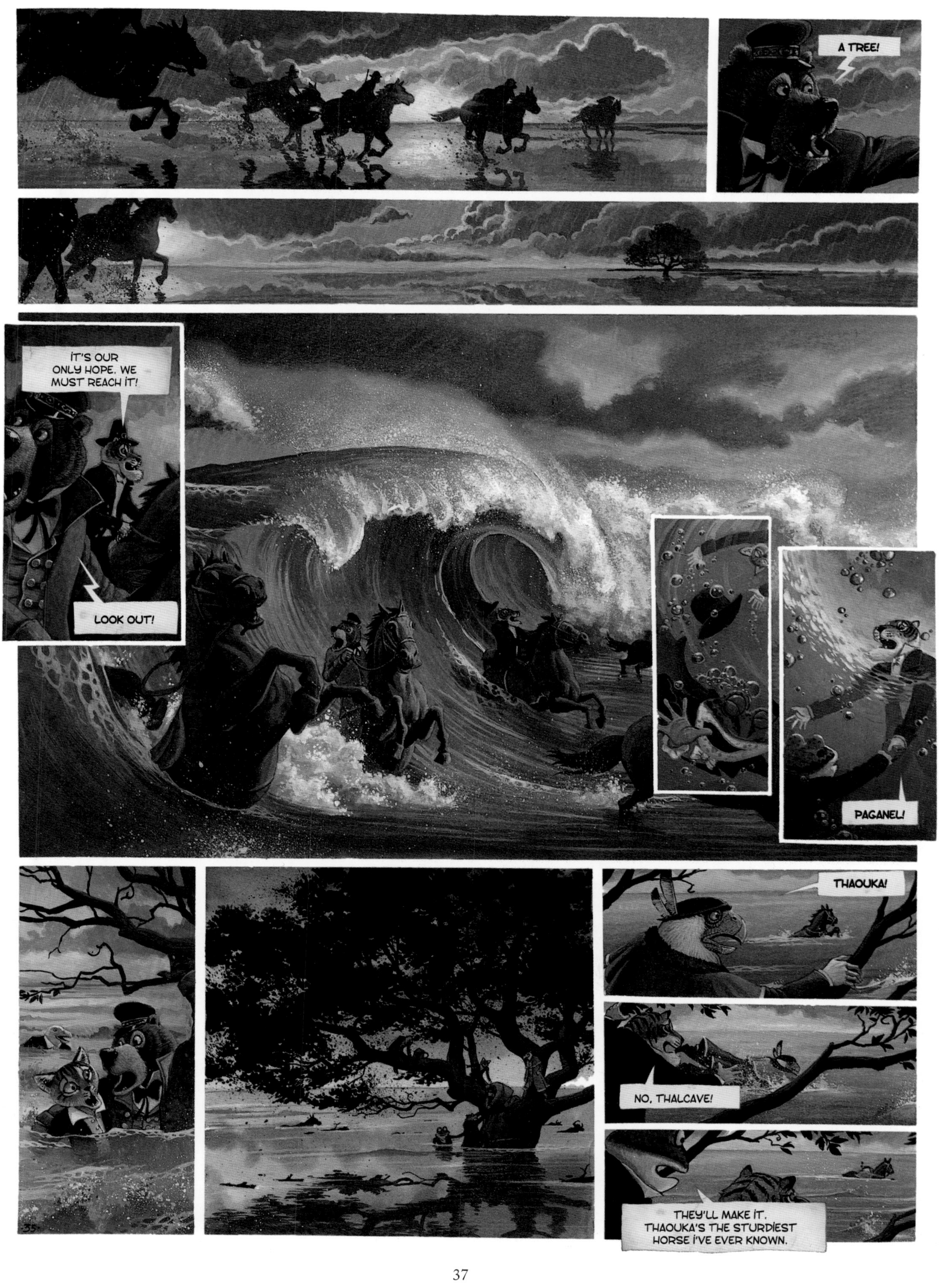
A TREE!
IT'S OUR ONLY HOPE. WE MUST REACH IT!
LOOK OUT!
PAGANEL!
THAOUKA!
NO, THALCAVE!
THEY'LL MAKE IT. THAOUKA'S THE STURDIEST HORSE I'VE EVER KNOWN.

Chapter 6
The Life of Birds

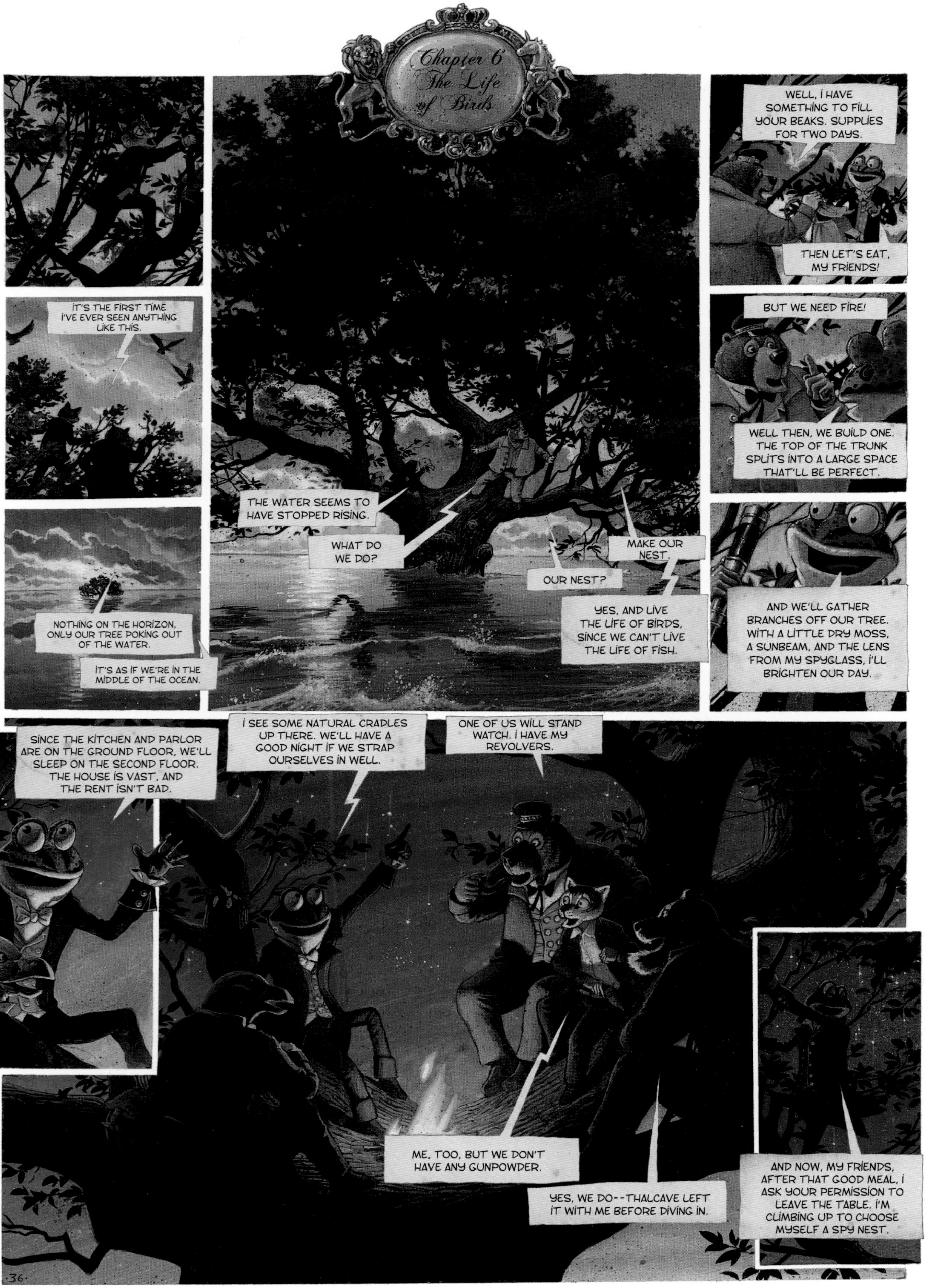

IT'S THE FIRST TIME I'VE EVER SEEN ANYTHING LIKE THIS.
NOTHING ON THE HORIZON, ONLY OUR TREE POKING OUT OF THE WATER.
IT'S AS IF WE'RE IN THE MIDDLE OF THE OCEAN.
THE WATER SEEMS TO HAVE STOPPED RISING.
WHAT DO WE DO?
MAKE OUR NEST.
OUR NEST?
YES, AND LIVE THE LIFE OF BIRDS, SINCE WE CAN'T LIVE THE LIFE OF FISH.
WELL, I HAVE SOMETHING TO FILL YOUR BEAKS. SUPPLIES FOR TWO DAYS.
THEN LET'S EAT, MY FRIENDS!
BUT WE NEED FIRE!
WELL THEN, WE BUILD ONE. THE TOP OF THE TRUNK SPLITS INTO A LARGE SPACE THAT'LL BE PERFECT.
AND WE'LL GATHER BRANCHES OFF OUR TREE. WITH A LITTLE DRY MOSS, A SUNBEAM, AND THE LENS FROM MY SPYGLASS, I'LL BRIGHTEN OUR DAY.
SINCE THE KITCHEN AND PARLOR ARE ON THE GROUND FLOOR, WE'LL SLEEP ON THE SECOND FLOOR. THE HOUSE IS VAST, AND THE RENT ISN'T BAD.
I SEE SOME NATURAL CRADLES UP THERE. WE'LL HAVE A GOOD NIGHT IF WE STRAP OURSELVES IN WELL.
ONE OF US WILL STAND WATCH. I HAVE MY REVOLVERS.
ME, TOO, BUT WE DON'T HAVE ANY GUNPOWDER.
YES, WE DO--THALCAVE LEFT IT WITH ME BEFORE DIVING IN.
AND NOW, MY FRIENDS, AFTER THAT GOOD MEAL, I ASK YOUR PERMISSION TO LEAVE THE TABLE. I'M CLIMBING UP TO CHOOSE MYSELF A SPY NEST.
·36·

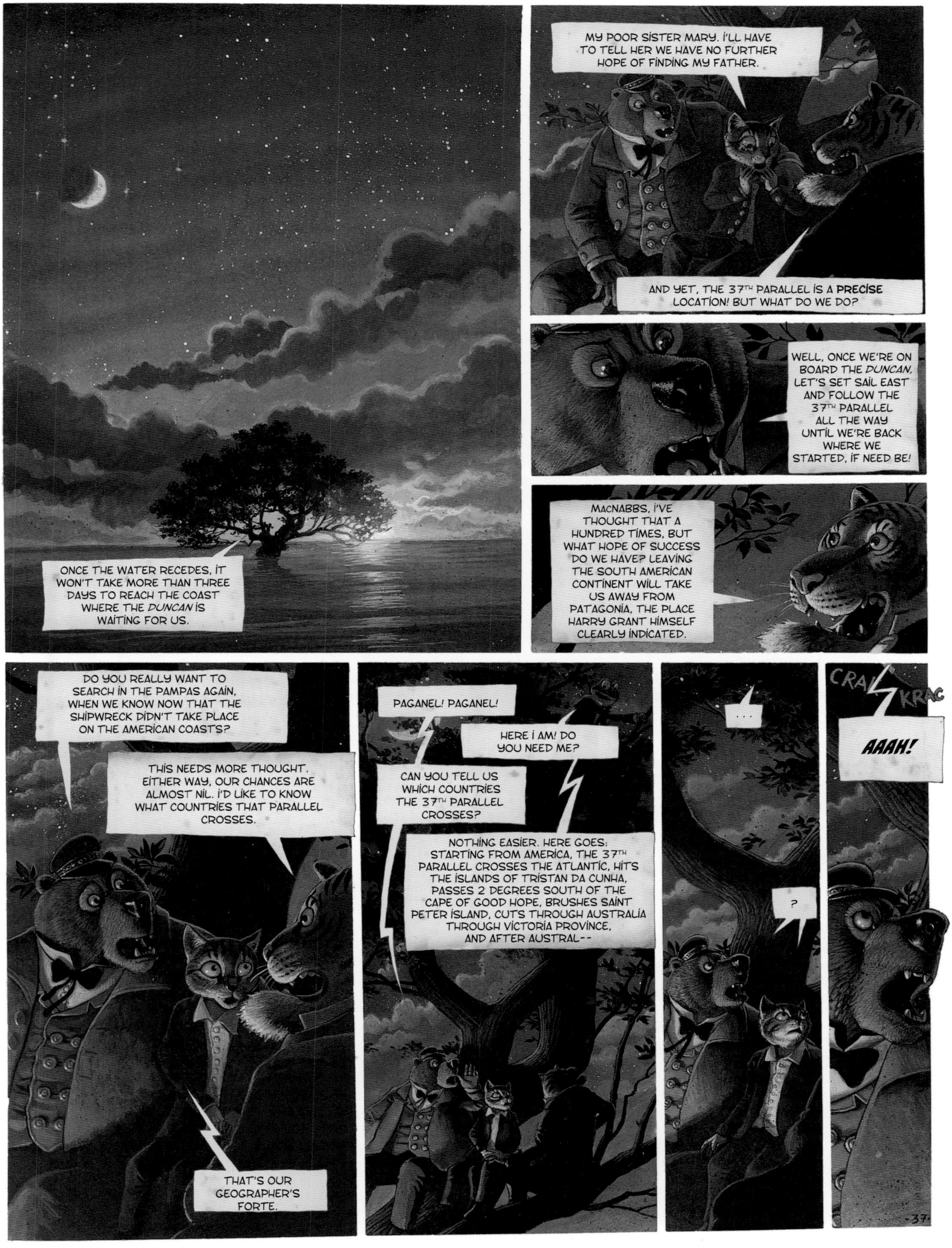
ONCE THE WATER RECEDES, IT WON'T TAKE MORE THAN THREE DAYS TO REACH THE COAST WHERE THE *DUNCAN* IS WAITING FOR US.
MY POOR SISTER MARY. I'LL HAVE TO TELL HER WE HAVE NO FURTHER HOPE OF FINDING MY FATHER.
AND YET, THE 37TH PARALLEL IS A **PRECISE** LOCATION! BUT WHAT DO WE DO?
WELL, ONCE WE'RE ON BOARD THE *DUNCAN*, LET'S SET SAIL EAST AND FOLLOW THE 37TH PARALLEL ALL THE WAY UNTIL WE'RE BACK WHERE WE STARTED, IF NEED BE!
MACNABBS, I'VE THOUGHT THAT A HUNDRED TIMES, BUT WHAT HOPE OF SUCCESS DO WE HAVE? LEAVING THE SOUTH AMERICAN CONTINENT WILL TAKE US AWAY FROM PATAGONIA, THE PLACE HARRY GRANT HIMSELF CLEARLY INDICATED.
DO YOU REALLY WANT TO SEARCH IN THE PAMPAS AGAIN, WHEN WE KNOW NOW THAT THE SHIPWRECK DIDN'T TAKE PLACE ON THE AMERICAN COASTS?
THIS NEEDS MORE THOUGHT. EITHER WAY, OUR CHANCES ARE ALMOST NIL. I'D LIKE TO KNOW WHAT COUNTRIES THAT PARALLEL CROSSES.
THAT'S OUR GEOGRAPHER'S FORTE.
PAGANEL! PAGANEL!
HERE I AM! DO YOU NEED ME?
CAN YOU TELL US WHICH COUNTRIES THE 37TH PARALLEL CROSSES?
NOTHING EASIER. HERE GOES: STARTING FROM AMERICA, THE 37TH PARALLEL CROSSES THE ATLANTIC, HITS THE ISLANDS OF TRISTAN DA CUNHA, PASSES 2 DEGREES SOUTH OF THE CAPE OF GOOD HOPE, BRUSHES SAINT PETER ISLAND, CUTS THROUGH AUSTRALIA THROUGH VICTORIA PROVINCE, AND AFTER AUSTRAL--
...
?
CRAK KRAC
AAAH!
-37-

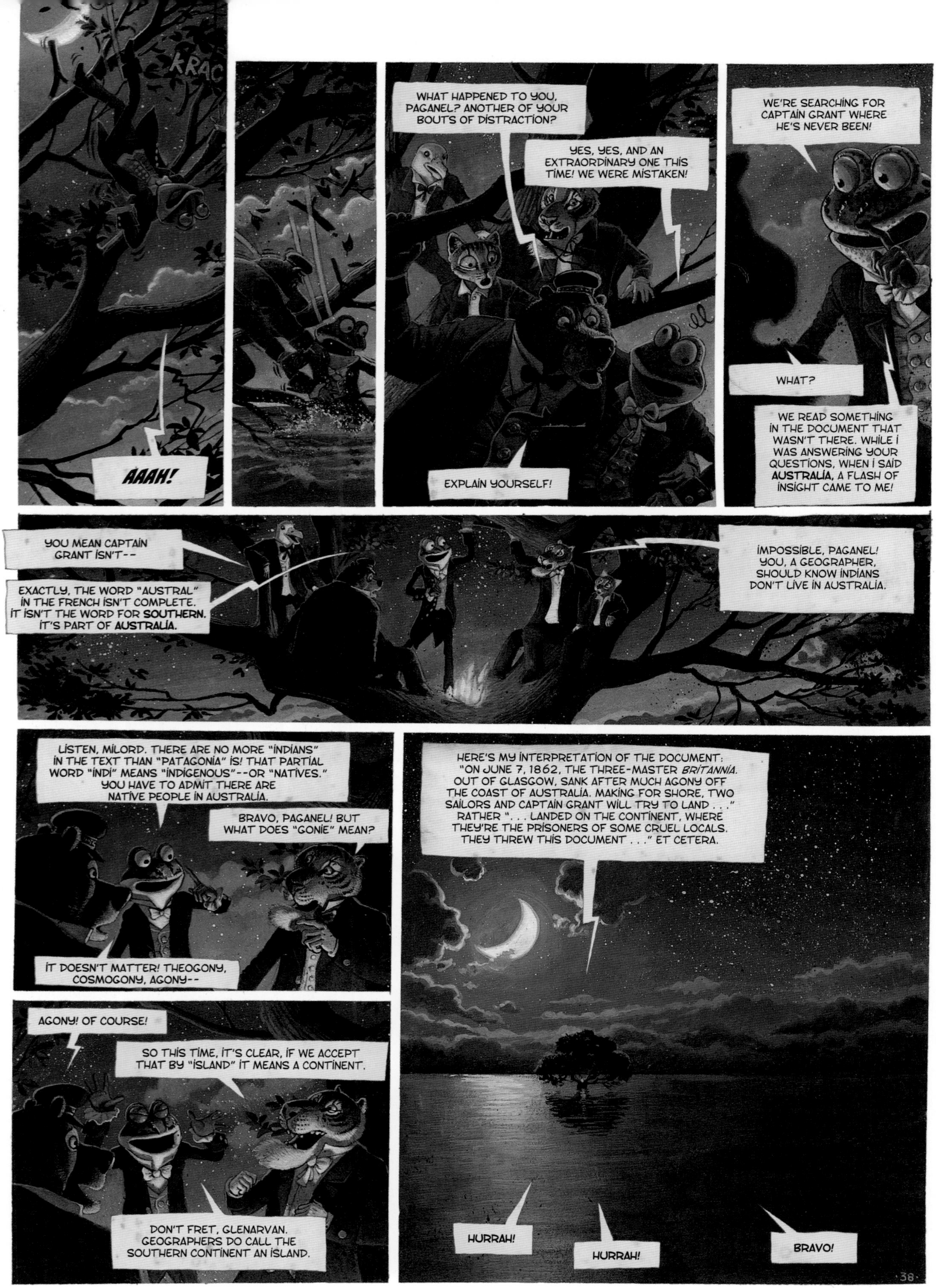
KRAC
AAAH!
WHAT HAPPENED TO YOU, PAGANEL? ANOTHER OF YOUR BOUTS OF DISTRACTION?
YES, YES, AND AN EXTRAORDINARY ONE THIS TIME! WE WERE MISTAKEN!
EXPLAIN YOURSELF!
WE'RE SEARCHING FOR CAPTAIN GRANT WHERE HE'S NEVER BEEN!
WHAT?
WE READ SOMETHING IN THE DOCUMENT THAT WASN'T THERE. WHILE I WAS ANSWERING YOUR QUESTIONS, WHEN I SAID AUSTRALIA, A FLASH OF INSIGHT CAME TO ME!
YOU MEAN CAPTAIN GRANT ISN'T--
EXACTLY, THE WORD "AUSTRAL" IN THE FRENCH ISN'T COMPLETE. IT ISN'T THE WORD FOR SOUTHERN. IT'S PART OF AUSTRALIA.
IMPOSSIBLE, PAGANEL! YOU, A GEOGRAPHER, SHOULD KNOW INDIANS DON'T LIVE IN AUSTRALIA.
LISTEN, MILORD. THERE ARE NO MORE "INDIANS" IN THE TEXT THAN "PATAGONIA" IS! THAT PARTIAL WORD "INDI" MEANS "INDIGENOUS"--OR "NATIVES." YOU HAVE TO ADMIT THERE ARE NATIVE PEOPLE IN AUSTRALIA.
BRAVO, PAGANEL! BUT WHAT DOES "GONIE" MEAN?
IT DOESN'T MATTER! THEOGONY, COSMOGONY, AGONY--
AGONY! OF COURSE!
SO THIS TIME, IT'S CLEAR, IF WE ACCEPT THAT BY "ISLAND" IT MEANS A CONTINENT.
DON'T FRET, GLENARVAN. GEOGRAPHERS DO CALL THE SOUTHERN CONTINENT AN ISLAND.
HERE'S MY INTERPRETATION OF THE DOCUMENT: "ON JUNE 7, 1862, THE THREE-MASTER BRITANNIA, OUT OF GLASGOW, SANK AFTER MUCH AGONY OFF THE COAST OF AUSTRALIA. MAKING FOR SHORE, TWO SAILORS AND CAPTAIN GRANT WILL TRY TO LAND . . ." RATHER ". . . LANDED ON THE CONTINENT, WHERE THEY'RE THE PRISONERS OF SOME CRUEL LOCALS. THEY THREW THIS DOCUMENT . . ." ET CETERA.
HURRAH!
HURRAH!
BRAVO!
·38·

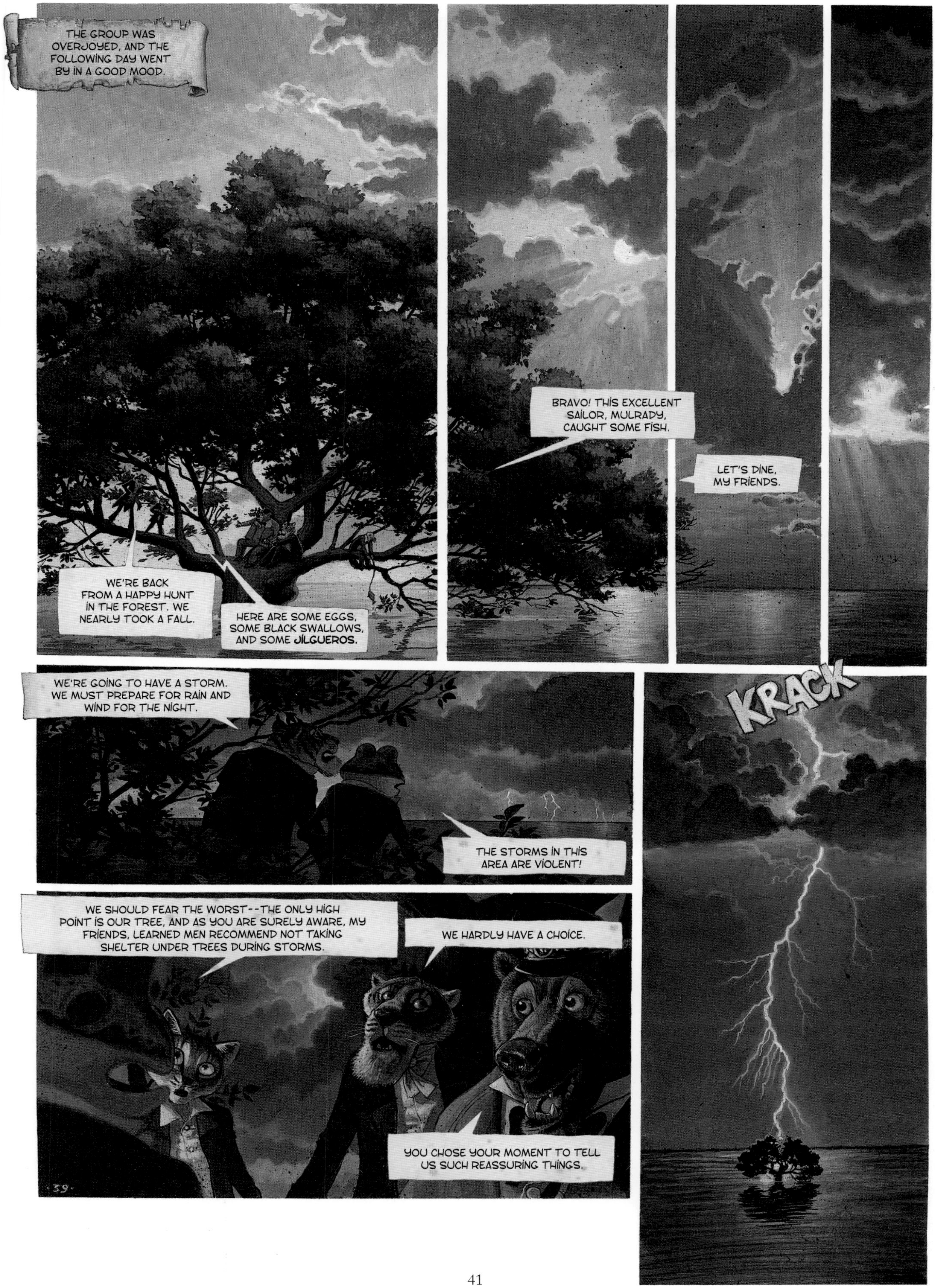
THE GROUP WAS OVERJOYED, AND THE FOLLOWING DAY WENT BY IN A GOOD MOOD.
WE'RE BACK FROM A HAPPY HUNT IN THE FOREST. WE NEARLY TOOK A FALL.
HERE ARE SOME EGGS, SOME BLACK SWALLOWS, AND SOME JILGUEROS.
BRAVO! THIS EXCELLENT SAILOR, MULRADY, CAUGHT SOME FISH.
LET'S DINE, MY FRIENDS.
WE'RE GOING TO HAVE A STORM. WE MUST PREPARE FOR RAIN AND WIND FOR THE NIGHT.
THE STORMS IN THIS AREA ARE VIOLENT!
WE SHOULD FEAR THE WORST--THE ONLY HIGH POINT IS OUR TREE, AND AS YOU ARE SURELY AWARE, MY FRIENDS, LEARNED MEN RECOMMEND NOT TAKING SHELTER UNDER TREES DURING STORMS.
WE HARDLY HAVE A CHOICE.
YOU CHOSE YOUR MOMENT TO TELL US SUCH REASSURING THINGS.
-39-
KRACK

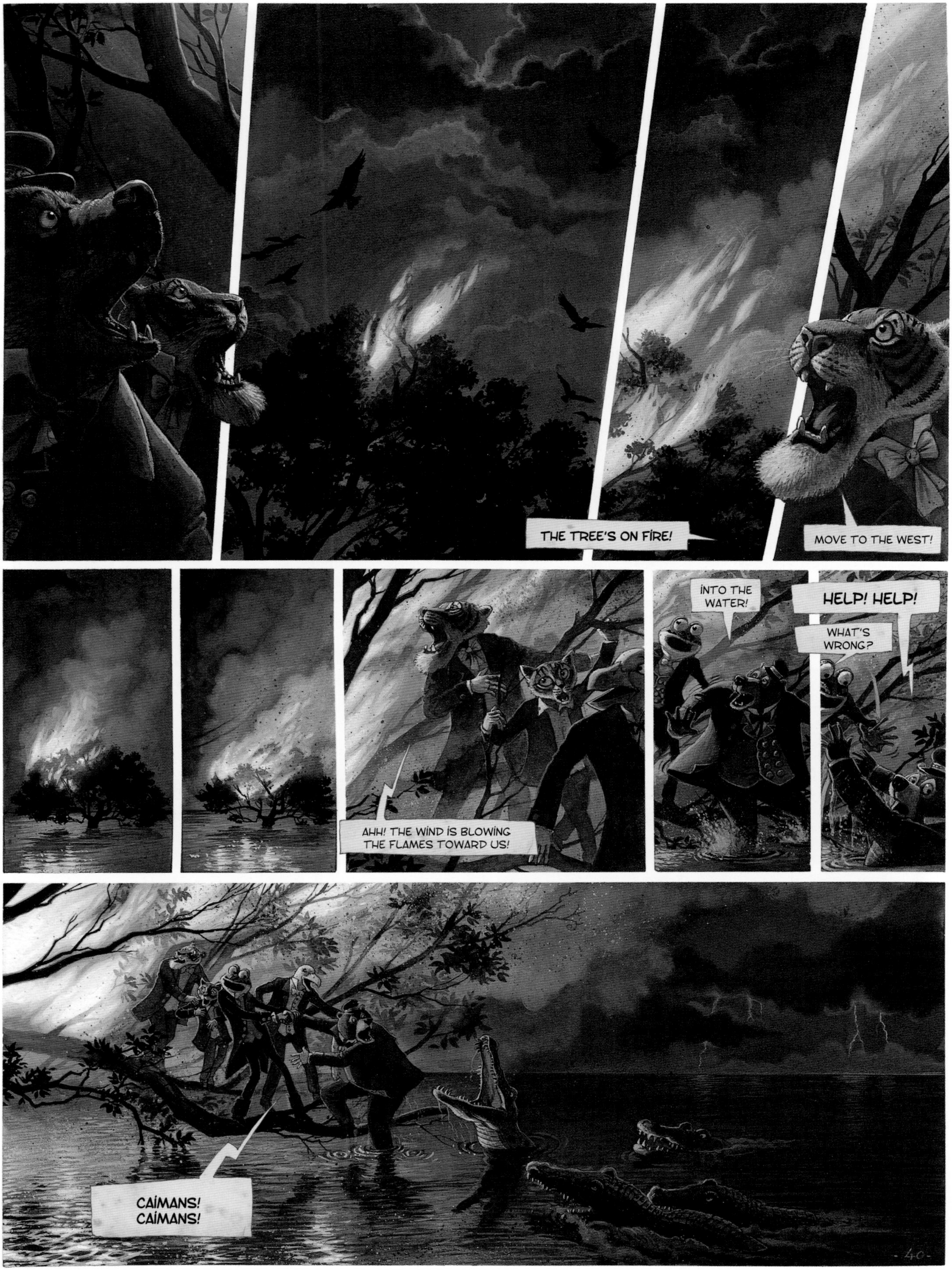
THE TREE'S ON FIRE!
MOVE TO THE WEST!
AHH! THE WIND IS BLOWING THE FLAMES TOWARD US!
INTO THE WATER!
HELP! HELP!
WHAT'S WRONG?
CAIMANS! CAIMANS!
-40-

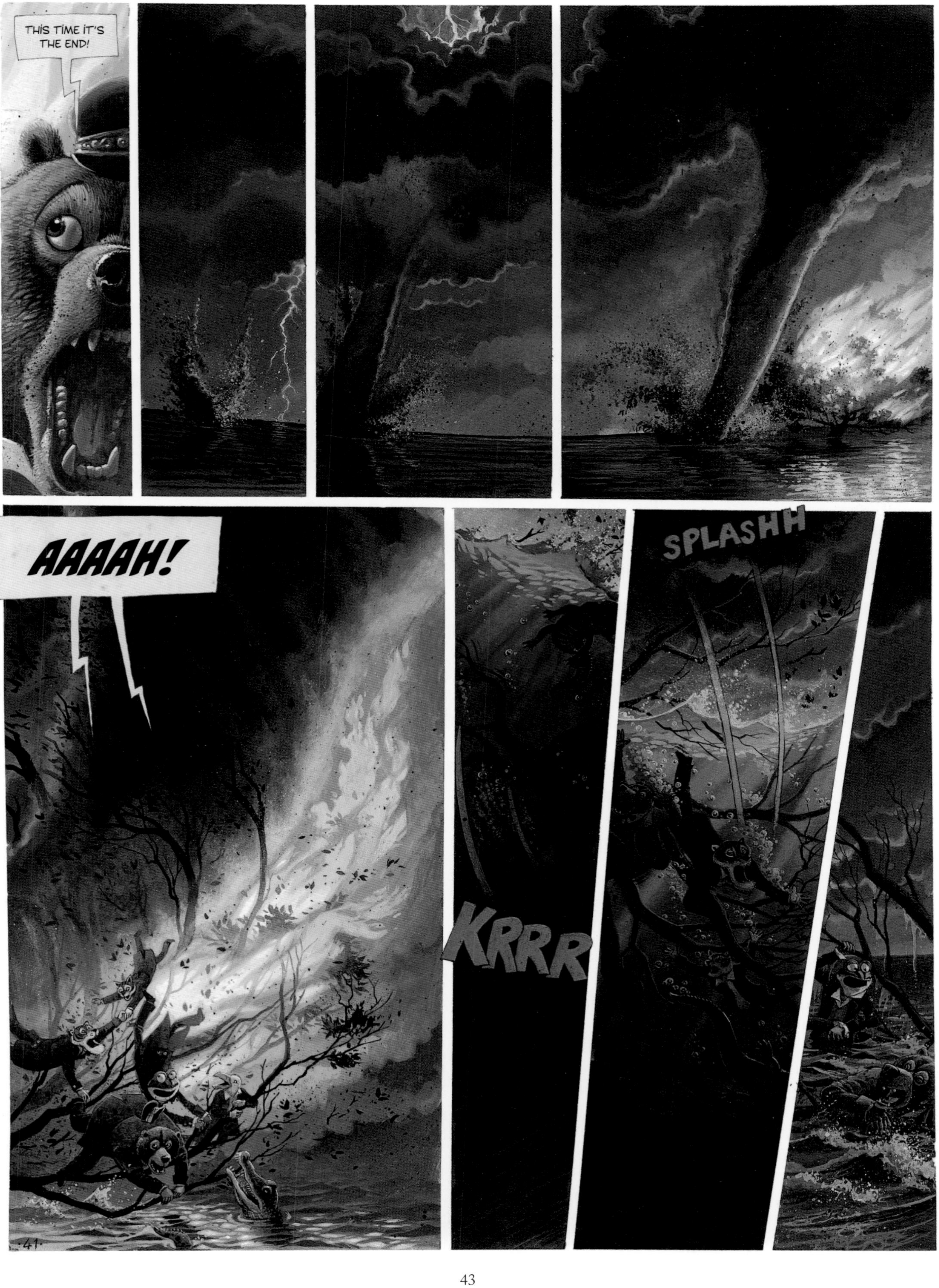
THIS TIME IT'S THE END!
AAAAH!
KRRR
SPLASHH
41

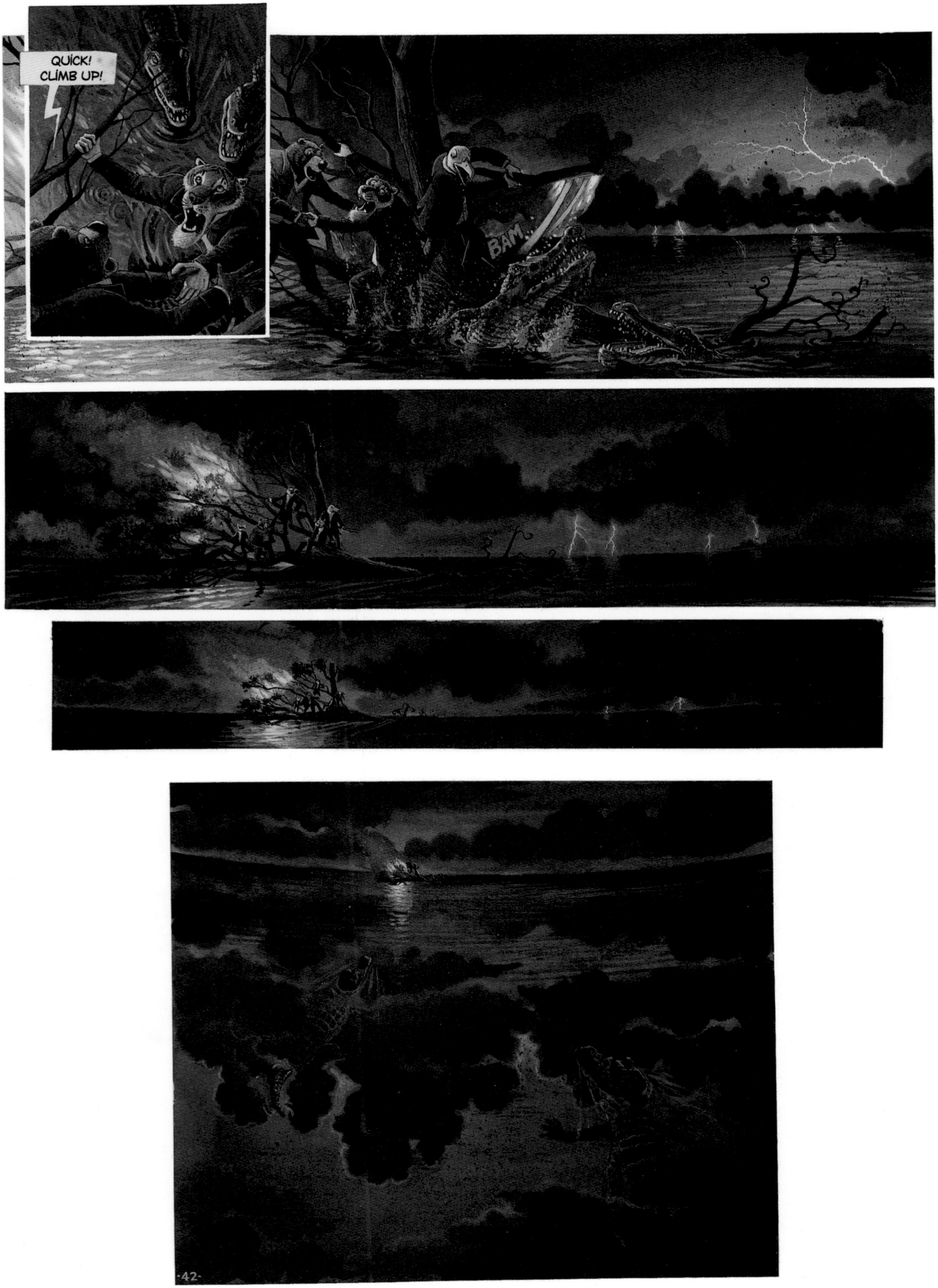
QUICK!
CLIMB UP!
BAM
-42-

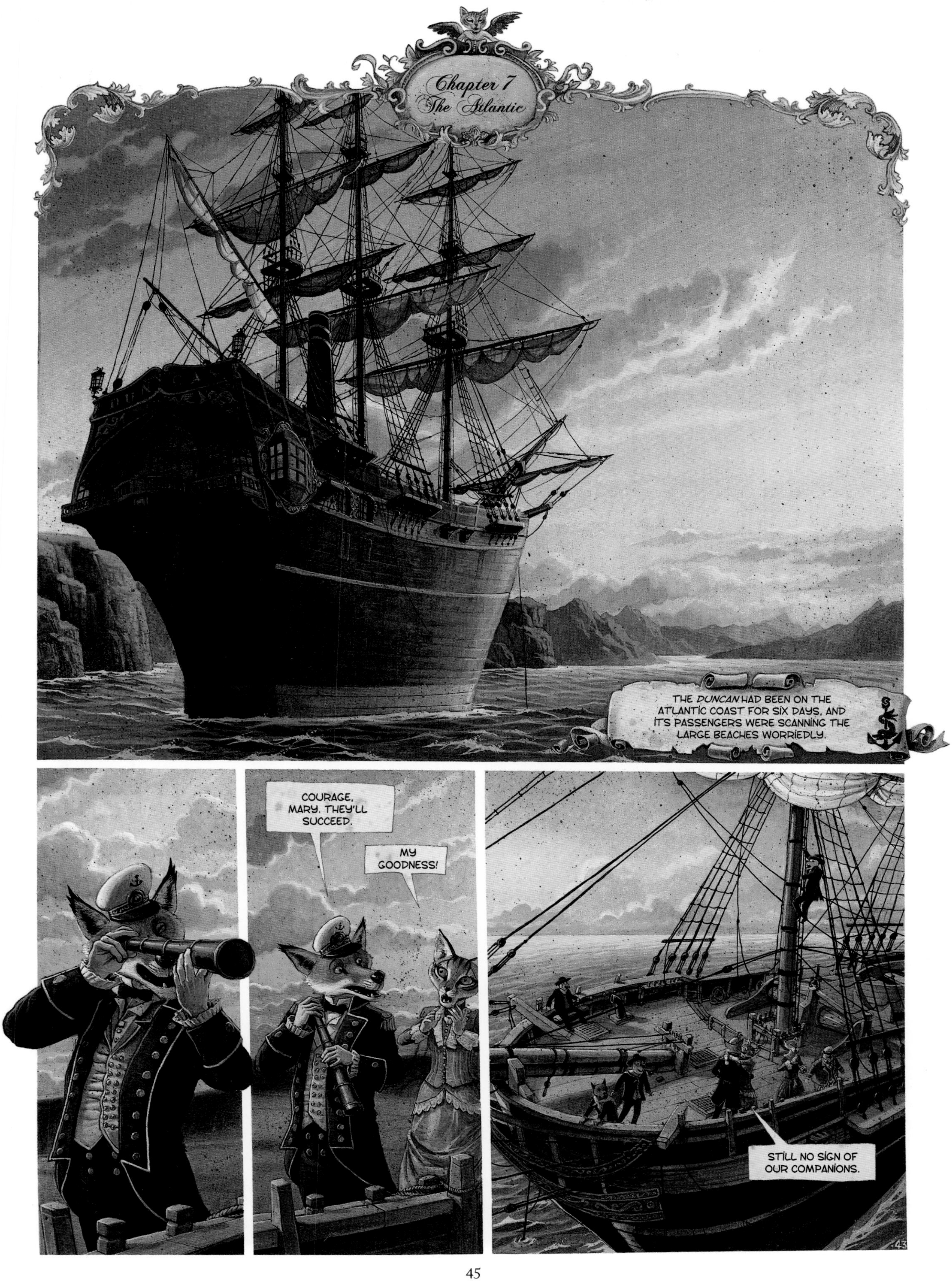
Chapter 7
The Atlantic
THE DUNCAN HAD BEEN ON THE ATLANTIC COAST FOR SIX DAYS, AND ITS PASSENGERS WERE SCANNING THE LARGE BEACHES WORRIEDLY.
COURAGE, MARY. THEY'LL SUCCEED.
MY GOODNESS!
STILL NO SIGN OF OUR COMPANIONS.

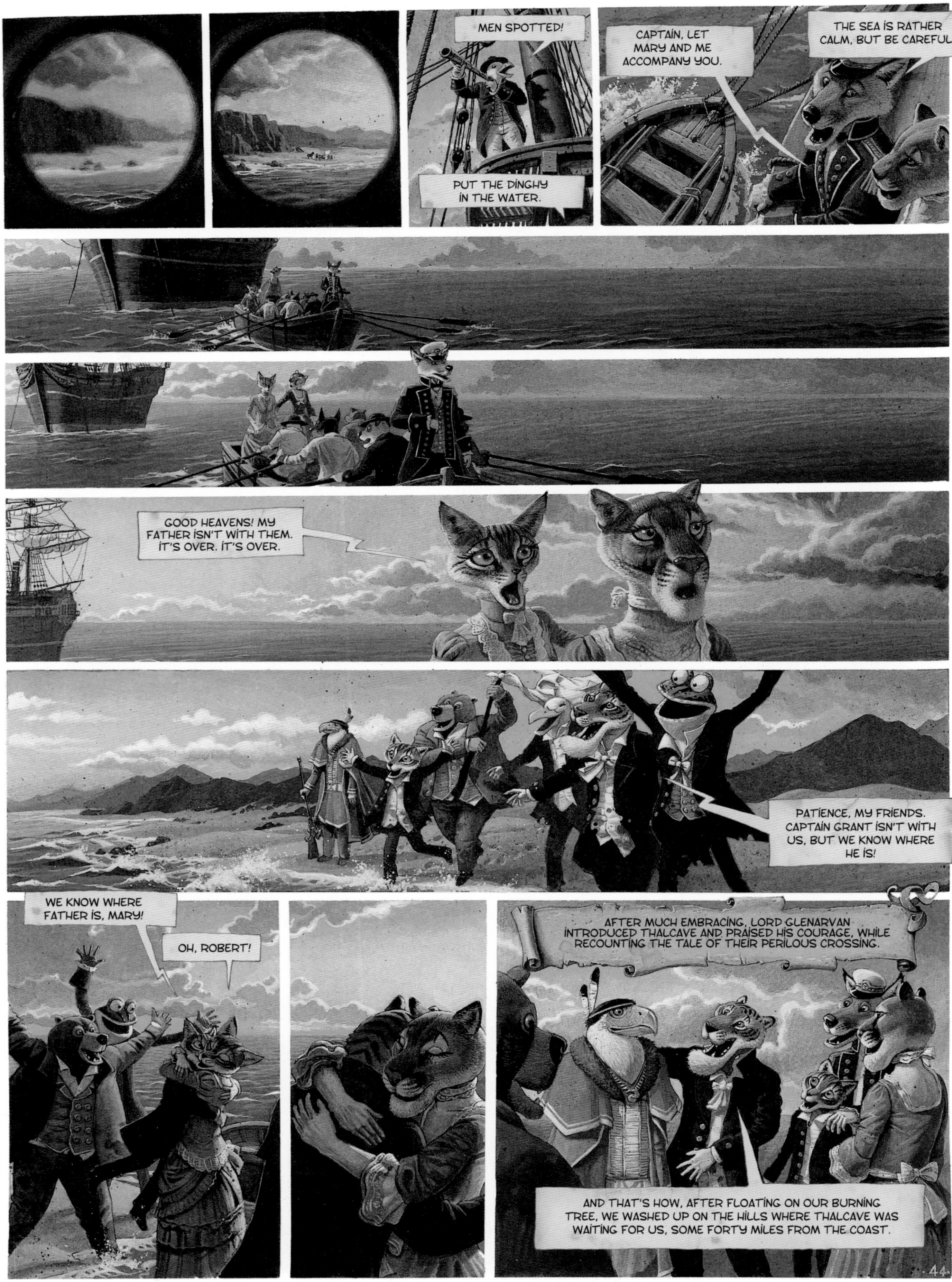
MEN SPOTTED!
PUT THE DINGHY IN THE WATER.
CAPTAIN, LET MARY AND ME ACCOMPANY YOU.
THE SEA IS RATHER CALM, BUT BE CAREFUL.
GOOD HEAVENS! MY FATHER ISN'T WITH THEM. IT'S OVER. IT'S OVER.
PATIENCE, MY FRIENDS. CAPTAIN GRANT ISN'T WITH US, BUT WE KNOW WHERE HE IS!
WE KNOW WHERE FATHER IS, MARY!
OH, ROBERT!
AFTER MUCH EMBRACING, LORD GLENARVAN INTRODUCED THALCAVE AND PRAISED HIS COURAGE, WHILE RECOUNTING THE TALE OF THEIR PERILOUS CROSSING.
AND THAT'S HOW, AFTER FLOATING ON OUR BURNING TREE, WE WASHED UP ON THE HILLS WHERE THALCAVE WAS WAITING FOR US, SOME FORTY MILES FROM THE COAST.
44

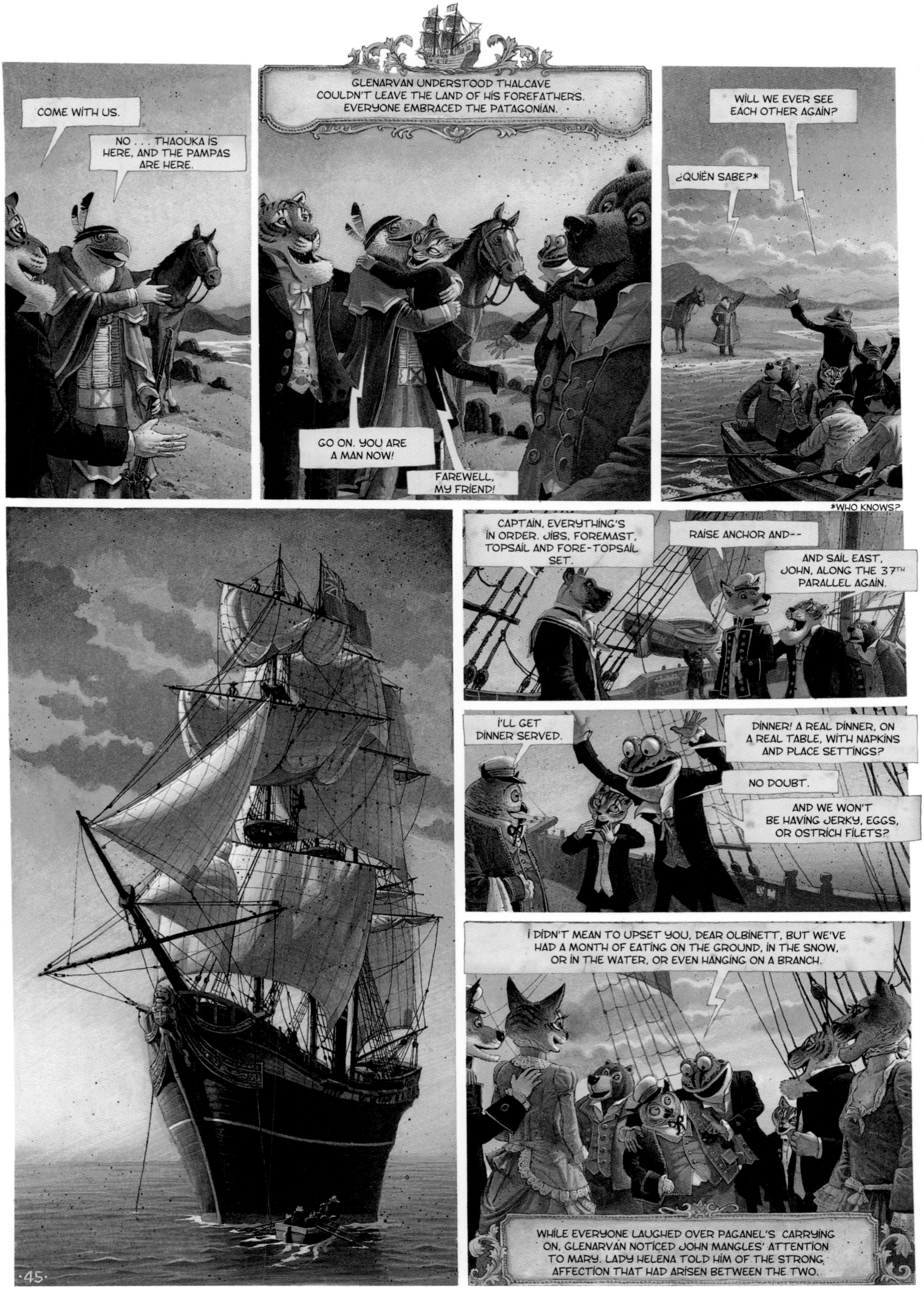
COME WITH US.
NO . . . THAOUKA IS HERE, AND THE PAMPAS ARE HERE.
GLENARVAN UNDERSTOOD THALCAVE COULDN'T LEAVE THE LAND OF HIS FOREFATHERS. EVERYONE EMBRACED THE PATAGONIAN.
GO ON. YOU ARE A MAN NOW!
FAREWELL, MY FRIEND!
WILL WE EVER SEE EACH OTHER AGAIN?
¿QUIÉN SABE?*
*WHO KNOWS?
CAPTAIN, EVERYTHING'S IN ORDER. JIBS, FOREMAST, TOPSAIL AND FORE-TOPSAIL SET.
RAISE ANCHOR AND--
AND SAIL EAST, JOHN, ALONG THE 37TH PARALLEL AGAIN.
I'LL GET DINNER SERVED.
DINNER! A REAL DINNER, ON A REAL TABLE, WITH NAPKINS AND PLACE SETTINGS?
NO DOUBT.
AND WE WON'T BE HAVING JERKY, EGGS, OR OSTRICH FILETS?
I DIDN'T MEAN TO UPSET YOU, DEAR OLBINETT, BUT WE'VE HAD A MONTH OF EATING ON THE GROUND, IN THE SNOW, OR IN THE WATER, OR EVEN HANGING ON A BRANCH.
WHILE EVERYONE LAUGHED OVER PAGANEL'S CARRYING ON, GLENARVAN NOTICED JOHN MANGLES' ATTENTION TO MARY. LADY HELENA TOLD HIM OF THE STRONG AFFECTION THAT HAD ARISEN BETWEEN THE TWO.
·45·

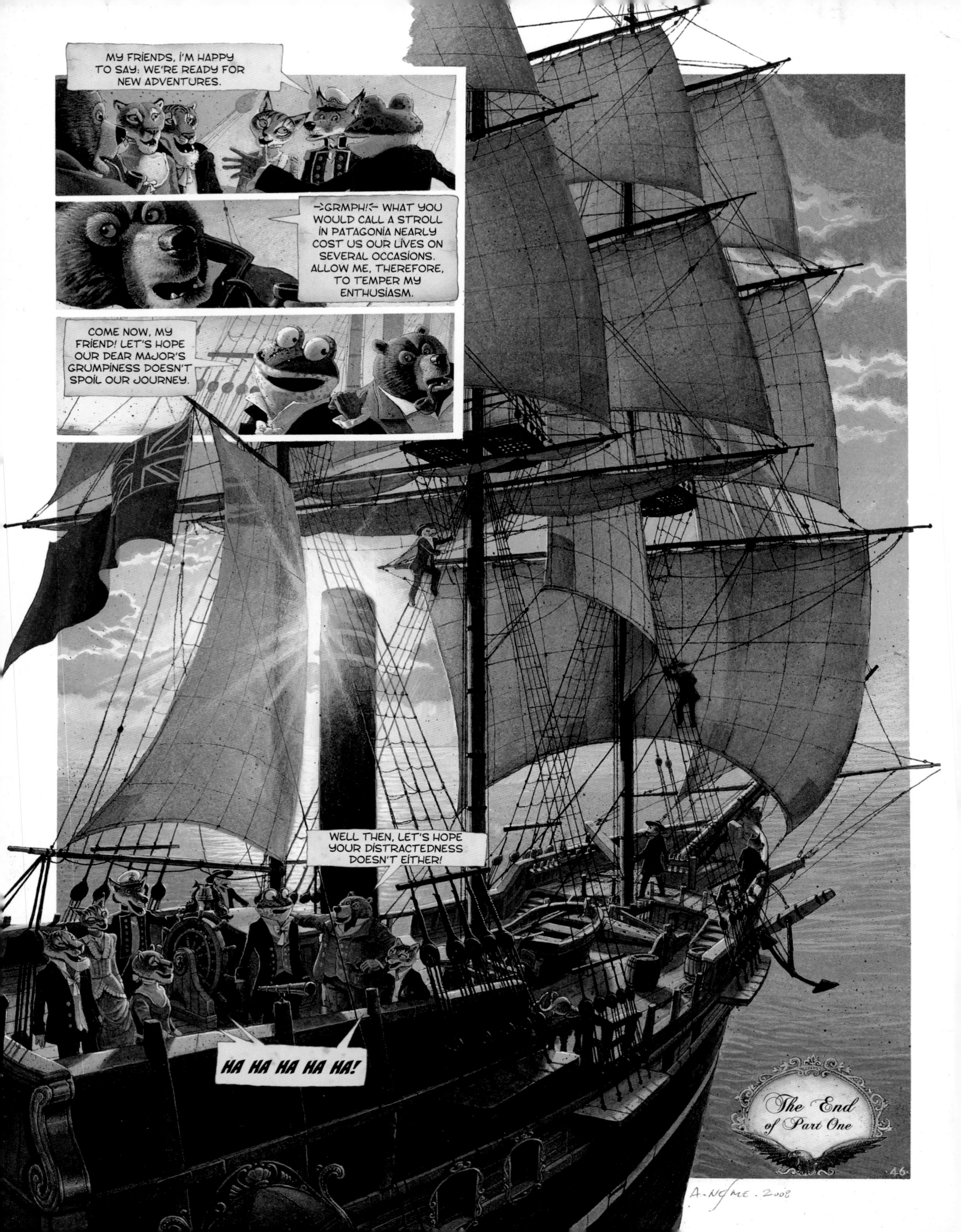
MY FRIENDS, I'M HAPPY TO SAY: WE'RE READY FOR NEW ADVENTURES.
–GRMPH!– WHAT YOU WOULD CALL A STROLL IN PATAGONIA NEARLY COST US OUR LIVES ON SEVERAL OCCASIONS. ALLOW ME, THEREFORE, TO TEMPER MY ENTHUSIASM.
COME NOW, MY FRIEND! LET'S HOPE OUR DEAR MAJOR'S GRUMPINESS DOESN'T SPOIL OUR JOURNEY.
WELL THEN, LET'S HOPE YOUR DISTRACTEDNESS DOESN'T EITHER!
HA HA HA HA HA!
The End of Part One
A. NOME . 2008

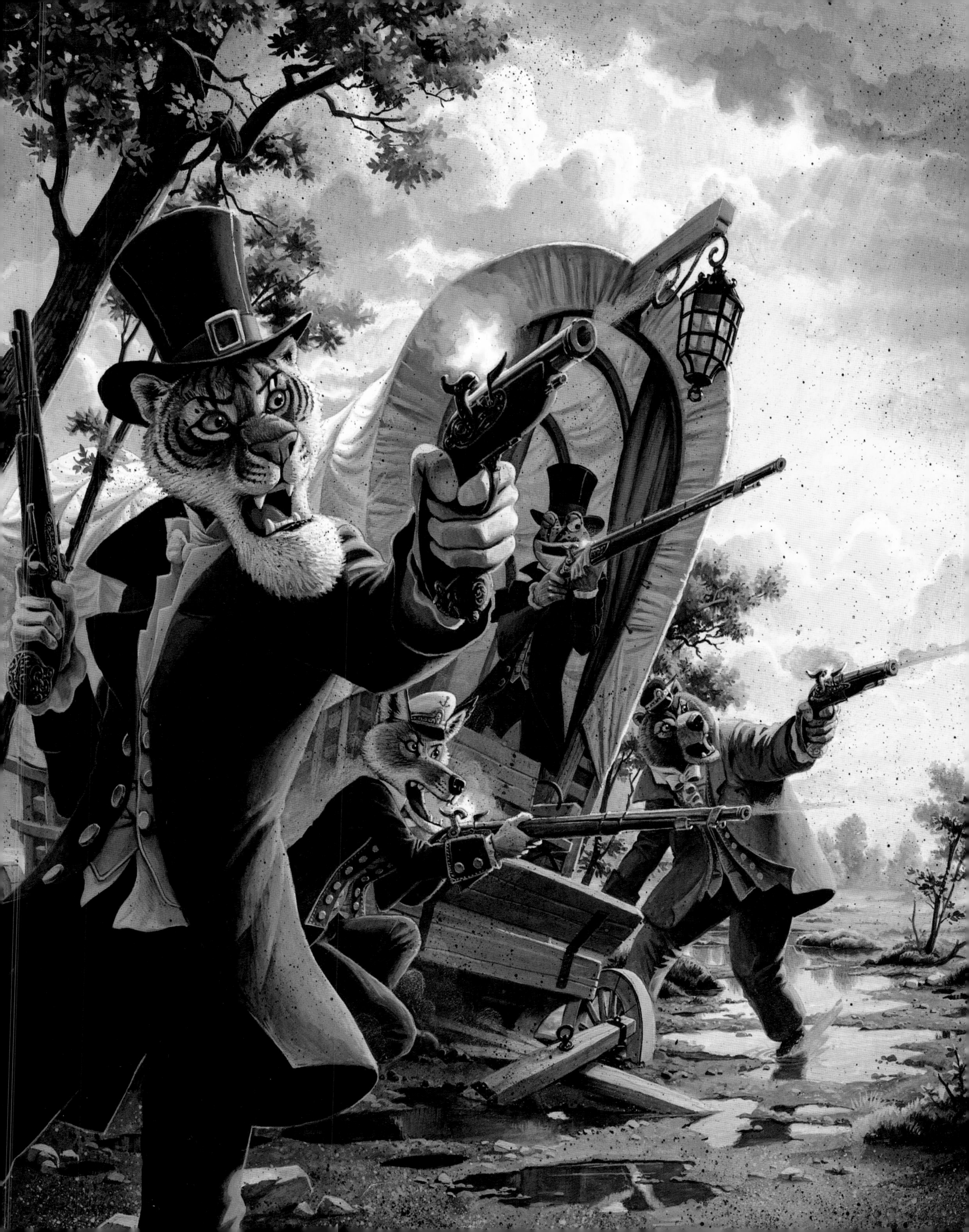

Part 2

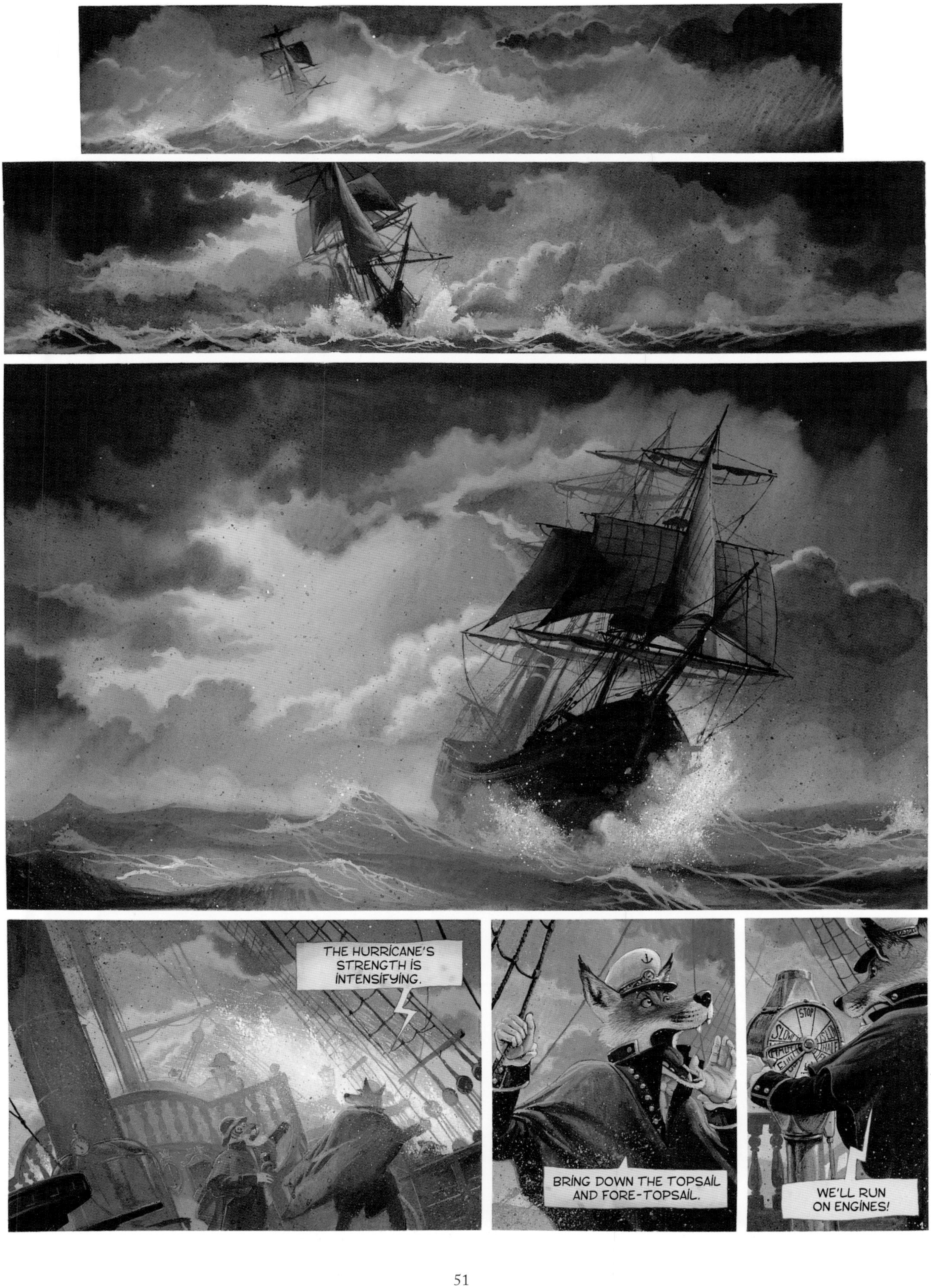
THE HURRICANE'S STRENGTH IS INTENSIFYING.
BRING DOWN THE TOPSAIL AND FORE-TOPSAIL.
WE'LL RUN ON ENGINES!

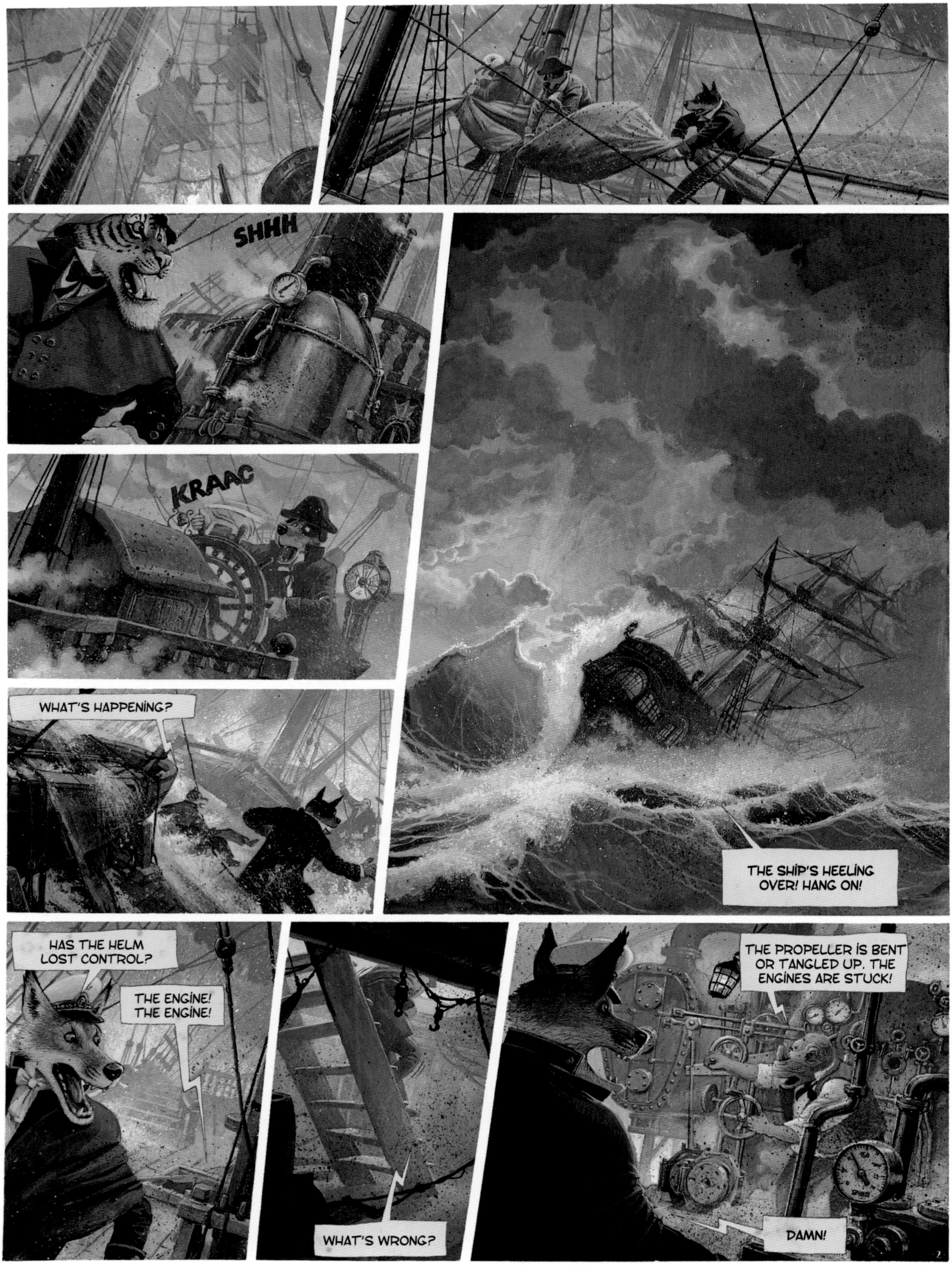
SHHH
KRAAC
WHAT'S HAPPENING?
THE SHIP'S HEELING OVER! HANG ON!
HAS THE HELM LOST CONTROL?
THE ENGINE! THE ENGINE!
WHAT'S WRONG?
THE PROPELLER IS BENT OR TANGLED UP. THE ENGINES ARE STUCK!
DAMN!

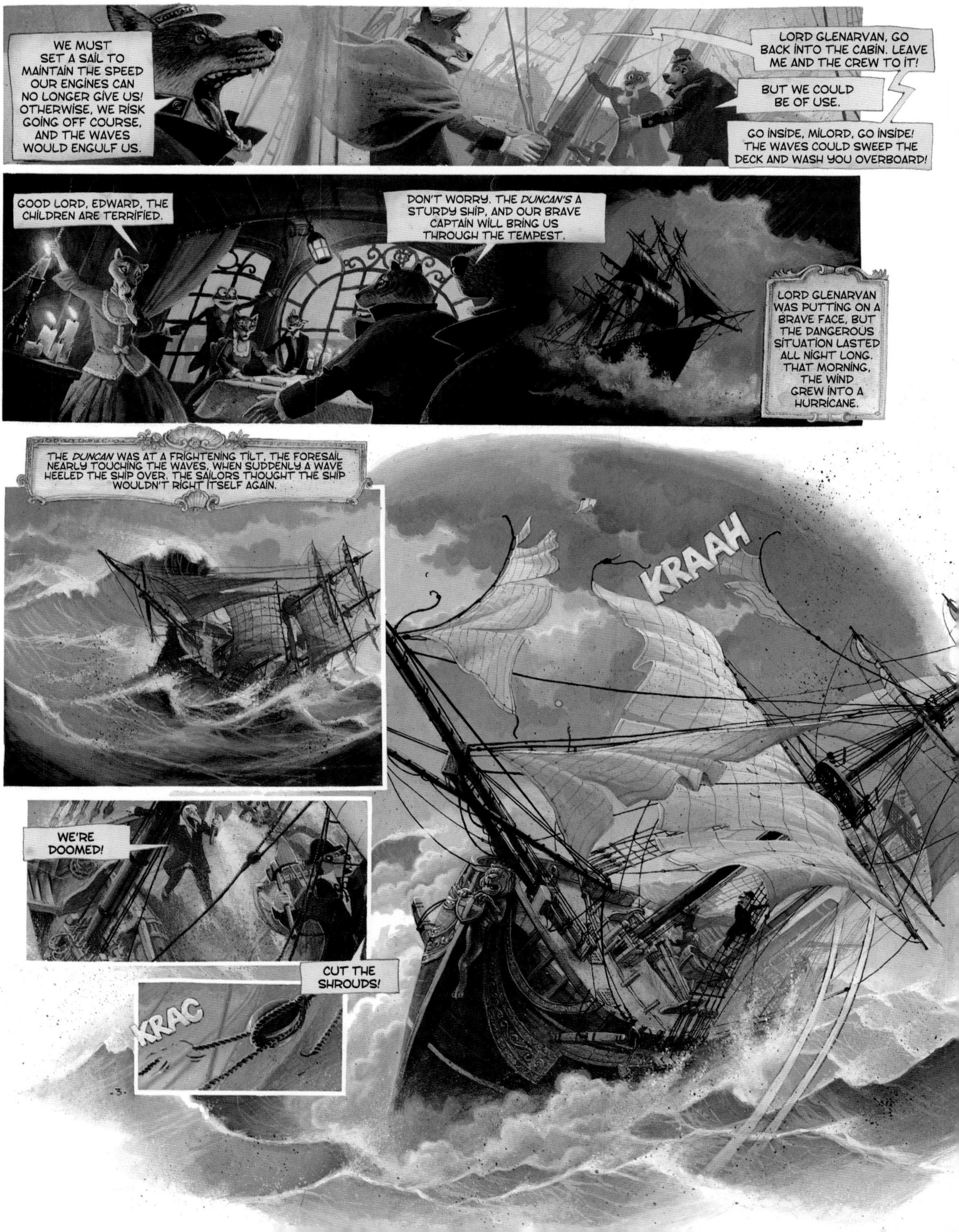
WE MUST SET A SAIL TO MAINTAIN THE SPEED OUR ENGINES CAN NO LONGER GIVE US! OTHERWISE, WE RISK GOING OFF COURSE, AND THE WAVES WOULD ENGULF US.
LORD GLENARVAN, GO BACK INTO THE CABIN. LEAVE ME AND THE CREW TO IT!
BUT WE COULD BE OF USE.
GO INSIDE, MILORD, GO INSIDE! THE WAVES COULD SWEEP THE DECK AND WASH YOU OVERBOARD!
GOOD LORD, EDWARD, THE CHILDREN ARE TERRIFIED.
DON'T WORRY. THE *DUNCAN'S* A STURDY SHIP, AND OUR BRAVE CAPTAIN WILL BRING US THROUGH THE TEMPEST.
LORD GLENARVAN WAS PUTTING ON A BRAVE FACE, BUT THE DANGEROUS SITUATION LASTED ALL NIGHT LONG. THAT MORNING, THE WIND GREW INTO A HURRICANE.
THE *DUNCAN* WAS AT A FRIGHTENING TILT, THE FORESAIL NEARLY TOUCHING THE WAVES, WHEN SUDDENLY A WAVE HEELED THE SHIP OVER. THE SAILORS THOUGHT THE SHIP WOULDN'T RIGHT ITSELF AGAIN.
KRAAH
WE'RE DOOMED!
CUT THE SHROUDS!
KRAC

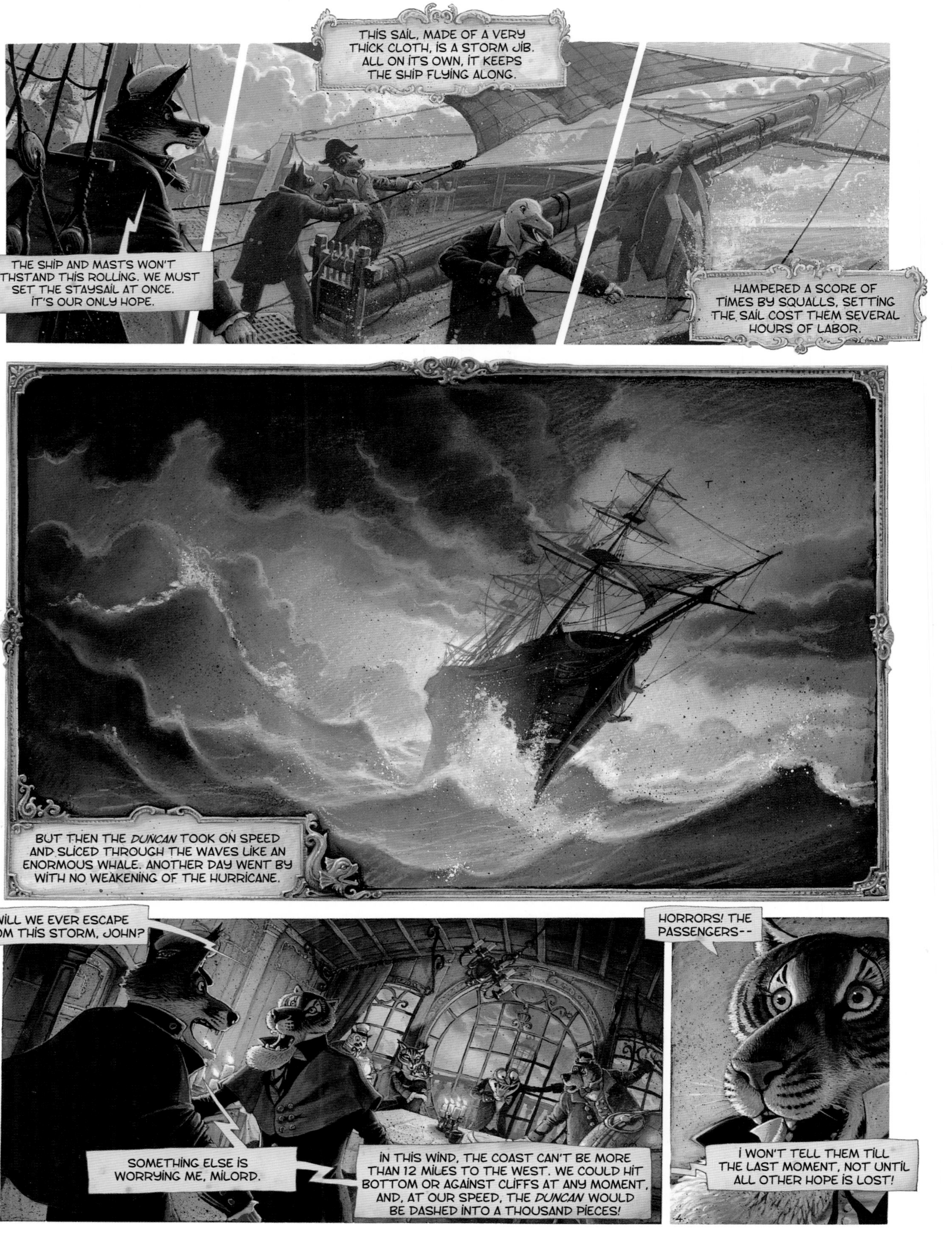

THE SHIP AND MASTS WON'T WITHSTAND THIS ROLLING. WE MUST SET THE STAYSAIL AT ONCE. IT'S OUR ONLY HOPE.
THIS SAIL, MADE OF A VERY THICK CLOTH, IS A STORM JIB. ALL ON ITS OWN, IT KEEPS THE SHIP FLYING ALONG.
HAMPERED A SCORE OF TIMES BY SQUALLS, SETTING THE SAIL COST THEM SEVERAL HOURS OF LABOR.
BUT THEN THE *DUNCAN* TOOK ON SPEED AND SLICED THROUGH THE WAVES LIKE AN ENORMOUS WHALE. ANOTHER DAY WENT BY WITH NO WEAKENING OF THE HURRICANE.
WILL WE EVER ESCAPE FROM THIS STORM, JOHN?
SOMETHING ELSE IS WORRYING ME, MILORD.
IN THIS WIND, THE COAST CAN'T BE MORE THAN 12 MILES TO THE WEST. WE COULD HIT BOTTOM OR AGAINST CLIFFS AT ANY MOMENT, AND, AT OUR SPEED, THE *DUNCAN* WOULD BE DASHED INTO A THOUSAND PIECES!
HORRORS! THE PASSENGERS--
I WON'T TELL THEM TILL THE LAST MOMENT, NOT UNTIL ALL OTHER HOPE IS LOST!

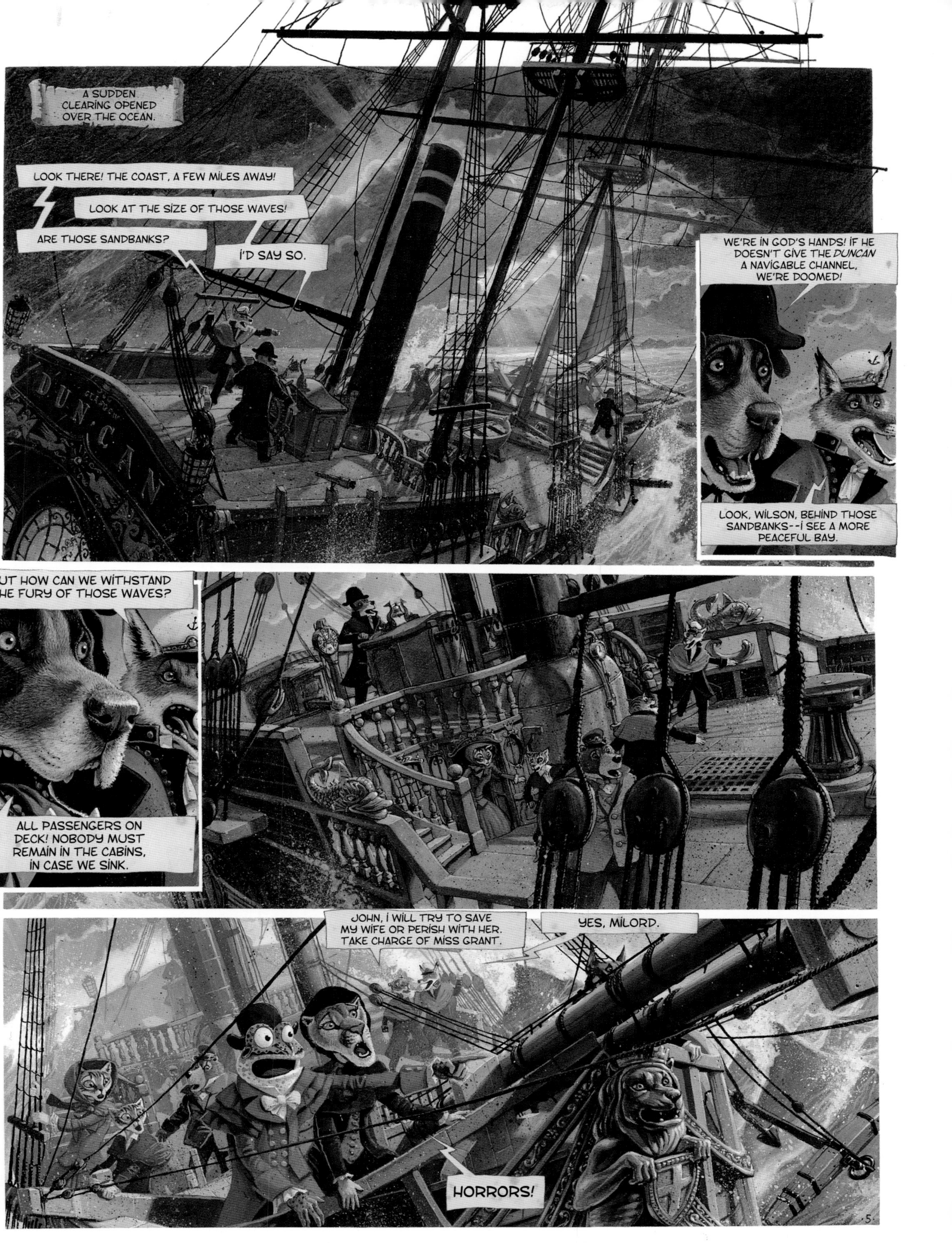
A SUDDEN CLEARING OPENED OVER THE OCEAN.
LOOK THERE! THE COAST, A FEW MILES AWAY!
LOOK AT THE SIZE OF THOSE WAVES!
ARE THOSE SANDBANKS?
I'D SAY SO.
WE'RE IN GOD'S HANDS! IF HE DOESN'T GIVE THE *DUNCAN* A NAVIGABLE CHANNEL, WE'RE DOOMED!
LOOK, WILSON, BEHIND THOSE SANDBANKS--I SEE A MORE PEACEFUL BAY.
BUT HOW CAN WE WITHSTAND THE FURY OF THOSE WAVES?
ALL PASSENGERS ON DECK! NOBODY MUST REMAIN IN THE CABINS, IN CASE WE SINK.
JOHN, I WILL TRY TO SAVE MY WIFE OR PERISH WITH HER. TAKE CHARGE OF MISS GRANT.
YES, MILORD.
HORRORS!
5

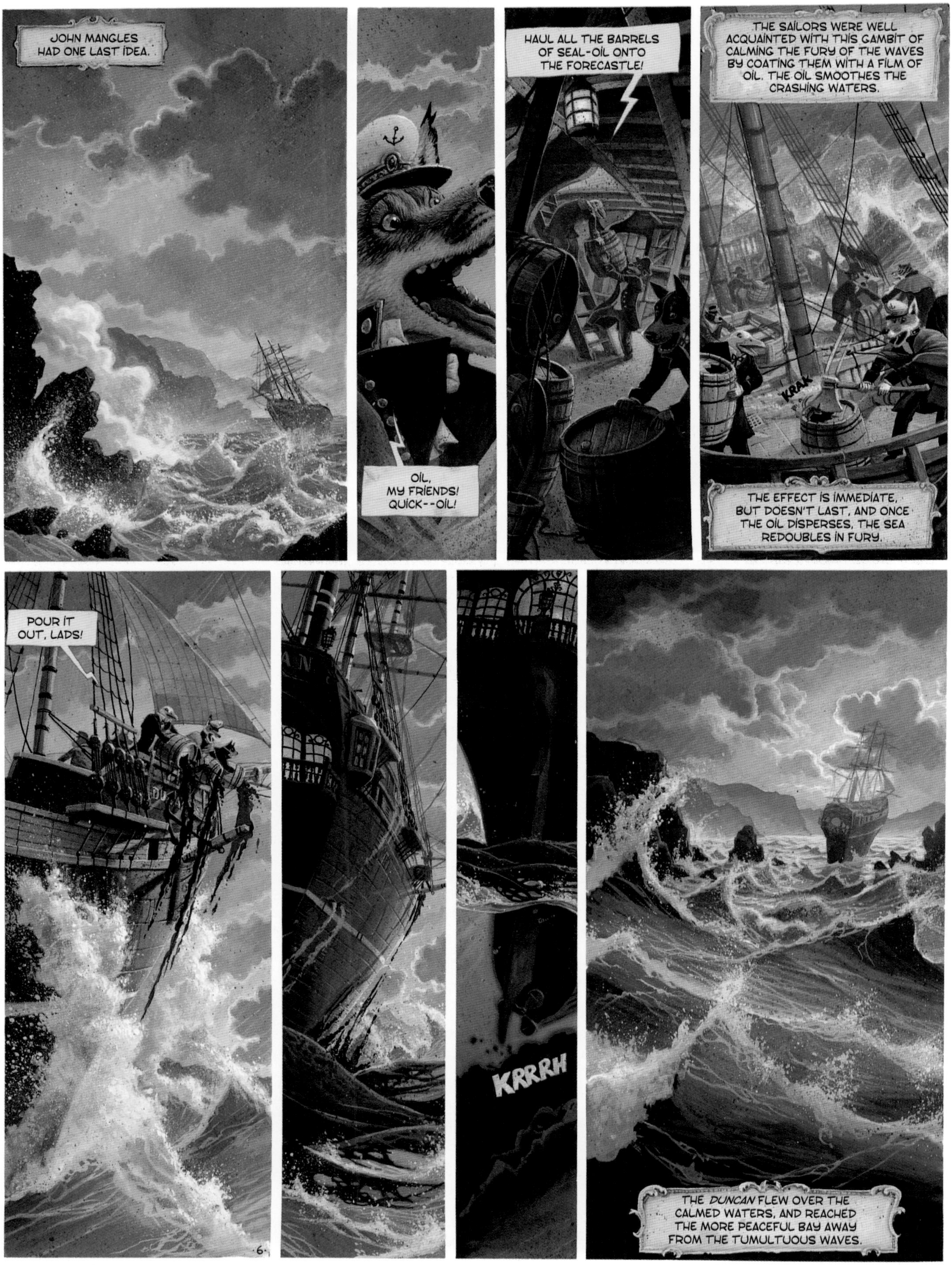
JOHN MANGLES HAD ONE LAST IDEA.
OIL, MY FRIENDS! QUICK--OIL!
HAUL ALL THE BARRELS OF SEAL-OIL ONTO THE FORECASTLE!
THE SAILORS WERE WELL ACQUAINTED WITH THIS GAMBIT OF CALMING THE FURY OF THE WAVES BY COATING THEM WITH A FILM OF OIL. THE OIL SMOOTHES THE CRASHING WATERS.
KRAK
THE EFFECT IS IMMEDIATE, BUT DOESN'T LAST, AND ONCE THE OIL DISPERSES, THE SEA REDOUBLES IN FURY.
POUR IT OUT, LADS!
KRRRH
THE *DUNCAN* FLEW OVER THE CALMED WATERS, AND REACHED THE MORE PEACEFUL BAY AWAY FROM THE TUMULTUOUS WAVES.

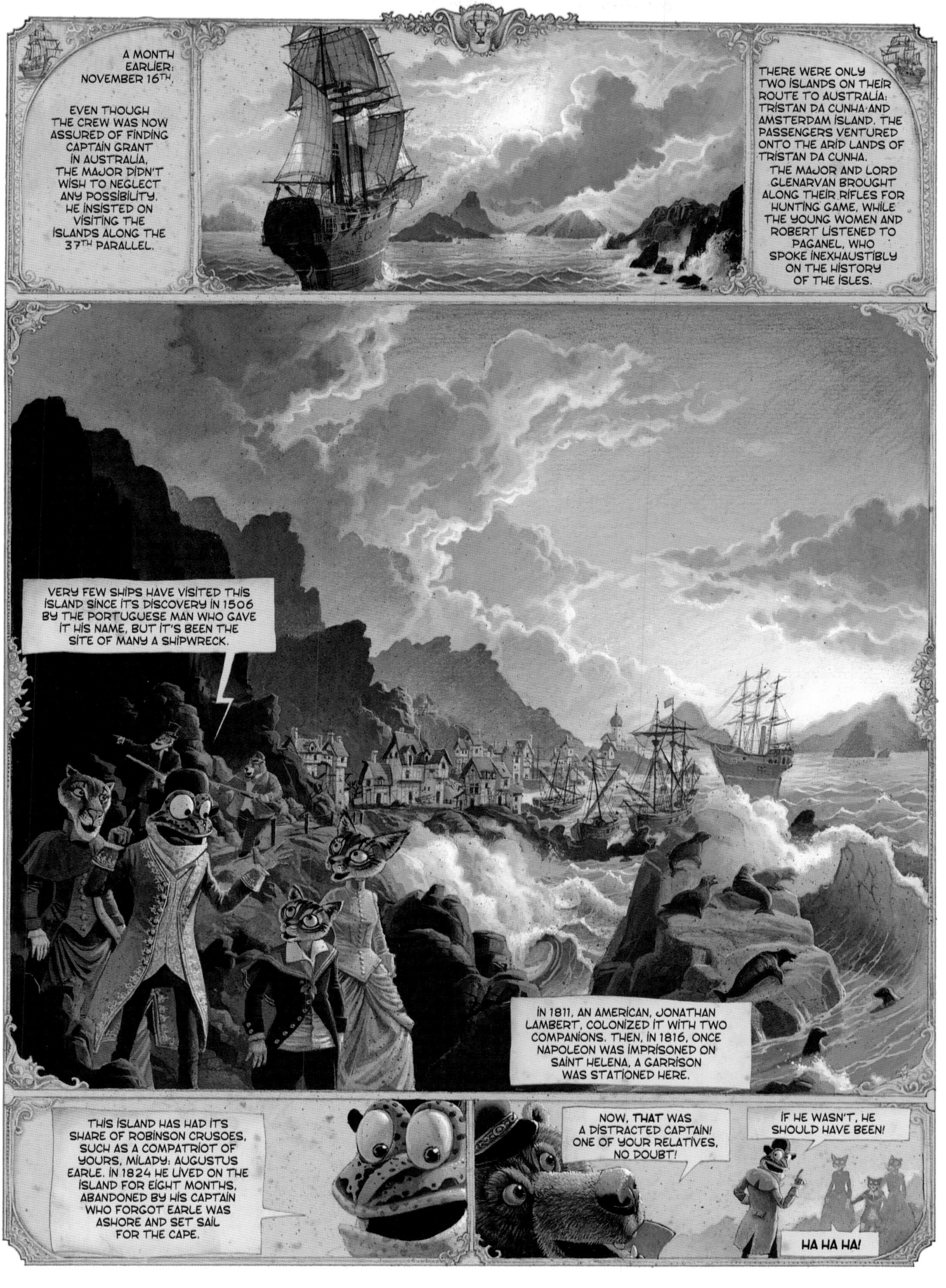
A MONTH EARLIER: NOVEMBER 16TH.
EVEN THOUGH THE CREW WAS NOW ASSURED OF FINDING CAPTAIN GRANT IN AUSTRALIA, THE MAJOR DIDN'T WISH TO NEGLECT ANY POSSIBILITY. HE INSISTED ON VISITING THE ISLANDS ALONG THE 37TH PARALLEL.
THERE WERE ONLY TWO ISLANDS ON THEIR ROUTE TO AUSTRALIA: TRISTAN DA CUNHA AND AMSTERDAM ISLAND. THE PASSENGERS VENTURED ONTO THE ARID LANDS OF TRISTAN DA CUNHA. THE MAJOR AND LORD GLENARVAN BROUGHT ALONG THEIR RIFLES FOR HUNTING GAME, WHILE THE YOUNG WOMEN AND ROBERT LISTENED TO PAGANEL, WHO SPOKE INEXHAUSTIBLY ON THE HISTORY OF THE ISLES.
VERY FEW SHIPS HAVE VISITED THIS ISLAND SINCE ITS DISCOVERY IN 1506 BY THE PORTUGUESE MAN WHO GAVE IT HIS NAME, BUT IT'S BEEN THE SITE OF MANY A SHIPWRECK.
IN 1811, AN AMERICAN, JONATHAN LAMBERT, COLONIZED IT WITH TWO COMPANIONS. THEN, IN 1816, ONCE NAPOLEON WAS IMPRISONED ON SAINT HELENA, A GARRISON WAS STATIONED HERE.
THIS ISLAND HAS HAD ITS SHARE OF ROBINSON CRUSOES, SUCH AS A COMPATRIOT OF YOURS, MILADY: AUGUSTUS EARLE. IN 1824 HE LIVED ON THE ISLAND FOR EIGHT MONTHS, ABANDONED BY HIS CAPTAIN WHO FORGOT EARLE WAS ASHORE AND SET SAIL FOR THE CAPE.
NOW, THAT WAS A DISTRACTED CAPTAIN! ONE OF YOUR RELATIVES, NO DOUBT!
IF HE WASN'T, HE SHOULD HAVE BEEN!
HA HA HA!

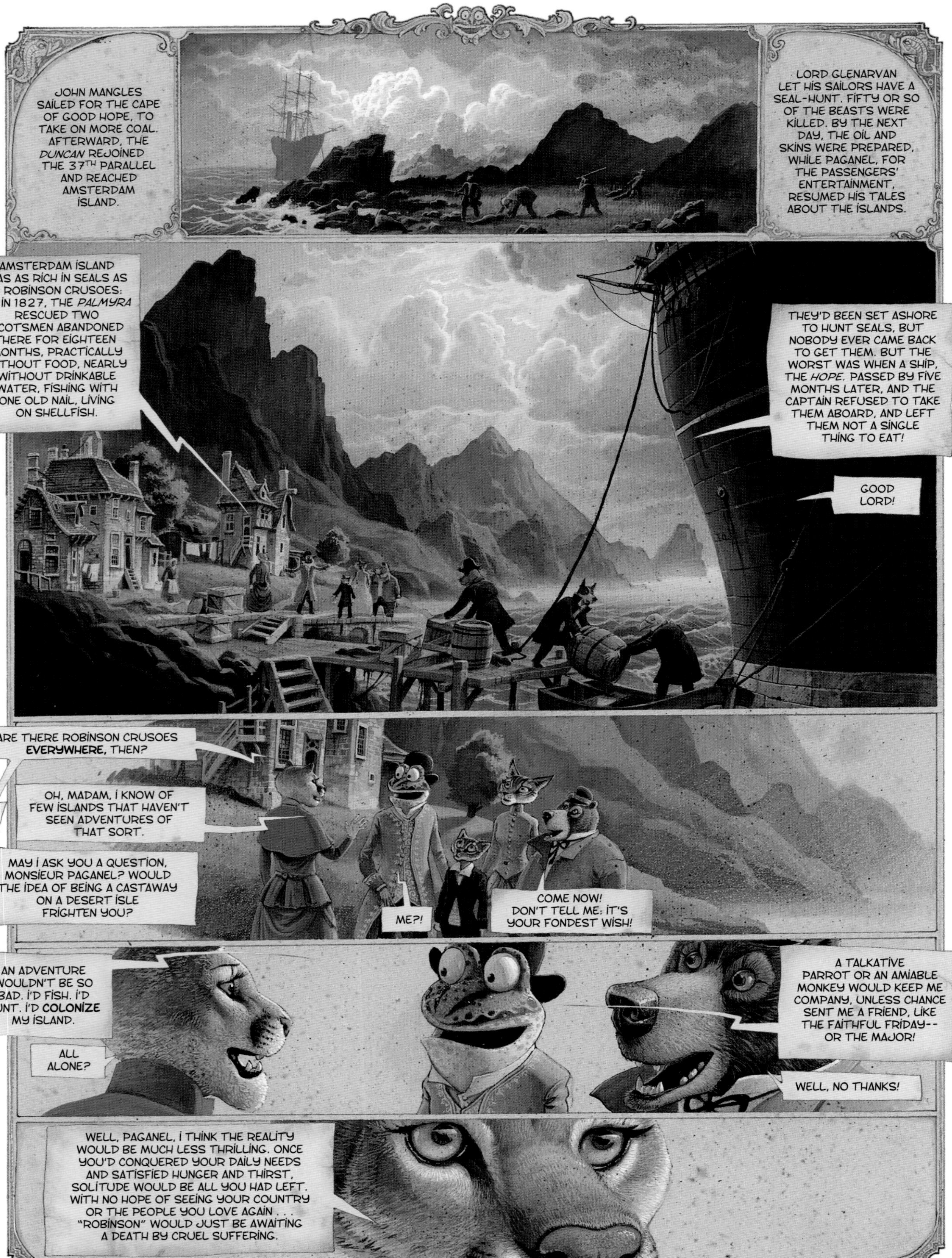
JOHN MANGLES SAILED FOR THE CAPE OF GOOD HOPE, TO TAKE ON MORE COAL. AFTERWARD, THE *DUNCAN* REJOINED THE 37TH PARALLEL AND REACHED AMSTERDAM ISLAND.
LORD GLENARVAN LET HIS SAILORS HAVE A SEAL-HUNT. FIFTY OR SO OF THE BEASTS WERE KILLED. BY THE NEXT DAY, THE OIL AND SKINS WERE PREPARED, WHILE PAGANEL, FOR THE PASSENGERS' ENTERTAINMENT, RESUMED HIS TALES ABOUT THE ISLANDS.
AMSTERDAM ISLAND WAS AS RICH IN SEALS AS IN ROBINSON CRUSOES: IN 1827, THE *PALMYRA* RESCUED TWO SCOTSMEN ABANDONED THERE FOR EIGHTEEN MONTHS, PRACTICALLY WITHOUT FOOD, NEARLY WITHOUT DRINKABLE WATER, FISHING WITH ONE OLD NAIL, LIVING ON SHELLFISH.
THEY'D BEEN SET ASHORE TO HUNT SEALS, BUT NOBODY EVER CAME BACK TO GET THEM. BUT THE WORST WAS WHEN A SHIP, THE *HOPE,* PASSED BY FIVE MONTHS LATER, AND THE CAPTAIN REFUSED TO TAKE THEM ABOARD, AND LEFT THEM NOT A SINGLE THING TO EAT!
GOOD LORD!
ARE THERE ROBINSON CRUSOES **EVERYWHERE,** THEN?
OH, MADAM, I KNOW OF FEW ISLANDS THAT HAVEN'T SEEN ADVENTURES OF THAT SORT.
MAY I ASK YOU A QUESTION, MONSIEUR PAGANEL? WOULD THE IDEA OF BEING A CASTAWAY ON A DESERT ISLE FRIGHTEN YOU?
ME?!
COME NOW! DON'T TELL ME: IT'S YOUR FONDEST WISH!
AN ADVENTURE WOULDN'T BE SO BAD. I'D FISH. I'D HUNT. I'D **COLONIZE** MY ISLAND.
ALL ALONE?
A TALKATIVE PARROT OR AN AMIABLE MONKEY WOULD KEEP ME COMPANY, UNLESS CHANCE SENT ME A FRIEND, LIKE THE FAITHFUL FRIDAY-- OR THE MAJOR!
WELL, NO THANKS!
WELL, PAGANEL, I THINK THE REALITY WOULD BE MUCH LESS THRILLING. ONCE YOU'D CONQUERED YOUR DAILY NEEDS AND SATISFIED HUNGER AND THIRST, SOLITUDE WOULD BE ALL YOU HAD LEFT. WITH NO HOPE OF SEEING YOUR COUNTRY OR THE PEOPLE YOU LOVE AGAIN . . . "ROBINSON" WOULD JUST BE AWAITING A DEATH BY CRUEL SUFFERING.

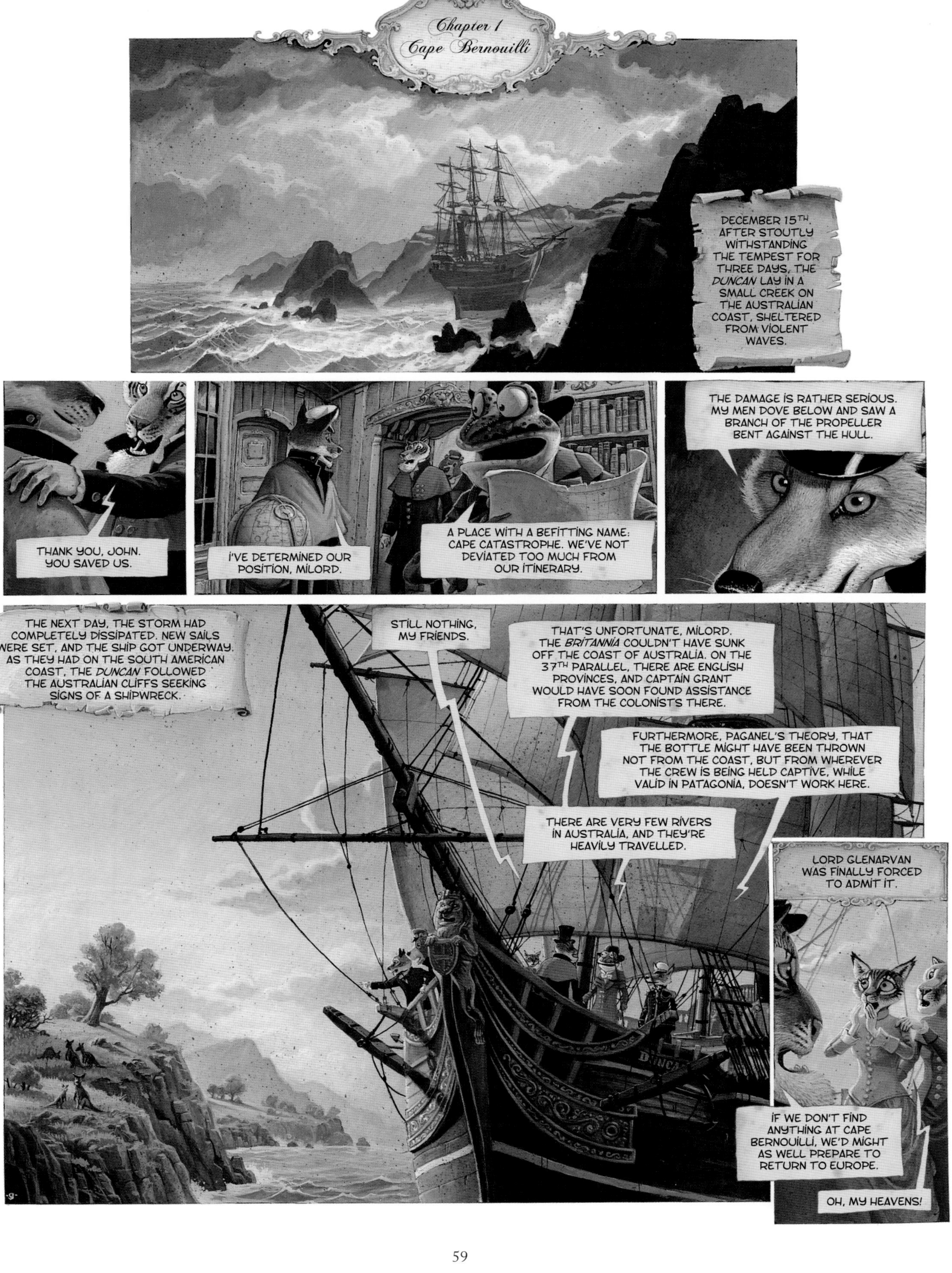
Chapter 1
Cape Bernouilli
DECEMBER 15TH. AFTER STOUTLY WITHSTANDING THE TEMPEST FOR THREE DAYS, THE DUNCAN LAY IN A SMALL CREEK ON THE AUSTRALIAN COAST, SHELTERED FROM VIOLENT WAVES.
THANK YOU, JOHN. YOU SAVED US.
I'VE DETERMINED OUR POSITION, MILORD.
A PLACE WITH A BEFITTING NAME: CAPE CATASTROPHE. WE'VE NOT DEVIATED TOO MUCH FROM OUR ITINERARY.
THE DAMAGE IS RATHER SERIOUS. MY MEN DOVE BELOW AND SAW A BRANCH OF THE PROPELLER BENT AGAINST THE HULL.
THE NEXT DAY, THE STORM HAD COMPLETELY DISSIPATED. NEW SAILS WERE SET, AND THE SHIP GOT UNDERWAY. AS THEY HAD ON THE SOUTH AMERICAN COAST, THE DUNCAN FOLLOWED THE AUSTRALIAN CLIFFS SEEKING SIGNS OF A SHIPWRECK.
STILL NOTHING, MY FRIENDS.
THAT'S UNFORTUNATE, MILORD. THE BRITANNIA COULDN'T HAVE SUNK OFF THE COAST OF AUSTRALIA. ON THE 37TH PARALLEL, THERE ARE ENGLISH PROVINCES, AND CAPTAIN GRANT WOULD HAVE SOON FOUND ASSISTANCE FROM THE COLONISTS THERE.
FURTHERMORE, PAGANEL'S THEORY, THAT THE BOTTLE MIGHT HAVE BEEN THROWN NOT FROM THE COAST, BUT FROM WHEREVER THE CREW IS BEING HELD CAPTIVE, WHILE VALID IN PATAGONIA, DOESN'T WORK HERE.
THERE ARE VERY FEW RIVERS IN AUSTRALIA, AND THEY'RE HEAVILY TRAVELLED.
LORD GLENARVAN WAS FINALLY FORCED TO ADMIT IT.
IF WE DON'T FIND ANYTHING AT CAPE BERNOUILLI, WE'D MIGHT AS WELL PREPARE TO RETURN TO EUROPE.
OH, MY HEAVENS!

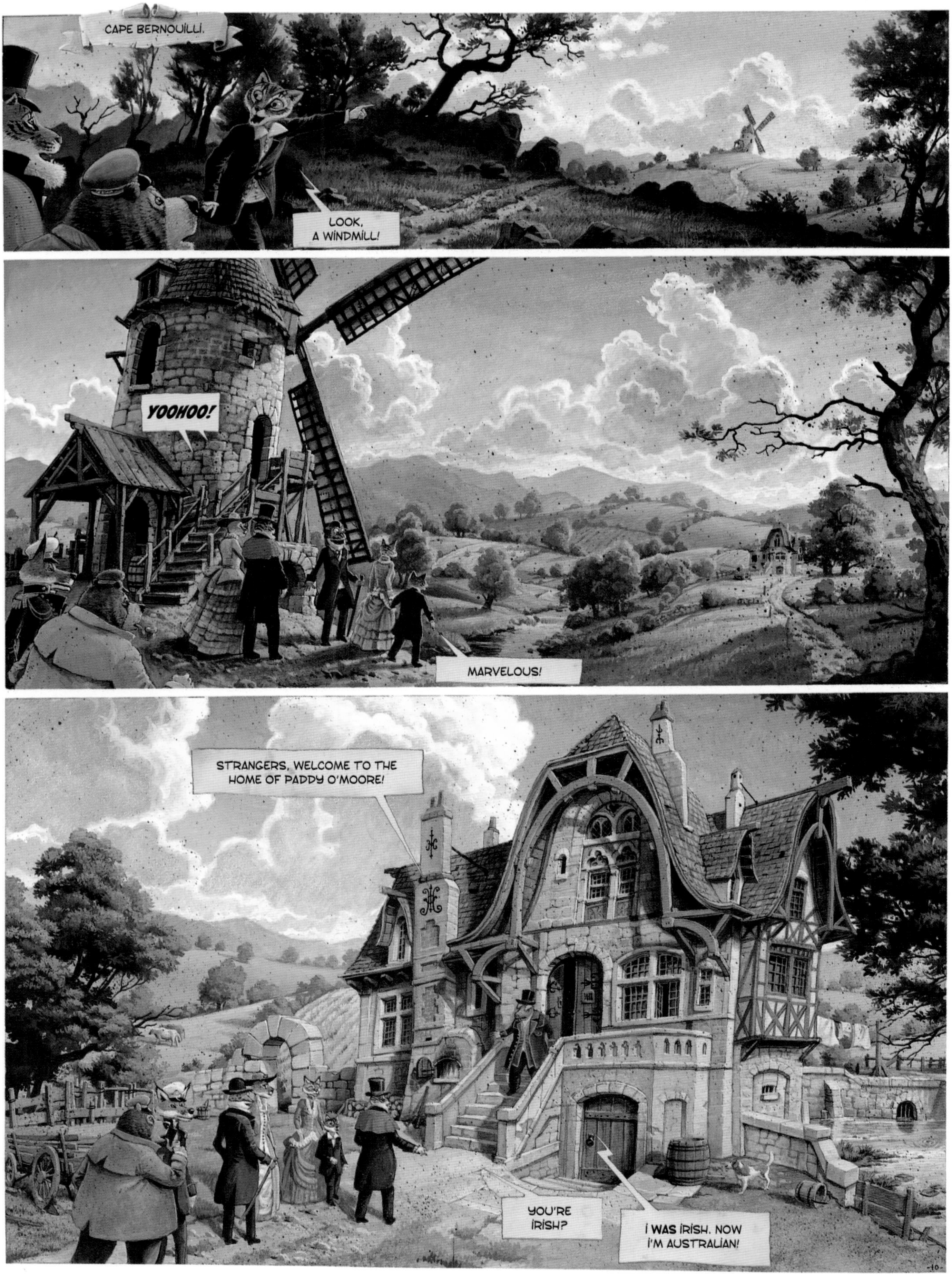
CAPE BERNOUILLI.
LOOK, A WINDMILL!
YOOHOO!
MARVELOUS!
STRANGERS, WELCOME TO THE HOME OF PADDY O'MOORE!
YOU'RE IRISH?
I WAS IRISH. NOW I'M AUSTRALIAN!

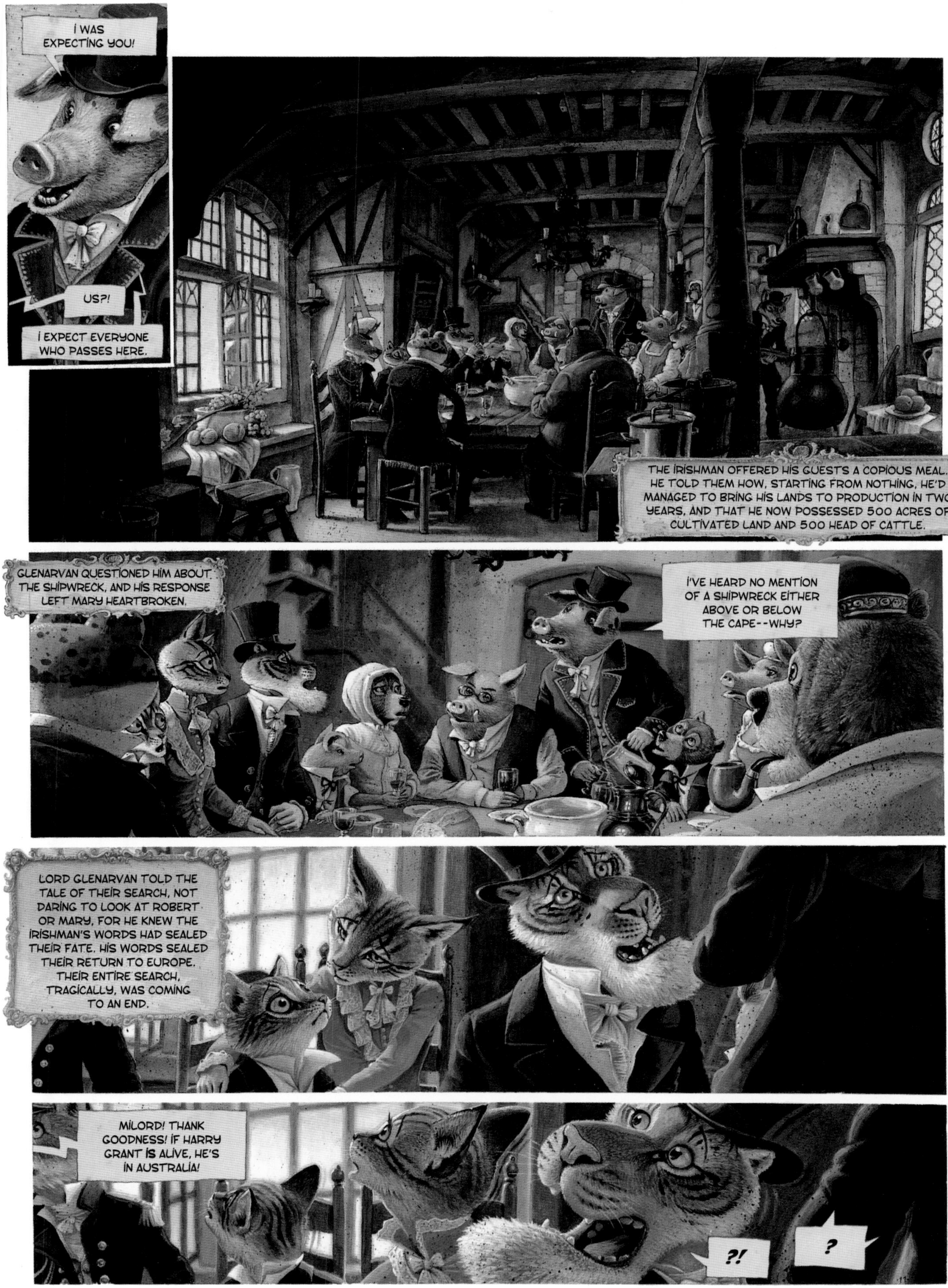
I WAS EXPECTING YOU!
US?!
I EXPECT EVERYONE WHO PASSES HERE.
THE IRISHMAN OFFERED HIS GUESTS A COPIOUS MEAL. HE TOLD THEM HOW, STARTING FROM NOTHING, HE'D MANAGED TO BRING HIS LANDS TO PRODUCTION IN TWO YEARS, AND THAT HE NOW POSSESSED 500 ACRES OF CULTIVATED LAND AND 500 HEAD OF CATTLE.
GLENARVAN QUESTIONED HIM ABOUT THE SHIPWRECK, AND HIS RESPONSE LEFT MARY HEARTBROKEN.
I'VE HEARD NO MENTION OF A SHIPWRECK EITHER ABOVE OR BELOW THE CAPE--WHY?
LORD GLENARVAN TOLD THE TALE OF THEIR SEARCH, NOT DARING TO LOOK AT ROBERT OR MARY, FOR HE KNEW THE IRISHMAN'S WORDS HAD SEALED THEIR FATE. HIS WORDS SEALED THEIR RETURN TO EUROPE. THEIR ENTIRE SEARCH, TRAGICALLY, WAS COMING TO AN END.
MILORD! THANK GOODNESS! IF HARRY GRANT IS ALIVE, HE'S IN AUSTRALIA!
?!
?

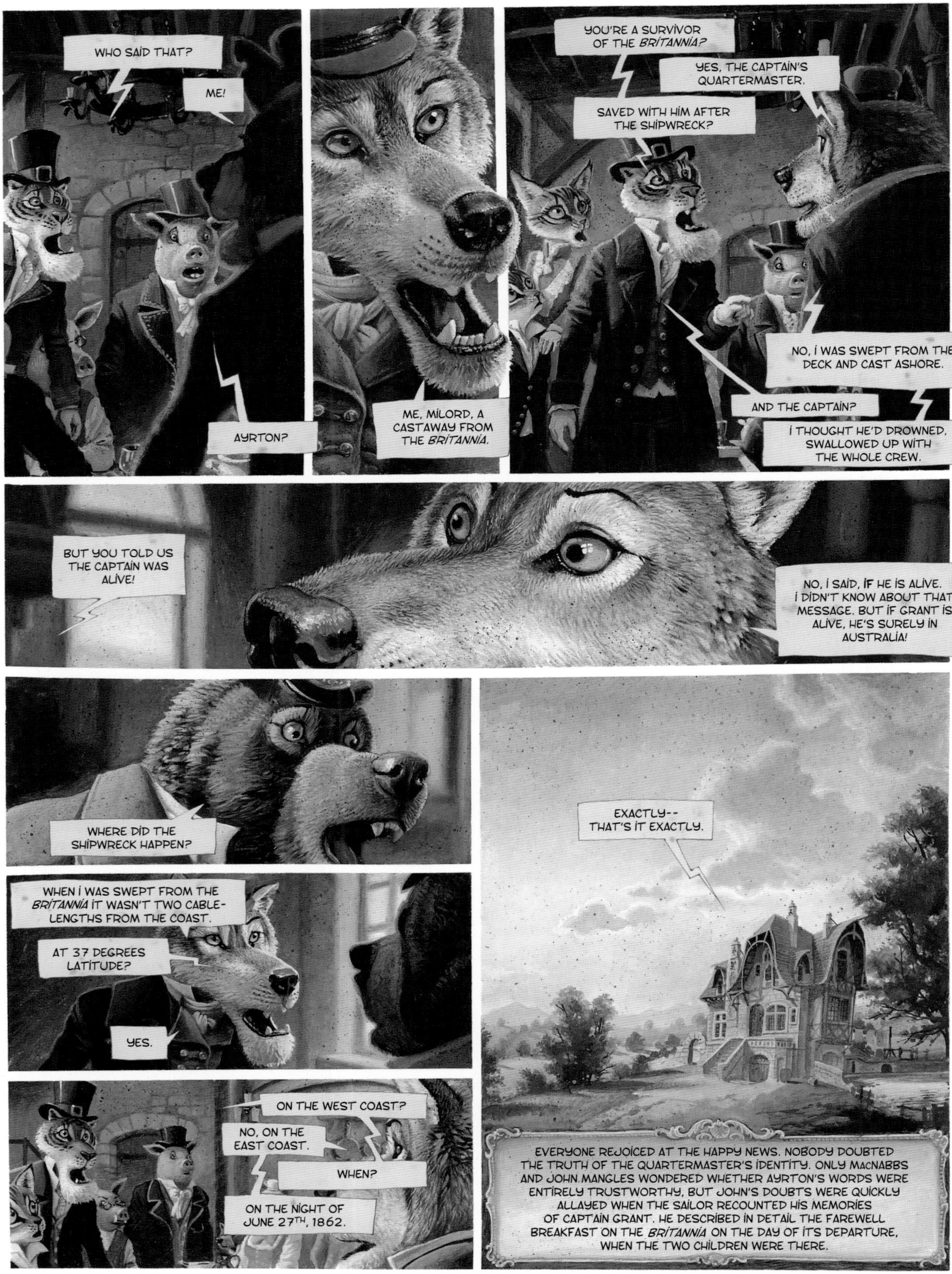
WHO SAID THAT?
ME!
AYRTON?
ME, MILORD, A CASTAWAY FROM THE BRITANNIA.
YOU'RE A SURVIVOR OF THE BRITANNIA?
YES, THE CAPTAIN'S QUARTERMASTER.
SAVED WITH HIM AFTER THE SHIPWRECK?
NO, I WAS SWEPT FROM THE DECK AND CAST ASHORE.
AND THE CAPTAIN?
I THOUGHT HE'D DROWNED, SWALLOWED UP WITH THE WHOLE CREW.
BUT YOU TOLD US THE CAPTAIN WAS ALIVE!
NO, I SAID, IF HE IS ALIVE. I DIDN'T KNOW ABOUT THAT MESSAGE. BUT IF GRANT IS ALIVE, HE'S SURELY IN AUSTRALIA!
WHERE DID THE SHIPWRECK HAPPEN?
WHEN I WAS SWEPT FROM THE BRITANNIA IT WASN'T TWO CABLE-LENGTHS FROM THE COAST.
AT 37 DEGREES LATITUDE?
YES.
ON THE WEST COAST?
NO, ON THE EAST COAST.
WHEN?
ON THE NIGHT OF JUNE 27TH, 1862.
EXACTLY-- THAT'S IT EXACTLY.
EVERYONE REJOICED AT THE HAPPY NEWS. NOBODY DOUBTED THE TRUTH OF THE QUARTERMASTER'S IDENTITY. ONLY MACNABBS AND JOHN MANGLES WONDERED WHETHER AYRTON'S WORDS WERE ENTIRELY TRUSTWORTHY, BUT JOHN'S DOUBTS WERE QUICKLY ALLAYED WHEN THE SAILOR RECOUNTED HIS MEMORIES OF CAPTAIN GRANT. HE DESCRIBED IN DETAIL THE FAREWELL BREAKFAST ON THE BRITANNIA ON THE DAY OF ITS DEPARTURE, WHEN THE TWO CHILDREN WERE THERE.

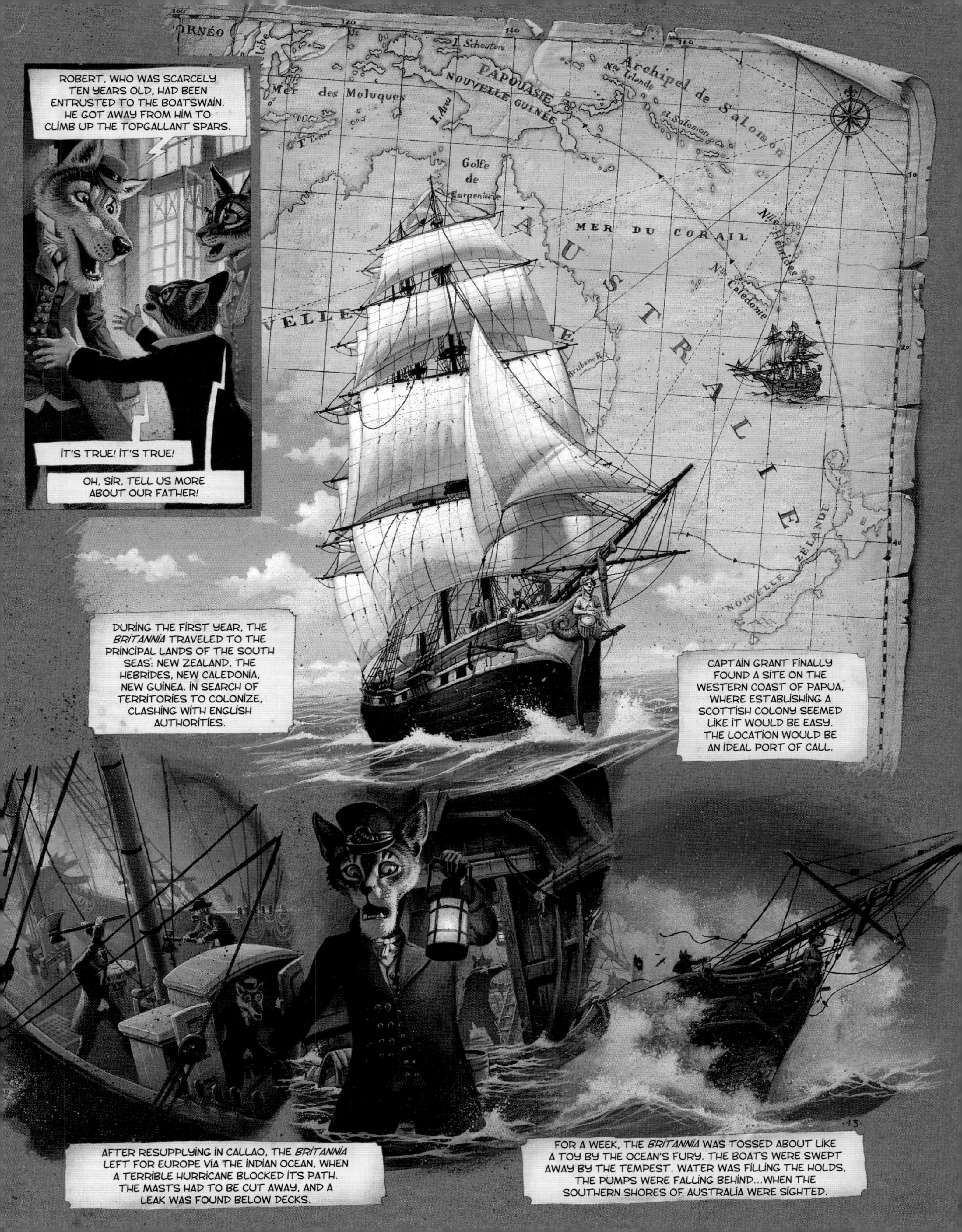
ROBERT, WHO WAS SCARCELY TEN YEARS OLD, HAD BEEN ENTRUSTED TO THE BOATSWAIN. HE GOT AWAY FROM HIM TO CLIMB UP THE TOPGALLANT SPARS.
IT'S TRUE! IT'S TRUE!
OH, SIR, TELL US MORE ABOUT OUR FATHER!
Archipel de Salomon
PAPOUASIE
NOUVELLE GUINÉE
Mer des Moluques
I. Schouten
Golfe de Carpentarie
MER DU CORAIL
AUSTRALIE
Nlle Hébrides
Nlle Calédonie
Brisbane R.
NOUVELLE ZÉLANDE
DURING THE FIRST YEAR, THE *BRITANNIA* TRAVELED TO THE PRINCIPAL LANDS OF THE SOUTH SEAS: NEW ZEALAND, THE HEBRIDES, NEW CALEDONIA, NEW GUINEA. IN SEARCH OF TERRITORIES TO COLONIZE, CLASHING WITH ENGLISH AUTHORITIES.
CAPTAIN GRANT FINALLY FOUND A SITE ON THE WESTERN COAST OF PAPUA, WHERE ESTABLISHING A SCOTTISH COLONY SEEMED LIKE IT WOULD BE EASY. THE LOCATION WOULD BE AN IDEAL PORT OF CALL.
AFTER RESUPPLYING IN CALLAO, THE *BRITANNIA* LEFT FOR EUROPE VIA THE INDIAN OCEAN, WHEN A TERRIBLE HURRICANE BLOCKED ITS PATH. THE MASTS HAD TO BE CUT AWAY, AND A LEAK WAS FOUND BELOW DECKS.
FOR A WEEK, THE *BRITANNIA* WAS TOSSED ABOUT LIKE A TOY BY THE OCEAN'S FURY. THE BOATS WERE SWEPT AWAY BY THE TEMPEST. WATER WAS FILLING THE HOLDS, THE PUMPS WERE FALLING BEHIND...WHEN THE SOUTHERN SHORES OF AUSTRALIA WERE SIGHTED.

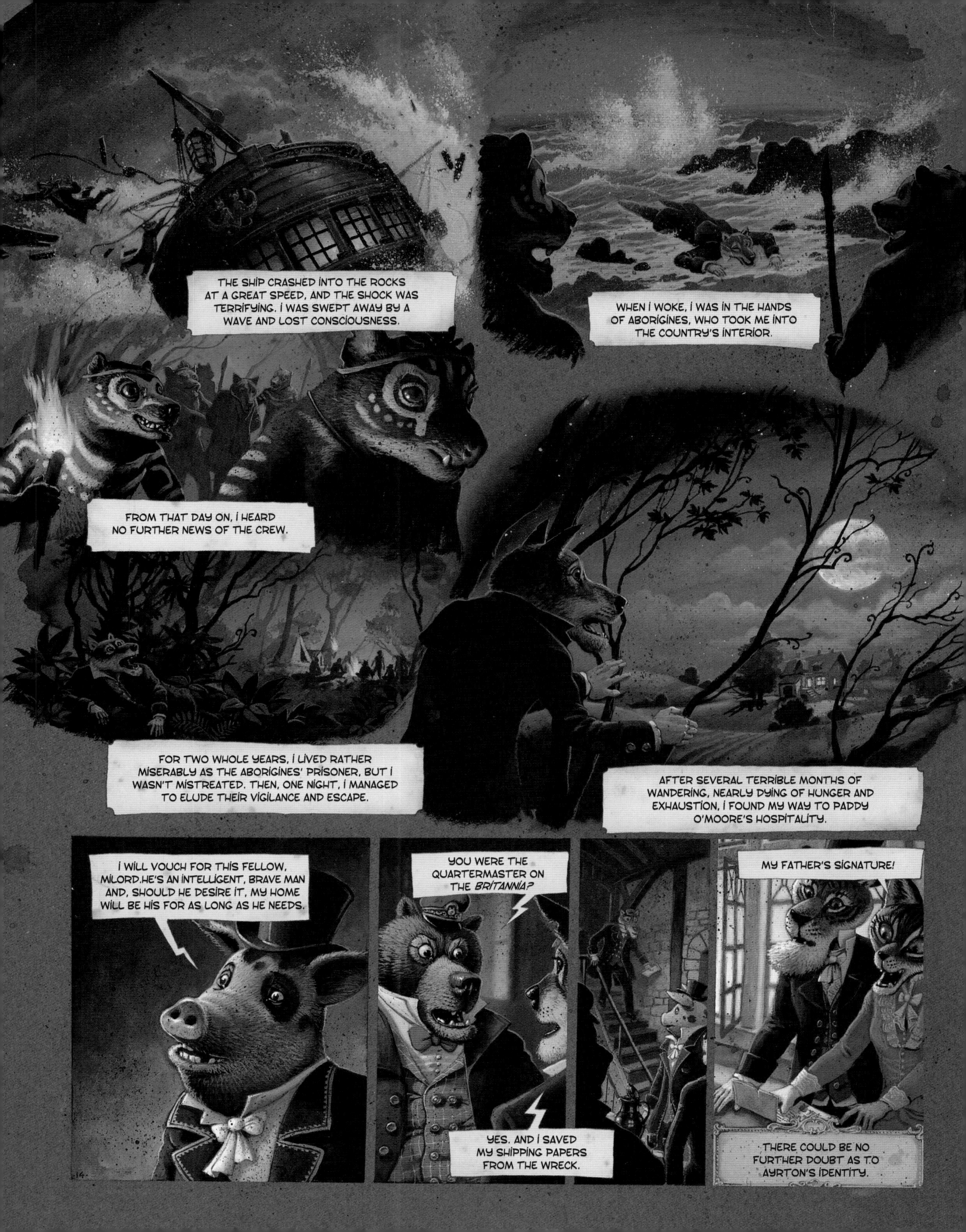
THE SHIP CRASHED INTO THE ROCKS AT A GREAT SPEED, AND THE SHOCK WAS TERRIFYING. I WAS SWEPT AWAY BY A WAVE AND LOST CONSCIOUSNESS.
WHEN I WOKE, I WAS IN THE HANDS OF ABORIGINES, WHO TOOK ME INTO THE COUNTRY'S INTERIOR.
FROM THAT DAY ON, I HEARD NO FURTHER NEWS OF THE CREW.
FOR TWO WHOLE YEARS, I LIVED RATHER MISERABLY AS THE ABORIGINES' PRISONER, BUT I WASN'T MISTREATED. THEN, ONE NIGHT, I MANAGED TO ELUDE THEIR VIGILANCE AND ESCAPE.
AFTER SEVERAL TERRIBLE MONTHS OF WANDERING, NEARLY DYING OF HUNGER AND EXHAUSTION, I FOUND MY WAY TO PADDY O'MOORE'S HOSPITALITY.
I WILL VOUCH FOR THIS FELLOW, MILORD.HE'S AN INTELLIGENT, BRAVE MAN AND, SHOULD HE DESIRE IT, MY HOME WILL BE HIS FOR AS LONG AS HE NEEDS.
YOU WERE THE QUARTERMASTER ON THE *BRITANNIA*?
YES. AND I SAVED MY SHIPPING PAPERS FROM THE WRECK.
MY FATHER'S SIGNATURE!
THERE COULD BE NO FURTHER DOUBT AS TO AYRTON'S IDENTITY.

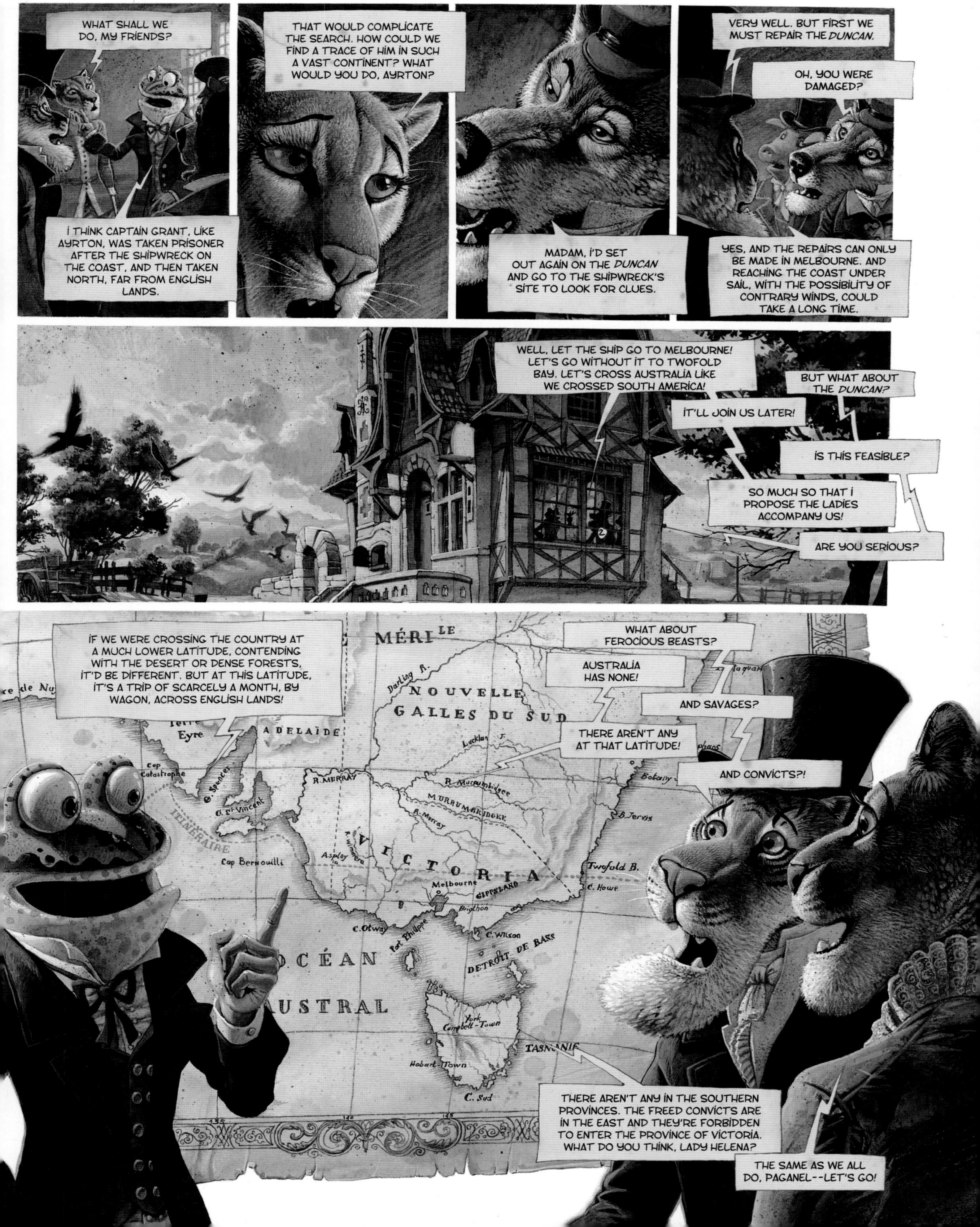

WHAT SHALL WE DO, MY FRIENDS?
I THINK CAPTAIN GRANT, LIKE AYRTON, WAS TAKEN PRISONER AFTER THE SHIPWRECK ON THE COAST, AND THEN TAKEN NORTH, FAR FROM ENGLISH LANDS.
THAT WOULD COMPLICATE THE SEARCH. HOW COULD WE FIND A TRACE OF HIM IN SUCH A VAST CONTINENT? WHAT WOULD YOU DO, AYRTON?
MADAM, I'D SET OUT AGAIN ON THE *DUNCAN* AND GO TO THE SHIPWRECK'S SITE TO LOOK FOR CLUES.
VERY WELL. BUT FIRST WE MUST REPAIR THE *DUNCAN.*
OH, YOU WERE DAMAGED?
YES, AND THE REPAIRS CAN ONLY BE MADE IN MELBOURNE. AND REACHING THE COAST UNDER SAIL, WITH THE POSSIBILITY OF CONTRARY WINDS, COULD TAKE A LONG TIME.
WELL, LET THE SHIP GO TO MELBOURNE! LET'S GO WITHOUT IT TO TWOFOLD BAY. LET'S CROSS AUSTRALIA LIKE WE CROSSED SOUTH AMERICA!
BUT WHAT ABOUT THE *DUNCAN?*
IT'LL JOIN US LATER!
IS THIS FEASIBLE?
SO MUCH SO THAT I PROPOSE THE LADIES ACCOMPANY US!
ARE YOU SERIOUS?
IF WE WERE CROSSING THE COUNTRY AT A MUCH LOWER LATITUDE, CONTENDING WITH THE DESERT OR DENSE FORESTS, IT'D BE DIFFERENT. BUT AT THIS LATITUDE, IT'S A TRIP OF SCARCELY A MONTH, BY WAGON, ACROSS ENGLISH LANDS!
WHAT ABOUT FEROCIOUS BEASTS?
AUSTRALIA HAS NONE!
AND SAVAGES?
THERE AREN'T ANY AT THAT LATITUDE!
AND CONVICTS?!
THERE AREN'T ANY IN THE SOUTHERN PROVINCES. THE FREED CONVICTS ARE IN THE EAST AND THEY'RE FORBIDDEN TO ENTER THE PROVINCE OF VICTORIA. WHAT DO YOU THINK, LADY HELENA?
THE SAME AS WE ALL DO, PAGANEL--LET'S GO!
NOUVELLE GALLES DU SUD
ADELAIDE
VICTORIA
Melbourne
Twofold B.
OCÉAN
AUSTRAL

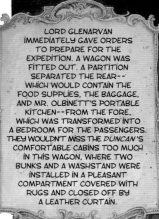

LORD GLENARVAN IMMEDIATELY GAVE ORDERS TO PREPARE FOR THE EXPEDITION. A WAGON WAS FITTED OUT. A PARTITION SEPARATED THE REAR--WHICH WOULD CONTAIN THE FOOD SUPPLIES, THE BAGGAGE, AND MR. OLBINETT'S PORTABLE KITCHEN--FROM THE FORE, WHICH WAS TRANSFORMED INTO A BEDROOM FOR THE PASSENGERS. THEY WOULDN'T MISS THE *DUNCAN'S* COMFORTABLE CABINS TOO MUCH IN THIS WAGON, WHERE TWO BUNKS AND A WASHSTAND WERE INSTALLED IN A PLEASANT COMPARTMENT COVERED WITH RUGS AND CLOSED OFF BY A LEATHER CURTAIN.

THE MEN WOULD TRAVEL ON HORSEBACK, EXCEPT FOR THE STEWARD OLBINETT, WHO PREFERRED TO REMAIN WITH THE BAGGAGE RATHER THAN TRY TO RIDE A HORSE.

LORD GLENARVAN ASKED AYRTON TO ACCOMPANY THEM, HOPING TO TAKE ADVANTAGE OF HIS KNOWLEDGE OF THE COUNTRY AND ITS INHABITANTS.

MILORD, I'D BE UNNEEDED ON BOARD, AND I HAVE COMPLETE FAITH IN WILSON, MY SECOND-IN-COMMAND, TO LEAD THE *DUNCAN*. MAY I JOIN YOU?

THE CAPTAIN COULD THINK OF MANY GOOD REASONS FOR HIM TO ACCOMPANY THE TRAVELERS, BUT GLENARVAN WAS CERTAINLY AWARE OF THE BEST REASON--WHICH MANGLES DARED NOT UTTER.

CERTAINLY, JOHN. IT'D BE GOOD FOR YOU TO BE THERE WHEN WE FIND MARY GRANT'S FATHER.

ON THE EVE OF THE DEPARTURE, THE IRISH FAMILY, ACCOMPANIED BY AYRTON, WAS INVITED TO A MAGNIFICENT DINNER ON BOARD THE *DUNCAN*.

PADDY O'MOORE WAS DAZZLED BY THE BEAUTY OF THE SHIP AND THE LUXURY OF ITS CABINS. AYRTON WAS ESPECIALLY INTERESTED IN THE RIGGING, ENGINES, AND WEAPONS.

YOU HAVE A BEAUTIFUL SHIP, MILORD.

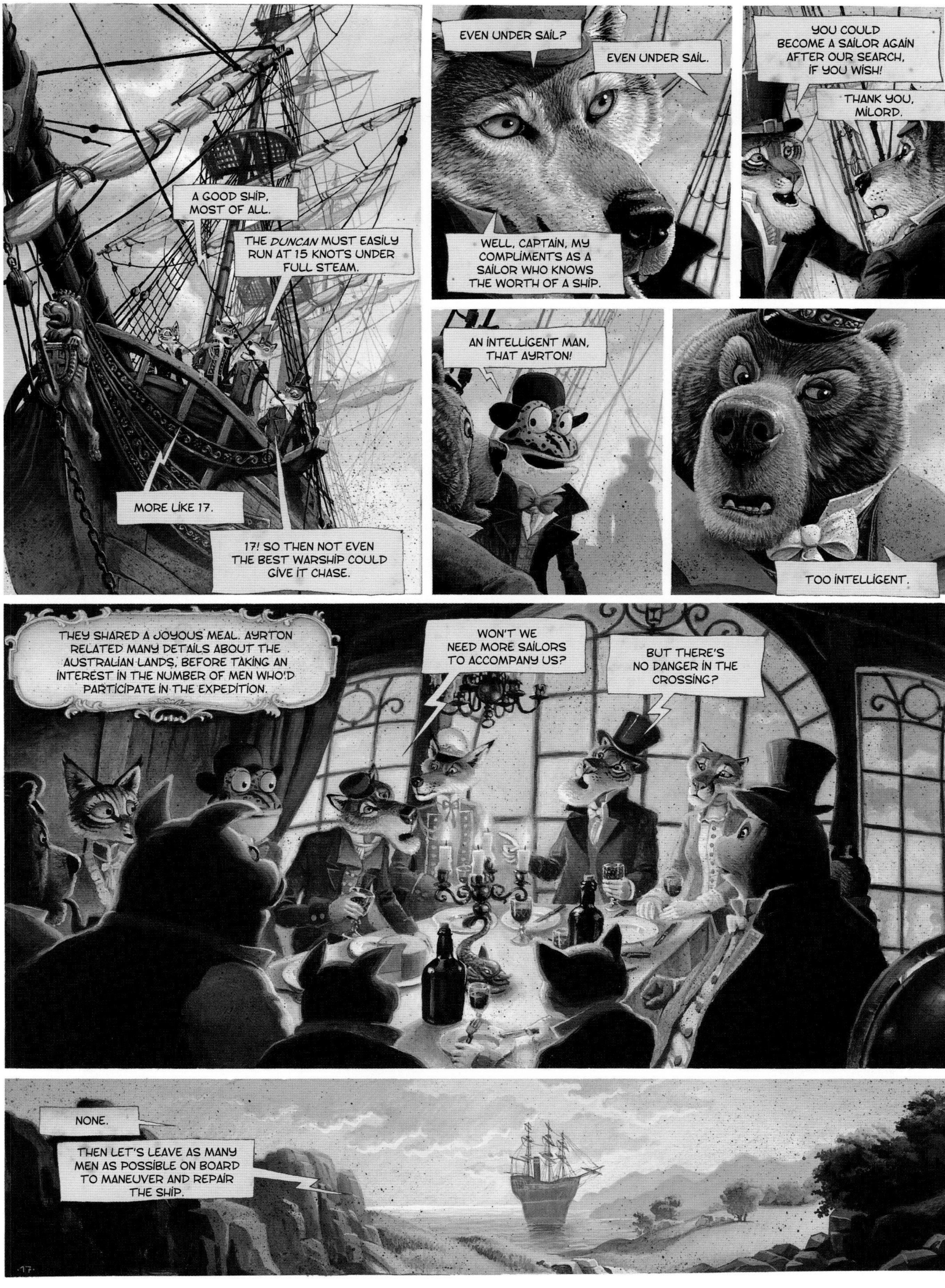
A GOOD SHIP, MOST OF ALL.
THE DUNCAN MUST EASILY RUN AT 15 KNOTS UNDER FULL STEAM.
MORE LIKE 17.
17! SO THEN NOT EVEN THE BEST WARSHIP COULD GIVE IT CHASE.
EVEN UNDER SAIL?
EVEN UNDER SAIL.
WELL, CAPTAIN, MY COMPLIMENTS AS A SAILOR WHO KNOWS THE WORTH OF A SHIP.
YOU COULD BECOME A SAILOR AGAIN AFTER OUR SEARCH, IF YOU WISH!
THANK YOU, MILORD.
AN INTELLIGENT MAN, THAT AYRTON!
TOO INTELLIGENT.
THEY SHARED A JOYOUS MEAL. AYRTON RELATED MANY DETAILS ABOUT THE AUSTRALIAN LANDS, BEFORE TAKING AN INTEREST IN THE NUMBER OF MEN WHO'D PARTICIPATE IN THE EXPEDITION.
WON'T WE NEED MORE SAILORS TO ACCOMPANY US?
BUT THERE'S NO DANGER IN THE CROSSING?
NONE.
THEN LET'S LEAVE AS MANY MEN AS POSSIBLE ON BOARD TO MANEUVER AND REPAIR THE SHIP.
17

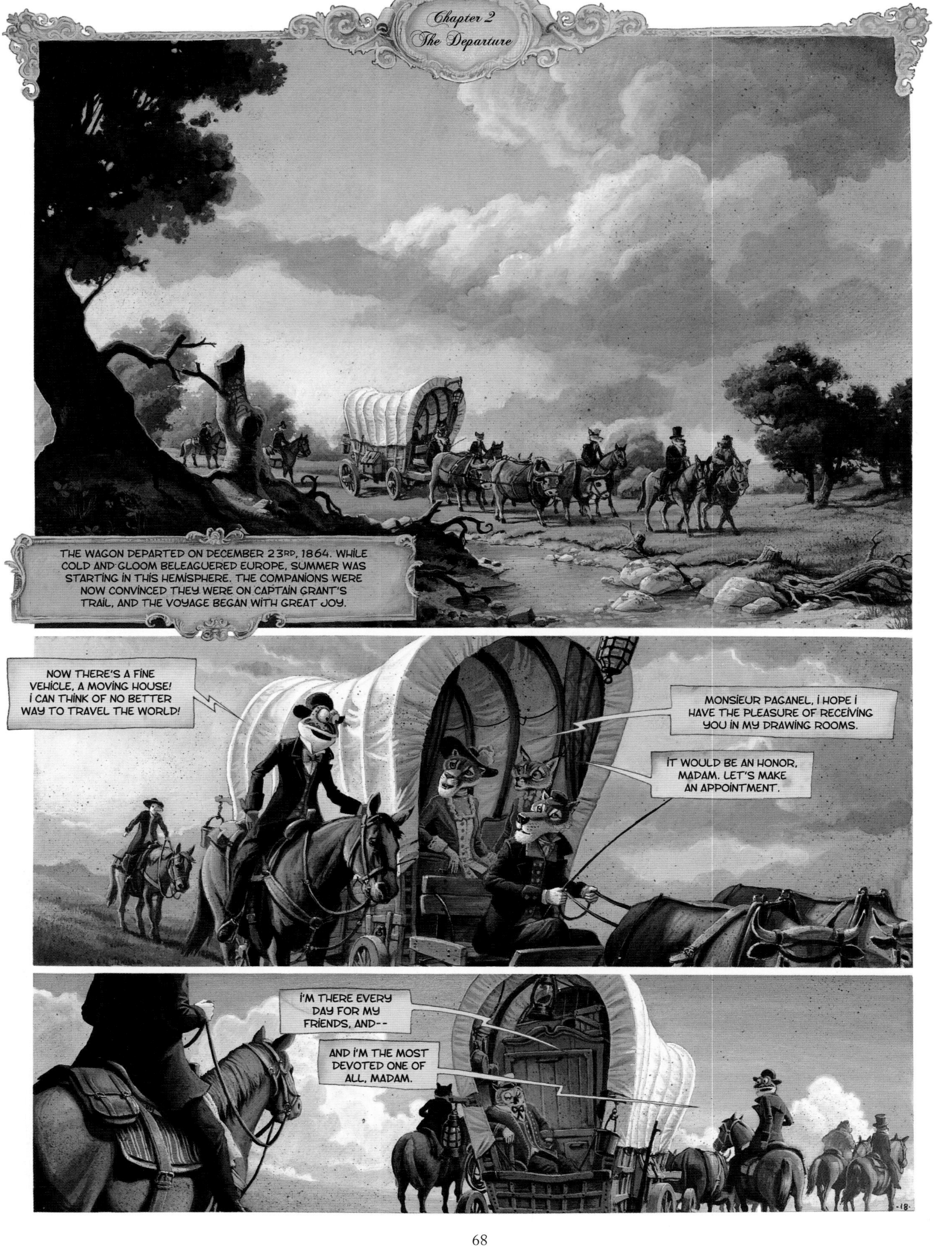
Chapter 2
The Departure
THE WAGON DEPARTED ON DECEMBER 23RD, 1864. WHILE COLD AND GLOOM BELEAGUERED EUROPE, SUMMER WAS STARTING IN THIS HEMISPHERE. THE COMPANIONS WERE NOW CONVINCED THEY WERE ON CAPTAIN GRANT'S TRAIL, AND THE VOYAGE BEGAN WITH GREAT JOY.
NOW THERE'S A FINE VEHICLE, A MOVING HOUSE! I CAN THINK OF NO BETTER WAY TO TRAVEL THE WORLD!
MONSIEUR PAGANEL, I HOPE I HAVE THE PLEASURE OF RECEIVING YOU IN MY DRAWING ROOMS.
IT WOULD BE AN HONOR, MADAM. LET'S MAKE AN APPOINTMENT.
I'M THERE EVERY DAY FOR MY FRIENDS, AND--
AND I'M THE MOST DEVOTED ONE OF ALL, MADAM.
-18-

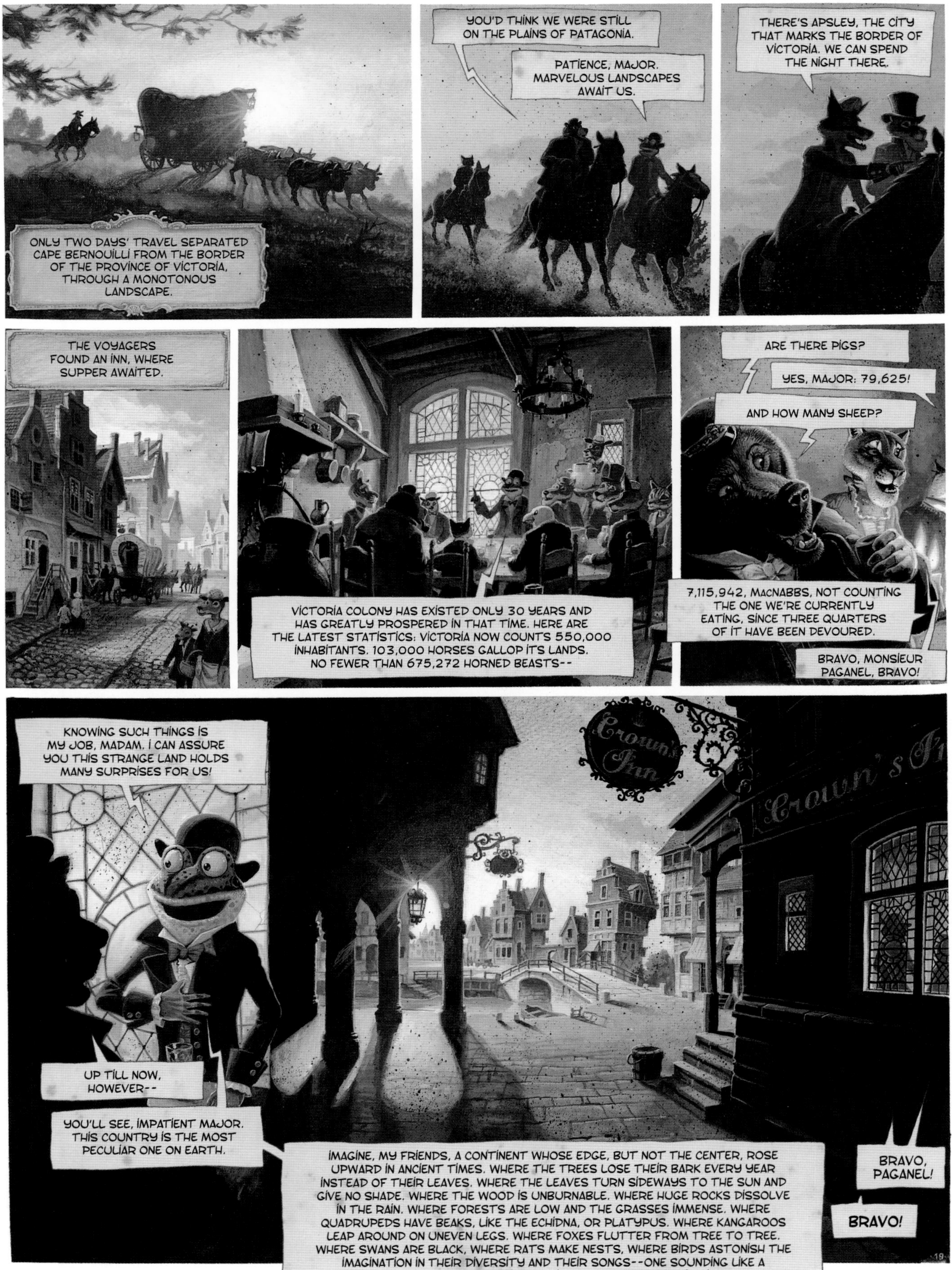
ONLY TWO DAYS' TRAVEL SEPARATED CAPE BERNOUILLI FROM THE BORDER OF THE PROVINCE OF VICTORIA, THROUGH A MONOTONOUS LANDSCAPE.
YOU'D THINK WE WERE STILL ON THE PLAINS OF PATAGONIA.
PATIENCE, MAJOR. MARVELOUS LANDSCAPES AWAIT US.
THERE'S APSLEY, THE CITY THAT MARKS THE BORDER OF VICTORIA. WE CAN SPEND THE NIGHT THERE.
THE VOYAGERS FOUND AN INN, WHERE SUPPER AWAITED.
VICTORIA COLONY HAS EXISTED ONLY 30 YEARS AND HAS GREATLY PROSPERED IN THAT TIME. HERE ARE THE LATEST STATISTICS: VICTORIA NOW COUNTS 550,000 INHABITANTS. 103,000 HORSES GALLOP ITS LANDS. NO FEWER THAN 675,272 HORNED BEASTS--
ARE THERE PIGS?
YES, MAJOR: 79,625!
AND HOW MANY SHEEP?
7,115,942, MACNABBS, NOT COUNTING THE ONE WE'RE CURRENTLY EATING, SINCE THREE QUARTERS OF IT HAVE BEEN DEVOURED.
BRAVO, MONSIEUR PAGANEL, BRAVO!
KNOWING SUCH THINGS IS MY JOB, MADAM. I CAN ASSURE YOU THIS STRANGE LAND HOLDS MANY SURPRISES FOR US!
Crown's Inn
Crown's In
UP TILL NOW, HOWEVER--
YOU'LL SEE, IMPATIENT MAJOR. THIS COUNTRY IS THE MOST PECULIAR ONE ON EARTH.
IMAGINE, MY FRIENDS, A CONTINENT WHOSE EDGE, BUT NOT THE CENTER, ROSE UPWARD IN ANCIENT TIMES. WHERE THE TREES LOSE THEIR BARK EVERY YEAR INSTEAD OF THEIR LEAVES. WHERE THE LEAVES TURN SIDEWAYS TO THE SUN AND GIVE NO SHADE. WHERE THE WOOD IS UNBURNABLE. WHERE HUGE ROCKS DISSOLVE IN THE RAIN. WHERE FORESTS ARE LOW AND THE GRASSES IMMENSE. WHERE QUADRUPEDS HAVE BEAKS, LIKE THE ECHIDNA, OR PLATYPUS. WHERE KANGAROOS LEAP AROUND ON UNEVEN LEGS. WHERE FOXES FLUTTER FROM TREE TO TREE. WHERE SWANS ARE BLACK, WHERE RATS MAKE NESTS, WHERE BIRDS ASTONISH THE IMAGINATION IN THEIR DIVERSITY AND THEIR SONGS--ONE SOUNDING LIKE A CLOCK, AND THE OTHER LIKE A GRINDER, AND ONE LAUGHING IN THE MORNING, AND ANOTHER WEEPING AT NIGHT.
BRAVO, PAGANEL!
BRAVO!
19

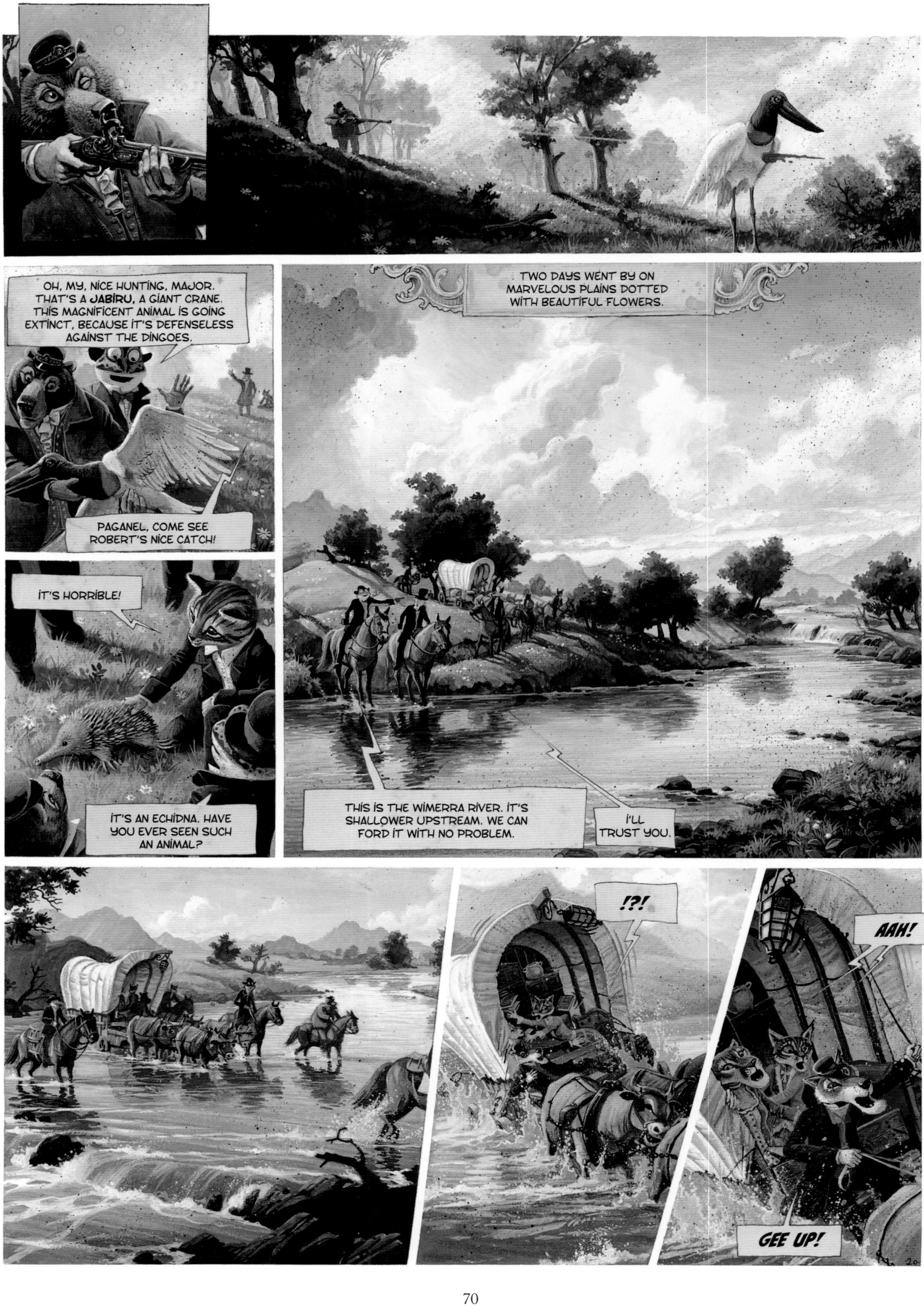
OH, MY, NICE HUNTING, MAJOR. THAT'S A **JABIRU**, A GIANT CRANE. THIS MAGNIFICENT ANIMAL IS GOING EXTINCT, BECAUSE IT'S DEFENSELESS AGAINST THE DINGOES.
PAGANEL, COME SEE ROBERT'S NICE CATCH!
IT'S HORRIBLE!
IT'S AN ECHIDNA. HAVE YOU EVER SEEN SUCH AN ANIMAL?
TWO DAYS WENT BY ON MARVELOUS PLAINS DOTTED WITH BEAUTIFUL FLOWERS.
THIS IS THE WIMERRA RIVER. IT'S SHALLOWER UPSTREAM. WE CAN FORD IT WITH NO PROBLEM.
I'LL TRUST YOU.
!?!
AAH!
GEE UP!

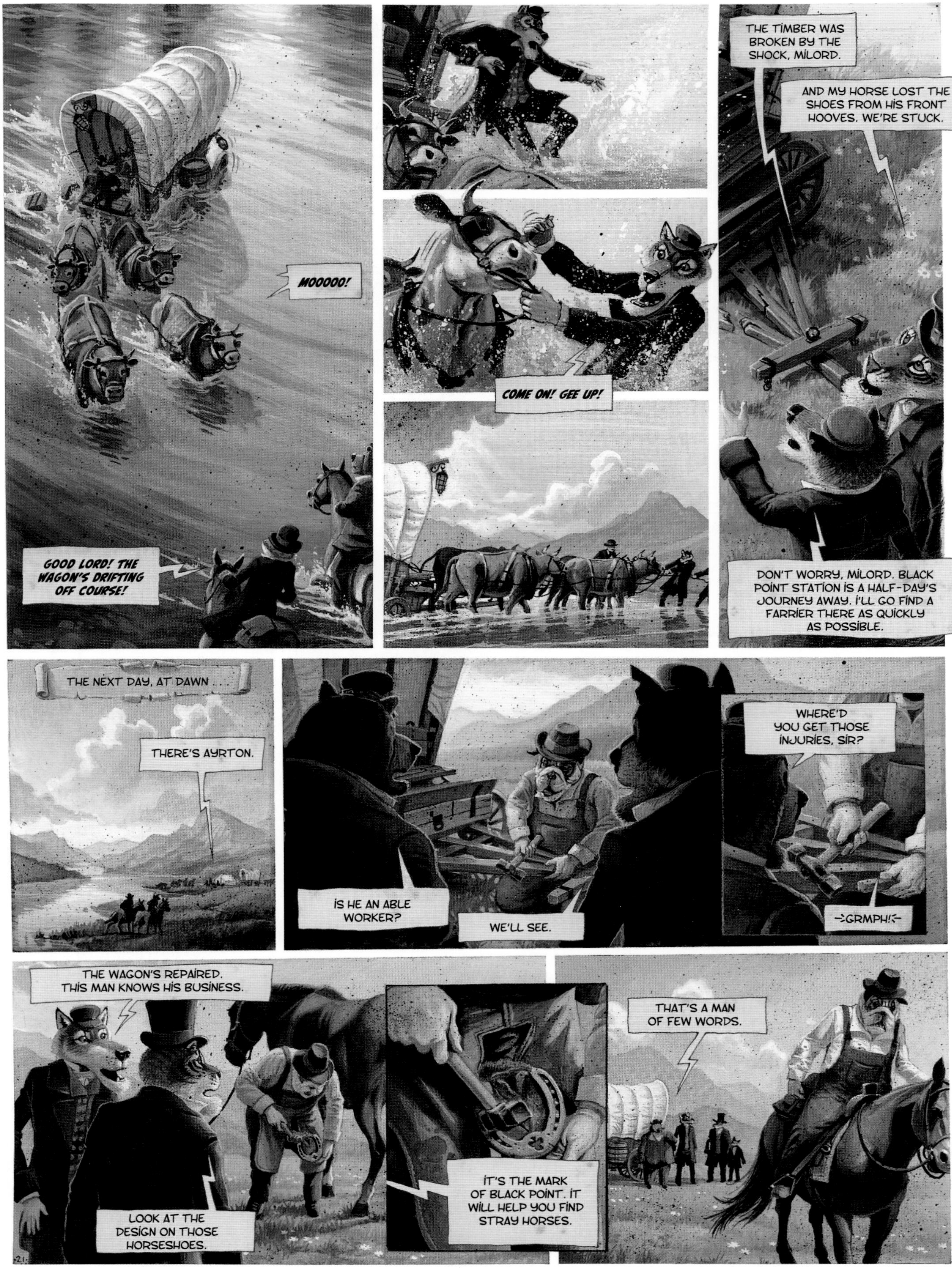
MOOOOO!
GOOD LORD! THE WAGON'S DRIFTING OFF COURSE!
COME ON! GEE UP!
THE TIMBER WAS BROKEN BY THE SHOCK, MILORD.
AND MY HORSE LOST THE SHOES FROM HIS FRONT HOOVES. WE'RE STUCK.
DON'T WORRY, MILORD. BLACK POINT STATION IS A HALF-DAY'S JOURNEY AWAY. I'LL GO FIND A FARRIER THERE AS QUICKLY AS POSSIBLE.
THE NEXT DAY, AT DAWN . . .
THERE'S AYRTON.
IS HE AN ABLE WORKER?
WE'LL SEE.
WHERE'D YOU GET THOSE INJURIES, SIR?
GRMPH!
THE WAGON'S REPAIRED. THIS MAN KNOWS HIS BUSINESS.
LOOK AT THE DESIGN ON THOSE HORSESHOES.
IT'S THE MARK OF BLACK POINT. IT WILL HELP YOU FIND STRAY HORSES.
THAT'S A MAN OF FEW WORDS.

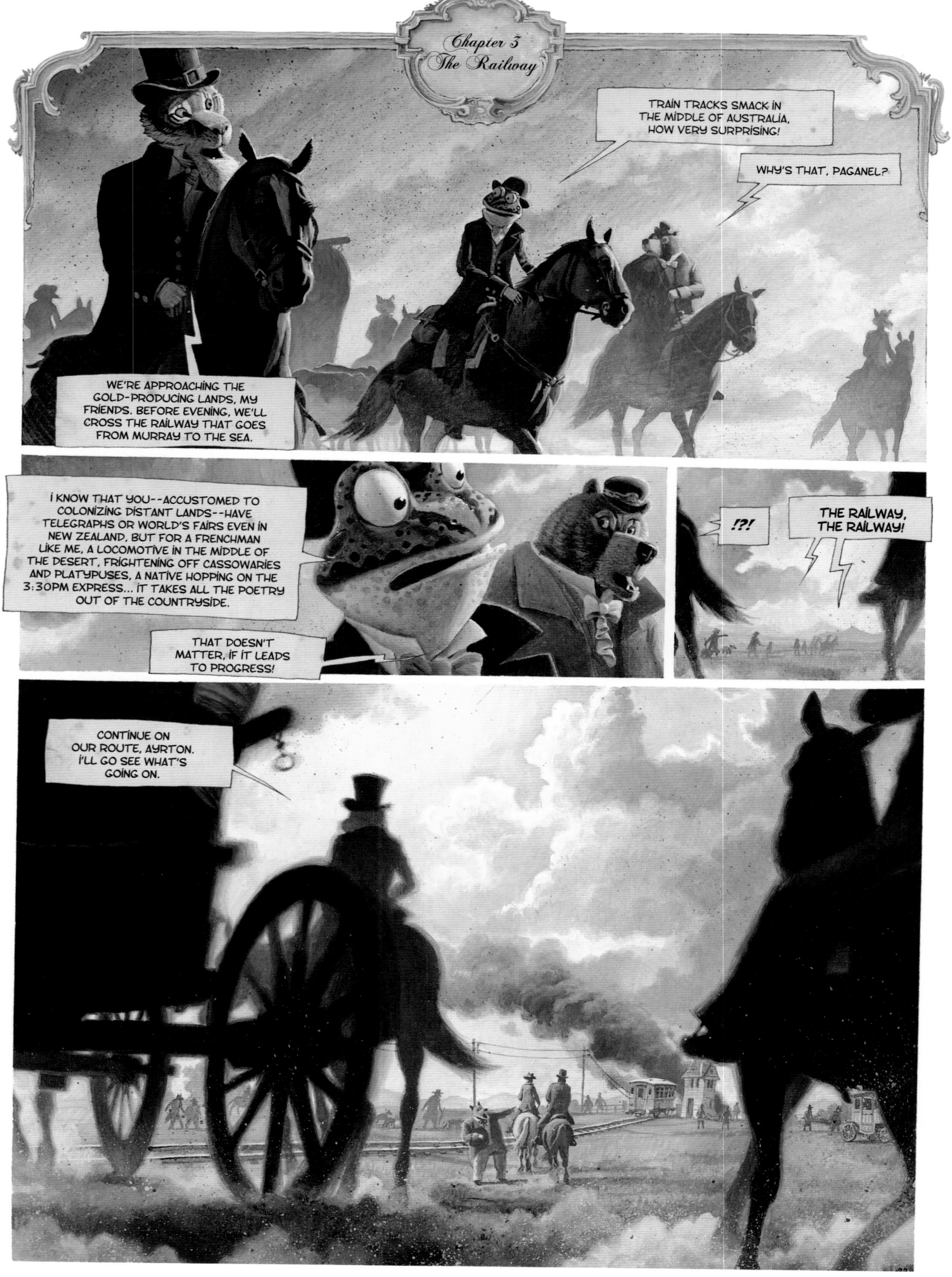
Chapter 3
The Railway
WE'RE APPROACHING THE GOLD-PRODUCING LANDS, MY FRIENDS. BEFORE EVENING, WE'LL CROSS THE RAILWAY THAT GOES FROM MURRAY TO THE SEA.
TRAIN TRACKS SMACK IN THE MIDDLE OF AUSTRALIA, HOW VERY SURPRISING!
WHY'S THAT, PAGANEL?
I KNOW THAT YOU--ACCUSTOMED TO COLONIZING DISTANT LANDS--HAVE TELEGRAPHS OR WORLD'S FAIRS EVEN IN NEW ZEALAND, BUT FOR A FRENCHMAN LIKE ME, A LOCOMOTIVE IN THE MIDDLE OF THE DESERT, FRIGHTENING OFF CASSOWARIES AND PLATYPUSES, A NATIVE HOPPING ON THE 3:30PM EXPRESS... IT TAKES ALL THE POETRY OUT OF THE COUNTRYSIDE.
THAT DOESN'T MATTER, IF IT LEADS TO PROGRESS!
!?!
THE RAILWAY, THE RAILWAY!
CONTINUE ON OUR ROUTE, AYRTON. I'LL GO SEE WHAT'S GOING ON.

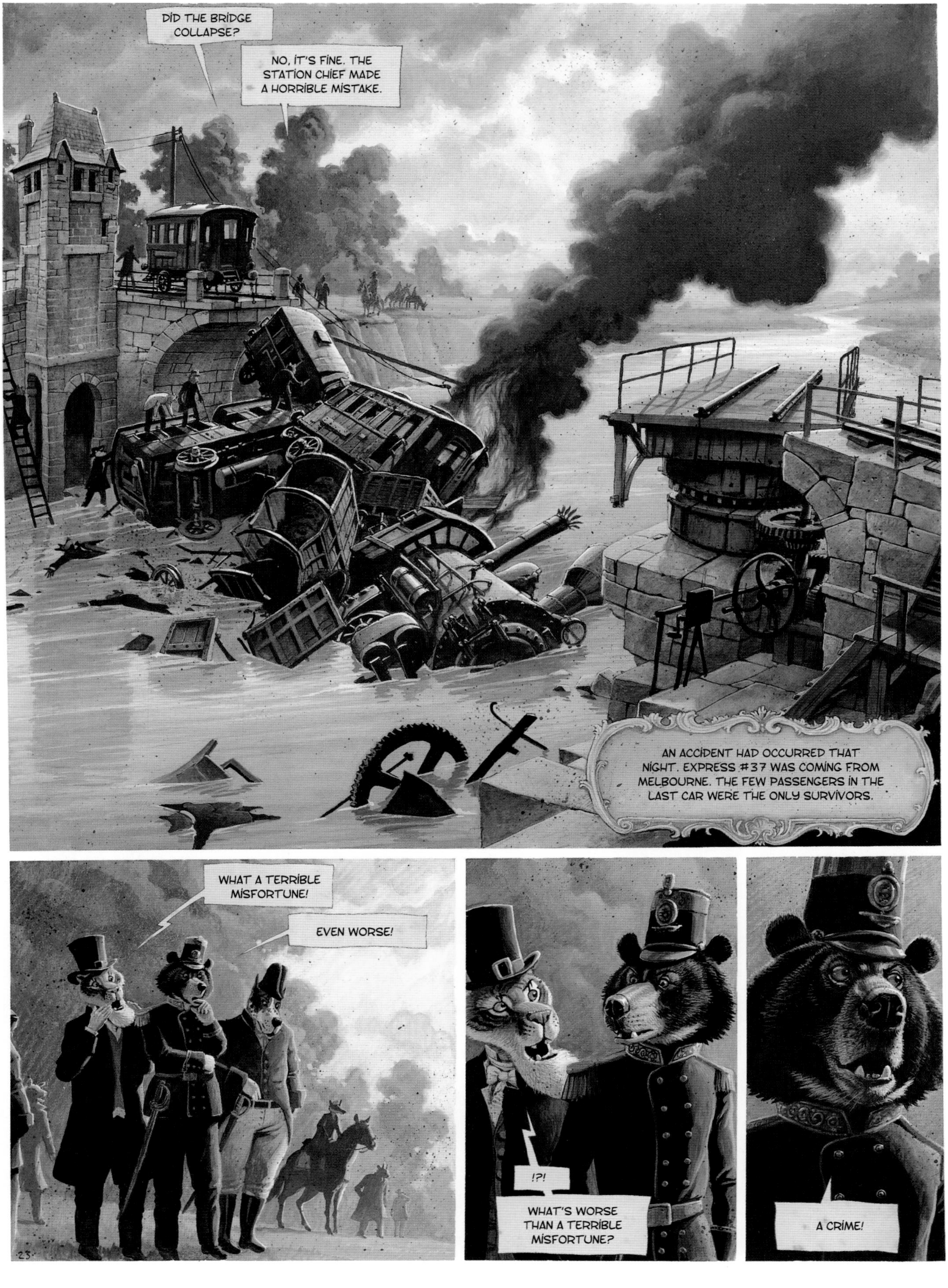
DID THE BRIDGE COLLAPSE?
NO, IT'S FINE. THE STATION CHIEF MADE A HORRIBLE MISTAKE.
AN ACCIDENT HAD OCCURRED THAT NIGHT. EXPRESS #37 WAS COMING FROM MELBOURNE. THE FEW PASSENGERS IN THE LAST CAR WERE THE ONLY SURVIVORS.
WHAT A TERRIBLE MISFORTUNE!
EVEN WORSE!
!?!
WHAT'S WORSE THAN A TERRIBLE MISFORTUNE?
A CRIME!

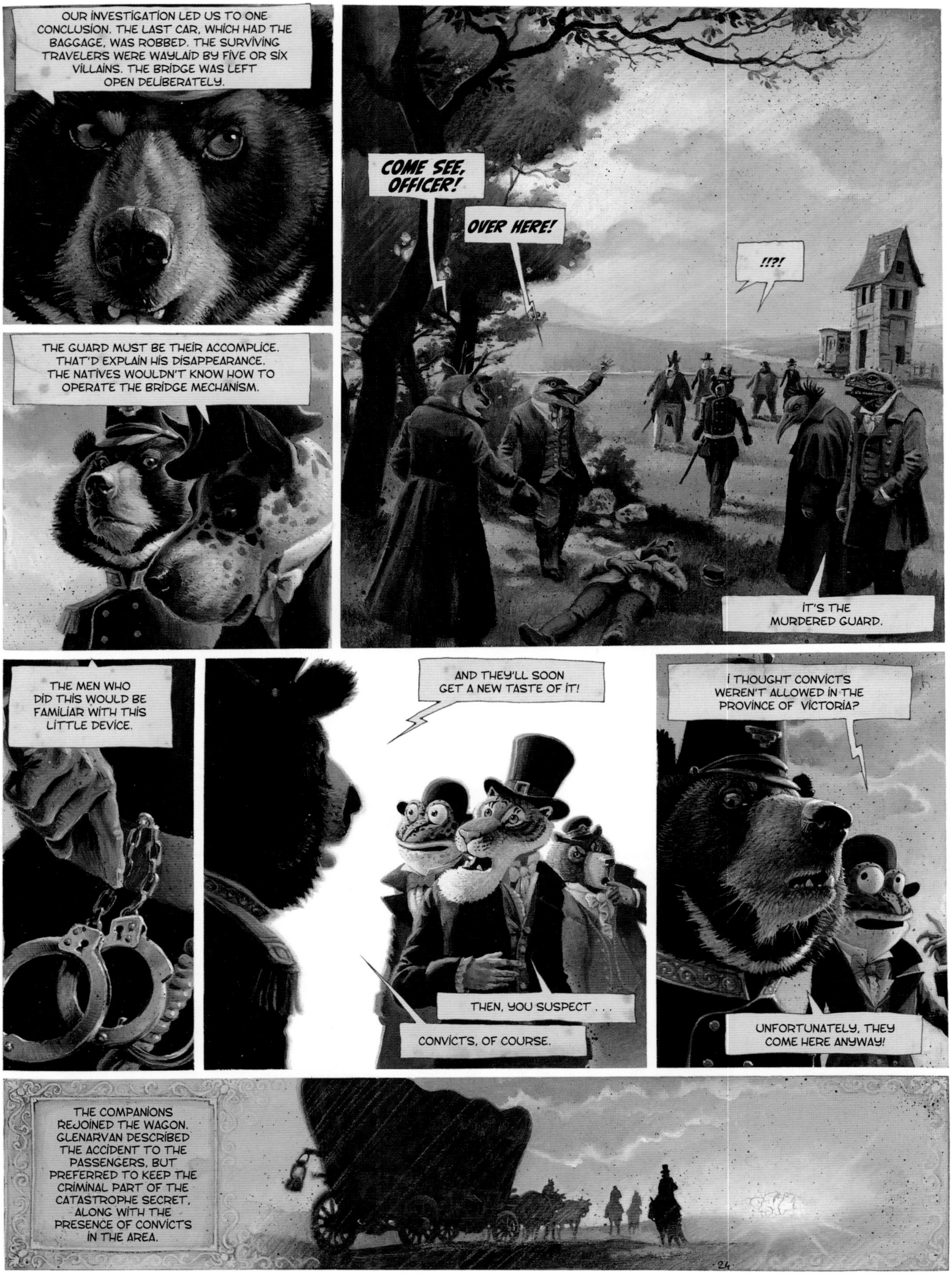
OUR INVESTIGATION LED US TO ONE CONCLUSION. THE LAST CAR, WHICH HAD THE BAGGAGE, WAS ROBBED. THE SURVIVING TRAVELERS WERE WAYLAID BY FIVE OR SIX VILLAINS. THE BRIDGE WAS LEFT OPEN DELIBERATELY.
THE GUARD MUST BE THEIR ACCOMPLICE. THAT'D EXPLAIN HIS DISAPPEARANCE. THE NATIVES WOULDN'T KNOW HOW TO OPERATE THE BRIDGE MECHANISM.
COME SEE, OFFICER!
OVER HERE!
!!?!
IT'S THE MURDERED GUARD.
THE MEN WHO DID THIS WOULD BE FAMILIAR WITH THIS LITTLE DEVICE.
AND THEY'LL SOON GET A NEW TASTE OF IT!
THEN, YOU SUSPECT . . .
CONVICTS, OF COURSE.
I THOUGHT CONVICTS WEREN'T ALLOWED IN THE PROVINCE OF VICTORIA?
UNFORTUNATELY, THEY COME HERE ANYWAY!
THE COMPANIONS REJOINED THE WAGON. GLENARVAN DESCRIBED THE ACCIDENT TO THE PASSENGERS, BUT PREFERRED TO KEEP THE CRIMINAL PART OF THE CATASTROPHE SECRET, ALONG WITH THE PRESENCE OF CONVICTS IN THE AREA.
24

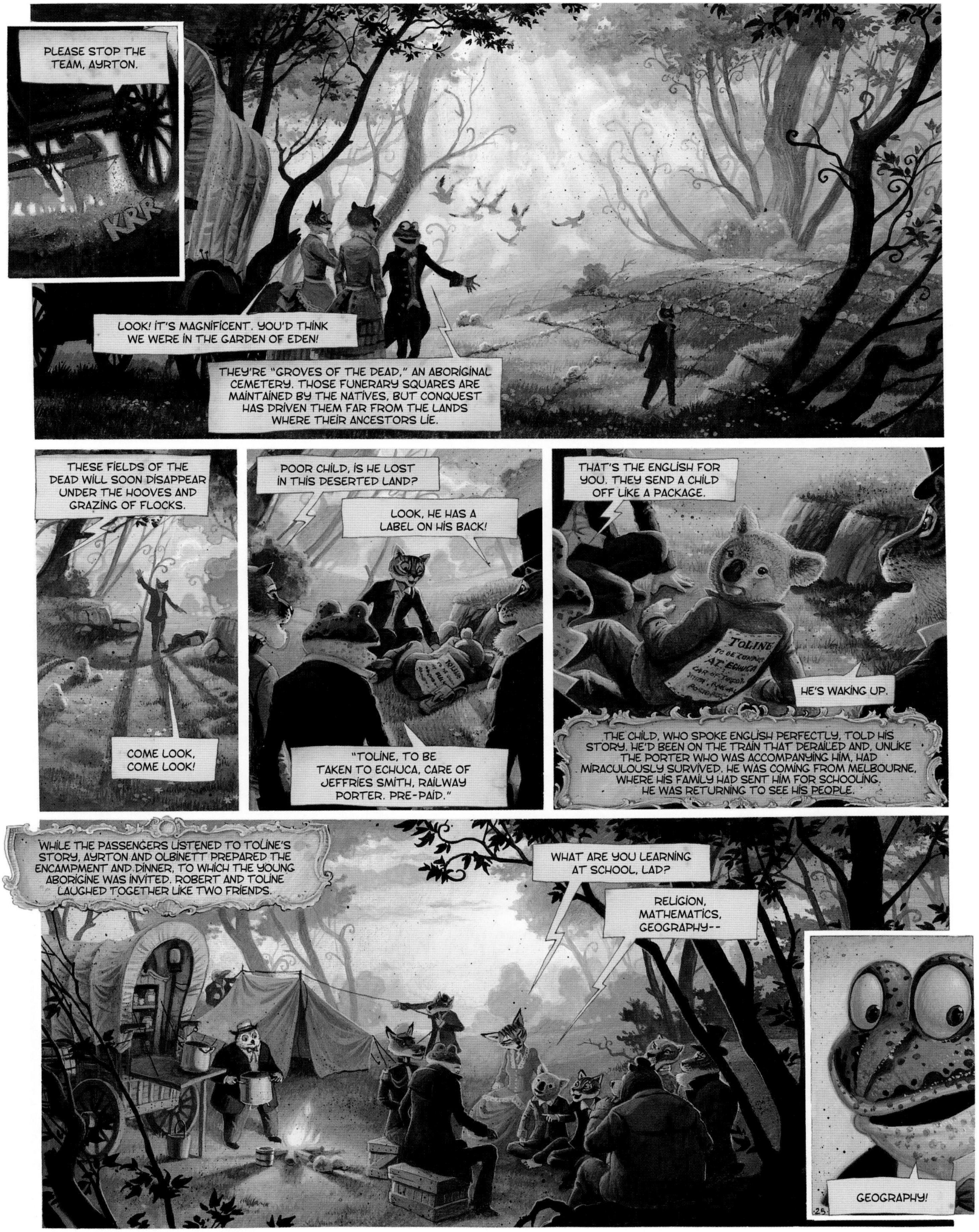
PLEASE STOP THE TEAM, AYRTON.
KRR
LOOK! IT'S MAGNIFICENT. YOU'D THINK WE WERE IN THE GARDEN OF EDEN!
THEY'RE "GROVES OF THE DEAD," AN ABORIGINAL CEMETERY. THOSE FUNERARY SQUARES ARE MAINTAINED BY THE NATIVES, BUT CONQUEST HAS DRIVEN THEM FAR FROM THE LANDS WHERE THEIR ANCESTORS LIE.
THESE FIELDS OF THE DEAD WILL SOON DISAPPEAR UNDER THE HOOVES AND GRAZING OF FLOCKS.
COME LOOK, COME LOOK!
POOR CHILD, IS HE LOST IN THIS DESERTED LAND?
LOOK, HE HAS A LABEL ON HIS BACK!
"TOLINE, TO BE TAKEN TO ECHUCA, CARE OF JEFFRIES SMITH, RAILWAY PORTER. PRE-PAID."
THAT'S THE ENGLISH FOR YOU. THEY SEND A CHILD OFF LIKE A PACKAGE.
TOLINE
HE'S WAKING UP.
THE CHILD, WHO SPOKE ENGLISH PERFECTLY, TOLD HIS STORY. HE'D BEEN ON THE TRAIN THAT DERAILED AND, UNLIKE THE PORTER WHO WAS ACCOMPANYING HIM, HAD MIRACULOUSLY SURVIVED. HE WAS COMING FROM MELBOURNE, WHERE HIS FAMILY HAD SENT HIM FOR SCHOOLING. HE WAS RETURNING TO SEE HIS PEOPLE.
WHILE THE PASSENGERS LISTENED TO TOLINE'S STORY, AYRTON AND OLBINETT PREPARED THE ENCAMPMENT AND DINNER, TO WHICH THE YOUNG ABORIGINE WAS INVITED. ROBERT AND TOLINE LAUGHED TOGETHER LIKE TWO FRIENDS.
WHAT ARE YOU LEARNING AT SCHOOL, LAD?
RELIGION, MATHEMATICS, GEOGRAPHY--
GEOGRAPHY!

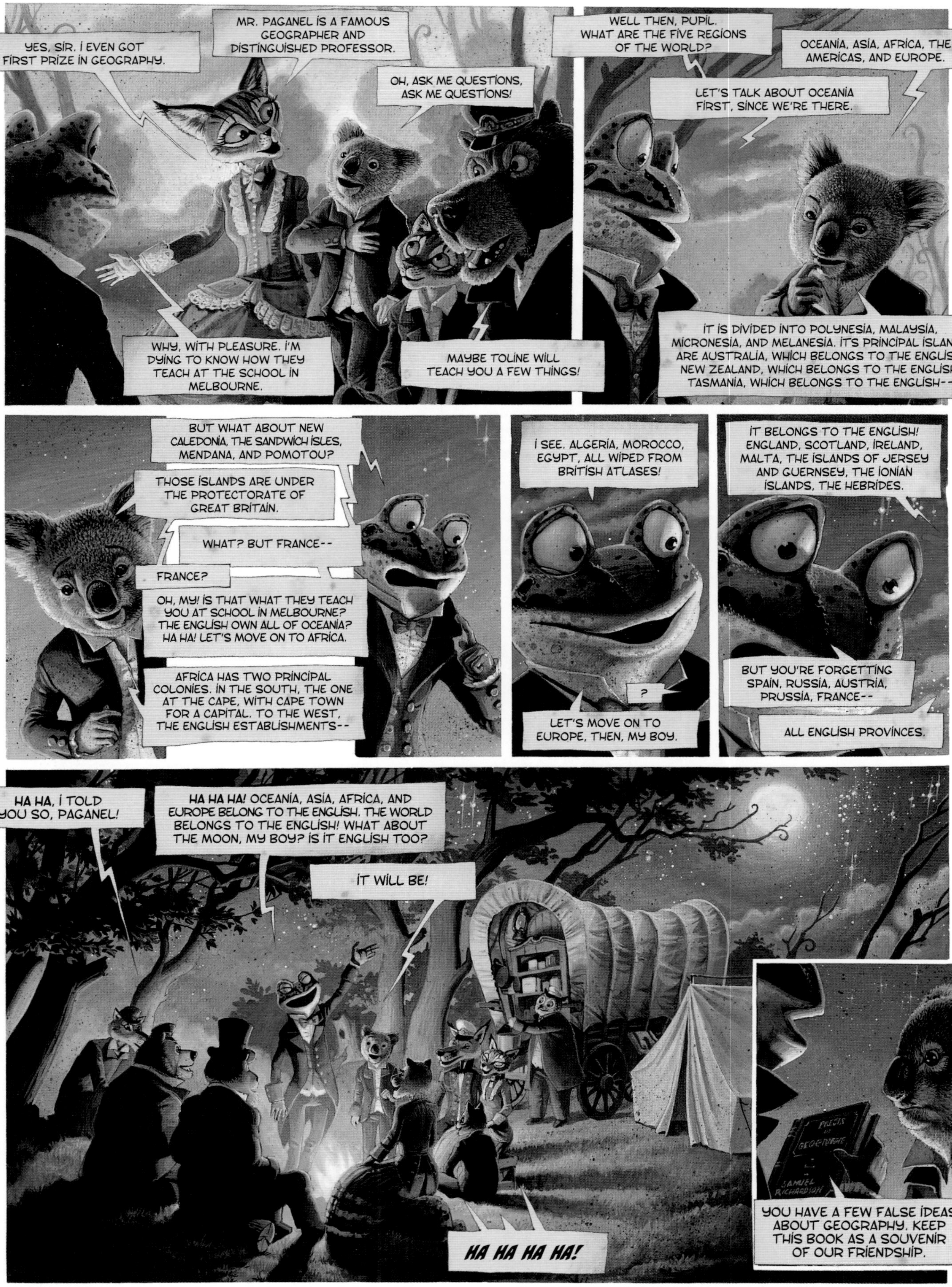
YES, SIR. I EVEN GOT FIRST PRIZE IN GEOGRAPHY.
MR. PAGANEL IS A FAMOUS GEOGRAPHER AND DISTINGUISHED PROFESSOR.
OH, ASK ME QUESTIONS, ASK ME QUESTIONS!
WHY, WITH PLEASURE. I'M DYING TO KNOW HOW THEY TEACH AT THE SCHOOL IN MELBOURNE.
MAYBE TOLINE WILL TEACH YOU A FEW THINGS!
WELL THEN, PUPIL. WHAT ARE THE FIVE REGIONS OF THE WORLD?
OCEANIA, ASIA, AFRICA, THE AMERICAS, AND EUROPE.
LET'S TALK ABOUT OCEANIA FIRST, SINCE WE'RE THERE.
IT IS DIVIDED INTO POLYNESIA, MALAYSIA, MICRONESIA, AND MELANESIA. ITS PRINCIPAL ISLANDS ARE AUSTRALIA, WHICH BELONGS TO THE ENGLISH, NEW ZEALAND, WHICH BELONGS TO THE ENGLISH, TASMANIA, WHICH BELONGS TO THE ENGLISH--
BUT WHAT ABOUT NEW CALEDONIA, THE SANDWICH ISLES, MENDANA, AND POMOTOU?
THOSE ISLANDS ARE UNDER THE PROTECTORATE OF GREAT BRITAIN.
WHAT? BUT FRANCE--
FRANCE?
OH, MY! IS THAT WHAT THEY TEACH YOU AT SCHOOL IN MELBOURNE? THE ENGLISH OWN ALL OF OCEANIA? HA HA! LET'S MOVE ON TO AFRICA.
AFRICA HAS TWO PRINCIPAL COLONIES. IN THE SOUTH, THE ONE AT THE CAPE, WITH CAPE TOWN FOR A CAPITAL. TO THE WEST, THE ENGLISH ESTABLISHMENTS--
I SEE. ALGERIA, MOROCCO, EGYPT, ALL WIPED FROM BRITISH ATLASES!
?
LET'S MOVE ON TO EUROPE, THEN, MY BOY.
IT BELONGS TO THE ENGLISH! ENGLAND, SCOTLAND, IRELAND, MALTA, THE ISLANDS OF JERSEY AND GUERNSEY, THE IONIAN ISLANDS, THE HEBRIDES.
BUT YOU'RE FORGETTING SPAIN, RUSSIA, AUSTRIA, PRUSSIA, FRANCE--
ALL ENGLISH PROVINCES.
HA HA, I TOLD YOU SO, PAGANEL!
HA HA HA! OCEANIA, ASIA, AFRICA, AND EUROPE BELONG TO THE ENGLISH. THE WORLD BELONGS TO THE ENGLISH! WHAT ABOUT THE MOON, MY BOY? IS IT ENGLISH TOO?
IT WILL BE!
HA HA HA HA!
YOU HAVE A FEW FALSE IDEAS ABOUT GEOGRAPHY. KEEP THIS BOOK AS A SOUVENIR OF OUR FRIENDSHIP.

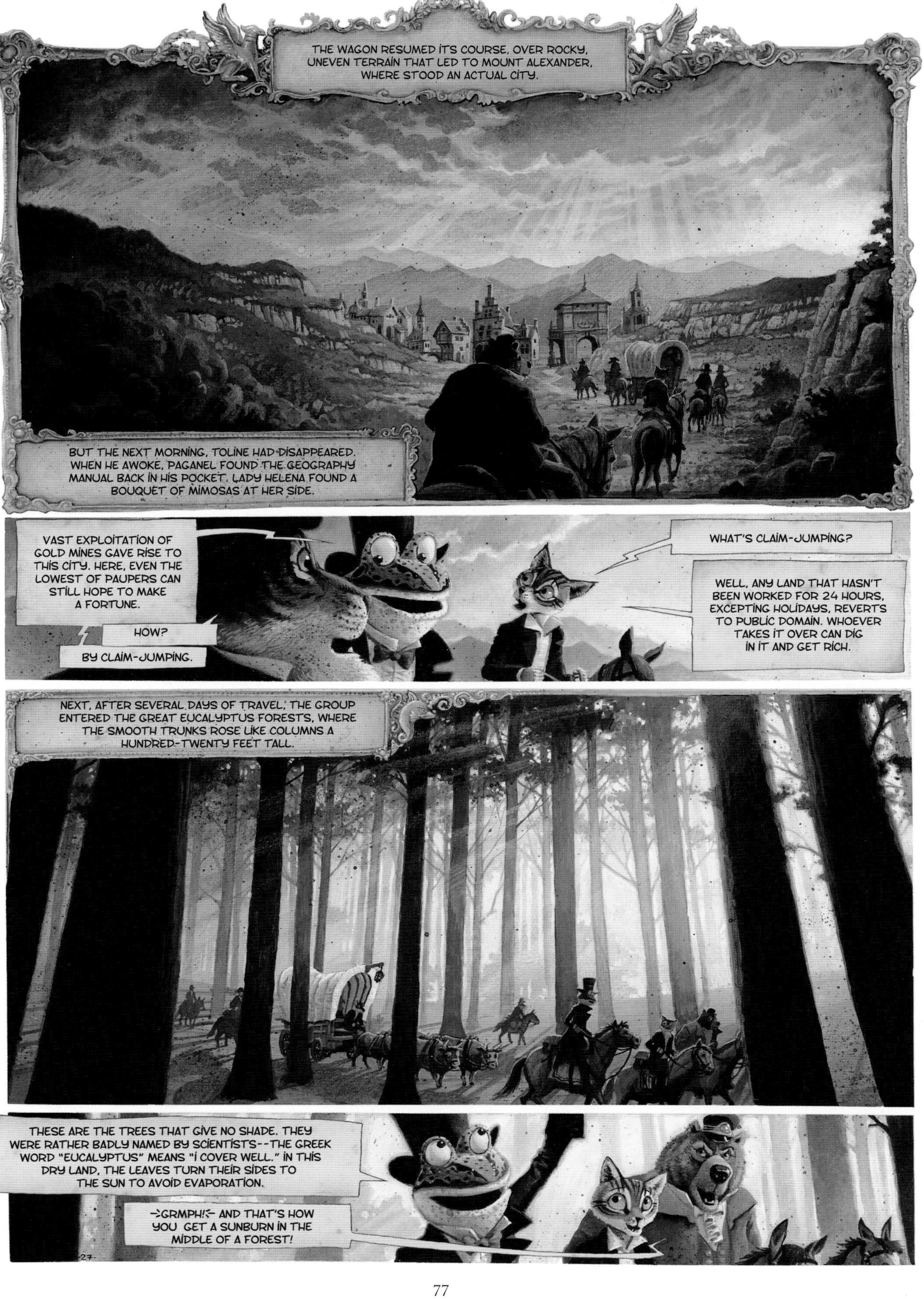
THE WAGON RESUMED ITS COURSE, OVER ROCKY, UNEVEN TERRAIN THAT LED TO MOUNT ALEXANDER, WHERE STOOD AN ACTUAL CITY.
BUT THE NEXT MORNING, TOLINE HAD DISAPPEARED. WHEN HE AWOKE, PAGANEL FOUND THE GEOGRAPHY MANUAL BACK IN HIS POCKET. LADY HELENA FOUND A BOUQUET OF MIMOSAS AT HER SIDE.
VAST EXPLOITATION OF GOLD MINES GAVE RISE TO THIS CITY. HERE, EVEN THE LOWEST OF PAUPERS CAN STILL HOPE TO MAKE A FORTUNE.
HOW?
BY CLAIM-JUMPING.
WHAT'S CLAIM-JUMPING?
WELL, ANY LAND THAT HASN'T BEEN WORKED FOR 24 HOURS, EXCEPTING HOLIDAYS, REVERTS TO PUBLIC DOMAIN. WHOEVER TAKES IT OVER CAN DIG IN IT AND GET RICH.
NEXT, AFTER SEVERAL DAYS OF TRAVEL, THE GROUP ENTERED THE GREAT EUCALYPTUS FORESTS, WHERE THE SMOOTH TRUNKS ROSE LIKE COLUMNS A HUNDRED-TWENTY FEET TALL.
THESE ARE THE TREES THAT GIVE NO SHADE. THEY WERE RATHER BADLY NAMED BY SCIENTISTS--THE GREEK WORD "EUCALYPTUS" MEANS "I COVER WELL." IN THIS DRY LAND, THE LEAVES TURN THEIR SIDES TO THE SUN TO AVOID EVAPORATION.
-GRMPH!- AND THAT'S HOW YOU GET A SUNBURN IN THE MIDDLE OF A FOREST!
-27-

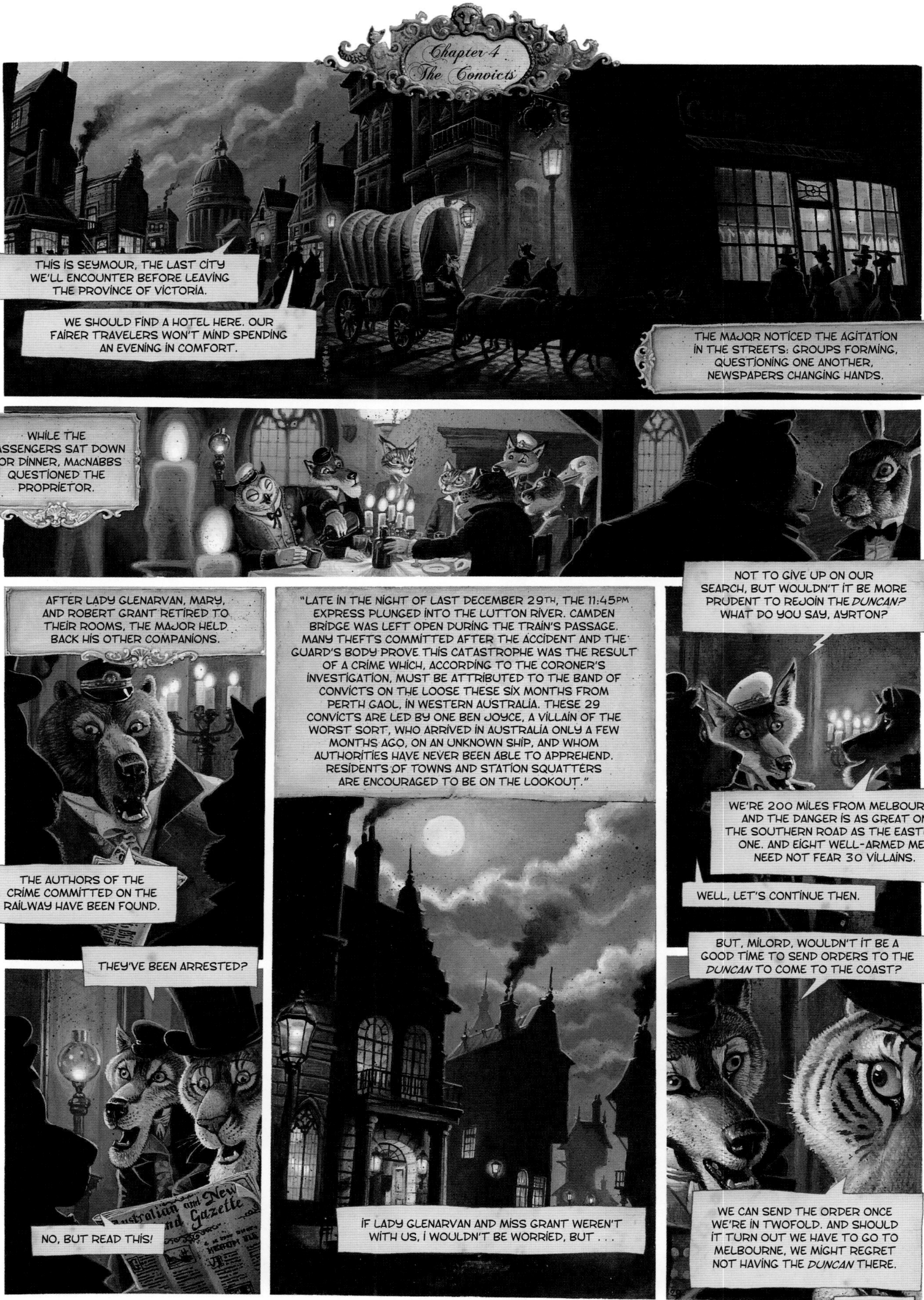
Chapter 4
The Convicts
THIS IS SEYMOUR, THE LAST CITY WE'LL ENCOUNTER BEFORE LEAVING THE PROVINCE OF VICTORIA.
WE SHOULD FIND A HOTEL HERE. OUR FAIRER TRAVELERS WON'T MIND SPENDING AN EVENING IN COMFORT.
THE MAJOR NOTICED THE AGITATION IN THE STREETS: GROUPS FORMING, QUESTIONING ONE ANOTHER, NEWSPAPERS CHANGING HANDS.
WHILE THE PASSENGERS SAT DOWN FOR DINNER, MACNABBS QUESTIONED THE PROPRIETOR.
AFTER LADY GLENARVAN, MARY, AND ROBERT GRANT RETIRED TO THEIR ROOMS, THE MAJOR HELD BACK HIS OTHER COMPANIONS.
THE AUTHORS OF THE CRIME COMMITTED ON THE RAILWAY HAVE BEEN FOUND.
THEY'VE BEEN ARRESTED?
NO, BUT READ THIS!
"LATE IN THE NIGHT OF LAST DECEMBER 29TH, THE 11:45PM EXPRESS PLUNGED INTO THE LUTTON RIVER. CAMDEN BRIDGE WAS LEFT OPEN DURING THE TRAIN'S PASSAGE. MANY THEFTS COMMITTED AFTER THE ACCIDENT AND THE GUARD'S BODY PROVE THIS CATASTROPHE WAS THE RESULT OF A CRIME WHICH, ACCORDING TO THE CORONER'S INVESTIGATION, MUST BE ATTRIBUTED TO THE BAND OF CONVICTS ON THE LOOSE THESE SIX MONTHS FROM PERTH GAOL, IN WESTERN AUSTRALIA. THESE 29 CONVICTS ARE LED BY ONE BEN JOYCE, A VILLAIN OF THE WORST SORT, WHO ARRIVED IN AUSTRALIA ONLY A FEW MONTHS AGO, ON AN UNKNOWN SHIP, AND WHOM AUTHORITIES HAVE NEVER BEEN ABLE TO APPREHEND. RESIDENTS OF TOWNS AND STATION SQUATTERS ARE ENCOURAGED TO BE ON THE LOOKOUT."
IF LADY GLENARVAN AND MISS GRANT WEREN'T WITH US, I WOULDN'T BE WORRIED, BUT . . .
NOT TO GIVE UP ON OUR SEARCH, BUT WOULDN'T IT BE MORE PRUDENT TO REJOIN THE *DUNCAN*? WHAT DO YOU SAY, AYRTON?
WE'RE 200 MILES FROM MELBOURNE, AND THE DANGER IS AS GREAT ON THE SOUTHERN ROAD AS THE EASTERN ONE. AND EIGHT WELL-ARMED MEN NEED NOT FEAR 30 VILLAINS.
WELL, LET'S CONTINUE THEN.
BUT, MILORD, WOULDN'T IT BE A GOOD TIME TO SEND ORDERS TO THE *DUNCAN* TO COME TO THE COAST?
WE CAN SEND THE ORDER ONCE WE'RE IN TWOFOLD. AND SHOULD IT TURN OUT WE HAVE TO GO TO MELBOURNE, WE MIGHT REGRET NOT HAVING THE *DUNCAN* THERE.
ALL RIGHT.

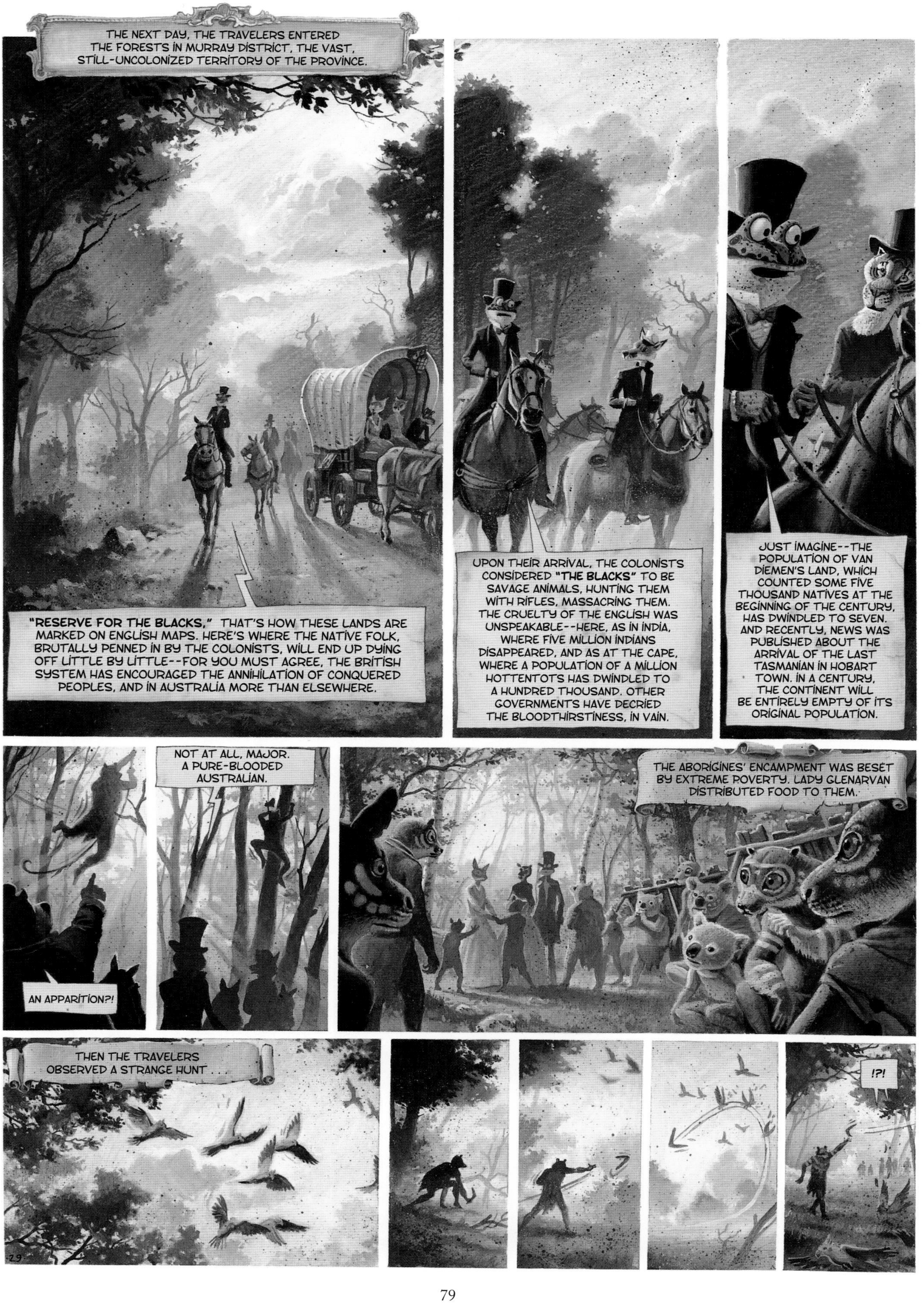
THE NEXT DAY, THE TRAVELERS ENTERED THE FORESTS IN MURRAY DISTRICT, THE VAST, STILL-UNCOLONIZED TERRITORY OF THE PROVINCE.
"RESERVE FOR THE BLACKS," THAT'S HOW THESE LANDS ARE MARKED ON ENGLISH MAPS. HERE'S WHERE THE NATIVE FOLK, BRUTALLY PENNED IN BY THE COLONISTS, WILL END UP DYING OFF LITTLE BY LITTLE--FOR YOU MUST AGREE, THE BRITISH SYSTEM HAS ENCOURAGED THE ANNIHILATION OF CONQUERED PEOPLES, AND IN AUSTRALIA MORE THAN ELSEWHERE.
UPON THEIR ARRIVAL, THE COLONISTS CONSIDERED "THE BLACKS" TO BE SAVAGE ANIMALS, HUNTING THEM WITH RIFLES, MASSACRING THEM. THE CRUELTY OF THE ENGLISH WAS UNSPEAKABLE--HERE, AS IN INDIA, WHERE FIVE MILLION INDIANS DISAPPEARED, AND AS AT THE CAPE, WHERE A POPULATION OF A MILLION HOTTENTOTS HAS DWINDLED TO A HUNDRED THOUSAND. OTHER GOVERNMENTS HAVE DECRIED THE BLOODTHIRSTINESS, IN VAIN.
JUST IMAGINE--THE POPULATION OF VAN DIEMEN'S LAND, WHICH COUNTED SOME FIVE THOUSAND NATIVES AT THE BEGINNING OF THE CENTURY, HAS DWINDLED TO SEVEN. AND RECENTLY, NEWS WAS PUBLISHED ABOUT THE ARRIVAL OF THE LAST TASMANIAN IN HOBART TOWN. IN A CENTURY, THE CONTINENT WILL BE ENTIRELY EMPTY OF ITS ORIGINAL POPULATION.
AN APPARITION?!
NOT AT ALL, MAJOR. A PURE-BLOODED AUSTRALIAN.
THE ABORIGINES' ENCAMPMENT WAS BESET BY EXTREME POVERTY. LADY GLENARVAN DISTRIBUTED FOOD TO THEM.
THEN THE TRAVELERS OBSERVED A STRANGE HUNT . . .
!?!

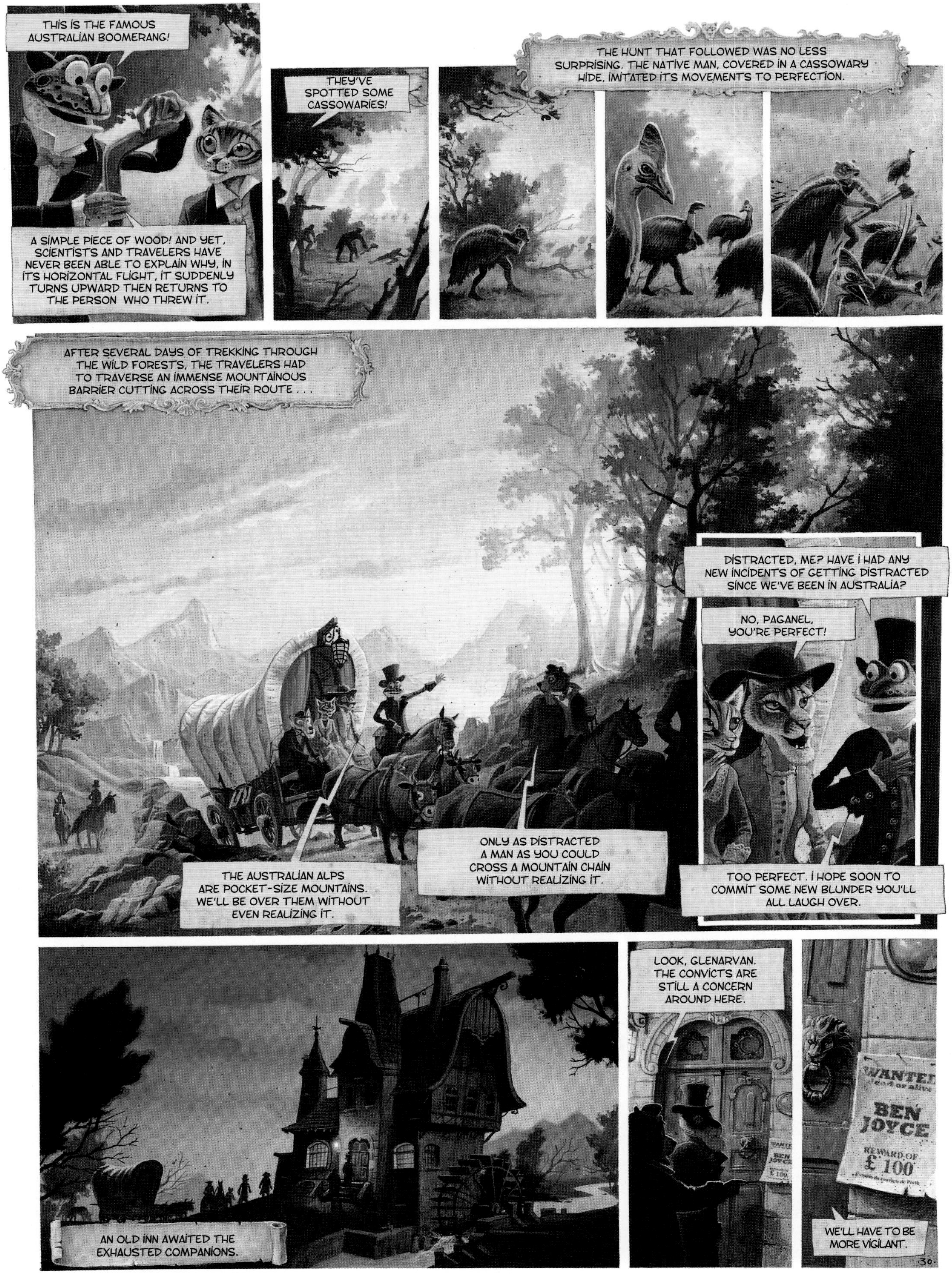

THIS IS THE FAMOUS AUSTRALIAN BOOMERANG!
A SIMPLE PIECE OF WOOD! AND YET, SCIENTISTS AND TRAVELERS HAVE NEVER BEEN ABLE TO EXPLAIN WHY, IN ITS HORIZONTAL FLIGHT, IT SUDDENLY TURNS UPWARD THEN RETURNS TO THE PERSON WHO THREW IT.
THEY'VE SPOTTED SOME CASSOWARIES!
THE HUNT THAT FOLLOWED WAS NO LESS SURPRISING. THE NATIVE MAN, COVERED IN A CASSOWARY HIDE, IMITATED ITS MOVEMENTS TO PERFECTION.
AFTER SEVERAL DAYS OF TREKKING THROUGH THE WILD FORESTS, THE TRAVELERS HAD TO TRAVERSE AN IMMENSE MOUNTAINOUS BARRIER CUTTING ACROSS THEIR ROUTE . . .
THE AUSTRALIAN ALPS ARE POCKET-SIZE MOUNTAINS. WE'LL BE OVER THEM WITHOUT EVEN REALIZING IT.
ONLY AS DISTRACTED A MAN AS YOU COULD CROSS A MOUNTAIN CHAIN WITHOUT REALIZING IT.
DISTRACTED, ME? HAVE I HAD ANY NEW INCIDENTS OF GETTING DISTRACTED SINCE WE'VE BEEN IN AUSTRALIA?
NO, PAGANEL, YOU'RE PERFECT!
TOO PERFECT. I HOPE SOON TO COMMIT SOME NEW BLUNDER YOU'LL ALL LAUGH OVER.
AN OLD INN AWAITED THE EXHAUSTED COMPANIONS.
LOOK, GLENARVAN. THE CONVICTS ARE STILL A CONCERN AROUND HERE.
WANTED
dead or alive
BEN JOYCE
REWARD OF
£ 100
WE'LL HAVE TO BE MORE VIGILANT.
-30-

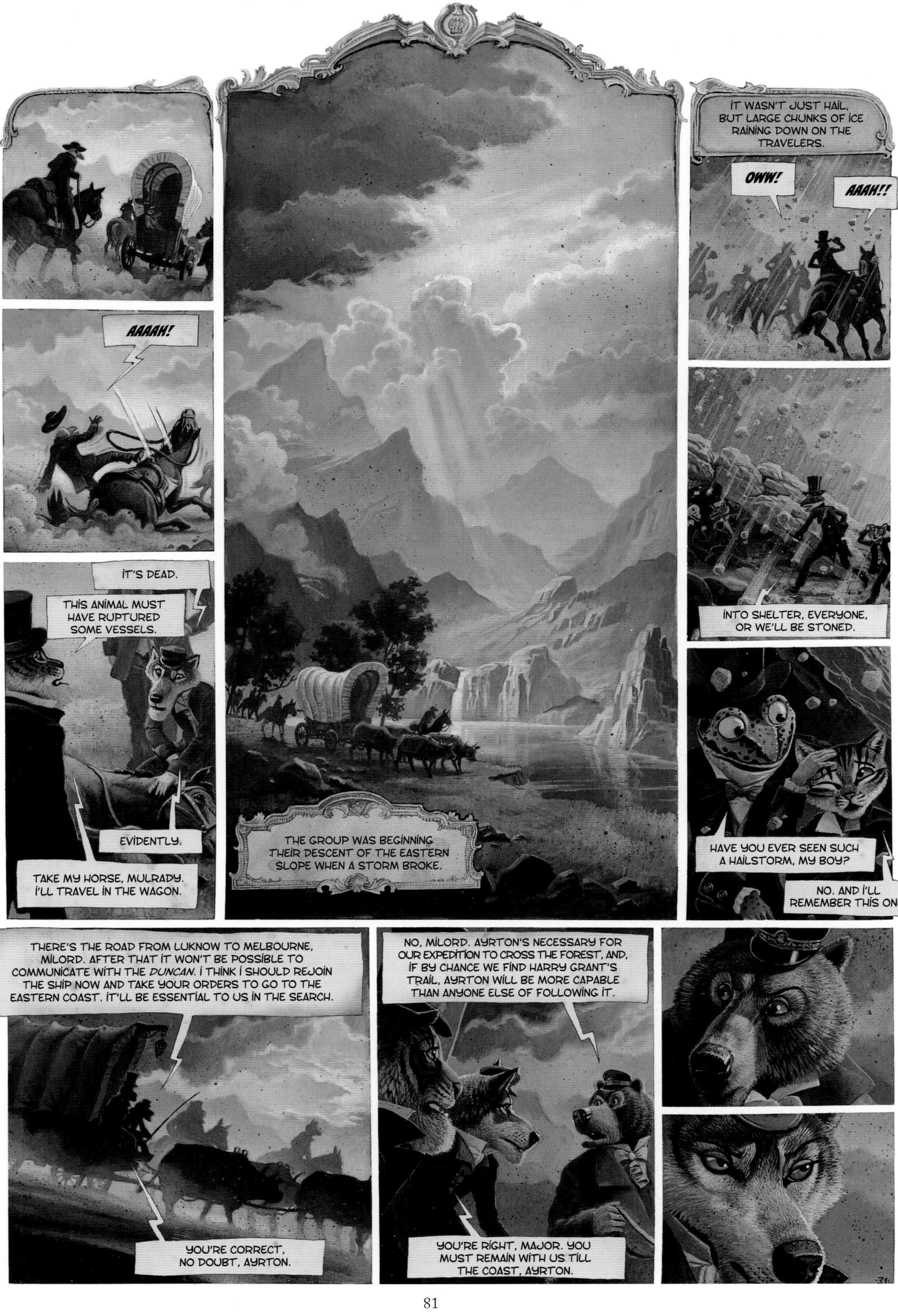
AAAAH!
IT'S DEAD.
THIS ANIMAL MUST HAVE RUPTURED SOME VESSELS.
EVIDENTLY.
TAKE MY HORSE, MULRADY. I'LL TRAVEL IN THE WAGON.
THE GROUP WAS BEGINNING THEIR DESCENT OF THE EASTERN SLOPE WHEN A STORM BROKE.
IT WASN'T JUST HAIL, BUT LARGE CHUNKS OF ICE RAINING DOWN ON THE TRAVELERS.
OWW!
AAAH!!
INTO SHELTER, EVERYONE, OR WE'LL BE STONED.
HAVE YOU EVER SEEN SUCH A HAILSTORM, MY BOY?
NO. AND I'LL REMEMBER THIS ONE.
THERE'S THE ROAD FROM LUKNOW TO MELBOURNE, MILORD. AFTER THAT IT WON'T BE POSSIBLE TO COMMUNICATE WITH THE DUNCAN. I THINK I SHOULD REJOIN THE SHIP NOW AND TAKE YOUR ORDERS TO GO TO THE EASTERN COAST. IT'LL BE ESSENTIAL TO US IN THE SEARCH.
YOU'RE CORRECT, NO DOUBT, AYRTON.
NO, MILORD. AYRTON'S NECESSARY FOR OUR EXPEDITION TO CROSS THE FOREST, AND, IF BY CHANCE WE FIND HARRY GRANT'S TRAIL, AYRTON WILL BE MORE CAPABLE THAN ANYONE ELSE OF FOLLOWING IT.
YOU'RE RIGHT, MAJOR. YOU MUST REMAIN WITH US TILL THE COAST, AYRTON.

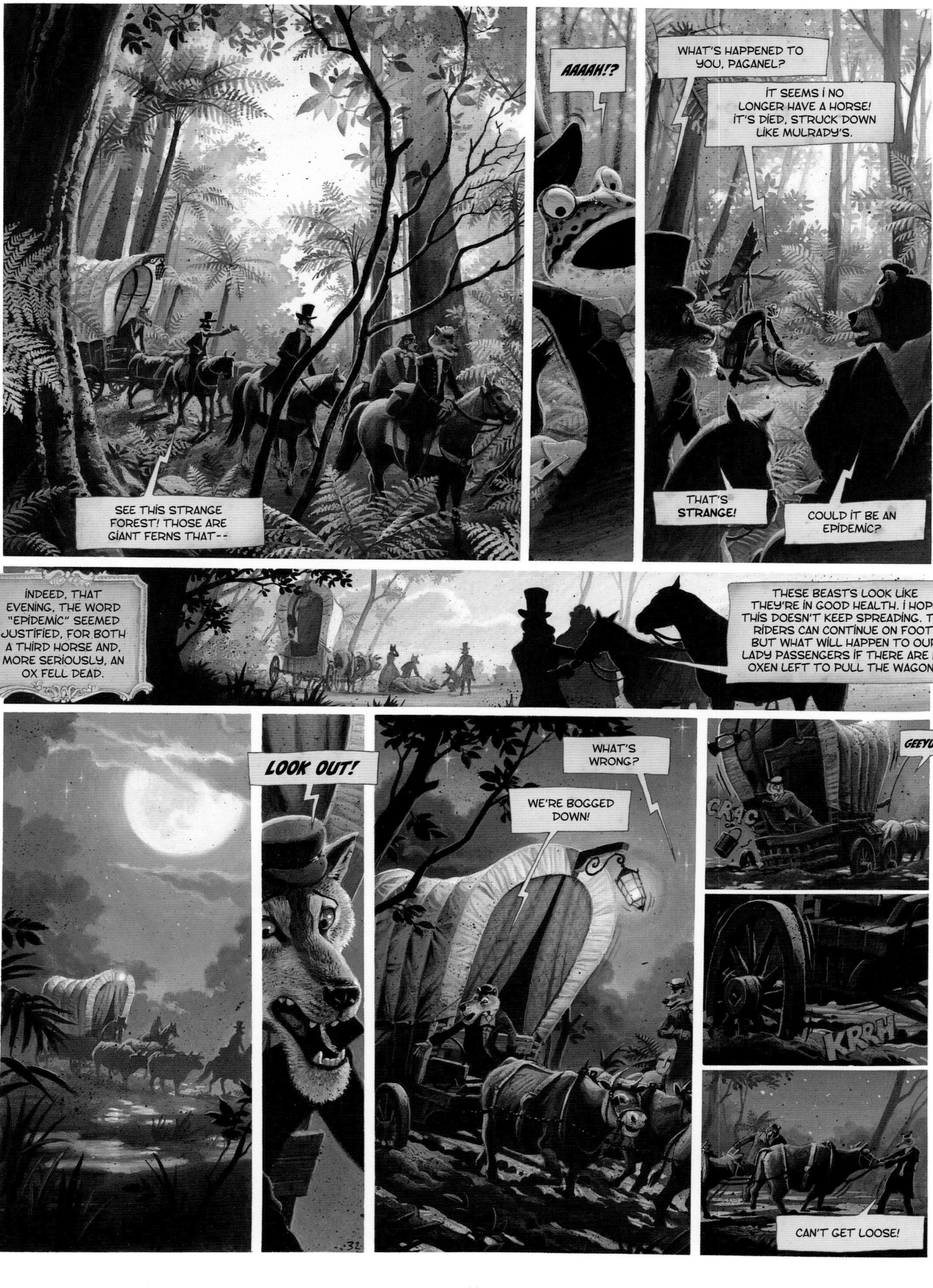
SEE THIS STRANGE FOREST! THOSE ARE GIANT FERNS THAT--
AAAAH!?
WHAT'S HAPPENED TO YOU, PAGANEL?
IT SEEMS I NO LONGER HAVE A HORSE! IT'S DIED, STRUCK DOWN LIKE MULRADY'S.
THAT'S STRANGE!
COULD IT BE AN EPIDEMIC?
INDEED, THAT EVENING, THE WORD "EPIDEMIC" SEEMED JUSTIFIED, FOR BOTH A THIRD HORSE AND, MORE SERIOUSLY, AN OX FELL DEAD.
THESE BEASTS LOOK LIKE THEY'RE IN GOOD HEALTH. I HOPE THIS DOESN'T KEEP SPREADING. THE RIDERS CAN CONTINUE ON FOOT, BUT WHAT WILL HAPPEN TO OUR LADY PASSENGERS IF THERE ARE NO OXEN LEFT TO PULL THE WAGON?
LOOK OUT!
WHAT'S WRONG?
WE'RE BOGGED DOWN!
GEEYUP!
CRAC
KRRH
CAN'T GET LOOSE!

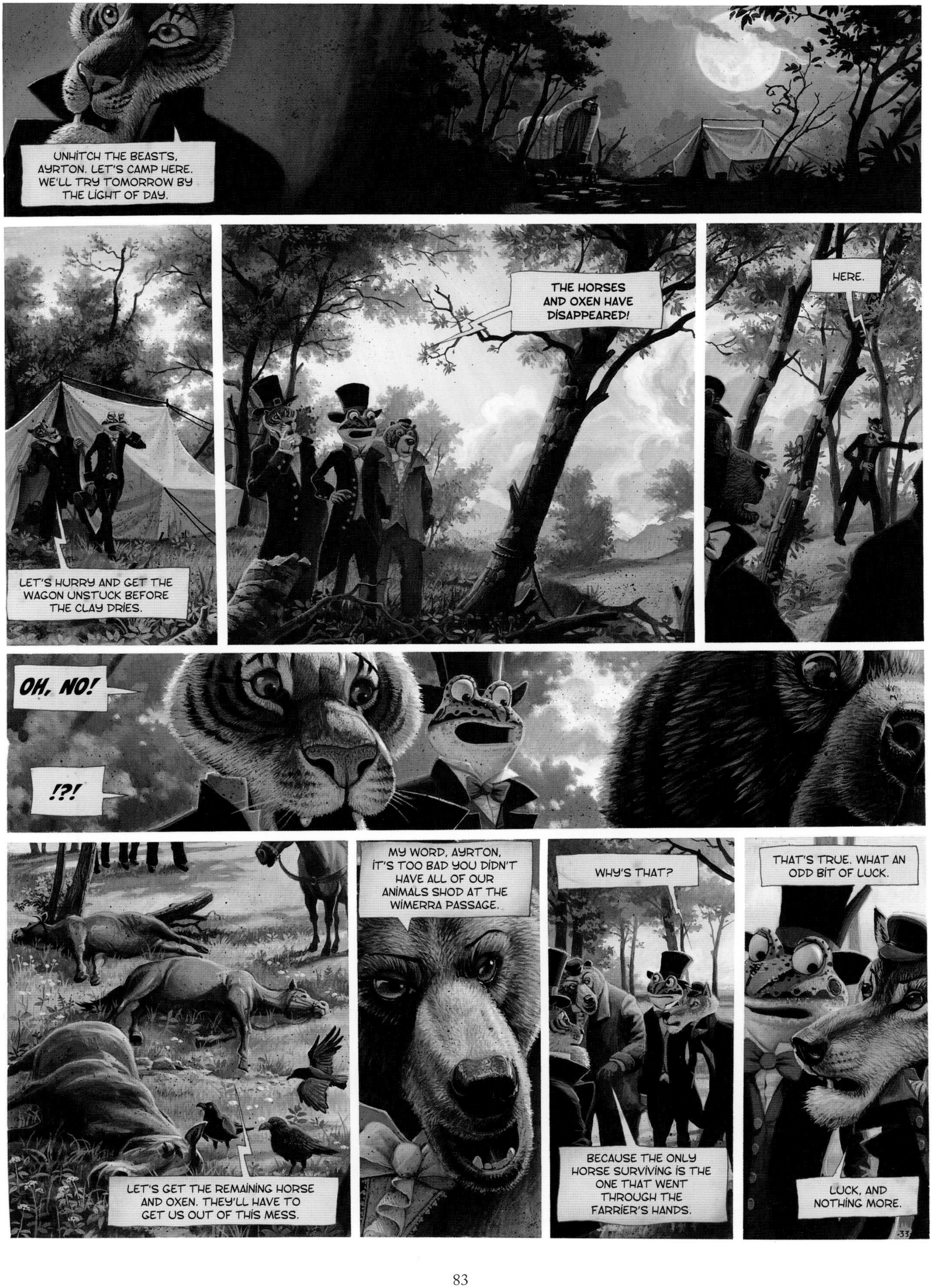
UNHITCH THE BEASTS, AYRTON. LET'S CAMP HERE. WE'LL TRY TOMORROW BY THE LIGHT OF DAY.
LET'S HURRY AND GET THE WAGON UNSTUCK BEFORE THE CLAY DRIES.
THE HORSES AND OXEN HAVE DISAPPEARED!
HERE.
OH, NO!
!?!
LET'S GET THE REMAINING HORSE AND OXEN. THEY'LL HAVE TO GET US OUT OF THIS MESS.
MY WORD, AYRTON, IT'S TOO BAD YOU DIDN'T HAVE ALL OF OUR ANIMALS SHOD AT THE WIMERRA PASSAGE.
WHY'S THAT?
BECAUSE THE ONLY HORSE SURVIVING IS THE ONE THAT WENT THROUGH THE FARRIER'S HANDS.
THAT'S TRUE. WHAT AN ODD BIT OF LUCK.
LUCK, AND NOTHING MORE.

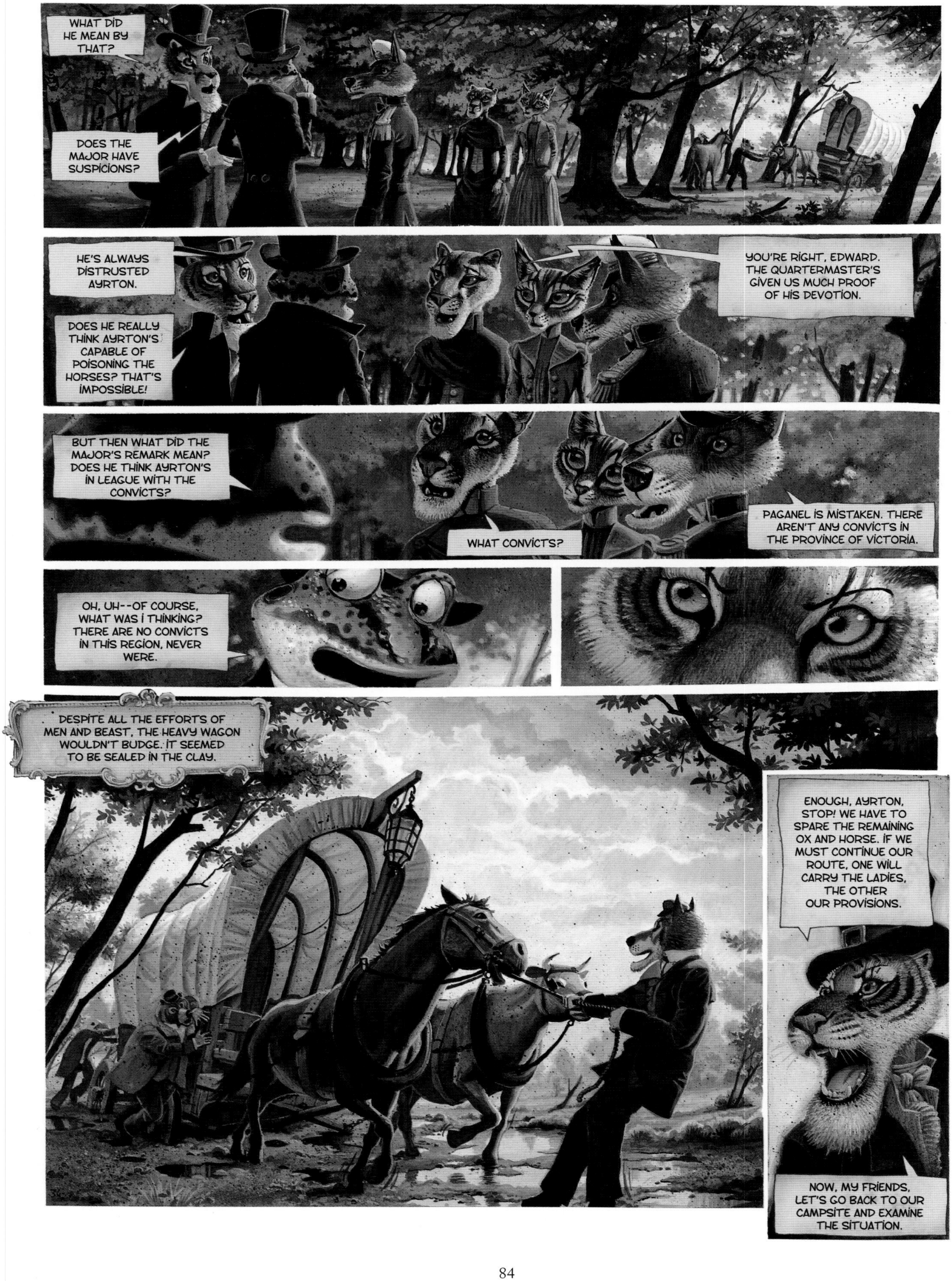
WHAT DID HE MEAN BY THAT?
DOES THE MAJOR HAVE SUSPICIONS?
HE'S ALWAYS DISTRUSTED AYRTON.
DOES HE REALLY THINK AYRTON'S CAPABLE OF POISONING THE HORSES? THAT'S IMPOSSIBLE!
YOU'RE RIGHT, EDWARD. THE QUARTERMASTER'S GIVEN US MUCH PROOF OF HIS DEVOTION.
BUT THEN WHAT DID THE MAJOR'S REMARK MEAN? DOES HE THINK AYRTON'S IN LEAGUE WITH THE CONVICTS?
WHAT CONVICTS?
PAGANEL IS MISTAKEN. THERE AREN'T ANY CONVICTS IN THE PROVINCE OF VICTORIA.
OH, UH--OF COURSE, WHAT WAS I THINKING? THERE ARE NO CONVICTS IN THIS REGION, NEVER WERE.
DESPITE ALL THE EFFORTS OF MEN AND BEAST, THE HEAVY WAGON WOULDN'T BUDGE. IT SEEMED TO BE SEALED IN THE CLAY.
ENOUGH, AYRTON, STOP! WE HAVE TO SPARE THE REMAINING OX AND HORSE. IF WE MUST CONTINUE OUR ROUTE, ONE WILL CARRY THE LADIES, THE OTHER OUR PROVISIONS.
NOW, MY FRIENDS, LET'S GO BACK TO OUR CAMPSITE AND EXAMINE THE SITUATION.

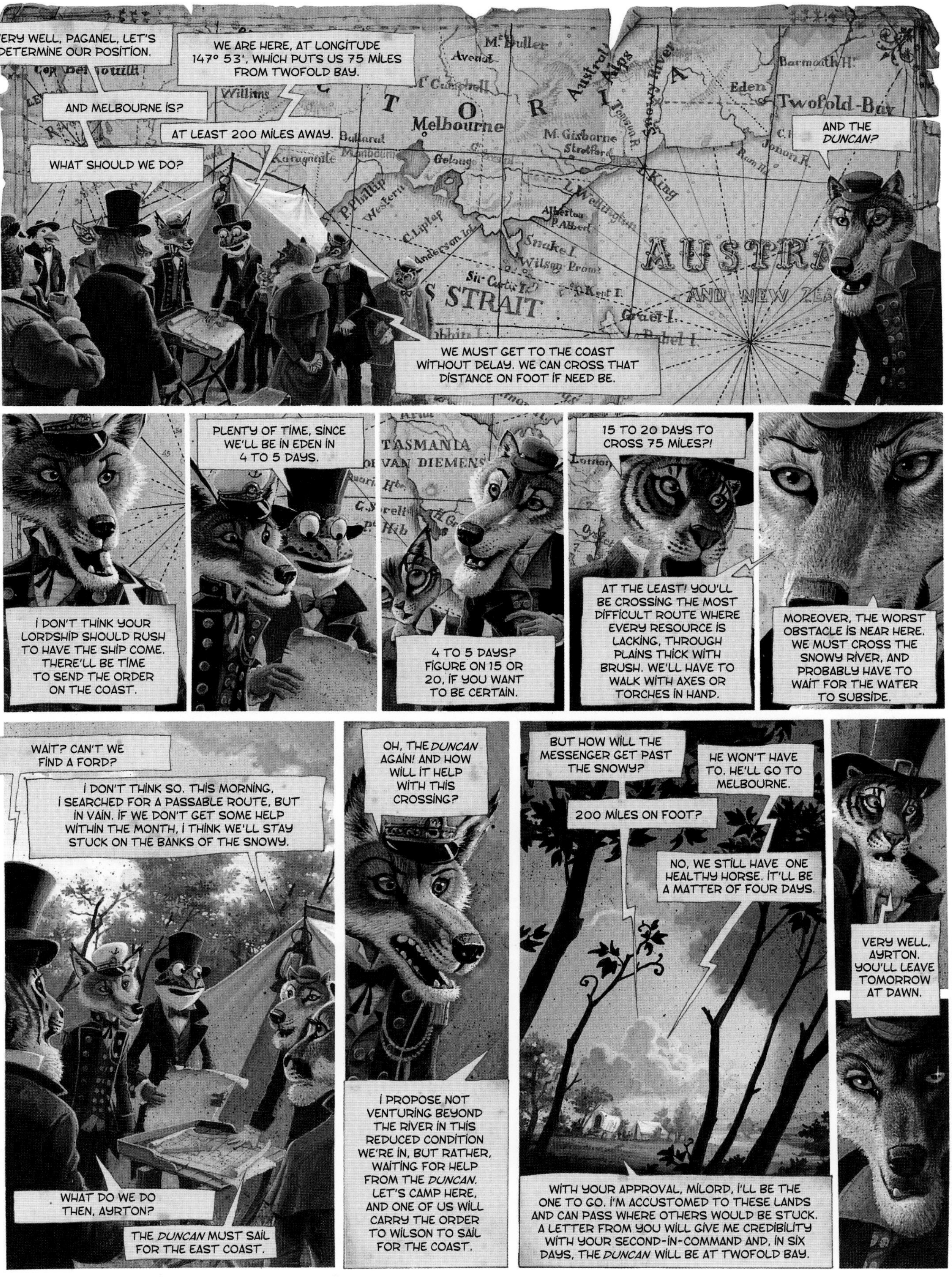
VERY WELL, PAGANEL, LET'S DETERMINE OUR POSITION.
WE ARE HERE, AT LONGITUDE 147° 53', WHICH PUTS US 75 MILES FROM TWOFOLD BAY.
AND MELBOURNE IS?
AT LEAST 200 MILES AWAY.
WHAT SHOULD WE DO?
AND THE *DUNCAN*?
WE MUST GET TO THE COAST WITHOUT DELAY. WE CAN CROSS THAT DISTANCE ON FOOT IF NEED BE.
I DON'T THINK YOUR LORDSHIP SHOULD RUSH TO HAVE THE SHIP COME. THERE'LL BE TIME TO SEND THE ORDER ON THE COAST.
PLENTY OF TIME, SINCE WE'LL BE IN EDEN IN 4 TO 5 DAYS.
4 TO 5 DAYS? FIGURE ON 15 OR 20, IF YOU WANT TO BE CERTAIN.
15 TO 20 DAYS TO CROSS 75 MILES?!
AT THE LEAST! YOU'LL BE CROSSING THE MOST DIFFICULT ROUTE WHERE EVERY RESOURCE IS LACKING, THROUGH PLAINS THICK WITH BRUSH. WE'LL HAVE TO WALK WITH AXES OR TORCHES IN HAND.
MOREOVER, THE WORST OBSTACLE IS NEAR HERE. WE MUST CROSS THE SNOWY RIVER, AND PROBABLY HAVE TO WAIT FOR THE WATER TO SUBSIDE.
WAIT? CAN'T WE FIND A FORD?
I DON'T THINK SO. THIS MORNING, I SEARCHED FOR A PASSABLE ROUTE, BUT IN VAIN. IF WE DON'T GET SOME HELP WITHIN THE MONTH, I THINK WE'LL STAY STUCK ON THE BANKS OF THE SNOWY.
WHAT DO WE DO THEN, AYRTON?
THE *DUNCAN* MUST SAIL FOR THE EAST COAST.
OH, THE *DUNCAN* AGAIN! AND HOW WILL IT HELP WITH THIS CROSSING?
I PROPOSE NOT VENTURING BEYOND THE RIVER IN THIS REDUCED CONDITION WE'RE IN, BUT RATHER, WAITING FOR HELP FROM THE *DUNCAN*. LET'S CAMP HERE, AND ONE OF US WILL CARRY THE ORDER TO WILSON TO SAIL FOR THE COAST.
BUT HOW WILL THE MESSENGER GET PAST THE SNOWY?
HE WON'T HAVE TO. HE'LL GO TO MELBOURNE.
200 MILES ON FOOT?
NO, WE STILL HAVE ONE HEALTHY HORSE. IT'LL BE A MATTER OF FOUR DAYS.
WITH YOUR APPROVAL, MILORD, I'LL BE THE ONE TO GO. I'M ACCUSTOMED TO THESE LANDS AND CAN PASS WHERE OTHERS WOULD BE STUCK. A LETTER FROM YOU WILL GIVE ME CREDIBILITY WITH YOUR SECOND-IN-COMMAND AND, IN SIX DAYS, THE *DUNCAN* WILL BE AT TWOFOLD BAY.
VERY WELL, AYRTON. YOU'LL LEAVE TOMORROW AT DAWN.

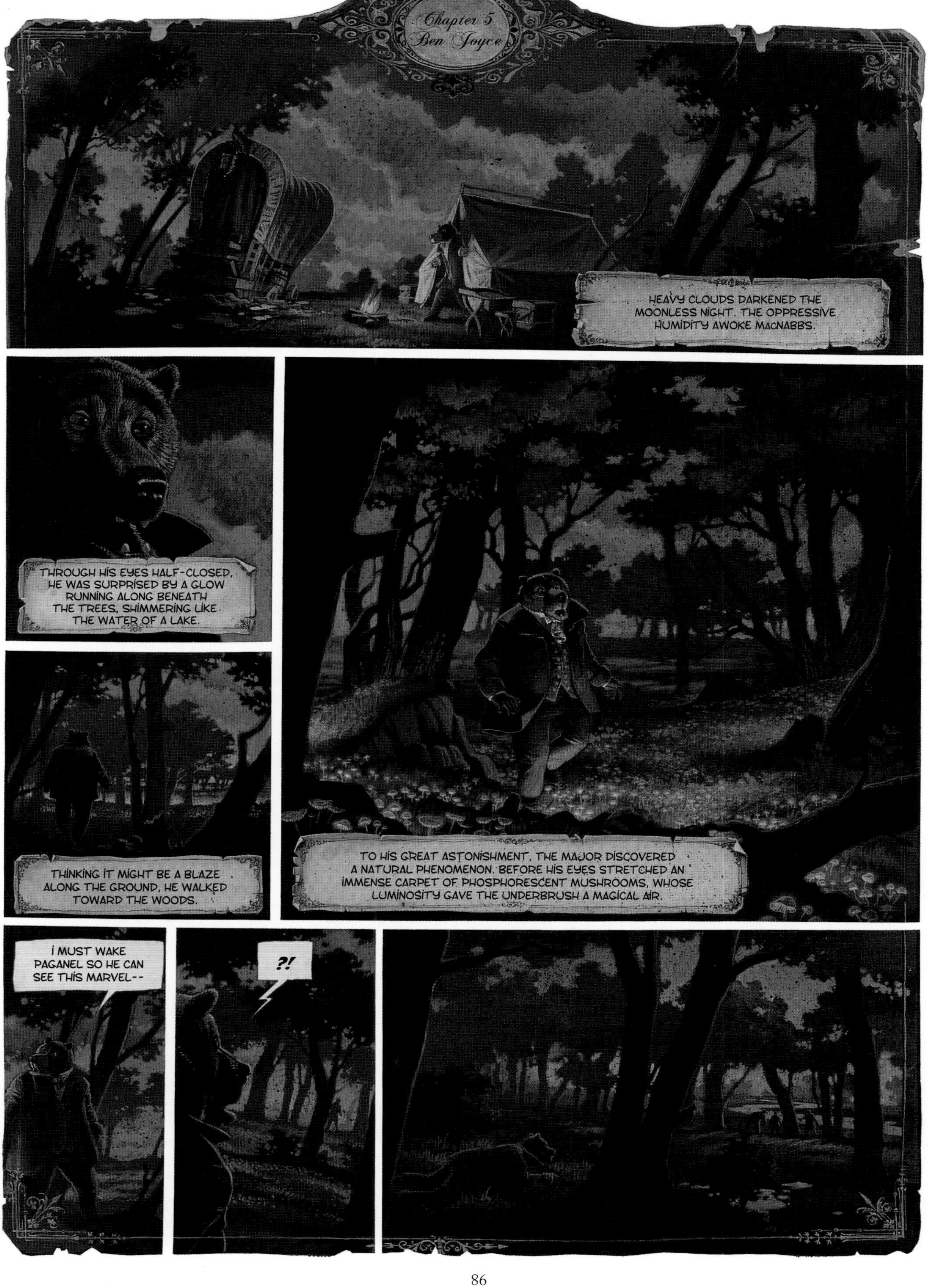
Chapter 5
Ben Joyce
HEAVY CLOUDS DARKENED THE MOONLESS NIGHT. THE OPPRESSIVE HUMIDITY AWOKE MACNABBS.
THROUGH HIS EYES HALF-CLOSED, HE WAS SURPRISED BY A GLOW RUNNING ALONG BENEATH THE TREES, SHIMMERING LIKE THE WATER OF A LAKE.
THINKING IT MIGHT BE A BLAZE ALONG THE GROUND, HE WALKED TOWARD THE WOODS.
TO HIS GREAT ASTONISHMENT, THE MAJOR DISCOVERED A NATURAL PHENOMENON. BEFORE HIS EYES STRETCHED AN IMMENSE CARPET OF PHOSPHORESCENT MUSHROOMS, WHOSE LUMINOSITY GAVE THE UNDERBRUSH A MAGICAL AIR.
I MUST WAKE PAGANEL SO HE CAN SEE THIS MARVEL--
?!

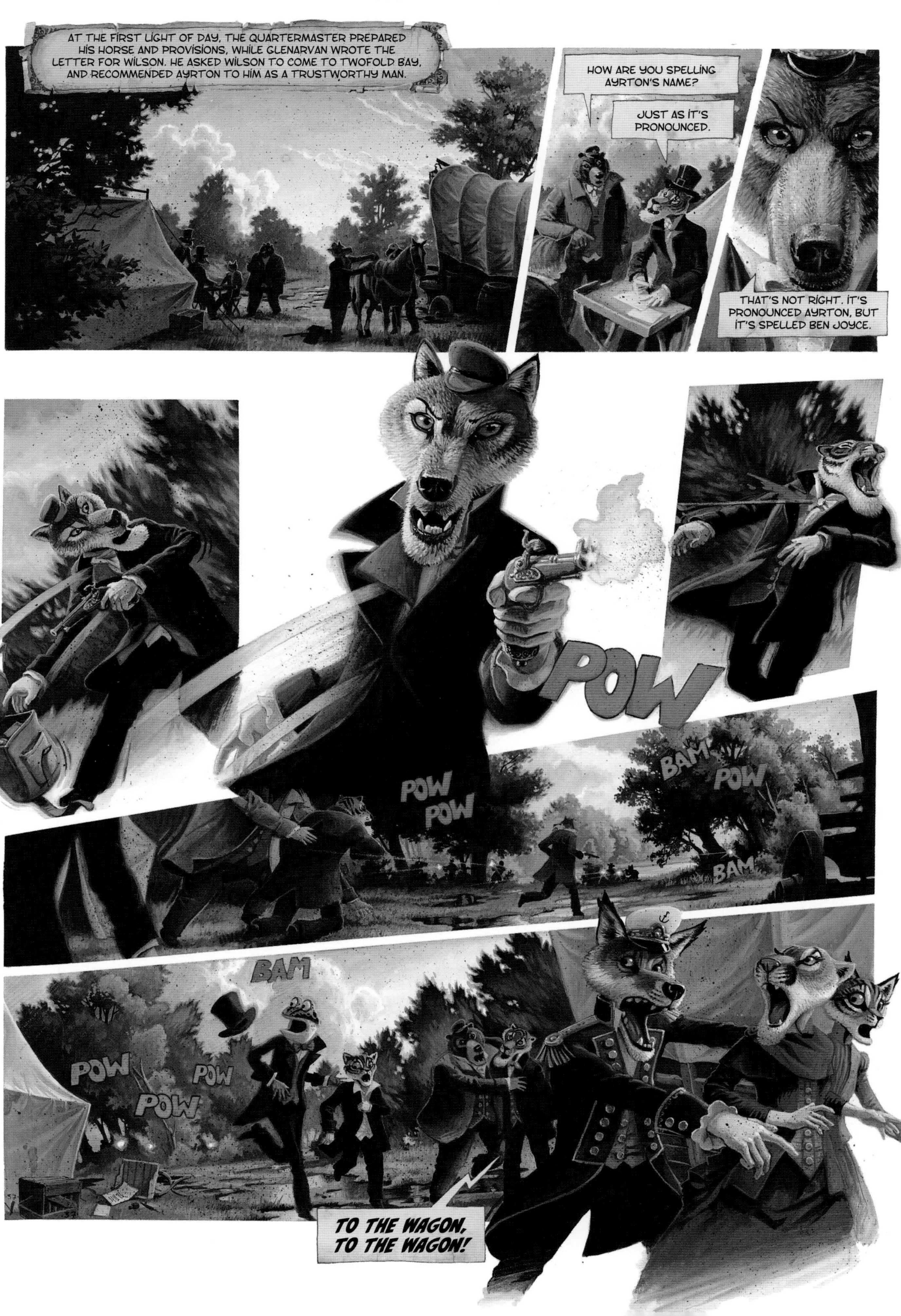
AT THE FIRST LIGHT OF DAY, THE QUARTERMASTER PREPARED HIS HORSE AND PROVISIONS, WHILE GLENARVAN WROTE THE LETTER FOR WILSON. HE ASKED WILSON TO COME TO TWOFOLD BAY, AND RECOMMENDED AYRTON TO HIM AS A TRUSTWORTHY MAN.
HOW ARE YOU SPELLING AYRTON'S NAME?
JUST AS IT'S PRONOUNCED.
THAT'S NOT RIGHT. IT'S PRONOUNCED AYRTON, BUT IT'S SPELLED BEN JOYCE.
POW
POW
POW
BAM
POW
BAM
BAM
POW
POW
POW
TO THE WAGON, TO THE WAGON!

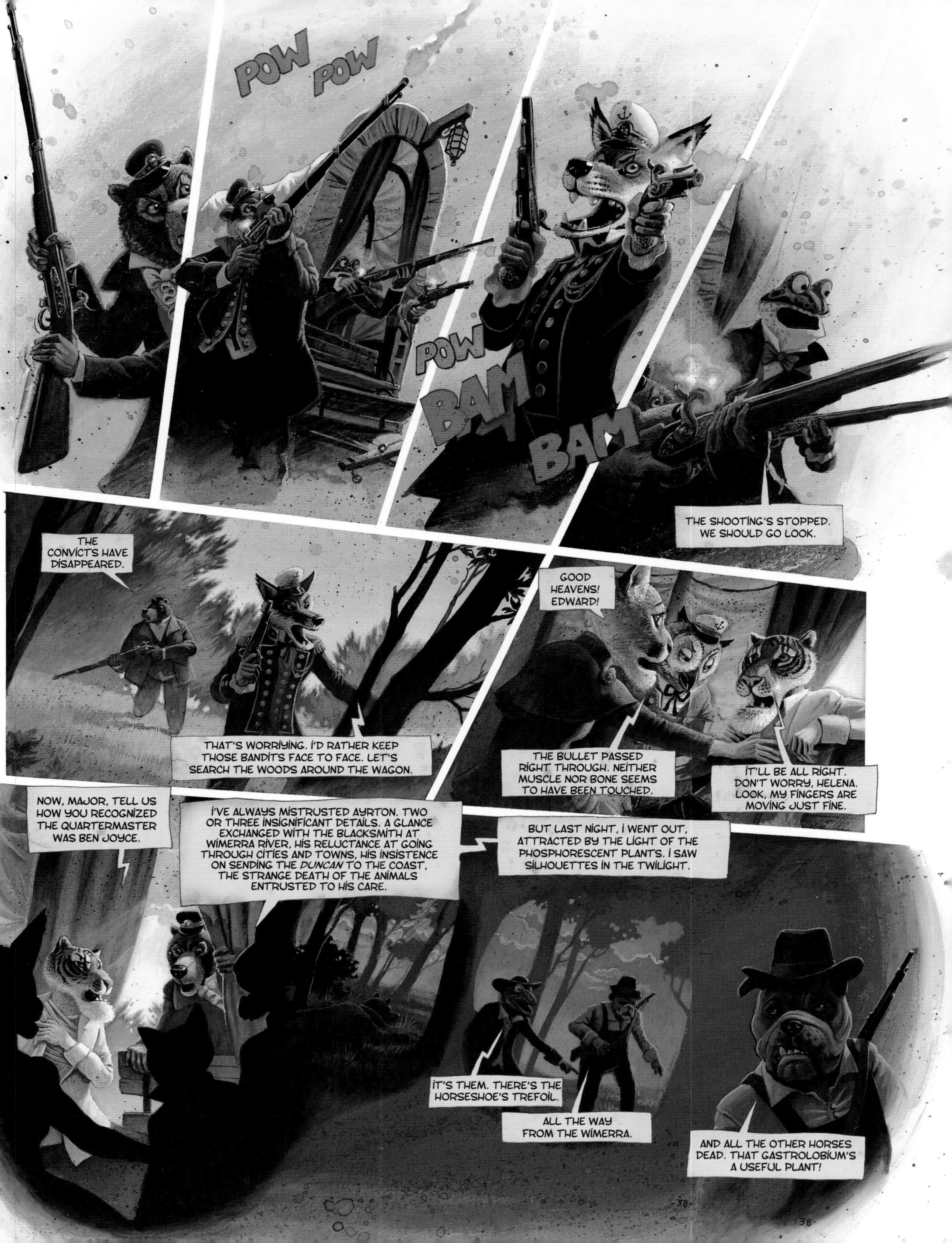
POW
POW
POW
BAM
BAM
THE SHOOTING'S STOPPED. WE SHOULD GO LOOK.
THE CONVICTS HAVE DISAPPEARED.
THAT'S WORRIYING. I'D RATHER KEEP THOSE BANDITS FACE TO FACE. LET'S SEARCH THE WOODS AROUND THE WAGON.
GOOD HEAVENS! EDWARD!
THE BULLET PASSED RIGHT THROUGH. NEITHER MUSCLE NOR BONE SEEMS TO HAVE BEEN TOUCHED.
IT'LL BE ALL RIGHT. DON'T WORRY, HELENA. LOOK, MY FINGERS ARE MOVING JUST FINE.
NOW, MAJOR, TELL US HOW YOU RECOGNIZED THE QUARTERMASTER WAS BEN JOYCE.
I'VE ALWAYS MISTRUSTED AYRTON. TWO OR THREE INSIGNIFICANT DETAILS. A GLANCE EXCHANGED WITH THE BLACKSMITH AT WIMERRA RIVER, HIS RELUCTANCE AT GOING THROUGH CITIES AND TOWNS, HIS INSISTENCE ON SENDING THE *DUNCAN* TO THE COAST, THE STRANGE DEATH OF THE ANIMALS ENTRUSTED TO HIS CARE.
BUT LAST NIGHT, I WENT OUT, ATTRACTED BY THE LIGHT OF THE PHOSPHORESCENT PLANTS. I SAW SILHOUETTES IN THE TWILIGHT.
IT'S THEM. THERE'S THE HORSESHOE'S TREFOIL.
ALL THE WAY FROM THE WIMERRA.
AND ALL THE OTHER HORSES DEAD. THAT GASTROLOBIUM'S A USEFUL PLANT!
-38-
38

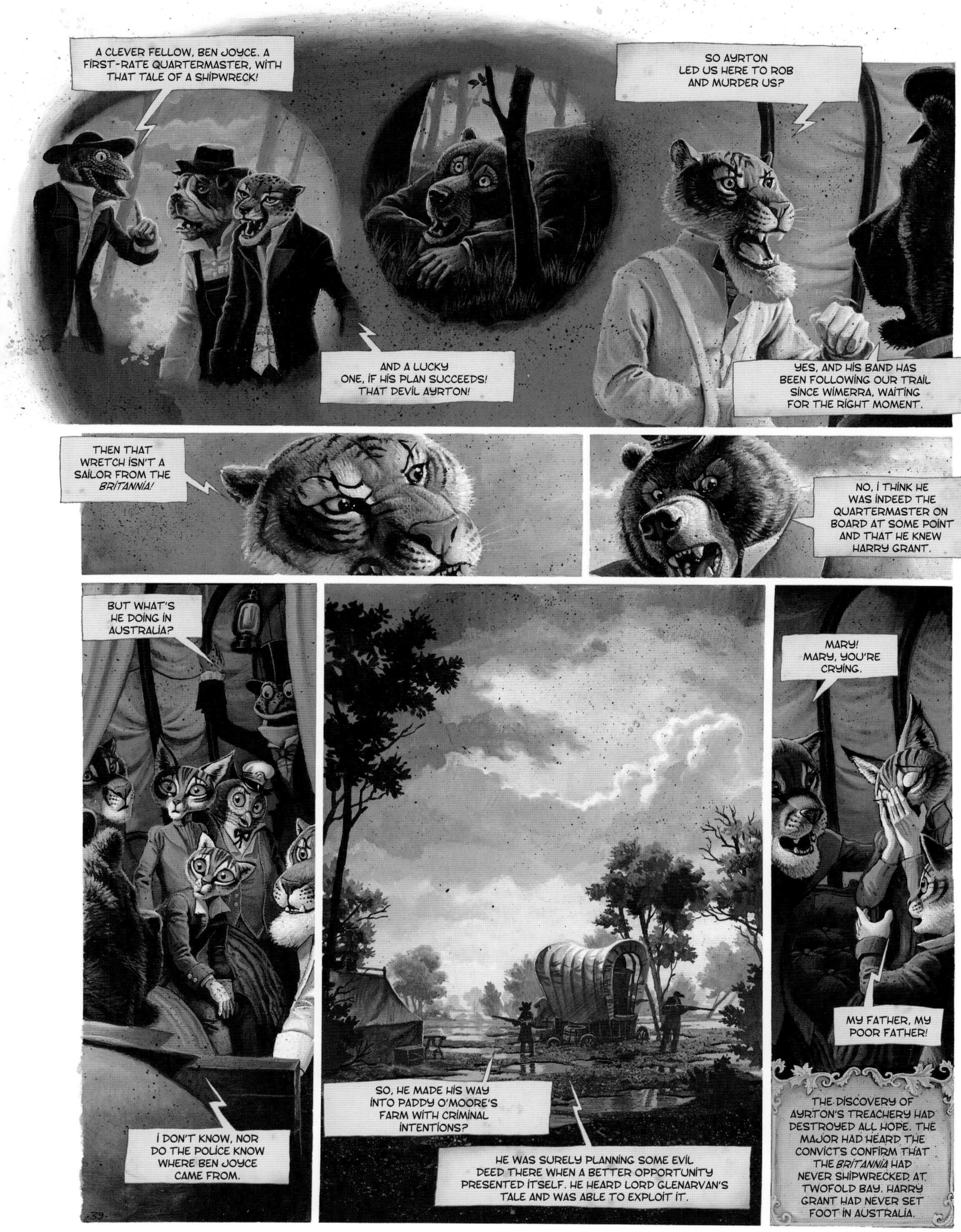
A CLEVER FELLOW, BEN JOYCE. A FIRST-RATE QUARTERMASTER, WITH THAT TALE OF A SHIPWRECK!
AND A LUCKY ONE, IF HIS PLAN SUCCEEDS! THAT DEVIL AYRTON!
SO AYRTON LED US HERE TO ROB AND MURDER US?
YES, AND HIS BAND HAS BEEN FOLLOWING OUR TRAIL SINCE WIMERRA, WAITING FOR THE RIGHT MOMENT.
THEN THAT WRETCH ISN'T A SAILOR FROM THE *BRITANNIA*!
NO, I THINK HE WAS INDEED THE QUARTERMASTER ON BOARD AT SOME POINT AND THAT HE KNEW HARRY GRANT.
BUT WHAT'S HE DOING IN AUSTRALIA?
I DON'T KNOW, NOR DO THE POLICE KNOW WHERE BEN JOYCE CAME FROM.
SO, HE MADE HIS WAY INTO PADDY O'MOORE'S FARM WITH CRIMINAL INTENTIONS?
HE WAS SURELY PLANNING SOME EVIL DEED THERE WHEN A BETTER OPPORTUNITY PRESENTED ITSELF. HE HEARD LORD GLENARVAN'S TALE AND WAS ABLE TO EXPLOIT IT.
MARY! MARY, YOU'RE CRYING.
MY FATHER, MY POOR FATHER!
THE DISCOVERY OF AYRTON'S TREACHERY HAD DESTROYED ALL HOPE. THE MAJOR HAD HEARD THE CONVICTS CONFIRM THAT THE *BRITANNIA* HAD NEVER SHIPWRECKED AT TWOFOLD BAY. HARRY GRANT HAD NEVER SET FOOT IN AUSTRALIA.
39

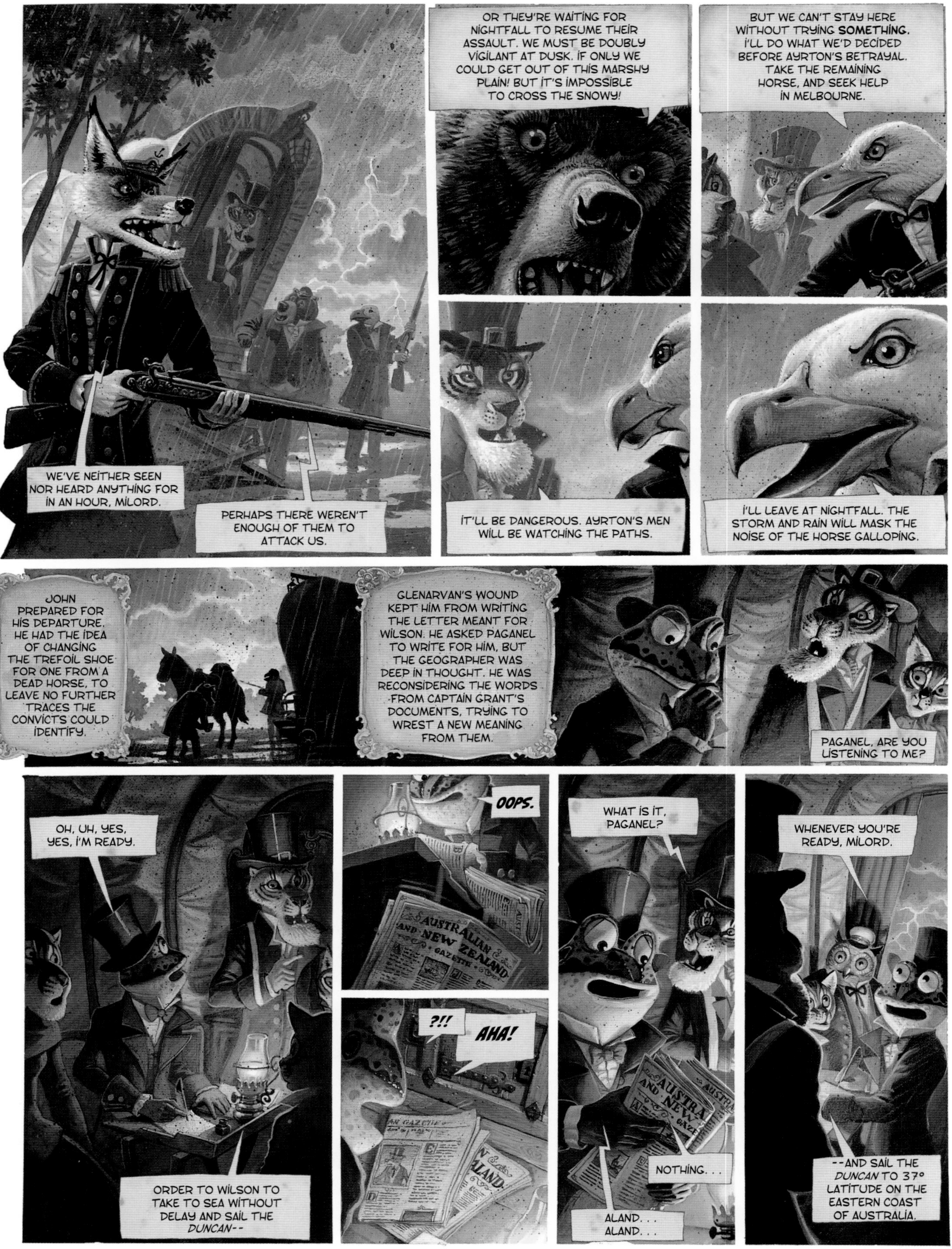
WE'VE NEITHER SEEN NOR HEARD ANYTHING FOR IN AN HOUR, MILORD.
PERHAPS THERE WEREN'T ENOUGH OF THEM TO ATTACK US.
OR THEY'RE WAITING FOR NIGHTFALL TO RESUME THEIR ASSAULT. WE MUST BE DOUBLY VIGILANT AT DUSK. IF ONLY WE COULD GET OUT OF THIS MARSHY PLAIN! BUT IT'S IMPOSSIBLE TO CROSS THE SNOWY!
BUT WE CAN'T STAY HERE WITHOUT TRYING **SOMETHING.** I'LL DO WHAT WE'D DECIDED BEFORE AYRTON'S BETRAYAL. TAKE THE REMAINING HORSE, AND SEEK HELP IN MELBOURNE.
IT'LL BE DANGEROUS. AYRTON'S MEN WILL BE WATCHING THE PATHS.
I'LL LEAVE AT NIGHTFALL. THE STORM AND RAIN WILL MASK THE NOISE OF THE HORSE GALLOPING.
JOHN PREPARED FOR HIS DEPARTURE. HE HAD THE IDEA OF CHANGING THE TREFOIL SHOE FOR ONE FROM A DEAD HORSE, TO LEAVE NO FURTHER TRACES THE CONVICTS COULD IDENTIFY.
GLENARVAN'S WOUND KEPT HIM FROM WRITING THE LETTER MEANT FOR WILSON. HE ASKED PAGANEL TO WRITE FOR HIM, BUT THE GEOGRAPHER WAS DEEP IN THOUGHT. HE WAS RECONSIDERING THE WORDS FROM CAPTAIN GRANT'S DOCUMENTS, TRYING TO WREST A NEW MEANING FROM THEM.
PAGANEL, ARE YOU LISTENING TO ME?
OH, UH, YES, YES, I'M READY.
ORDER TO WILSON TO TAKE TO SEA WITHOUT DELAY AND SAIL THE *DUNCAN*--
OOPS.
AUSTRALIAN AND NEW ZEALAND GAZETTE
?!!
AHA!
WHAT IS IT, PAGANEL?
NOTHING. . .
ALAND. . . ALAND. . .
WHENEVER YOU'RE READY, MILORD.
--AND SAIL THE *DUNCAN* TO 37° LATITUDE ON THE EASTERN COAST OF AUSTRALIA.

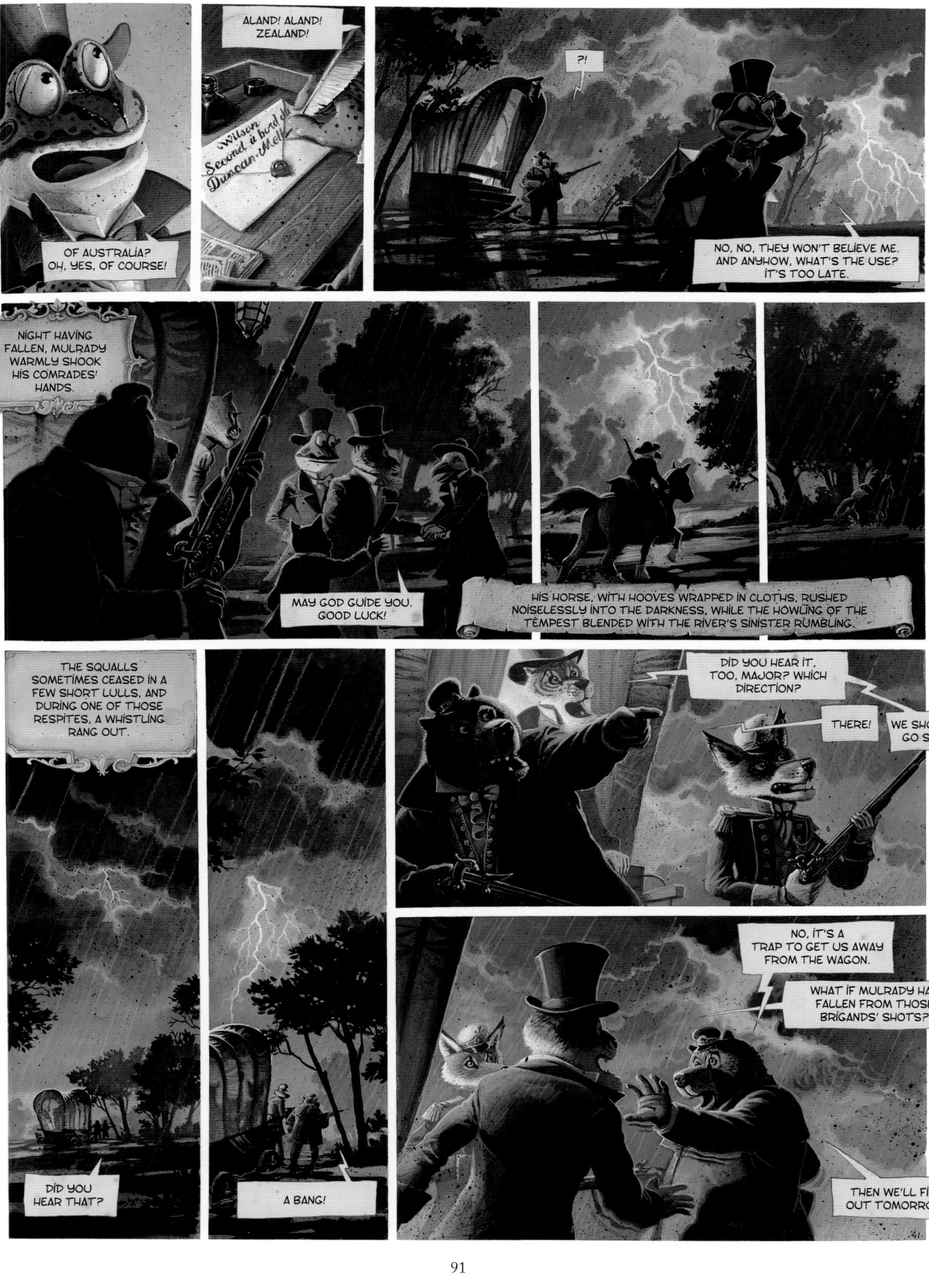
ALAND! ALAND! ZEALAND!
OF AUSTRALIA? OH, YES, OF COURSE!
Wilson Second it bord di Duncan-Mell
?!
NO, NO, THEY WON'T BELIEVE ME. AND ANYHOW, WHAT'S THE USE? IT'S TOO LATE.
NIGHT HAVING FALLEN, MULRADY WARMLY SHOOK HIS COMRADES' HANDS.
MAY GOD GUIDE YOU. GOOD LUCK!
HIS HORSE, WITH HOOVES WRAPPED IN CLOTHS, RUSHED NOISELESSLY INTO THE DARKNESS, WHILE THE HOWLING OF THE TEMPEST BLENDED WITH THE RIVER'S SINISTER RUMBLING.
THE SQUALLS SOMETIMES CEASED IN A FEW SHORT LULLS, AND DURING ONE OF THOSE RESPITES, A WHISTLING RANG OUT.
DID YOU HEAR THAT?
A BANG!
DID YOU HEAR IT, TOO, MAJOR? WHICH DIRECTION?
THERE!
WE SHOULD GO SEE!
NO, IT'S A TRAP TO GET US AWAY FROM THE WAGON.
WHAT IF MULRADY HAS FALLEN FROM THOSE BRIGANDS' SHOTS?
THEN WE'LL FIND OUT TOMORROW.
41.

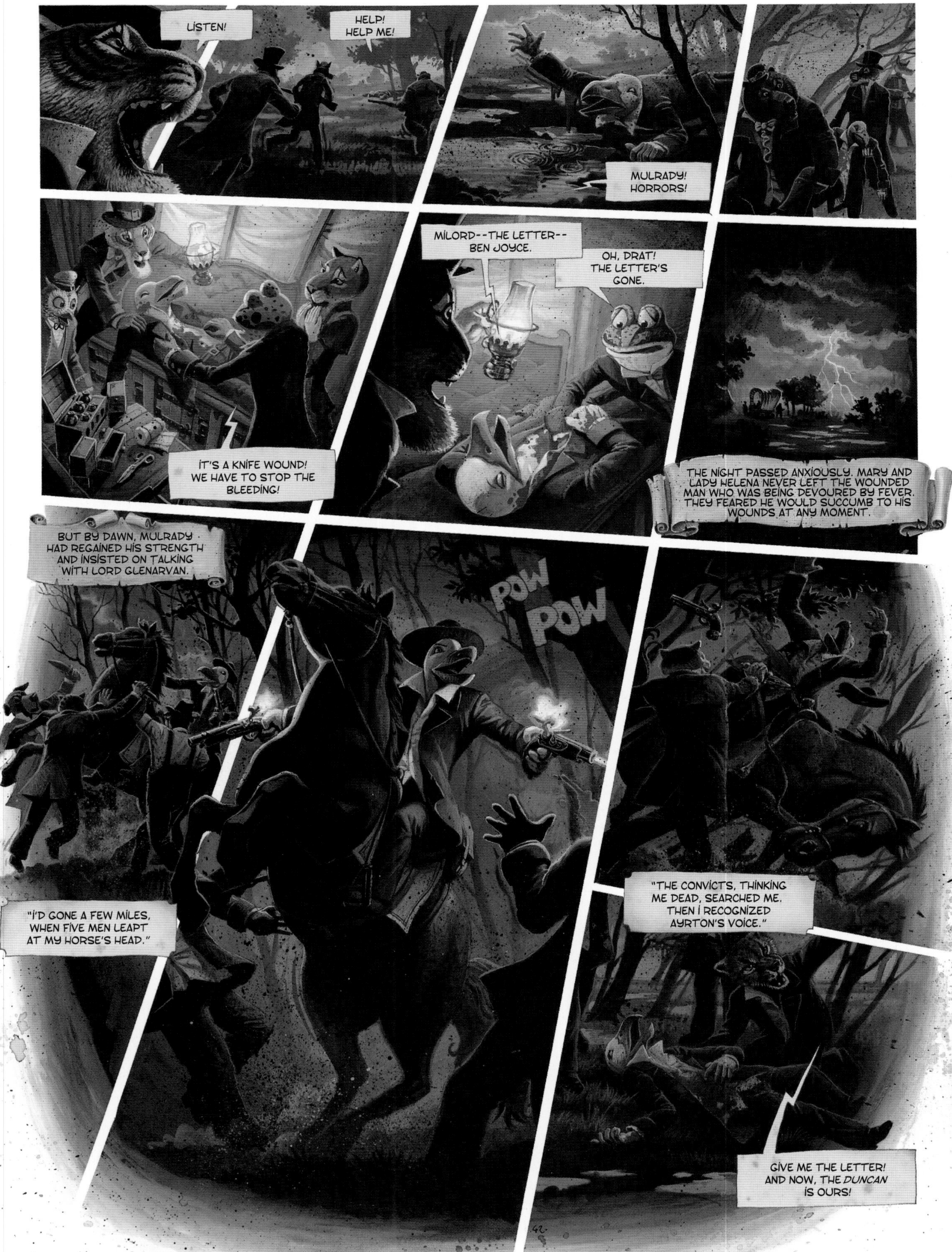
LISTEN!
HELP! HELP ME!
MULRADY! HORRORS!
MILORD--THE LETTER--BEN JOYCE.
OH, DRAT! THE LETTER'S GONE.
IT'S A KNIFE WOUND! WE HAVE TO STOP THE BLEEDING!
THE NIGHT PASSED ANXIOUSLY. MARY AND LADY HELENA NEVER LEFT THE WOUNDED MAN WHO WAS BEING DEVOURED BY FEVER. THEY FEARED HE WOULD SUCCUMB TO HIS WOUNDS AT ANY MOMENT.
BUT BY DAWN, MULRADY HAD REGAINED HIS STRENGTH AND INSISTED ON TALKING WITH LORD GLENARVAN.
POW
POW
"I'D GONE A FEW MILES, WHEN FIVE MEN LEAPT AT MY HORSE'S HEAD."
"THE CONVICTS, THINKING ME DEAD, SEARCHED ME. THEN I RECOGNIZED AYRTON'S VOICE."
GIVE ME THE LETTER! AND NOW, THE *DUNCAN* IS OURS!

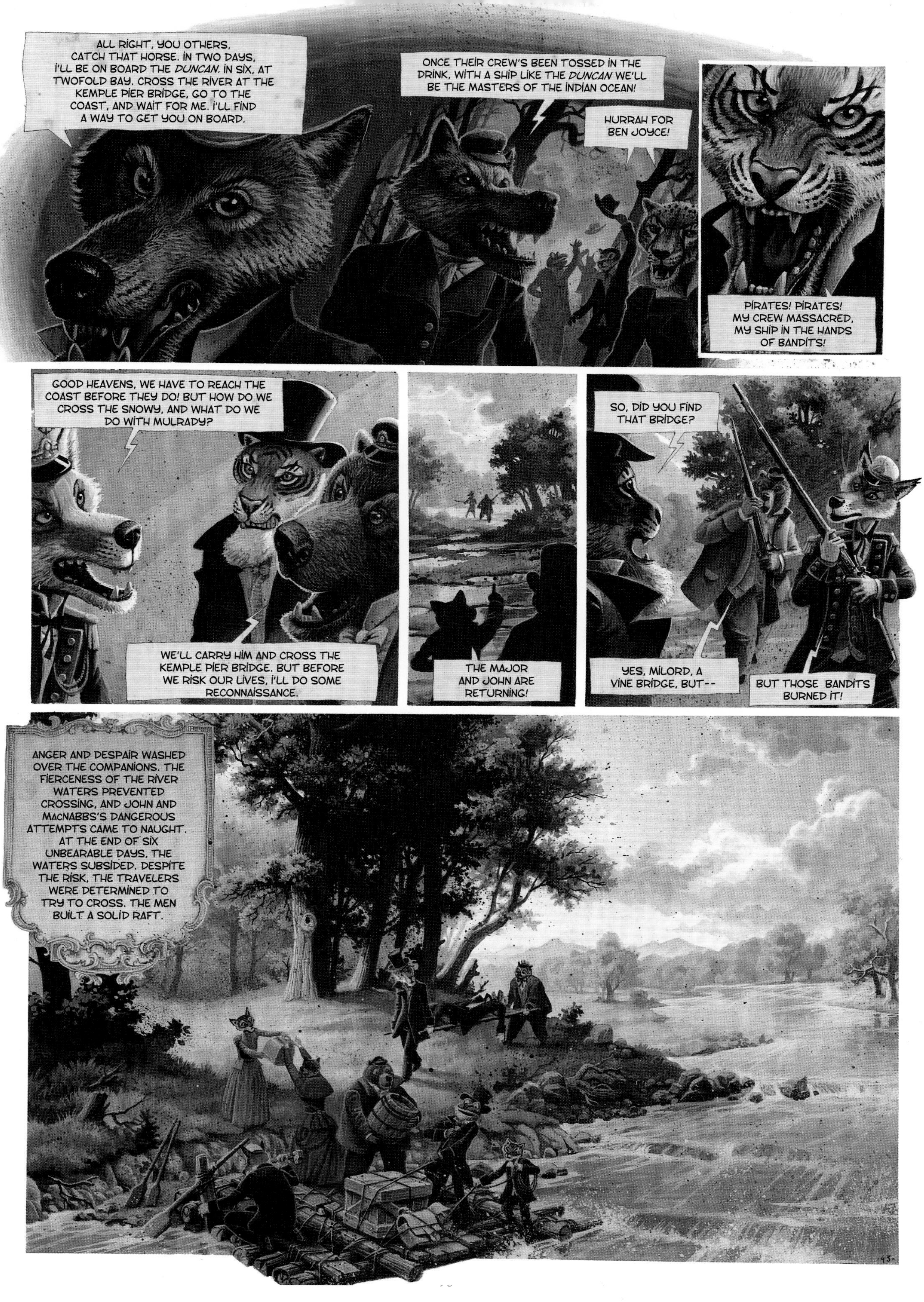
ALL RIGHT, YOU OTHERS, CATCH THAT HORSE. IN TWO DAYS, I'LL BE ON BOARD THE *DUNCAN*. IN SIX, AT TWOFOLD BAY. CROSS THE RIVER AT THE KEMPLE PIER BRIDGE, GO TO THE COAST, AND WAIT FOR ME. I'LL FIND A WAY TO GET YOU ON BOARD.
ONCE THEIR CREW'S BEEN TOSSED IN THE DRINK, WITH A SHIP LIKE THE *DUNCAN* WE'LL BE THE MASTERS OF THE INDIAN OCEAN!
HURRAH FOR BEN JOYCE!
PIRATES! PIRATES! MY CREW MASSACRED, MY SHIP IN THE HANDS OF BANDITS!
GOOD HEAVENS, WE HAVE TO REACH THE COAST BEFORE THEY DO! BUT HOW DO WE CROSS THE SNOWY, AND WHAT DO WE DO WITH MULRADY?
WE'LL CARRY HIM AND CROSS THE KEMPLE PIER BRIDGE. BUT BEFORE WE RISK OUR LIVES, I'LL DO SOME RECONNAISSANCE.
THE MAJOR AND JOHN ARE RETURNING!
SO, DID YOU FIND THAT BRIDGE?
YES, MILORD, A VINE BRIDGE, BUT--
BUT THOSE BANDITS BURNED IT!
ANGER AND DESPAIR WASHED OVER THE COMPANIONS. THE FIERCENESS OF THE RIVER WATERS PREVENTED CROSSING, AND JOHN AND MACNABBS'S DANGEROUS ATTEMPTS CAME TO NAUGHT. AT THE END OF SIX UNBEARABLE DAYS, THE WATERS SUBSIDED. DESPITE THE RISK, THE TRAVELERS WERE DETERMINED TO TRY TO CROSS. THE MEN BUILT A SOLID RAFT.

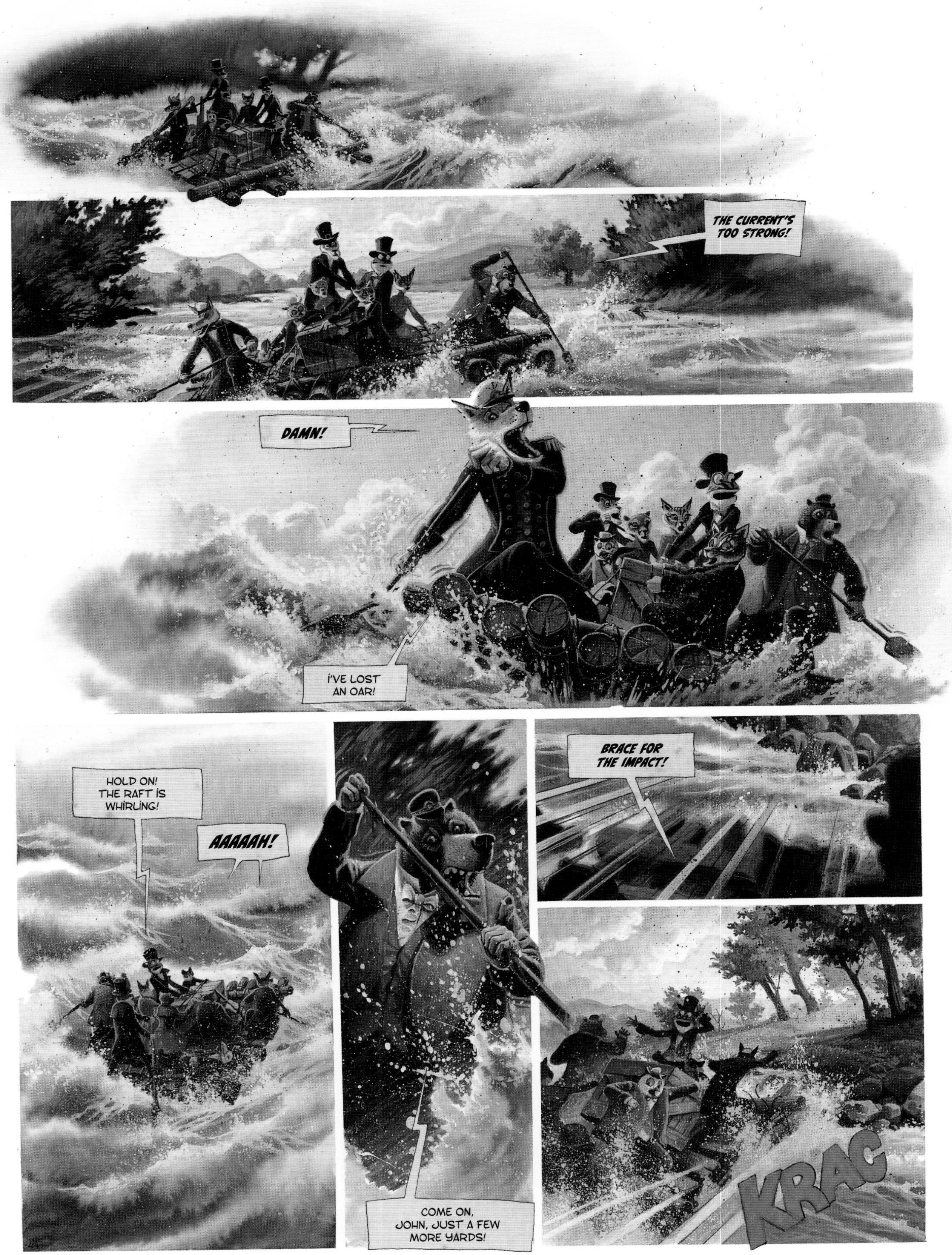
THE CURRENT'S TOO STRONG!
DAMN!
I'VE LOST AN OAR!
HOLD ON! THE RAFT IS WHIRLING!
AAAAAH!
COME ON, JOHN, JUST A FEW MORE YARDS!
BRACE FOR THE IMPACT!
KRAC

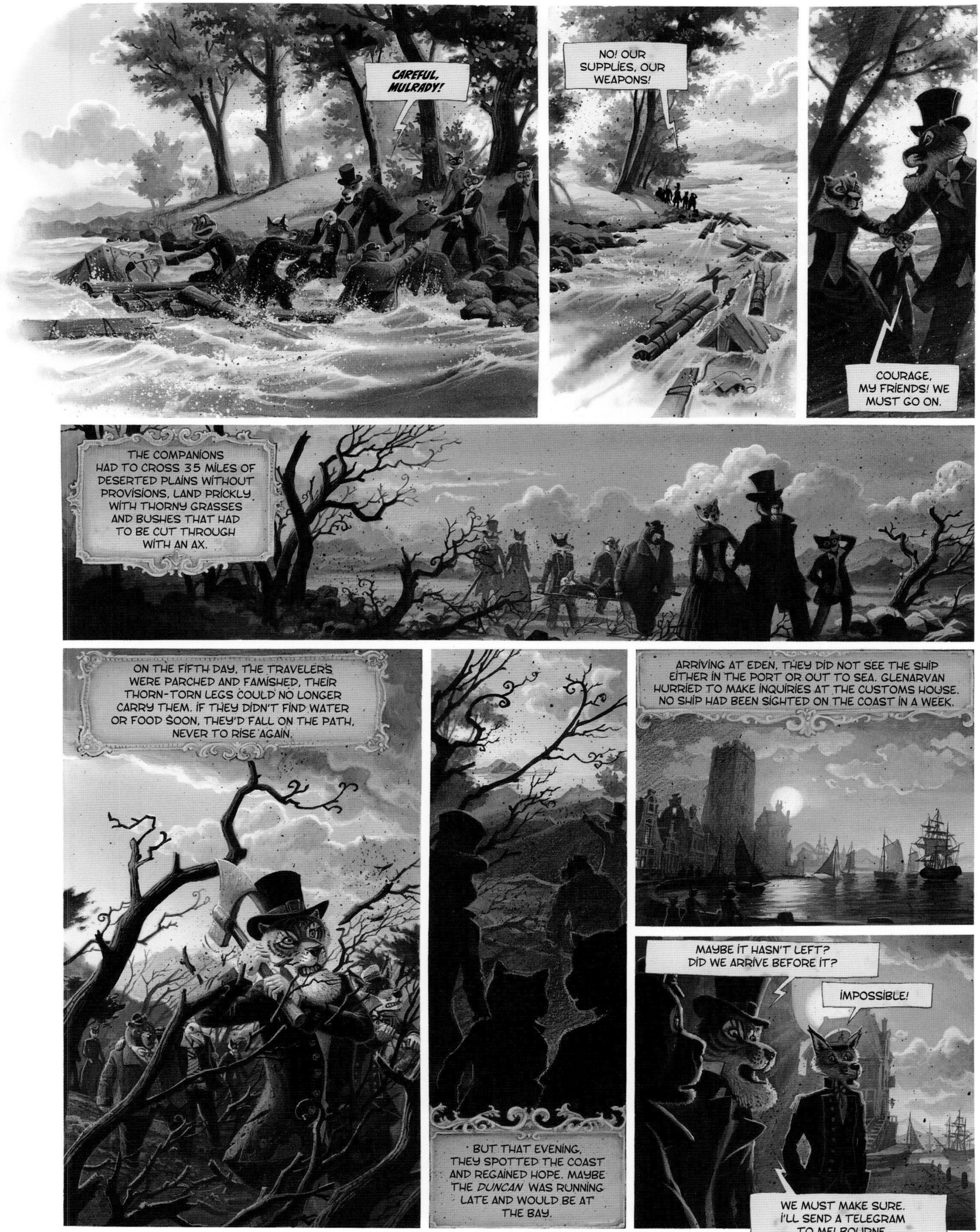
CAREFUL, MULRADY!
NO! OUR SUPPLIES, OUR WEAPONS!
COURAGE, MY FRIENDS! WE MUST GO ON.
THE COMPANIONS HAD TO CROSS 35 MILES OF DESERTED PLAINS WITHOUT PROVISIONS, LAND PRICKLY WITH THORNY GRASSES AND BUSHES THAT HAD TO BE CUT THROUGH WITH AN AX.
ON THE FIFTH DAY, THE TRAVELERS WERE PARCHED AND FAMISHED. THEIR THORN-TORN LEGS COULD NO LONGER CARRY THEM. IF THEY DIDN'T FIND WATER OR FOOD SOON, THEY'D FALL ON THE PATH, NEVER TO RISE AGAIN.
BUT THAT EVENING, THEY SPOTTED THE COAST AND REGAINED HOPE. MAYBE THE *DUNCAN* WAS RUNNING LATE AND WOULD BE AT THE BAY.
ARRIVING AT EDEN, THEY DID NOT SEE THE SHIP EITHER IN THE PORT OR OUT TO SEA. GLENARVAN HURRIED TO MAKE INQUIRIES AT THE CUSTOMS HOUSE. NO SHIP HAD BEEN SIGHTED ON THE COAST IN A WEEK.
MAYBE IT HASN'T LEFT? DID WE ARRIVE BEFORE IT?
IMPOSSIBLE!
WE MUST MAKE SURE. I'LL SEND A TELEGRAM TO MELBOURNE.

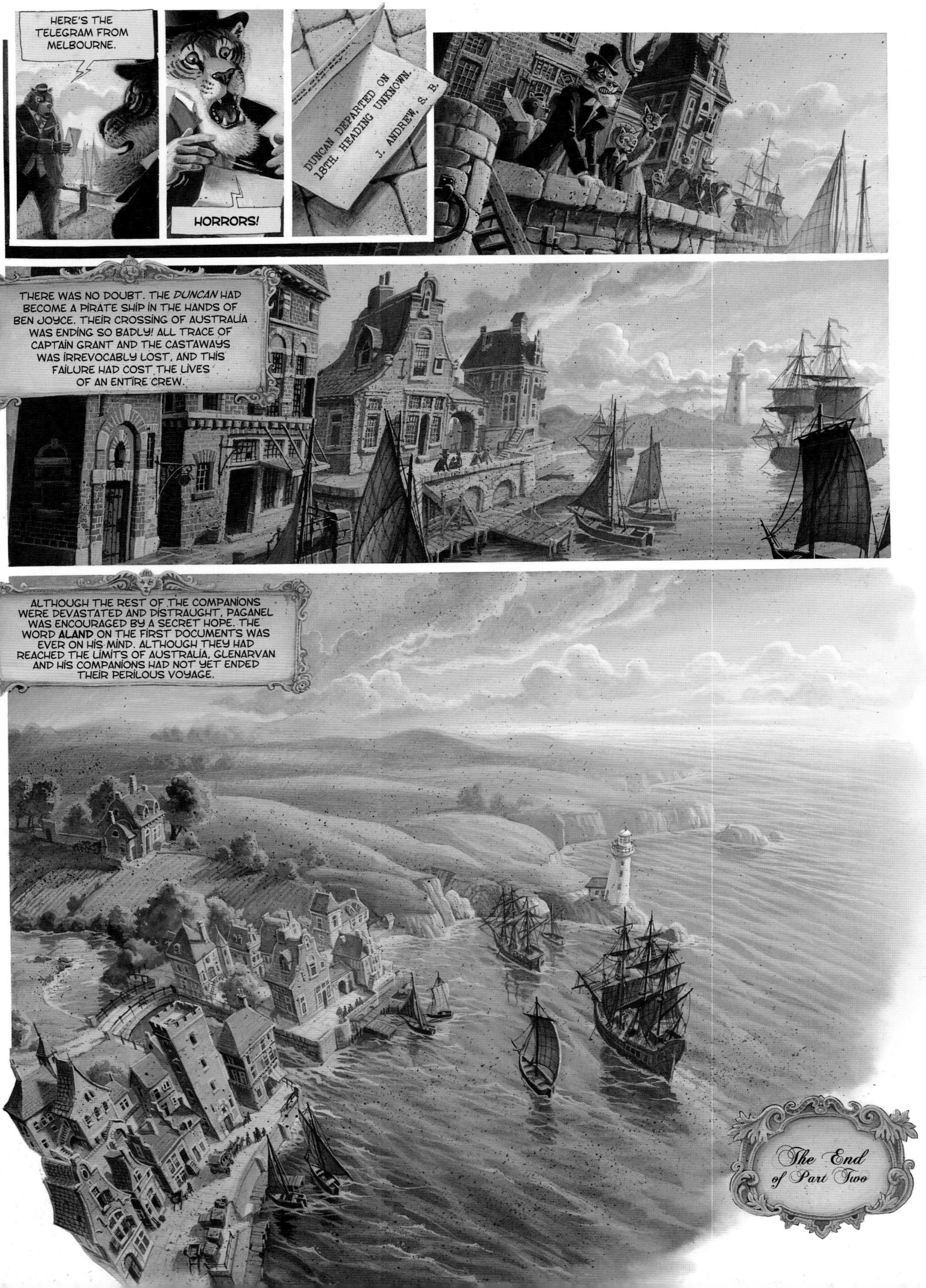
HERE'S THE TELEGRAM FROM MELBOURNE.
HORRORS!
DUNCAN DEPARTED ON 18TH. HEADING UNKNOWN.
J. ANDREW, S. B.
THERE WAS NO DOUBT. THE *DUNCAN* HAD BECOME A PIRATE SHIP IN THE HANDS OF BEN JOYCE. THEIR CROSSING OF AUSTRALIA WAS ENDING SO BADLY! ALL TRACE OF CAPTAIN GRANT AND THE CASTAWAYS WAS IRREVOCABLY LOST, AND THIS FAILURE HAD COST THE LIVES OF AN ENTIRE CREW.
ALTHOUGH THE REST OF THE COMPANIONS WERE DEVASTATED AND DISTRAUGHT, PAGANEL WAS ENCOURAGED BY A SECRET HOPE. THE WORD **ALAND** ON THE FIRST DOCUMENTS WAS EVER ON HIS MIND. ALTHOUGH THEY HAD REACHED THE LIMITS OF AUSTRALIA, GLENARVAN AND HIS COMPANIONS HAD NOT YET ENDED THEIR PERILOUS VOYAGE.
The End of Part Two

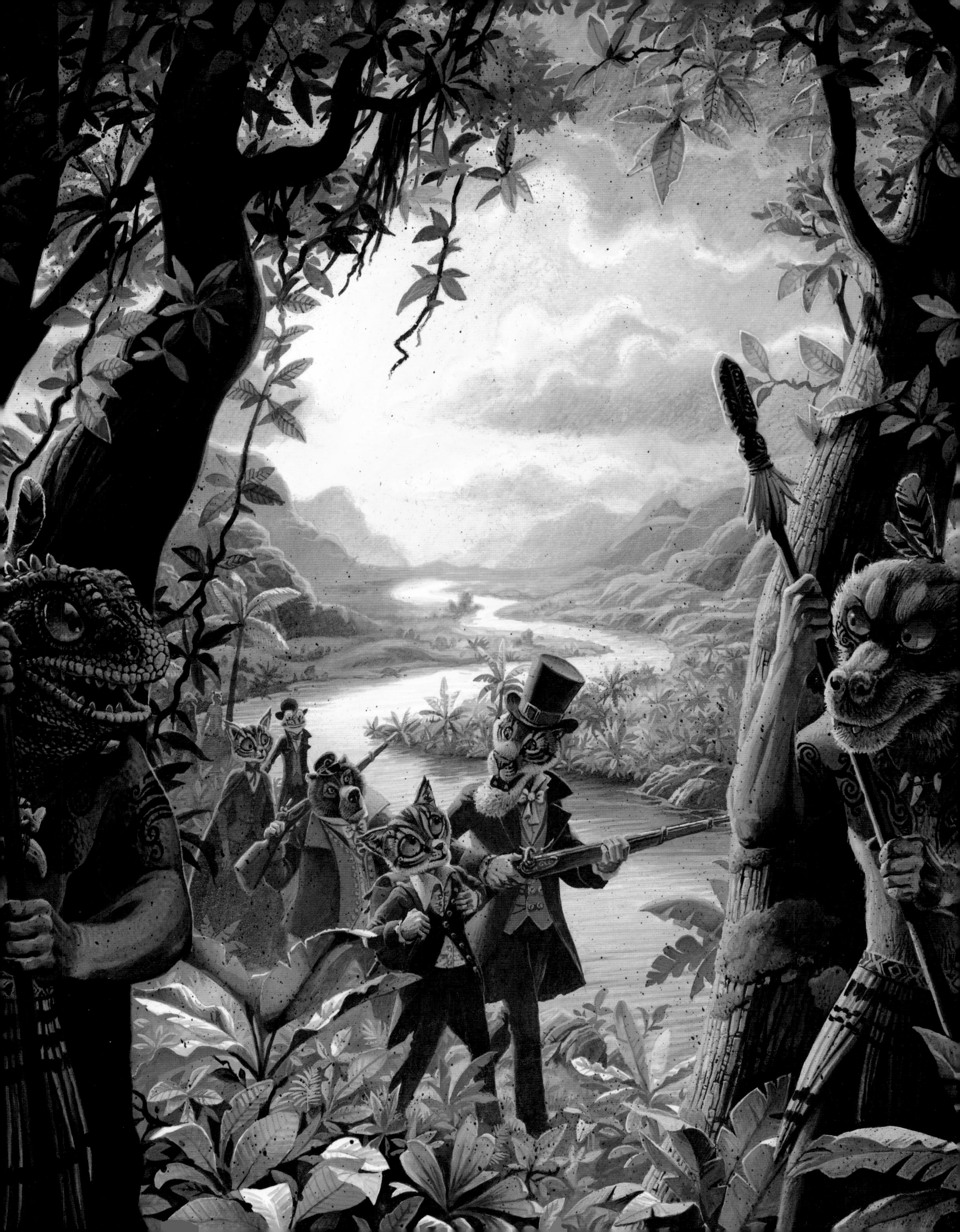

Part 3

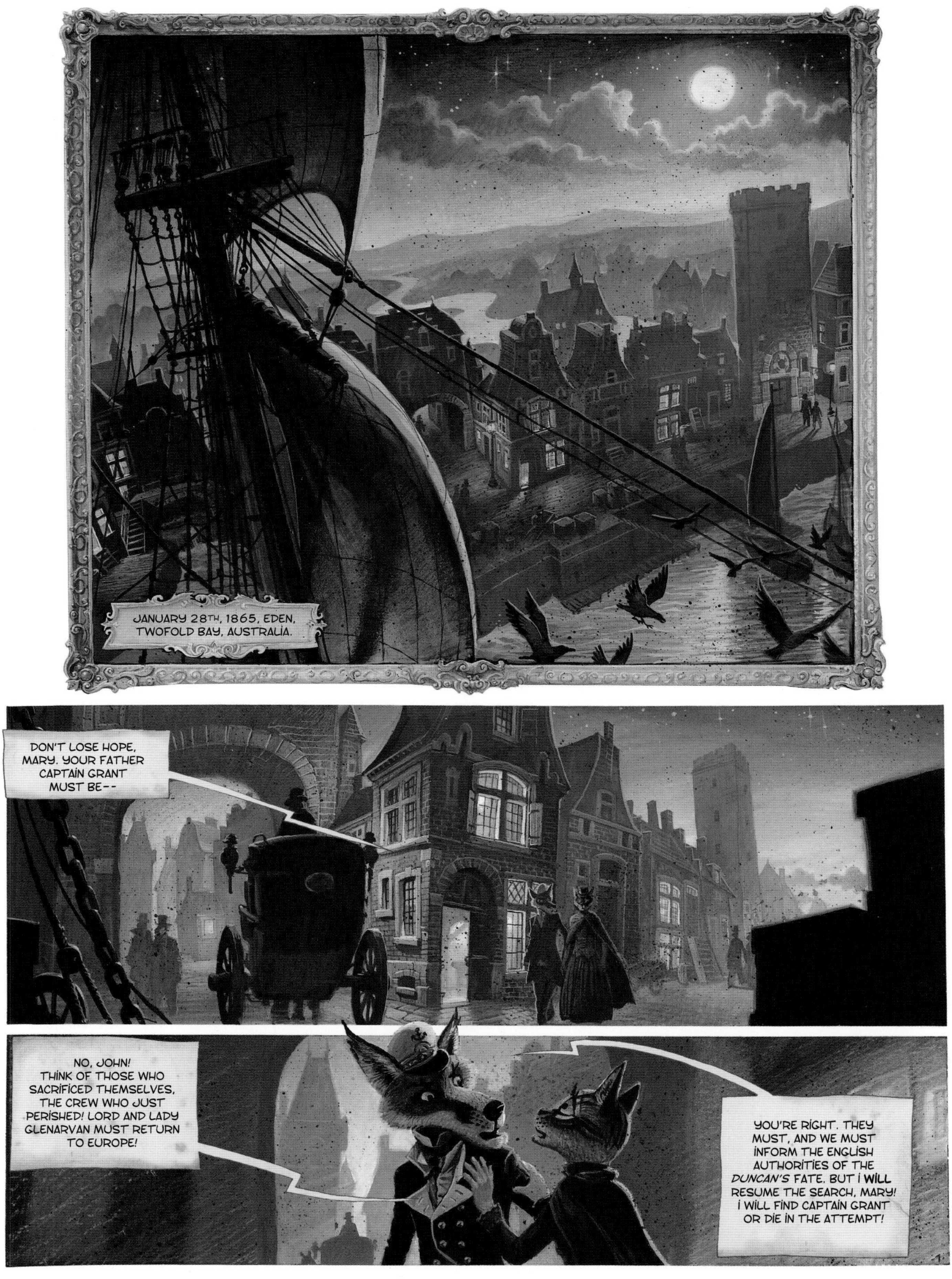
JANUARY 28TH, 1865, EDEN, TWOFOLD BAY, AUSTRALIA.
DON'T LOSE HOPE, MARY. YOUR FATHER CAPTAIN GRANT MUST BE--
NO, JOHN! THINK OF THOSE WHO SACRIFICED THEMSELVES, THE CREW WHO JUST PERISHED! LORD AND LADY GLENARVAN MUST RETURN TO EUROPE!
YOU'RE RIGHT. THEY MUST, AND WE MUST INFORM THE ENGLISH AUTHORITIES OF THE *DUNCAN'S* FATE. BUT I **WILL** RESUME THE SEARCH, MARY! I WILL FIND CAPTAIN GRANT OR DIE IN THE ATTEMPT!

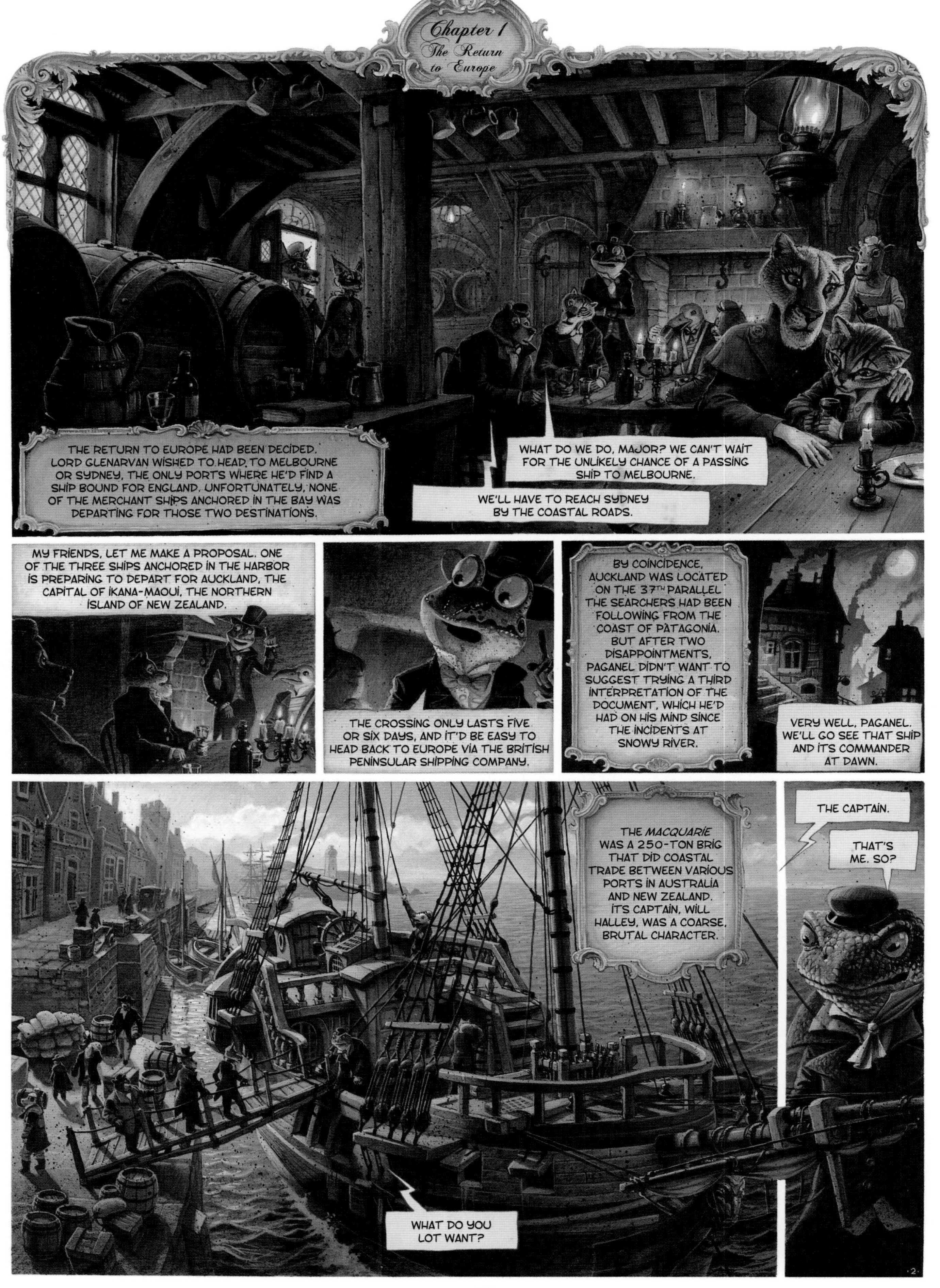
Chapter 1
The Return to Europe
THE RETURN TO EUROPE HAD BEEN DECIDED. LORD GLENARVAN WISHED TO HEAD TO MELBOURNE OR SYDNEY, THE ONLY PORTS WHERE HE'D FIND A SHIP BOUND FOR ENGLAND. UNFORTUNATELY, NONE OF THE MERCHANT SHIPS ANCHORED IN THE BAY WAS DEPARTING FOR THOSE TWO DESTINATIONS.
WHAT DO WE DO, MAJOR? WE CAN'T WAIT FOR THE UNLIKELY CHANCE OF A PASSING SHIP TO MELBOURNE.
WE'LL HAVE TO REACH SYDNEY BY THE COASTAL ROADS.
MY FRIENDS, LET ME MAKE A PROPOSAL. ONE OF THE THREE SHIPS ANCHORED IN THE HARBOR IS PREPARING TO DEPART FOR AUCKLAND, THE CAPITAL OF IKANA-MAOUI, THE NORTHERN ISLAND OF NEW ZEALAND.
THE CROSSING ONLY LASTS FIVE OR SIX DAYS, AND IT'D BE EASY TO HEAD BACK TO EUROPE VIA THE BRITISH PENINSULAR SHIPPING COMPANY.
BY COINCIDENCE, AUCKLAND WAS LOCATED ON THE 37TH PARALLEL THE SEARCHERS HAD BEEN FOLLOWING FROM THE COAST OF PATAGONIA. BUT AFTER TWO DISAPPOINTMENTS, PAGANEL DIDN'T WANT TO SUGGEST TRYING A THIRD INTERPRETATION OF THE DOCUMENT, WHICH HE'D HAD ON HIS MIND SINCE THE INCIDENTS AT SNOWY RIVER.
VERY WELL, PAGANEL. WE'LL GO SEE THAT SHIP AND ITS COMMANDER AT DAWN.
THE MACQUARIE WAS A 250-TON BRIG THAT DID COASTAL TRADE BETWEEN VARIOUS PORTS IN AUSTRALIA AND NEW ZEALAND. ITS CAPTAIN, WILL HALLEY, WAS A COARSE, BRUTAL CHARACTER.
WHAT DO YOU LOT WANT?
THE CAPTAIN.
THAT'S ME. SO?
2

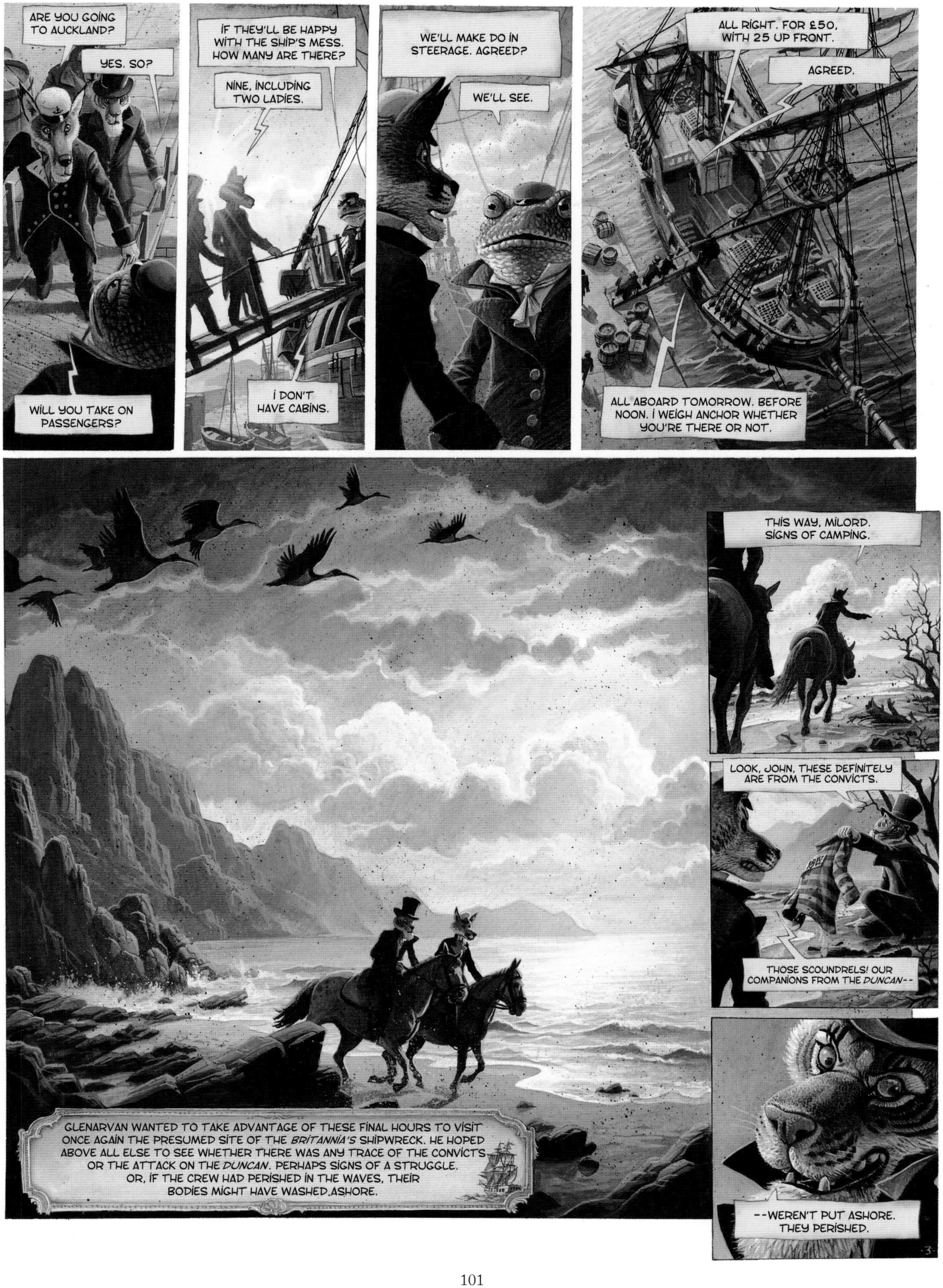
ARE YOU GOING TO AUCKLAND?
YES. SO?
WILL YOU TAKE ON PASSENGERS?
IF THEY'LL BE HAPPY WITH THE SHIP'S MESS. HOW MANY ARE THERE?
NINE, INCLUDING TWO LADIES.
I DON'T HAVE CABINS.
WE'LL MAKE DO IN STEERAGE. AGREED?
WE'LL SEE.
ALL RIGHT. FOR £50, WITH 25 UP FRONT.
AGREED.
ALL ABOARD TOMORROW. BEFORE NOON. I WEIGH ANCHOR WHETHER YOU'RE THERE OR NOT.
GLENARVAN WANTED TO TAKE ADVANTAGE OF THESE FINAL HOURS TO VISIT ONCE AGAIN THE PRESUMED SITE OF THE *BRITANNIA'S* SHIPWRECK. HE HOPED ABOVE ALL ELSE TO SEE WHETHER THERE WAS ANY TRACE OF THE CONVICTS OR THE ATTACK ON THE *DUNCAN*. PERHAPS SIGNS OF A STRUGGLE. OR, IF THE CREW HAD PERISHED IN THE WAVES, THEIR BODIES MIGHT HAVE WASHED ASHORE.
THIS WAY, MILORD. SIGNS OF CAMPING.
LOOK, JOHN, THESE DEFINITELY ARE FROM THE CONVICTS.
THOSE SCOUNDRELS! OUR COMPANIONS FROM THE *DUNCAN*--
--WEREN'T PUT ASHORE. THEY PERISHED.
-3-

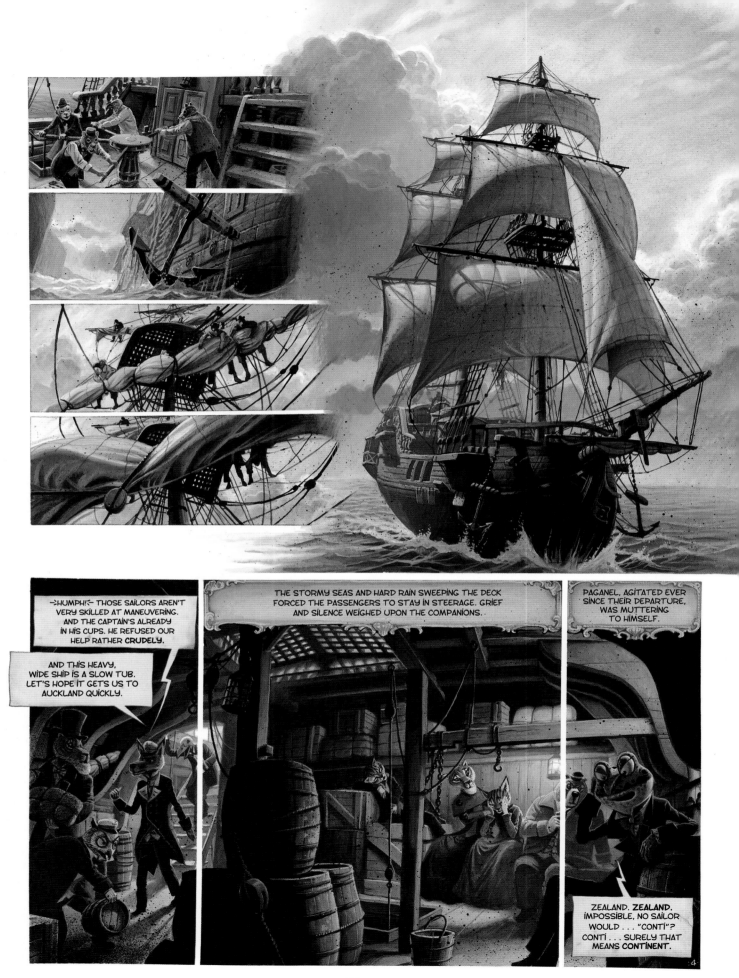

-:HUMPH!:- THOSE SAILORS AREN'T VERY SKILLED AT MANEUVERING. AND THE CAPTAIN'S ALREADY IN HIS CUPS. HE REFUSED OUR HELP RATHER CRUDELY.

AND THIS HEAVY, WIDE SHIP IS A SLOW TUB. LET'S HOPE IT GETS US TO AUCKLAND QUICKLY.

THE STORMY SEAS AND HARD RAIN SWEEPING THE DECK FORCED THE PASSENGERS TO STAY IN STEERAGE. GRIEF AND SILENCE WEIGHED UPON THE COMPANIONS.

PAGANEL, AGITATED EVER SINCE THEIR DEPARTURE, WAS MUTTERING TO HIMSELF.

ZEALAND. ZEALAND. IMPOSSIBLE, NO SAILOR WOULD . . . "CONTI"? CONTI . . . SURELY THAT MEANS CONTINENT.

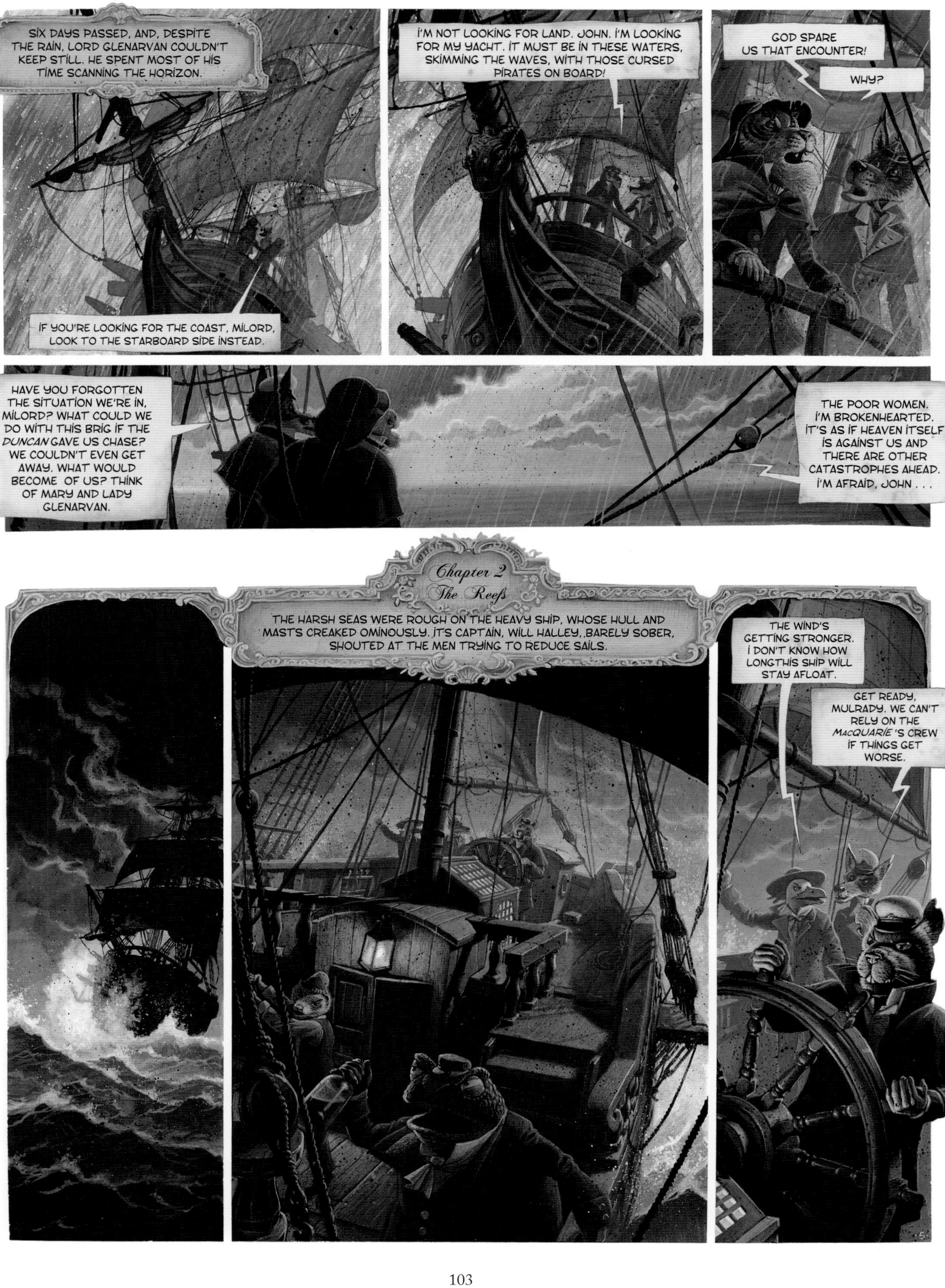
SIX DAYS PASSED, AND, DESPITE THE RAIN, LORD GLENARVAN COULDN'T KEEP STILL. HE SPENT MOST OF HIS TIME SCANNING THE HORIZON.
IF YOU'RE LOOKING FOR THE COAST, MILORD, LOOK TO THE STARBOARD SIDE INSTEAD.
I'M NOT LOOKING FOR LAND. JOHN. I'M LOOKING FOR MY YACHT. IT MUST BE IN THESE WATERS, SKIMMING THE WAVES, WITH THOSE CURSED PIRATES ON BOARD!
GOD SPARE US THAT ENCOUNTER!
WHY?
HAVE YOU FORGOTTEN THE SITUATION WE'RE IN, MILORD? WHAT COULD WE DO WITH THIS BRIG IF THE *DUNCAN* GAVE US CHASE? WE COULDN'T EVEN GET AWAY. WHAT WOULD BECOME OF US? THINK OF MARY AND LADY GLENARVAN.
THE POOR WOMEN. I'M BROKENHEARTED. IT'S AS IF HEAVEN ITSELF IS AGAINST US AND THERE ARE OTHER CATASTROPHES AHEAD. I'M AFRAID, JOHN . . .
Chapter 2
The Reefs
THE HARSH SEAS WERE ROUGH ON THE HEAVY SHIP, WHOSE HULL AND MASTS CREAKED OMINOUSLY. IT'S CAPTAIN, WILL HALLEY, ,BARELY SOBER, SHOUTED AT THE MEN TRYING TO REDUCE SAILS.
THE WIND'S GETTING STRONGER. I DON'T KNOW HOW LONGTHIS SHIP WILL STAY AFLOAT.
GET READY, MULRADY. WE CAN'T RELY ON THE *MACQUARIE*'S CREW IF THINGS GET WORSE.

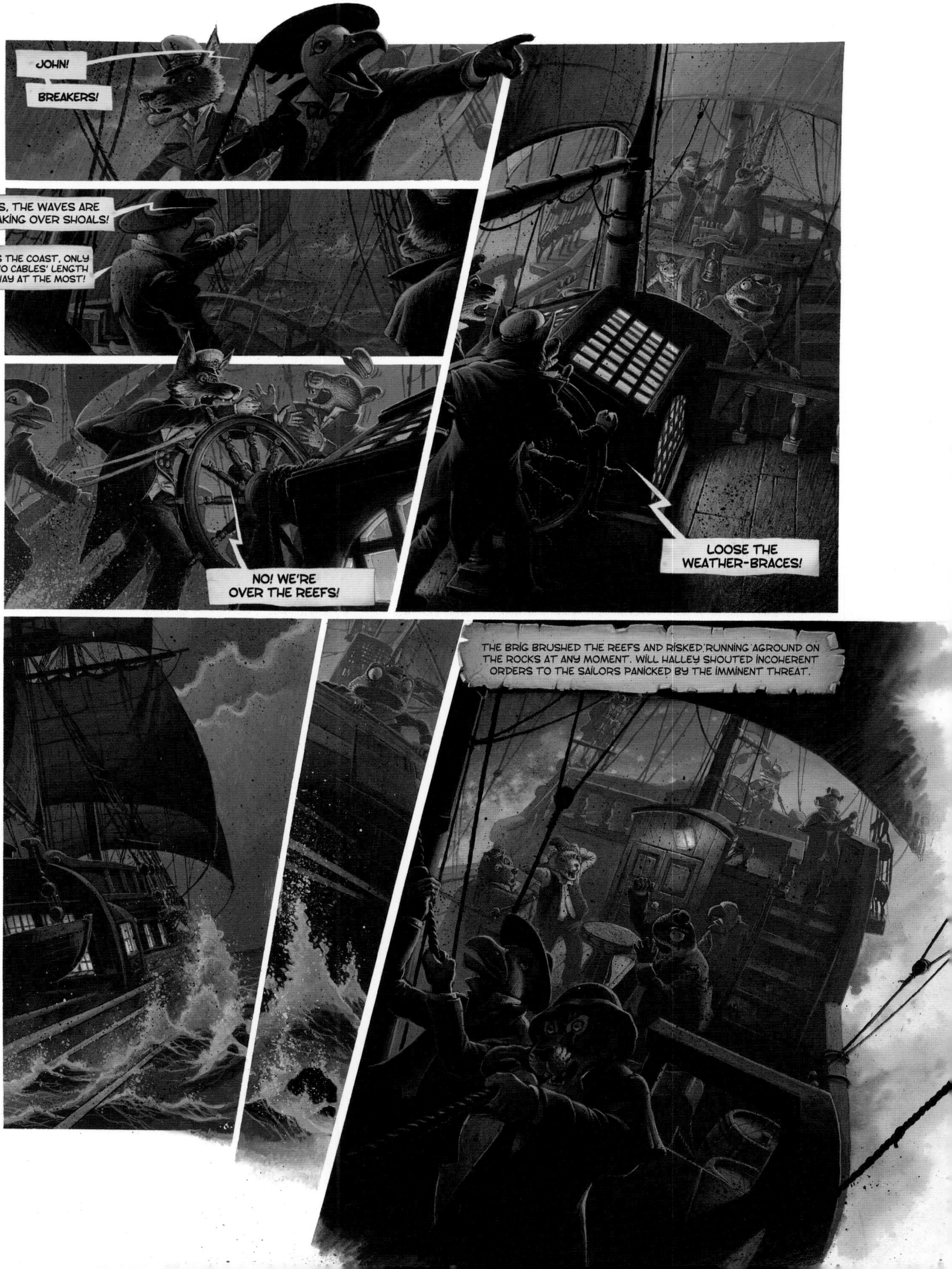
JOHN!
BREAKERS!
YES, THE WAVES ARE BREAKING OVER SHOALS!
IT'S THE COAST, ONLY TWO CABLES' LENGTH AWAY AT THE MOST!
NO! WE'RE OVER THE REEFS!
LOOSE THE WEATHER-BRACES!
THE BRIG BRUSHED THE REEFS AND RISKED RUNNING AGROUND ON THE ROCKS AT ANY MOMENT. WILL HALLEY SHOUTED INCOHERENT ORDERS TO THE SAILORS PANICKED BY THE IMMINENT THREAT.

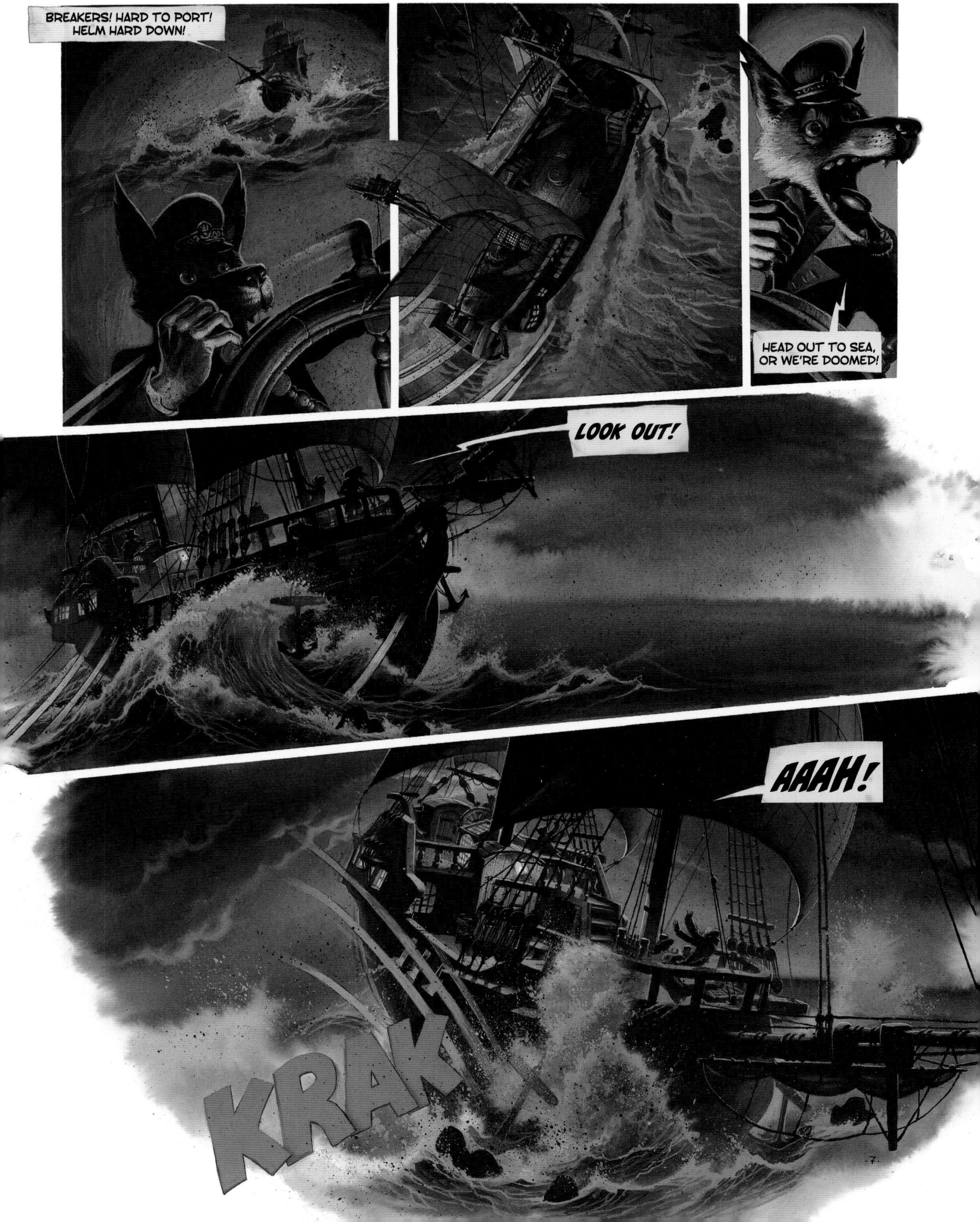
BREAKERS! HARD TO PORT!
HELM HARD DOWN!
HEAD OUT TO SEA,
OR WE'RE DOOMED!
LOOK OUT!
AAAH!
KRAK

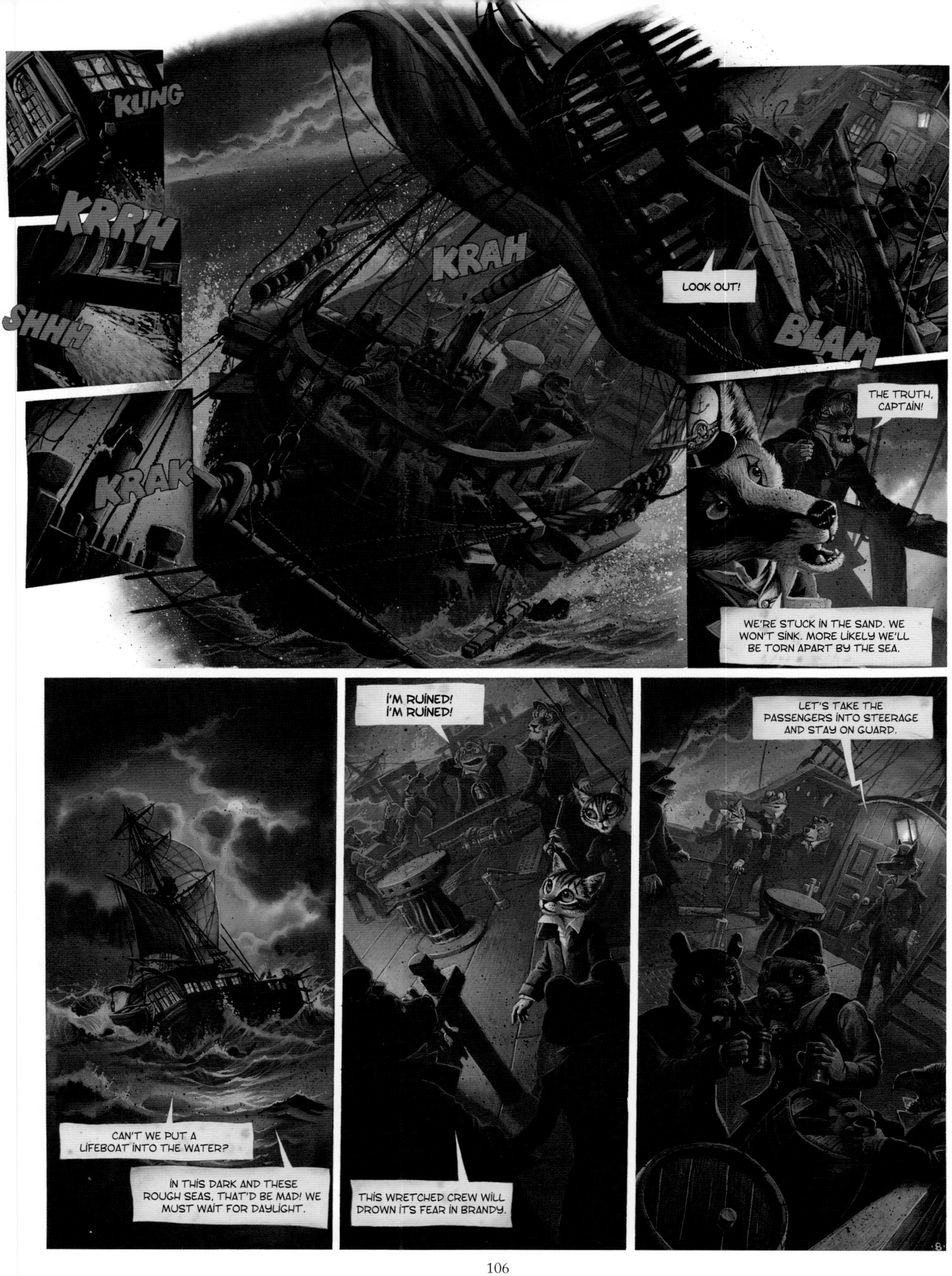
KLING
KRRH
SHHH
KRAK
KRAH
LOOK OUT!
BLAM
THE TRUTH, CAPTAIN!
WE'RE STUCK IN THE SAND. WE WON'T SINK. MORE LIKELY WE'LL BE TORN APART BY THE SEA.
CAN'T WE PUT A LIFEBOAT INTO THE WATER?
IN THIS DARK AND THESE ROUGH SEAS, THAT'D BE MAD! WE MUST WAIT FOR DAYLIGHT.
I'M RUINED! I'M RUINED!
THIS WRETCHED CREW WILL DROWN ITS FEAR IN BRANDY.
LET'S TAKE THE PASSENGERS INTO STEERAGE AND STAY ON GUARD.

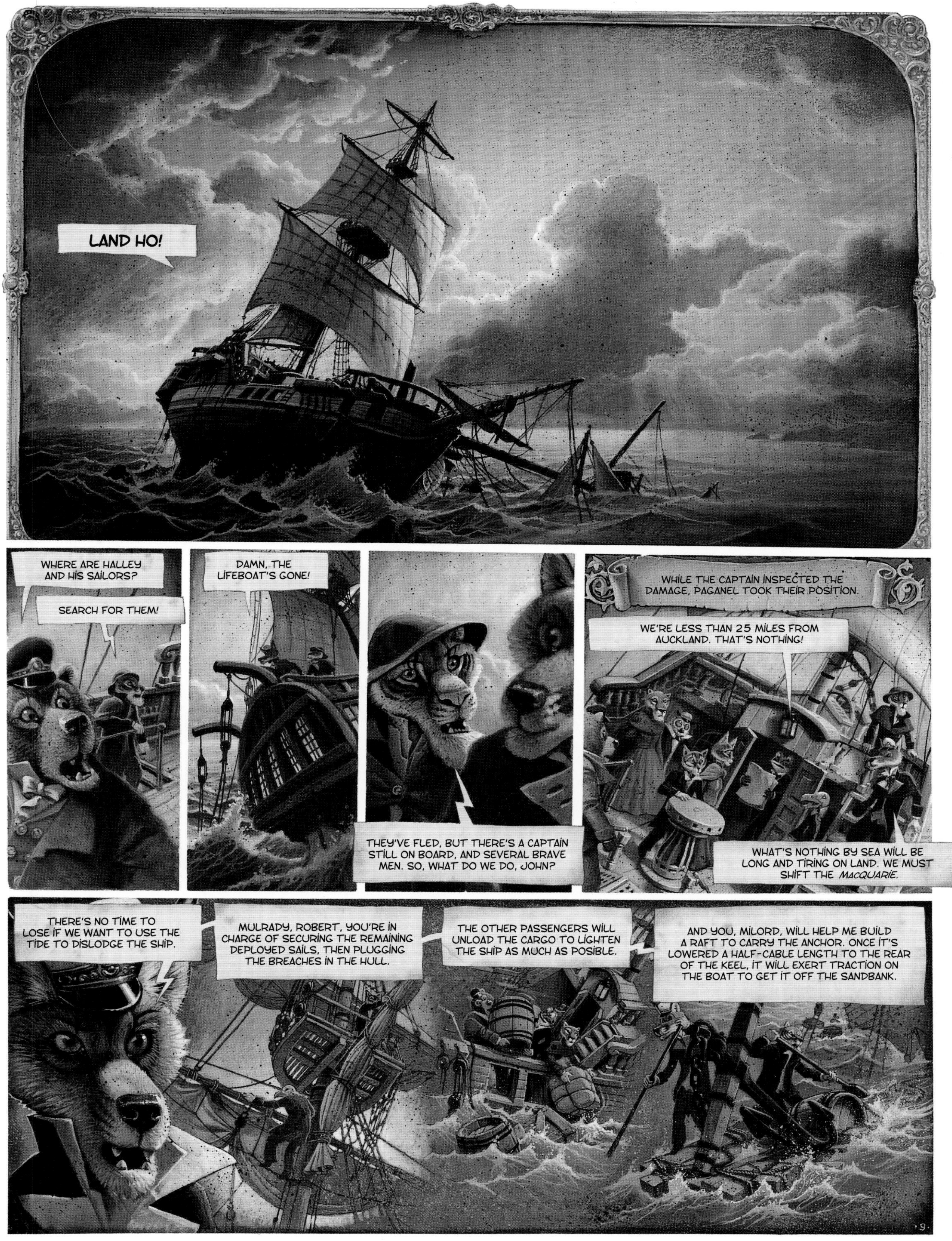

LAND HO!
WHERE ARE HALLEY AND HIS SAILORS?
SEARCH FOR THEM!
DAMN, THE LIFEBOAT'S GONE!
THEY'VE FLED, BUT THERE'S A CAPTAIN STILL ON BOARD, AND SEVERAL BRAVE MEN. SO, WHAT DO WE DO, JOHN?
WHILE THE CAPTAIN INSPECTED THE DAMAGE, PAGANEL TOOK THEIR POSITION.
WE'RE LESS THAN 25 MILES FROM AUCKLAND. THAT'S NOTHING!
WHAT'S NOTHING BY SEA WILL BE LONG AND TIRING ON LAND. WE MUST SHIFT THE *MACQUARIE*.
THERE'S NO TIME TO LOSE IF WE WANT TO USE THE TIDE TO DISLODGE THE SHIP.
MULRADY, ROBERT, YOU'RE IN CHARGE OF SECURING THE REMAINING DEPLOYED SAILS, THEN PLUGGING THE BREACHES IN THE HULL.
THE OTHER PASSENGERS WILL UNLOAD THE CARGO TO LIGHTEN THE SHIP AS MUCH AS POSIBLE.
AND YOU, MILORD, WILL HELP ME BUILD A RAFT TO CARRY THE ANCHOR. ONCE IT'S LOWERED A HALF-CABLE LENGTH TO THE REAR OF THE KEEL, IT WILL EXERT TRACTION ON THE BOAT TO GET IT OFF THE SANDBANK.
9

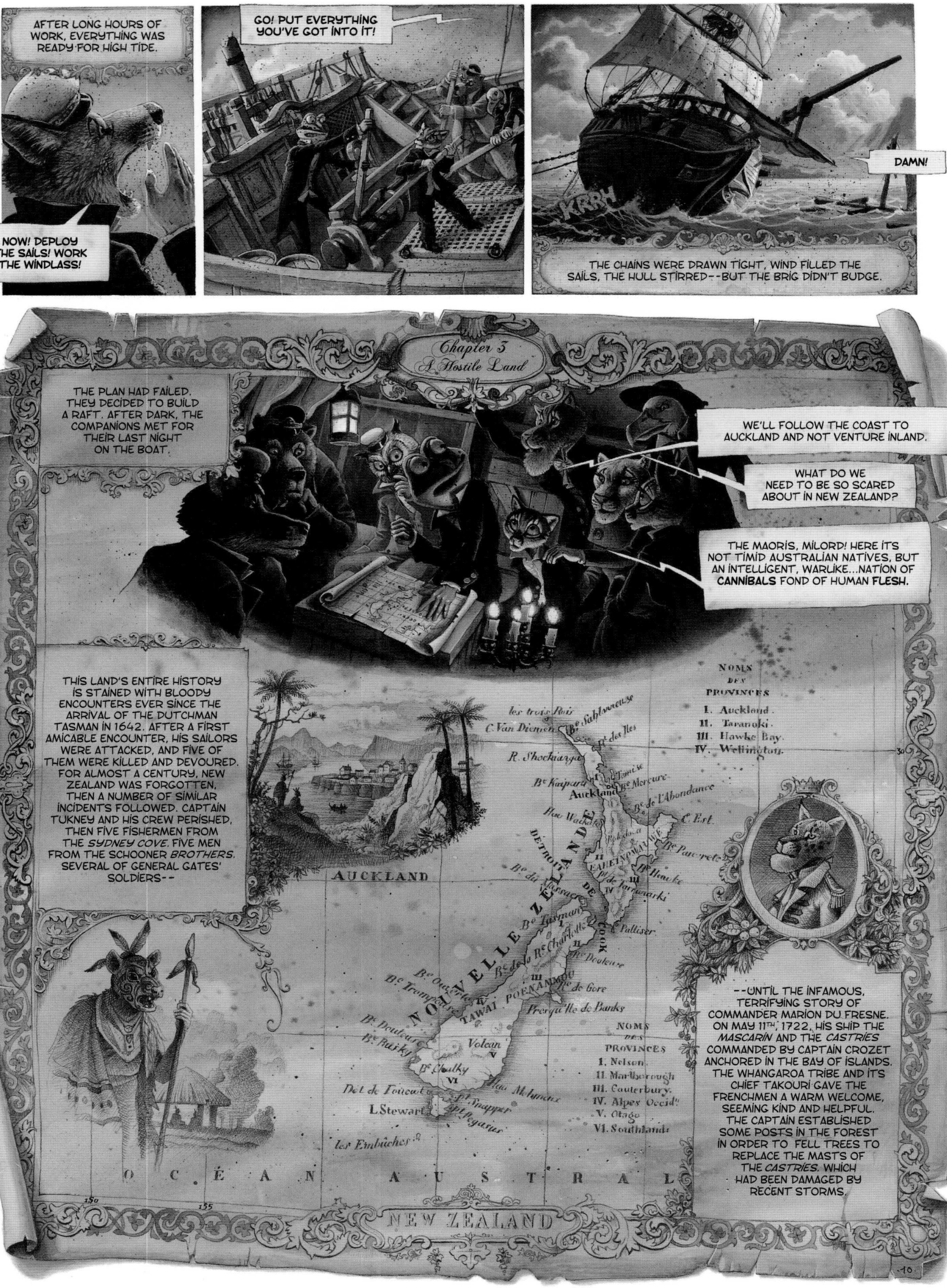
AFTER LONG HOURS OF WORK, EVERYTHING WAS READY FOR HIGH TIDE.
NOW! DEPLOY THE SAILS! WORK THE WINDLASS!
GO! PUT EVERYTHING YOU'VE GOT INTO IT!
KRRH
DAMN!
THE CHAINS WERE DRAWN TIGHT, WIND FILLED THE SAILS, THE HULL STIRRED--BUT THE BRIG DIDN'T BUDGE.
Chapter 3
A Hostile Land
THE PLAN HAD FAILED. THEY DECIDED TO BUILD A RAFT. AFTER DARK, THE COMPANIONS MET FOR THEIR LAST NIGHT ON THE BOAT.
WE'LL FOLLOW THE COAST TO AUCKLAND AND NOT VENTURE INLAND.
WHAT DO WE NEED TO BE SO SCARED ABOUT IN NEW ZEALAND?
THE MAORIS, MILORD! HERE IT'S NOT TIMID AUSTRALIAN NATIVES, BUT AN INTELLIGENT, WARLIKE...NATION OF **CANNIBALS** FOND OF HUMAN **FLESH.**
THIS LAND'S ENTIRE HISTORY IS STAINED WITH BLOODY ENCOUNTERS EVER SINCE THE ARRIVAL OF THE DUTCHMAN TASMAN IN 1642. AFTER A FIRST AMICABLE ENCOUNTER, HIS SAILORS WERE ATTACKED, AND FIVE OF THEM WERE KILLED AND DEVOURED. FOR ALMOST A CENTURY, NEW ZEALAND WAS FORGOTTEN, THEN A NUMBER OF SIMILAR INCIDENTS FOLLOWED. CAPTAIN TUKNEY AND HIS CREW PERISHED, THEN FIVE FISHERMEN FROM THE *SYDNEY COVE.* FIVE MEN FROM THE SCHOONER *BROTHERS.* SEVERAL OF GENERAL GATES' SOLDIERS--
AUCKLAND
NOMS DES PROVINCES
I. Auckland.
II. Taranaki.
III. Hawke Bay.
IV. Wellington.
NOUVELLE ZELANDE
DETROIT DE COOK
TAWAI POENAMMOU
NOMS DES PROVINCES
I. Nelson.
II. Marlborough
III. Canterbury.
IV. Alpes Occid.
V. Otago
VI. Southland.
I. Stewart
les Embuches
OCÉAN AUSTRAL
NEW ZEALAND
--UNTIL THE INFAMOUS, TERRIFYING STORY OF COMMANDER MARION DU FRESNE. ON MAY 11TH, 1722, HIS SHIP THE *MASCARIN* AND THE *CASTRIES* COMMANDED BY CAPTAIN CROZET ANCHORED IN THE BAY OF ISLANDS. THE WHANGAROA TRIBE AND ITS CHIEF TAKOURI GAVE THE FRENCHMEN A WARM WELCOME, SEEMING KIND AND HELPFUL. THE CAPTAIN ESTABLISHED SOME POSTS IN THE FOREST IN ORDER TO FELL TREES TO REPLACE THE MASTS OF THE *CASTRIES,* WHICH HAD BEEN DAMAGED BY RECENT STORMS.

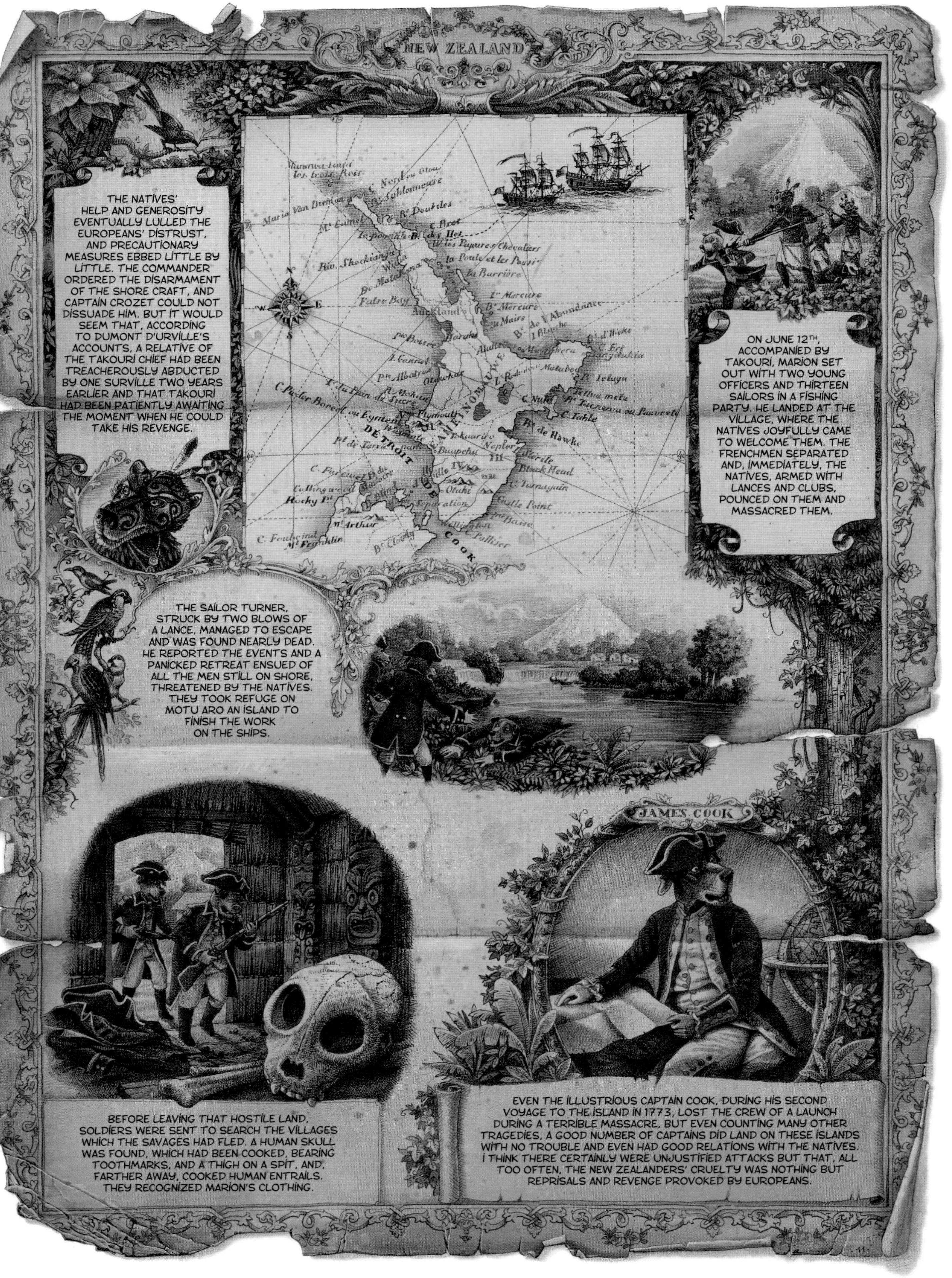
NEW ZEALAND
THE NATIVES' HELP AND GENEROSITY EVENTUALLY LULLED THE EUROPEANS' DISTRUST, AND PRECAUTIONARY MEASURES EBBED LITTLE BY LITTLE. THE COMMANDER ORDERED THE DISARMAMENT OF THE SHORE CRAFT, AND CAPTAIN CROZET COULD NOT DISSUADE HIM. BUT IT WOULD SEEM THAT, ACCORDING TO DUMONT D'URVILLE'S ACCOUNTS, A RELATIVE OF THE TAKOURI CHIEF HAD BEEN TREACHEROUSLY ABDUCTED BY ONE SURVILLE TWO YEARS EARLIER AND THAT TAKOURI HAD BEEN PATIENTLY AWAITING THE MOMENT WHEN HE COULD TAKE HIS REVENGE.
Auckland
False Bay
Plymouth
DETROIT DE COOK
Napier
Black Head
C. Table
ON JUNE 12TH, ACCOMPANIED BY TAKOURI, MARION SET OUT WITH TWO YOUNG OFFICERS AND THIRTEEN SAILORS IN A FISHING PARTY. HE LANDED AT THE VILLAGE, WHERE THE NATIVES JOYFULLY CAME TO WELCOME THEM. THE FRENCHMEN SEPARATED AND, IMMEDIATELY, THE NATIVES, ARMED WITH LANCES AND CLUBS, POUNCED ON THEM AND MASSACRED THEM.
THE SAILOR TURNER, STRUCK BY TWO BLOWS OF A LANCE, MANAGED TO ESCAPE AND WAS FOUND NEARLY DEAD. HE REPORTED THE EVENTS AND A PANICKED RETREAT ENSUED OF ALL THE MEN STILL ON SHORE, THREATENED BY THE NATIVES. THEY TOOK REFUGE ON MOTU ARO AN ISLAND TO FINISH THE WORK ON THE SHIPS.
JAMES COOK
BEFORE LEAVING THAT HOSTILE LAND, SOLDIERS WERE SENT TO SEARCH THE VILLAGES WHICH THE SAVAGES HAD FLED. A HUMAN SKULL WAS FOUND, WHICH HAD BEEN COOKED, BEARING TOOTHMARKS, AND A THIGH ON A SPIT, AND, FARTHER AWAY, COOKED HUMAN ENTRAILS. THEY RECOGNIZED MARION'S CLOTHING.
EVEN THE ILLUSTRIOUS CAPTAIN COOK, DURING HIS SECOND VOYAGE TO THE ISLAND IN 1773, LOST THE CREW OF A LAUNCH DURING A TERRIBLE MASSACRE, BUT EVEN COUNTING MANY OTHER TRAGEDIES, A GOOD NUMBER OF CAPTAINS DID LAND ON THESE ISLANDS WITH NO TROUBLE AND EVEN HAD GOOD RELATIONS WITH THE NATIVES. I THINK THERE CERTAINLY WERE UNJUSTIFIED ATTACKS BUT THAT, ALL TOO OFTEN, THE NEW ZEALANDERS' CRUELTY WAS NOTHING BUT REPRISALS AND REVENGE PROVOKED BY EUROPEANS.
11

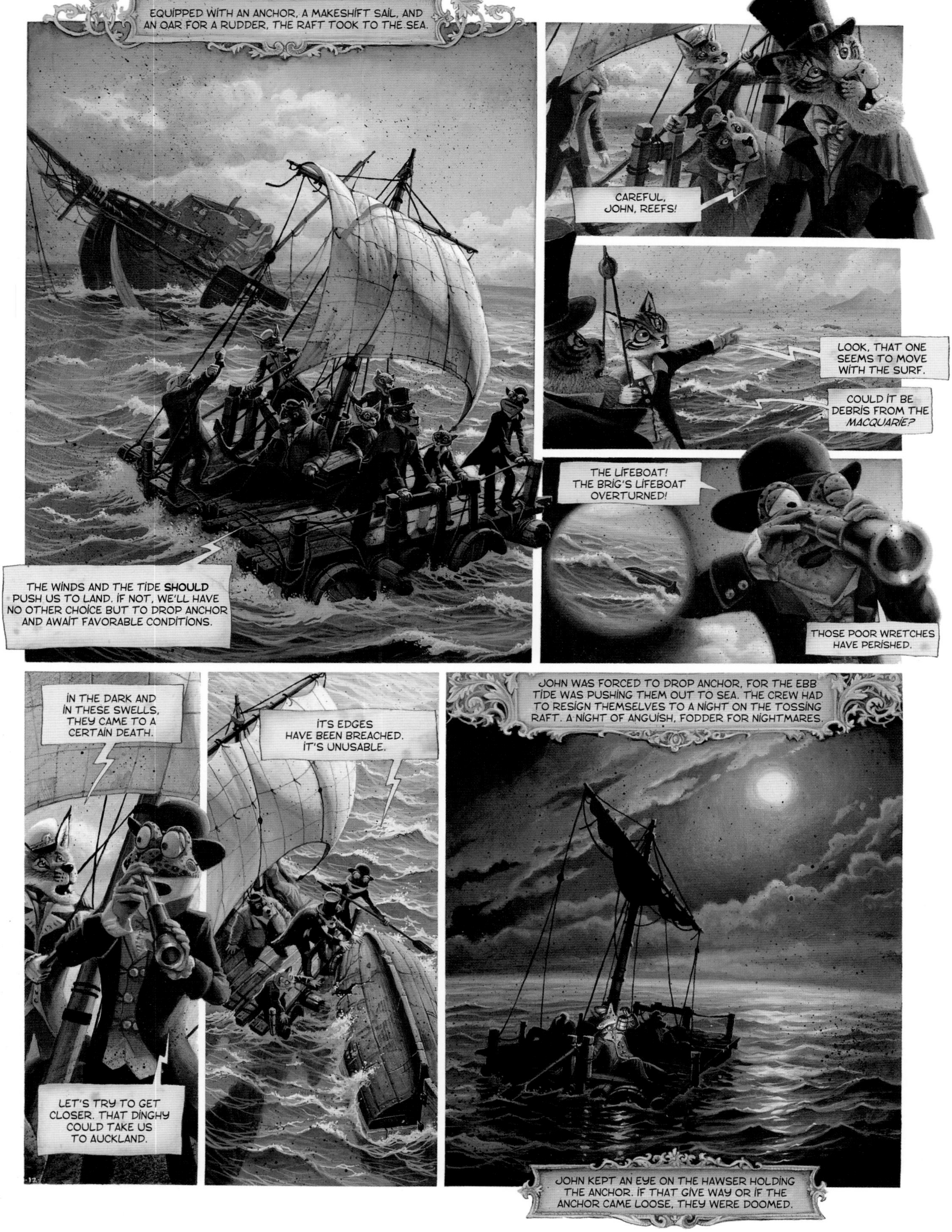

EQUIPPED WITH AN ANCHOR, A MAKESHIFT SAIL, AND AN OAR FOR A RUDDER, THE RAFT TOOK TO THE SEA.
THE WINDS AND THE TIDE **SHOULD** PUSH US TO LAND. IF NOT, WE'LL HAVE NO OTHER CHOICE BUT TO DROP ANCHOR AND AWAIT FAVORABLE CONDITIONS.
CAREFUL, JOHN, REEFS!
LOOK, THAT ONE SEEMS TO MOVE WITH THE SURF.
COULD IT BE DEBRIS FROM THE *MACQUARIE?*
THE LIFEBOAT! THE BRIG'S LIFEBOAT OVERTURNED!
THOSE POOR WRETCHES HAVE PERISHED.
IN THE DARK AND IN THESE SWELLS, THEY CAME TO A CERTAIN DEATH.
LET'S TRY TO GET CLOSER. THAT DINGHY COULD TAKE US TO AUCKLAND.
ITS EDGES HAVE BEEN BREACHED. IT'S UNUSABLE.
JOHN WAS FORCED TO DROP ANCHOR, FOR THE EBB TIDE WAS PUSHING THEM OUT TO SEA. THE CREW HAD TO RESIGN THEMSELVES TO A NIGHT ON THE TOSSING RAFT. A NIGHT OF ANGUISH, FODDER FOR NIGHTMARES.
JOHN KEPT AN EYE ON THE HAWSER HOLDING THE ANCHOR. IF THAT GIVE WAY OR IF THE ANCHOR CAME LOOSE, THEY WERE DOOMED.

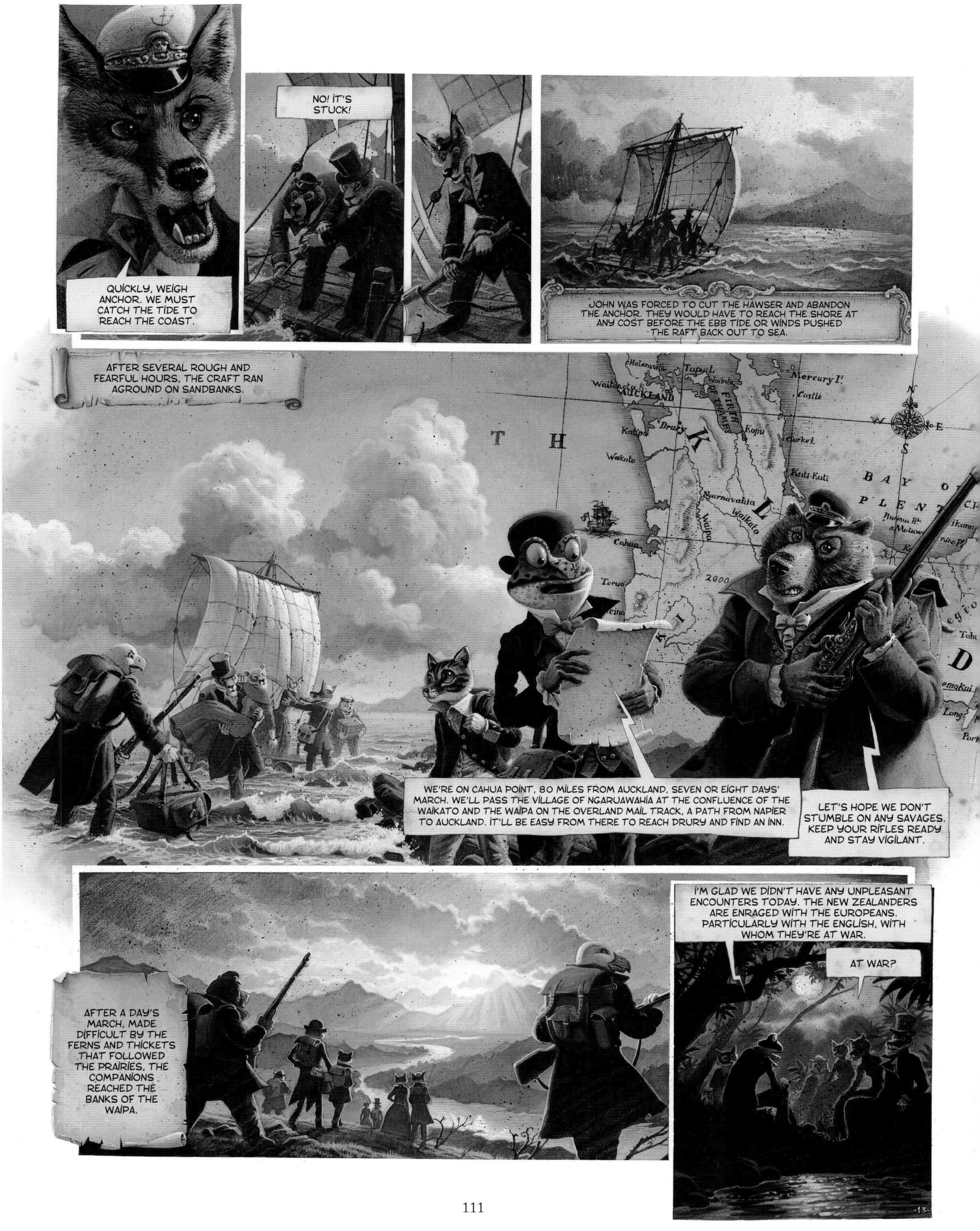
QUICKLY, WEIGH ANCHOR. WE MUST CATCH THE TIDE TO REACH THE COAST.
NO! IT'S STUCK!
JOHN WAS FORCED TO CUT THE HAWSER AND ABANDON THE ANCHOR. THEY WOULD HAVE TO REACH THE SHORE AT ANY COST BEFORE THE EBB TIDE OR WINDS PUSHED THE RAFT BACK OUT TO SEA.
AFTER SEVERAL ROUGH AND FEARFUL HOURS, THE CRAFT RAN AGROUND ON SANDBANKS.
AUCKLAND
Drury
Waikato
Kopu
Kati-Kati
WE'RE ON CAHUA POINT, 80 MILES FROM AUCKLAND, SEVEN OR EIGHT DAYS' MARCH. WE'LL PASS THE VILLAGE OF NGARUAWAHIA AT THE CONFLUENCE OF THE WAIKATO AND THE WAIPA ON THE OVERLAND MAIL TRACK, A PATH FROM NAPIER TO AUCKLAND. IT'LL BE EASY FROM THERE TO REACH DRURY AND FIND AN INN.
LET'S HOPE WE DON'T STUMBLE ON ANY SAVAGES. KEEP YOUR RIFLES READY AND STAY VIGILANT.
AFTER A DAY'S MARCH, MADE DIFFICULT BY THE FERNS AND THICKETS THAT FOLLOWED THE PRAIRIES, THE COMPANIONS REACHED THE BANKS OF THE WAIPA.
I'M GLAD WE DIDN'T HAVE ANY UNPLEASANT ENCOUNTERS TODAY. THE NEW ZEALANDERS ARE ENRAGED WITH THE EUROPEANS. PARTICULARLY WITH THE ENGLISH, WITH WHOM THEY'RE AT WAR.
AT WAR?
-13-

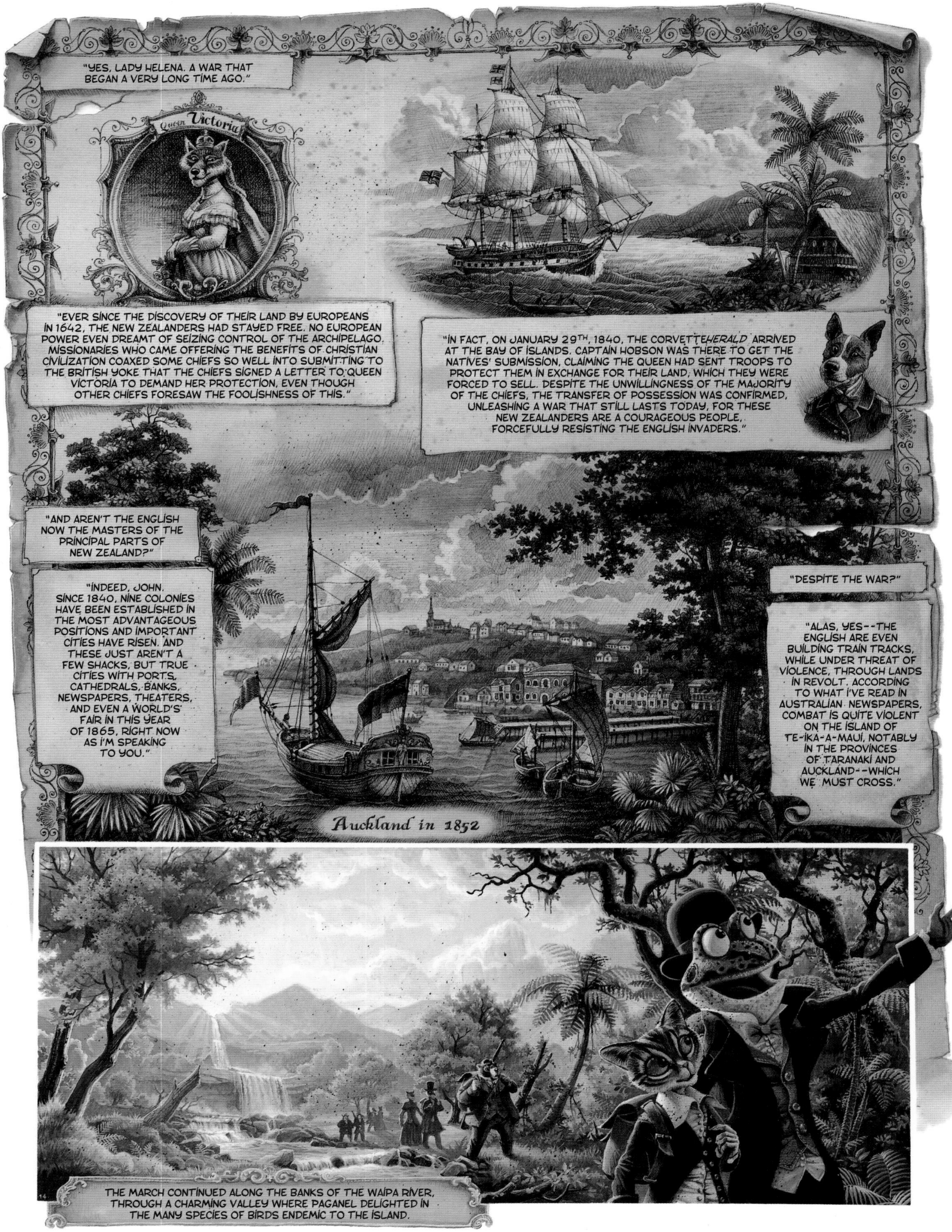
"YES, LADY HELENA. A WAR THAT BEGAN A VERY LONG TIME AGO."
Queen Victoria
"EVER SINCE THE DISCOVERY OF THEIR LAND BY EUROPEANS IN 1642, THE NEW ZEALANDERS HAD STAYED FREE. NO EUROPEAN POWER EVEN DREAMT OF SEIZING CONTROL OF THE ARCHIPELAGO. MISSIONARIES WHO CAME OFFERING THE BENEFITS OF CHRISTIAN CIVILIZATION COAXED SOME CHIEFS SO WELL INTO SUBMITTING TO THE BRITISH YOKE THAT THE CHIEFS SIGNED A LETTER TO QUEEN VICTORIA TO DEMAND HER PROTECTION, EVEN THOUGH OTHER CHIEFS FORESAW THE FOOLISHNESS OF THIS."
"IN FACT, ON JANUARY 29TH, 1840, THE CORVETTE *HERALD* ARRIVED AT THE BAY OF ISLANDS. CAPTAIN HOBSON WAS THERE TO GET THE NATIVES' SUBMISSION, CLAIMING THE QUEEN HAD SENT TROOPS TO PROTECT THEM IN EXCHANGE FOR THEIR LAND, WHICH THEY WERE FORCED TO SELL. DESPITE THE UNWILLINGNESS OF THE MAJORITY OF THE CHIEFS, THE TRANSFER OF POSSESSION WAS CONFIRMED, UNLEASHING A WAR THAT STILL LASTS TODAY, FOR THESE NEW ZEALANDERS ARE A COURAGEOUS PEOPLE, FORCEFULLY RESISTING THE ENGLISH INVADERS."
"AND AREN'T THE ENGLISH NOW THE MASTERS OF THE PRINCIPAL PARTS OF NEW ZEALAND?"
"INDEED, JOHN. SINCE 1840, NINE COLONIES HAVE BEEN ESTABLISHED IN THE MOST ADVANTAGEOUS POSITIONS AND IMPORTANT CITIES HAVE RISEN. AND THESE JUST AREN'T A FEW SHACKS, BUT TRUE CITIES WITH PORTS, CATHEDRALS, BANKS, NEWSPAPERS, THEATERS, AND EVEN A WORLD'S FAIR IN THIS YEAR OF 1865, RIGHT NOW AS I'M SPEAKING TO YOU."
"DESPITE THE WAR?"
"ALAS, YES--THE ENGLISH ARE EVEN BUILDING TRAIN TRACKS, WHILE UNDER THREAT OF VIOLENCE, THROUGH LANDS IN REVOLT. ACCORDING TO WHAT I'VE READ IN AUSTRALIAN NEWSPAPERS, COMBAT IS QUITE VIOLENT ON THE ISLAND OF TE-IKA-A-MAUI, NOTABLY IN THE PROVINCES OF TARANAKI AND AUCKLAND--WHICH WE MUST CROSS."
Auckland in 1852
THE MARCH CONTINUED ALONG THE BANKS OF THE WAIPA RIVER, THROUGH A CHARMING VALLEY WHERE PAGANEL DELIGHTED IN THE MANY SPECIES OF BIRDS ENDEMIC TO THE ISLAND.

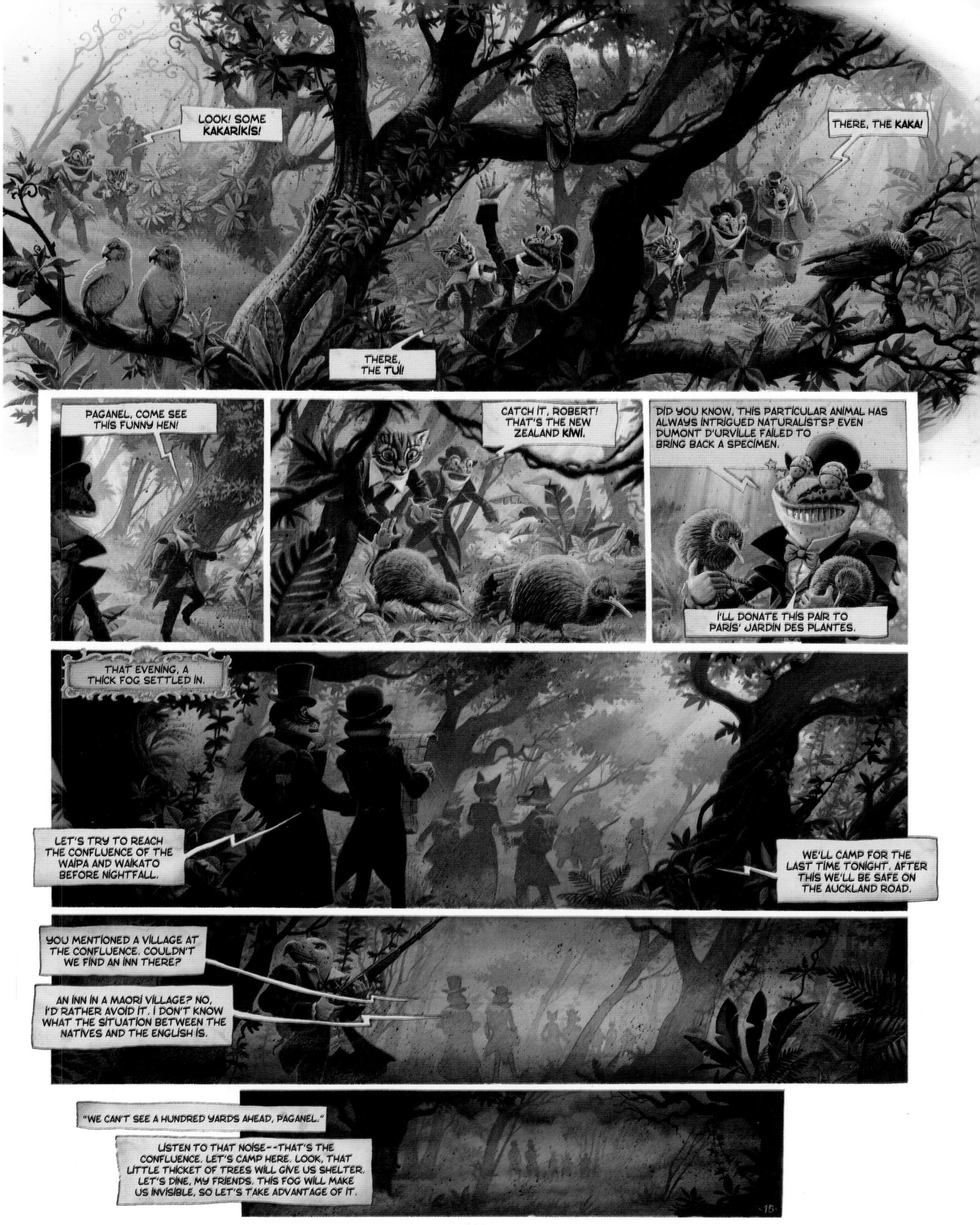
LOOK! SOME KAKARIKIS!
THERE, THE TUI!
THERE, THE KAKA!
PAGANEL, COME SEE THIS FUNNY HEN!
CATCH IT, ROBERT! THAT'S THE NEW ZEALAND KIWI.
DID YOU KNOW, THIS PARTICULAR ANIMAL HAS ALWAYS INTRIGUED NATURALISTS? EVEN DUMONT D'URVILLE FAILED TO BRING BACK A SPECIMEN.
I'LL DONATE THIS PAIR TO PARIS' JARDIN DES PLANTES.
THAT EVENING, A THICK FOG SETTLED IN.
LET'S TRY TO REACH THE CONFLUENCE OF THE WAIPA AND WAIKATO BEFORE NIGHTFALL.
WE'LL CAMP FOR THE LAST TIME TONIGHT. AFTER THIS WE'LL BE SAFE ON THE AUCKLAND ROAD.
YOU MENTIONED A VILLAGE AT THE CONFLUENCE. COULDN'T WE FIND AN INN THERE?
AN INN IN A MAORI VILLAGE? NO, I'D RATHER AVOID IT. I DON'T KNOW WHAT THE SITUATION BETWEEN THE NATIVES AND THE ENGLISH IS.
"WE CAN'T SEE A HUNDRED YARDS AHEAD, PAGANEL."
LISTEN TO THAT NOISE--THAT'S THE CONFLUENCE. LET'S CAMP HERE. LOOK, THAT LITTLE THICKET OF TREES WILL GIVE US SHELTER. LET'S DINE, MY FRIENDS. THIS FOG WILL MAKE US INVISIBLE, SO LET'S TAKE ADVANTAGE OF IT.
15

Chapter 4
The Maoris

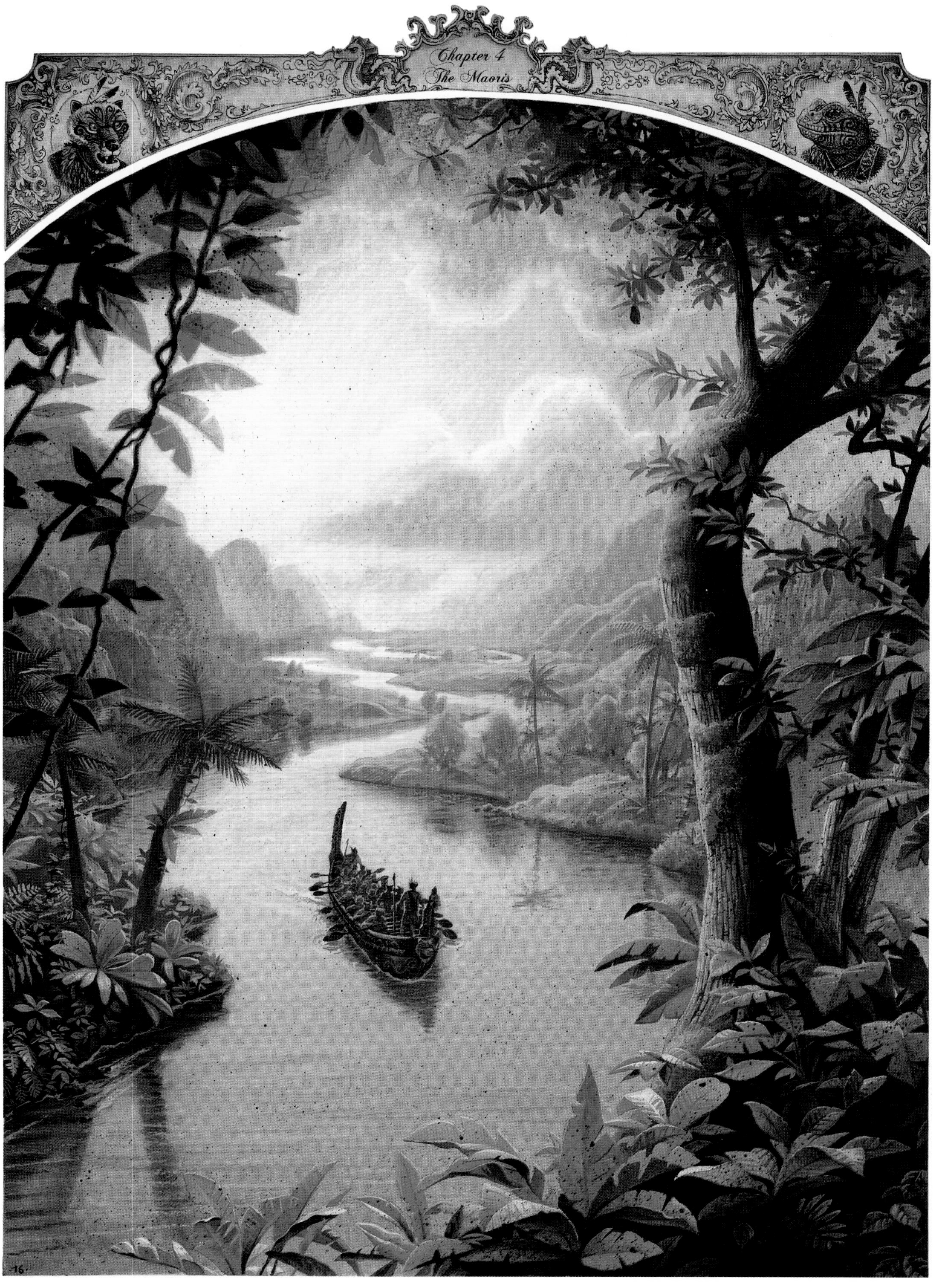

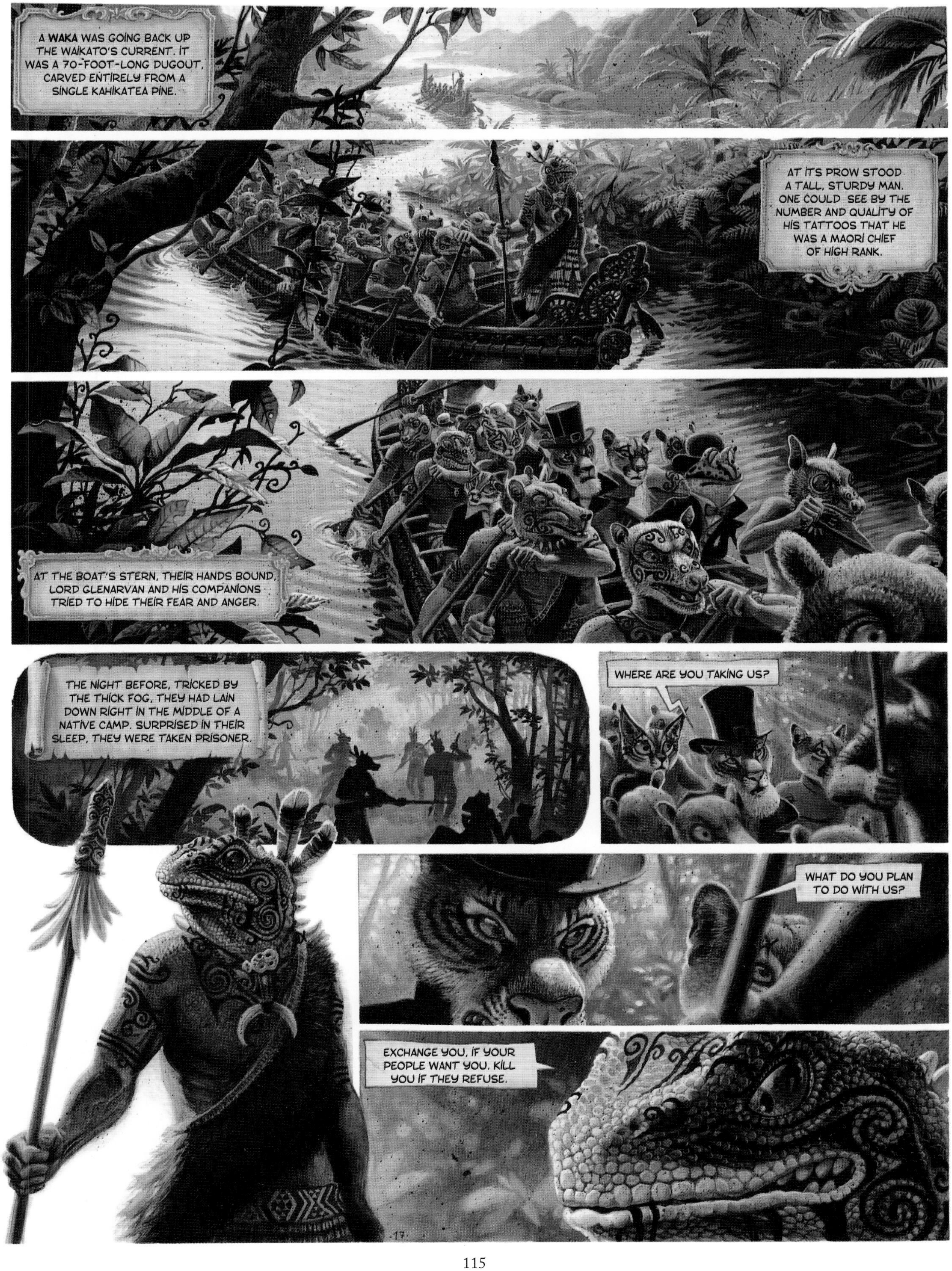
A WAKA WAS GOING BACK UP THE WAIKATO'S CURRENT. IT WAS A 70-FOOT-LONG DUGOUT, CARVED ENTIRELY FROM A SINGLE KAHIKATEA PINE.
AT ITS PROW STOOD A TALL, STURDY MAN. ONE COULD SEE BY THE NUMBER AND QUALITY OF HIS TATTOOS THAT HE WAS A MAORI CHIEF OF HIGH RANK.
AT THE BOAT'S STERN, THEIR HANDS BOUND, LORD GLENARVAN AND HIS COMPANIONS TRIED TO HIDE THEIR FEAR AND ANGER.
THE NIGHT BEFORE, TRICKED BY THE THICK FOG, THEY HAD LAIN DOWN RIGHT IN THE MIDDLE OF A NATIVE CAMP. SURPRISED IN THEIR SLEEP, THEY WERE TAKEN PRISONER.
WHERE ARE YOU TAKING US?
WHAT DO YOU PLAN TO DO WITH US?
EXCHANGE YOU, IF YOUR PEOPLE WANT YOU. KILL YOU IF THEY REFUSE.

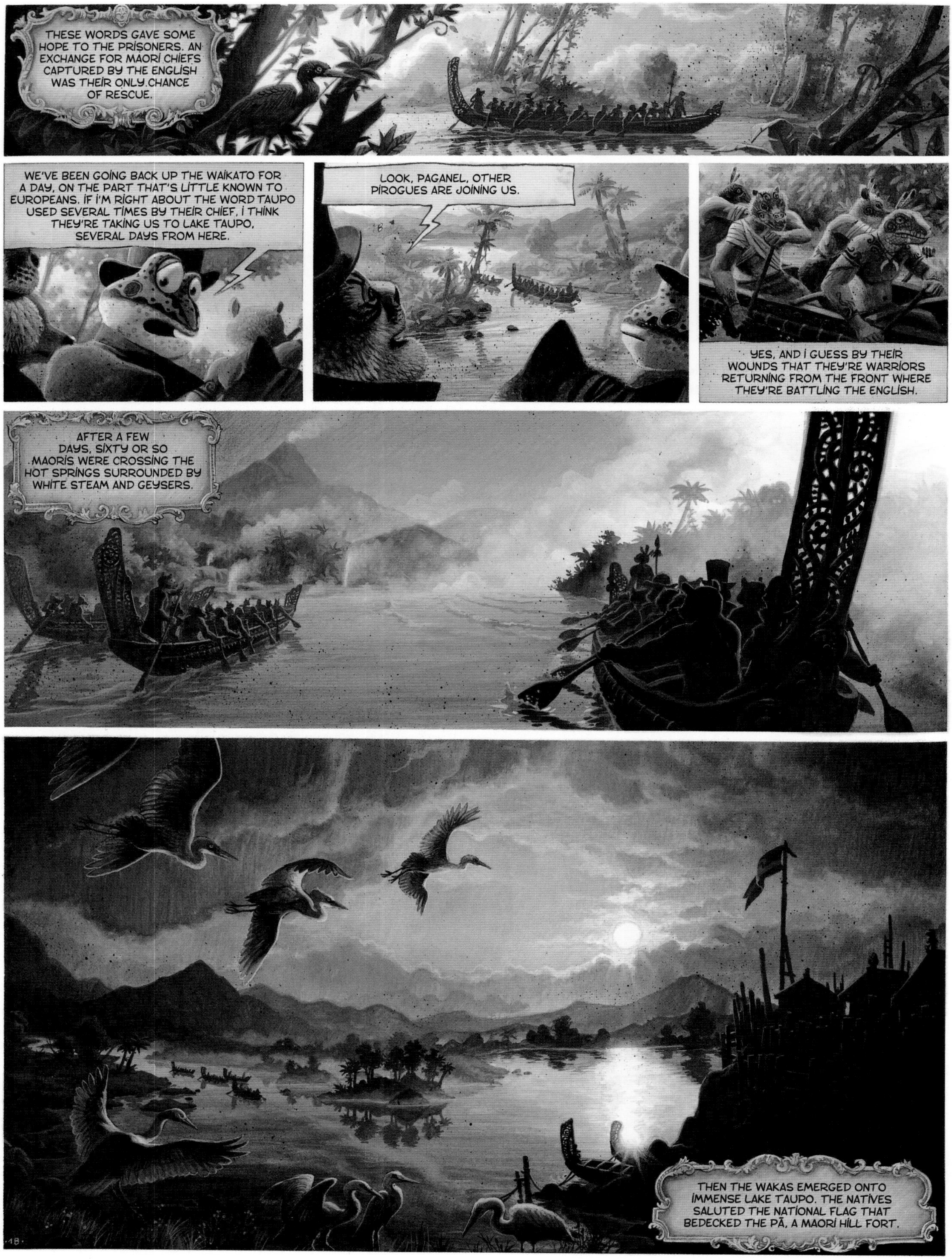
THESE WORDS GAVE SOME HOPE TO THE PRISONERS. AN EXCHANGE FOR MAORI CHIEFS CAPTURED BY THE ENGLISH WAS THEIR ONLY CHANCE OF RESCUE.
WE'VE BEEN GOING BACK UP THE WAIKATO FOR A DAY, ON THE PART THAT'S LITTLE KNOWN TO EUROPEANS. IF I'M RIGHT ABOUT THE WORD TAUPO USED SEVERAL TIMES BY THEIR CHIEF, I THINK THEY'RE TAKING US TO LAKE TAUPO, SEVERAL DAYS FROM HERE.
LOOK, PAGANEL, OTHER PIROGUES ARE JOINING US.
YES, AND I GUESS BY THEIR WOUNDS THAT THEY'RE WARRIORS RETURNING FROM THE FRONT WHERE THEY'RE BATTLING THE ENGLISH.
AFTER A FEW DAYS, SIXTY OR SO MAORIS WERE CROSSING THE HOT SPRINGS SURROUNDED BY WHITE STEAM AND GEYSERS.
THEN THE WAKAS EMERGED ONTO IMMENSE LAKE TAUPO. THE NATIVES SALUTED THE NATIONAL FLAG THAT BEDECKED THE PÃ, A MAORI HILL FORT.
18

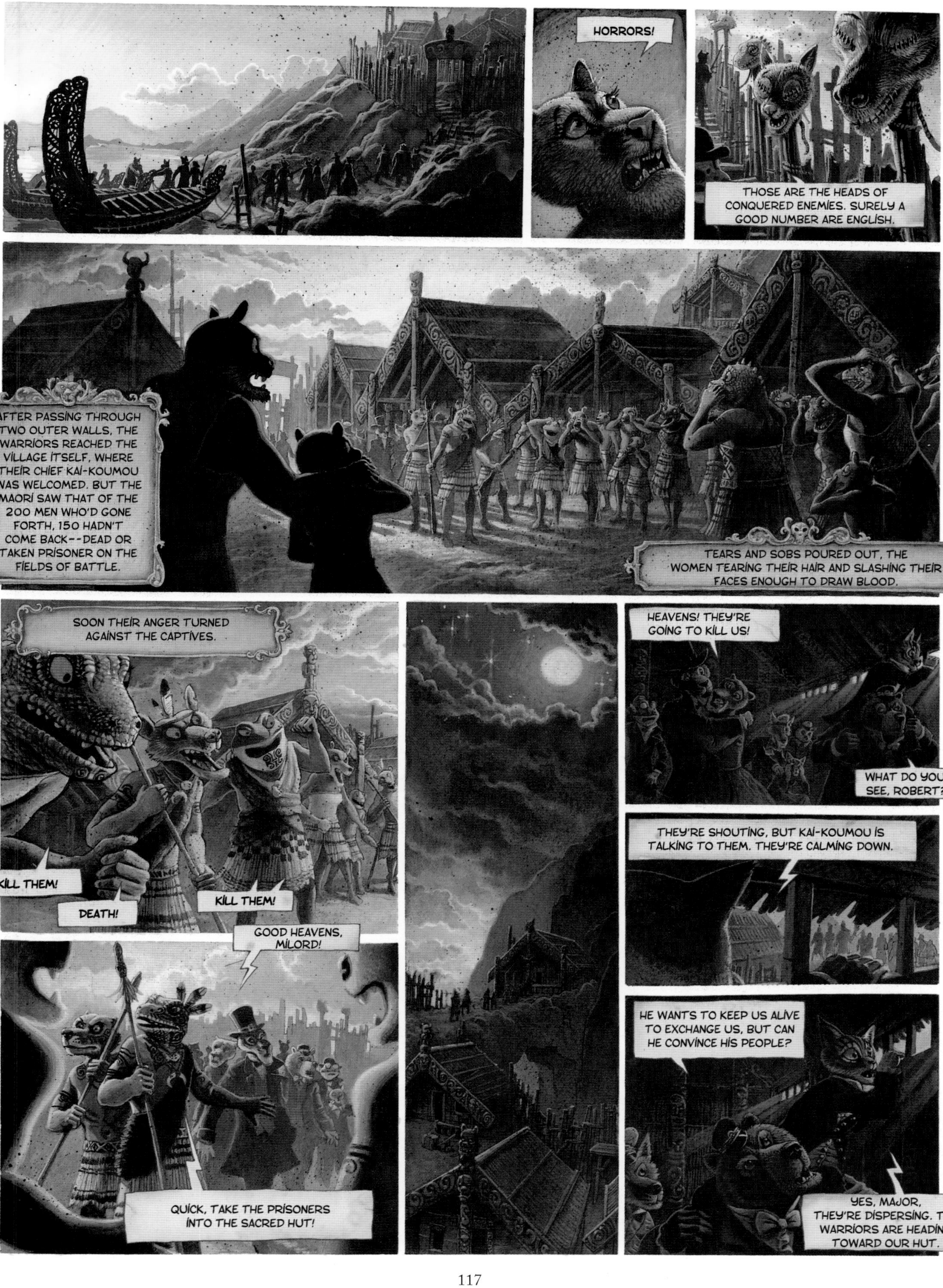
HORRORS!
THOSE ARE THE HEADS OF CONQUERED ENEMIES. SURELY A GOOD NUMBER ARE ENGLISH.
AFTER PASSING THROUGH TWO OUTER WALLS, THE WARRIORS REACHED THE VILLAGE ITSELF, WHERE THEIR CHIEF KAÏ-KOUMOU WAS WELCOMED. BUT THE MAORI SAW THAT OF THE 200 MEN WHO'D GONE FORTH, 150 HADN'T COME BACK--DEAD OR TAKEN PRISONER ON THE FIELDS OF BATTLE.
TEARS AND SOBS POURED OUT, THE WOMEN TEARING THEIR HAIR AND SLASHING THEIR FACES ENOUGH TO DRAW BLOOD.
SOON THEIR ANGER TURNED AGAINST THE CAPTIVES.
KILL THEM!
DEATH!
KILL THEM!
GOOD HEAVENS, MILORD!
QUICK, TAKE THE PRISONERS INTO THE SACRED HUT!
HEAVENS! THEY'RE GOING TO KILL US!
WHAT DO YOU SEE, ROBERT?
THEY'RE SHOUTING, BUT KAÏ-KOUMOU IS TALKING TO THEM. THEY'RE CALMING DOWN.
HE WANTS TO KEEP US ALIVE TO EXCHANGE US, BUT CAN HE CONVINCE HIS PEOPLE?
YES, MAJOR, THEY'RE DISPERSING. THE WARRIORS ARE HEADING TOWARD OUR HUT.

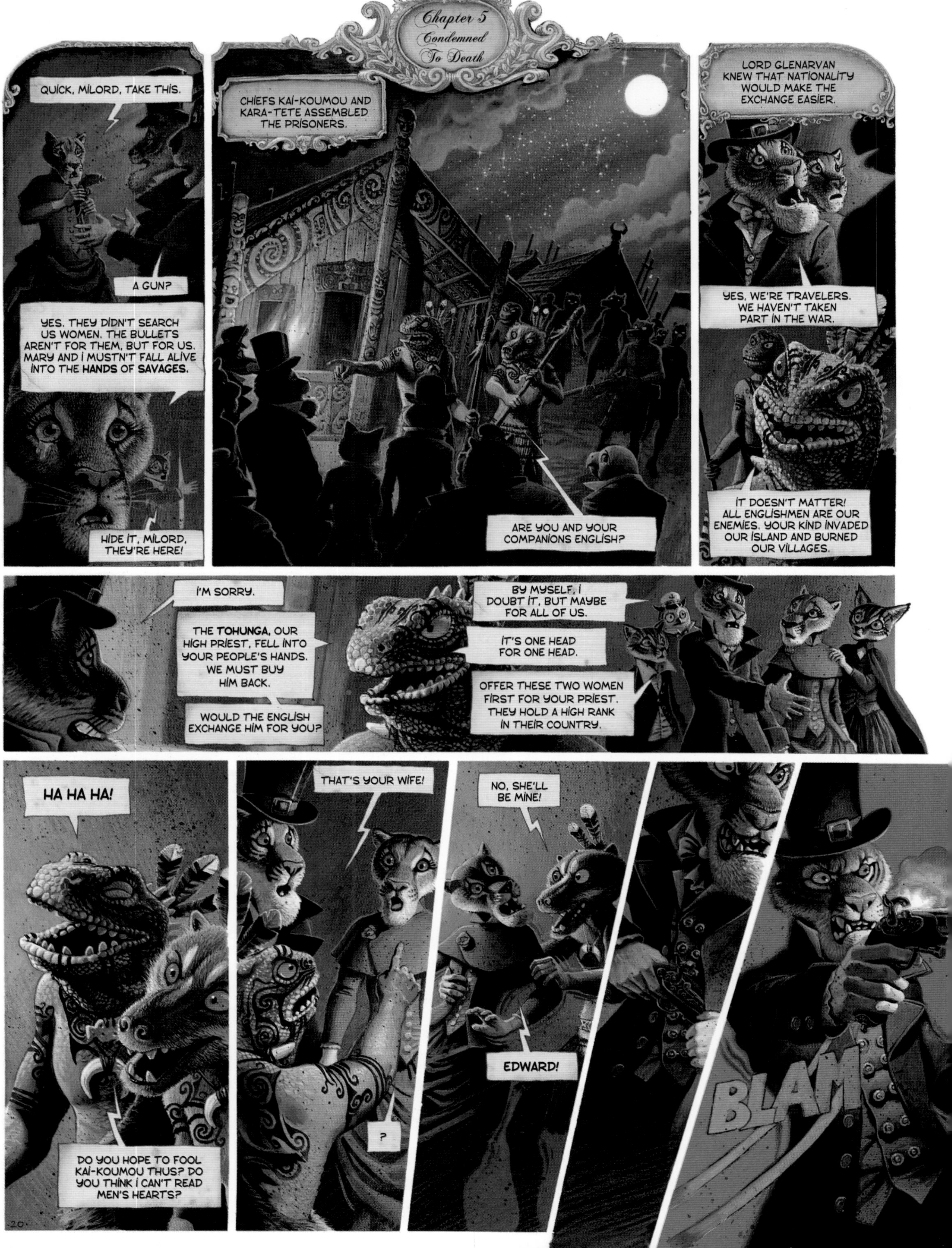
Chapter 5
Condemned To Death
QUICK, MILORD, TAKE THIS.
A GUN?
YES. THEY DIDN'T SEARCH US WOMEN. THE BULLETS AREN'T FOR THEM, BUT FOR US. MARY AND I MUSTN'T FALL ALIVE INTO THE HANDS OF SAVAGES.
HIDE IT, MILORD, THEY'RE HERE!
CHIEFS KAI-KOUMOU AND KARA-TETE ASSEMBLED THE PRISONERS.
ARE YOU AND YOUR COMPANIONS ENGLISH?
LORD GLENARVAN KNEW THAT NATIONALITY WOULD MAKE THE EXCHANGE EASIER.
YES, WE'RE TRAVELERS. WE HAVEN'T TAKEN PART IN THE WAR.
IT DOESN'T MATTER! ALL ENGLISHMEN ARE OUR ENEMIES. YOUR KIND INVADED OUR ISLAND AND BURNED OUR VILLAGES.
I'M SORRY.
THE TOHUNGA, OUR HIGH PRIEST, FELL INTO YOUR PEOPLE'S HANDS. WE MUST BUY HIM BACK.
WOULD THE ENGLISH EXCHANGE HIM FOR YOU?
BY MYSELF, I DOUBT IT, BUT MAYBE FOR ALL OF US.
IT'S ONE HEAD FOR ONE HEAD.
OFFER THESE TWO WOMEN FIRST FOR YOUR PRIEST. THEY HOLD A HIGH RANK IN THEIR COUNTRY.
HA HA HA!
DO YOU HOPE TO FOOL KAI-KOUMOU THUS? DO YOU THINK I CAN'T READ MEN'S HEARTS?
THAT'S YOUR WIFE!
?
NO, SHE'LL BE MINE!
EDWARD!
BLAM

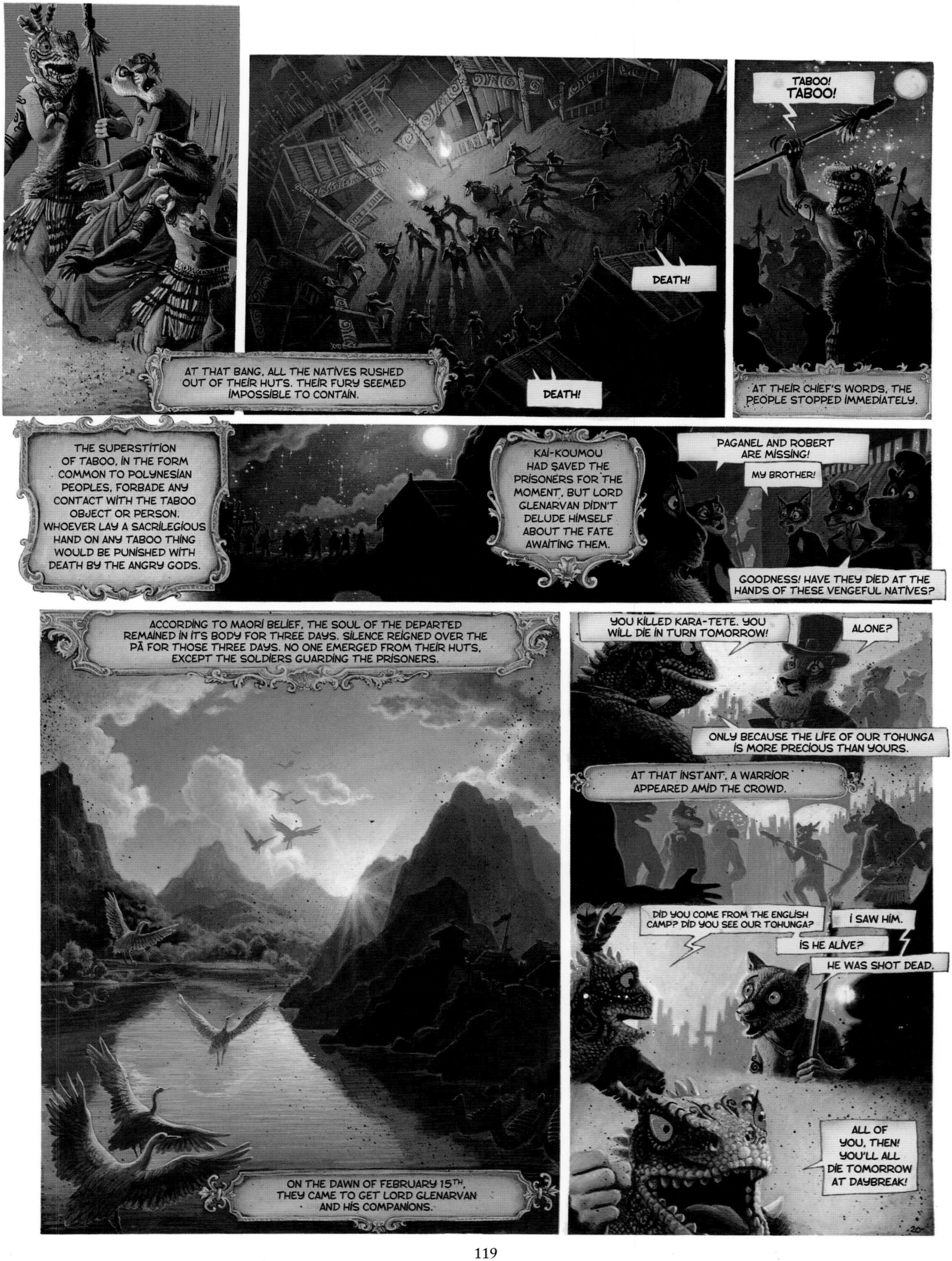

AT THAT BANG, ALL THE NATIVES RUSHED OUT OF THEIR HUTS. THEIR FURY SEEMED IMPOSSIBLE TO CONTAIN.
DEATH!
DEATH!
TABOO! TABOO!
AT THEIR CHIEF'S WORDS, THE PEOPLE STOPPED IMMEDIATELY.
THE SUPERSTITION OF TABOO, IN THE FORM COMMON TO POLYNESIAN PEOPLES, FORBADE ANY CONTACT WITH THE TABOO OBJECT OR PERSON. WHOEVER LAY A SACRILEGIOUS HAND ON ANY TABOO THING WOULD BE PUNISHED WITH DEATH BY THE ANGRY GODS.
KAI-KOUMOU HAD SAVED THE PRISONERS FOR THE MOMENT, BUT LORD GLENARVAN DIDN'T DELUDE HIMSELF ABOUT THE FATE AWAITING THEM.
PAGANEL AND ROBERT ARE MISSING!
MY BROTHER!
GOODNESS! HAVE THEY DIED AT THE HANDS OF THESE VENGEFUL NATIVES?
ACCORDING TO MAORI BELIEF, THE SOUL OF THE DEPARTED REMAINED IN ITS BODY FOR THREE DAYS. SILENCE REIGNED OVER THE PĀ FOR THOSE THREE DAYS. NO ONE EMERGED FROM THEIR HUTS, EXCEPT THE SOLDIERS GUARDING THE PRISONERS.
ON THE DAWN OF FEBRUARY 15TH, THEY CAME TO GET LORD GLENARVAN AND HIS COMPANIONS.
YOU KILLED KARA-TETE. YOU WILL DIE IN TURN TOMORROW!
ALONE?
ONLY BECAUSE THE LIFE OF OUR TOHUNGA IS MORE PRECIOUS THAN YOURS.
AT THAT INSTANT, A WARRIOR APPEARED AMID THE CROWD.
DID YOU COME FROM THE ENGLISH CAMP? DID YOU SEE OUR TOHUNGA?
I SAW HIM.
IS HE ALIVE?
HE WAS SHOT DEAD.
ALL OF YOU, THEN! YOU'LL ALL DIE TOMORROW AT DAYBREAK!
20

THE PRISONERS, WHO HAD ABANDONED ALL HOPE, ATTENDED A SPECTACLE WHOSE HORROR ONLY INCREASED THEIR ANGUISH.

THE CHIEF'S FUNERAL CEREMONIES BEGAN BEFORE THEIR TERRIFIED EYES WITH THE DEATH OF HIS SPOUSE AND SERVANTS SO THEY COULD ACCOMPANY HIM INTO THE OTHER WORLD.

THE EUROPEANS AVERTED THEIR GAZE, FOR THE SUBSEQUENT SCENE OF CANNIBALISM WAS UNBEARABLE TO THEM. THE NATIVES, YOUNG AND OLD ALIKE, SET TO THE RITUAL CONSUMING OF THE SERVANTS' BODIES. THE COMPANIONS FINALLY UNDERSTOOD THE ORDEAL AWAITING THEM.

FINALLY, THE CHIEF'S REMAINS AND THOSE OF HIS SPOUSE WERE BORNE IN A LONG PROCESSION TO HIS GRAVE, BUILT UPON THE SUMMIT OF MOUNT MAUNGANAMU, WHICH LOOMED OVER THE PÃ.

JOHN, THE PROMISE LORD GLENARVAN MADE NOT TO LET HIS WIFE FALL ALIVE INTO THE HANDS OF THOSE SAVAGES--A HUSBAND'S PROMISE TO HIS WIFE . . . WILL YOU MAKE ME THAT PROMISE, AS A FIANCÉ TO HIS FIANCÉE?

FROZEN WITH FEAR, LORD GLENARVAN AND HIS FRIENDS RETURNED TO THE HUT. DESPITE THEIR DESPONDENCY, THEY ATE THEIR LAST MEAL TOGETHER. LADY HELENA RECITED A PRAYER. THEY WOULD HAVE TO PREPARE THEMSELVES TO DIE.

HAVEN'T I LONG BEEN YOUR FIANCÉE IN YOUR HEART?

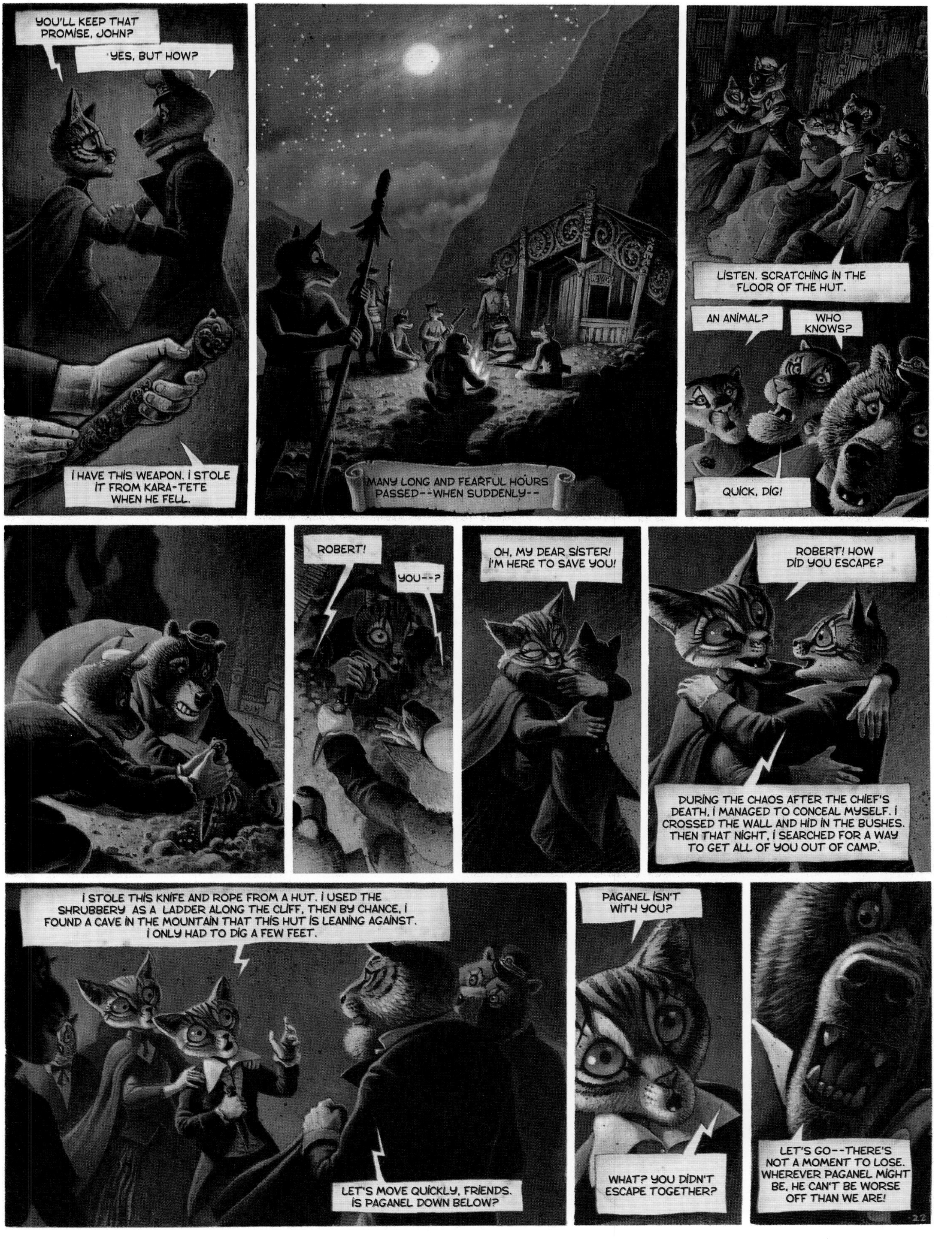
YOU'LL KEEP THAT PROMISE, JOHN?
YES, BUT HOW?
I HAVE THIS WEAPON. I STOLE IT FROM KARA-TETE WHEN HE FELL.
MANY LONG AND FEARFUL HOURS PASSED--WHEN SUDDENLY--
LISTEN. SCRATCHING IN THE FLOOR OF THE HUT.
AN ANIMAL?
WHO KNOWS?
QUICK, DIG!
ROBERT!
YOU--?
OH, MY DEAR SISTER! I'M HERE TO SAVE YOU!
ROBERT! HOW DID YOU ESCAPE?
DURING THE CHAOS AFTER THE CHIEF'S DEATH, I MANAGED TO CONCEAL MYSELF. I CROSSED THE WALL AND HID IN THE BUSHES. THEN THAT NIGHT, I SEARCHED FOR A WAY TO GET ALL OF YOU OUT OF CAMP.
I STOLE THIS KNIFE AND ROPE FROM A HUT. I USED THE SHRUBBERY AS A LADDER ALONG THE CLIFF, THEN BY CHANCE, I FOUND A CAVE IN THE MOUNTAIN THAT THIS HUT IS LEANING AGAINST. I ONLY HAD TO DIG A FEW FEET.
LET'S MOVE QUICKLY, FRIENDS. IS PAGANEL DOWN BELOW?
PAGANEL ISN'T WITH YOU?
WHAT? YOU DIDN'T ESCAPE TOGETHER?
LET'S GO--THERE'S NOT A MOMENT TO LOSE. WHEREVER PAGANEL MIGHT BE, HE CAN'T BE WORSE OFF THAN WE ARE!

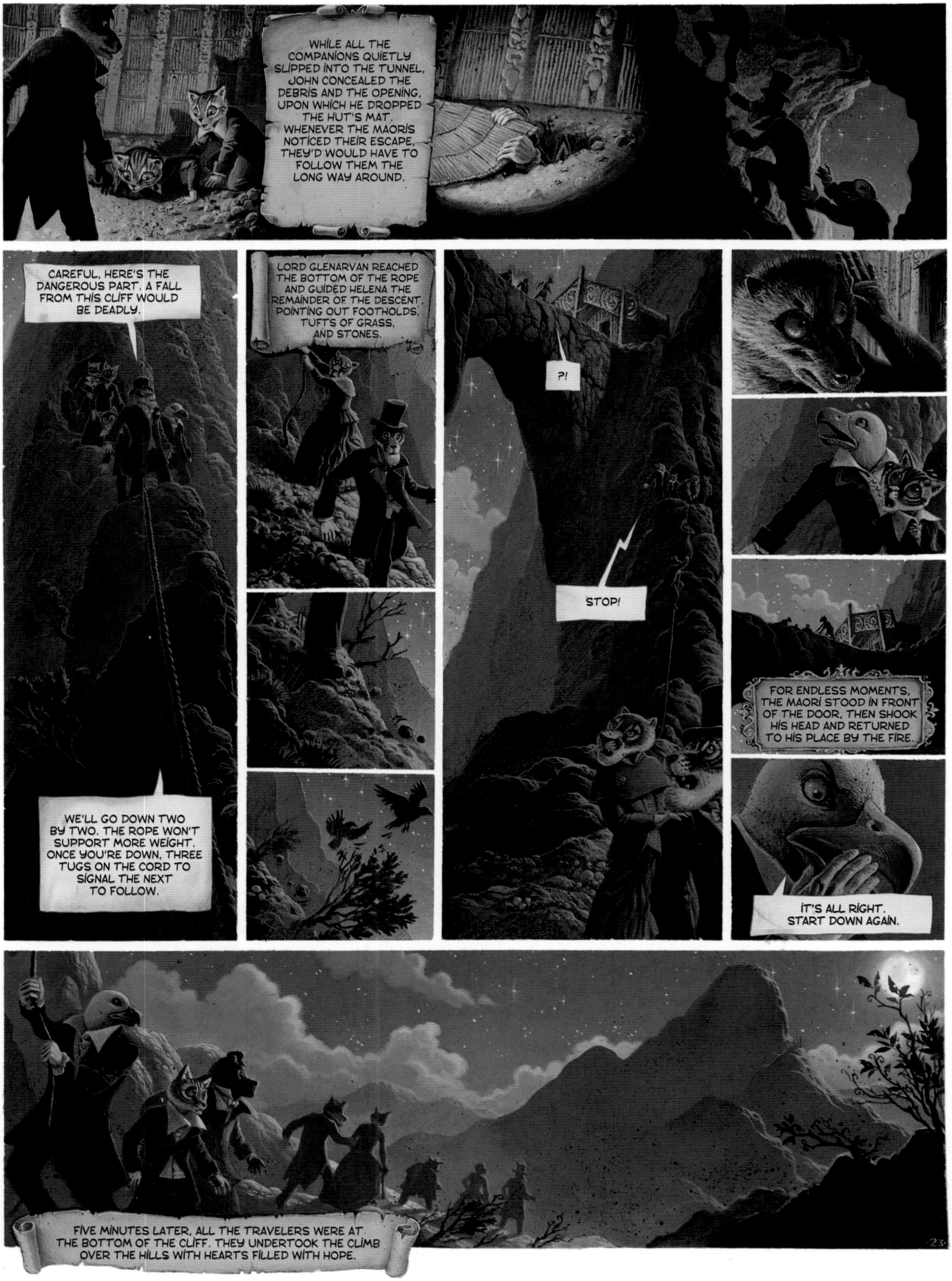
WHILE ALL THE COMPANIONS QUIETLY SLIPPED INTO THE TUNNEL, JOHN CONCEALED THE DEBRIS AND THE OPENING, UPON WHICH HE DROPPED THE HUT'S MAT. WHENEVER THE MAORIS NOTICED THEIR ESCAPE, THEY'D WOULD HAVE TO FOLLOW THEM THE LONG WAY AROUND.
CAREFUL, HERE'S THE DANGEROUS PART. A FALL FROM THIS CLIFF WOULD BE DEADLY.
WE'LL GO DOWN TWO BY TWO. THE ROPE WON'T SUPPORT MORE WEIGHT. ONCE YOU'RE DOWN, THREE TUGS ON THE CORD TO SIGNAL THE NEXT TO FOLLOW.
LORD GLENARVAN REACHED THE BOTTOM OF THE ROPE AND GUIDED HELENA THE REMAINDER OF THE DESCENT, POINTING OUT FOOTHOLDS, TUFTS OF GRASS, AND STONES.
?!
STOP!
FOR ENDLESS MOMENTS, THE MAORI STOOD IN FRONT OF THE DOOR, THEN SHOOK HIS HEAD AND RETURNED TO HIS PLACE BY THE FIRE.
IT'S ALL RIGHT. START DOWN AGAIN.
FIVE MINUTES LATER, ALL THE TRAVELERS WERE AT THE BOTTOM OF THE CLIFF. THEY UNDERTOOK THE CLIMB OVER THE HILLS WITH HEARTS FILLED WITH HOPE.
·23·

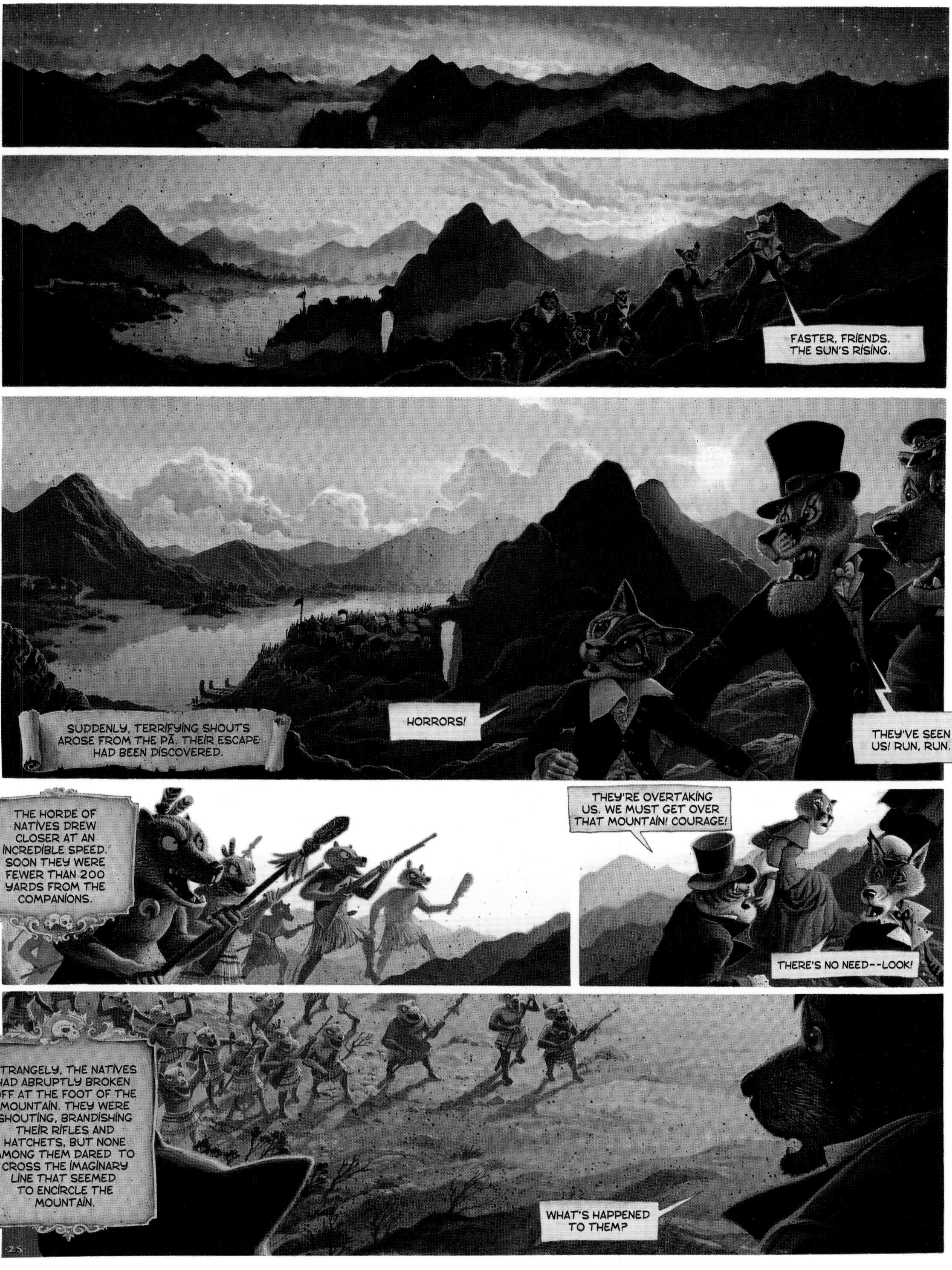
FASTER, FRIENDS. THE SUN'S RISING.
SUDDENLY, TERRIFYING SHOUTS AROSE FROM THE PĀ. THEIR ESCAPE HAD BEEN DISCOVERED.
HORRORS!
THEY'VE SEEN US! RUN, RUN.
THE HORDE OF NATIVES DREW CLOSER AT AN INCREDIBLE SPEED. SOON THEY WERE FEWER THAN 200 YARDS FROM THE COMPANIONS.
THEY'RE OVERTAKING US. WE MUST GET OVER THAT MOUNTAIN! COURAGE!
THERE'S NO NEED--LOOK!
STRANGELY, THE NATIVES HAD ABRUPTLY BROKEN OFF AT THE FOOT OF THE MOUNTAIN. THEY WERE SHOUTING, BRANDISHING THEIR RIFLES AND HATCHETS, BUT NONE AMONG THEM DARED TO CROSS THE IMAGINARY LINE THAT SEEMED TO ENCIRCLE THE MOUNTAIN.
WHAT'S HAPPENED TO THEM?
-25-

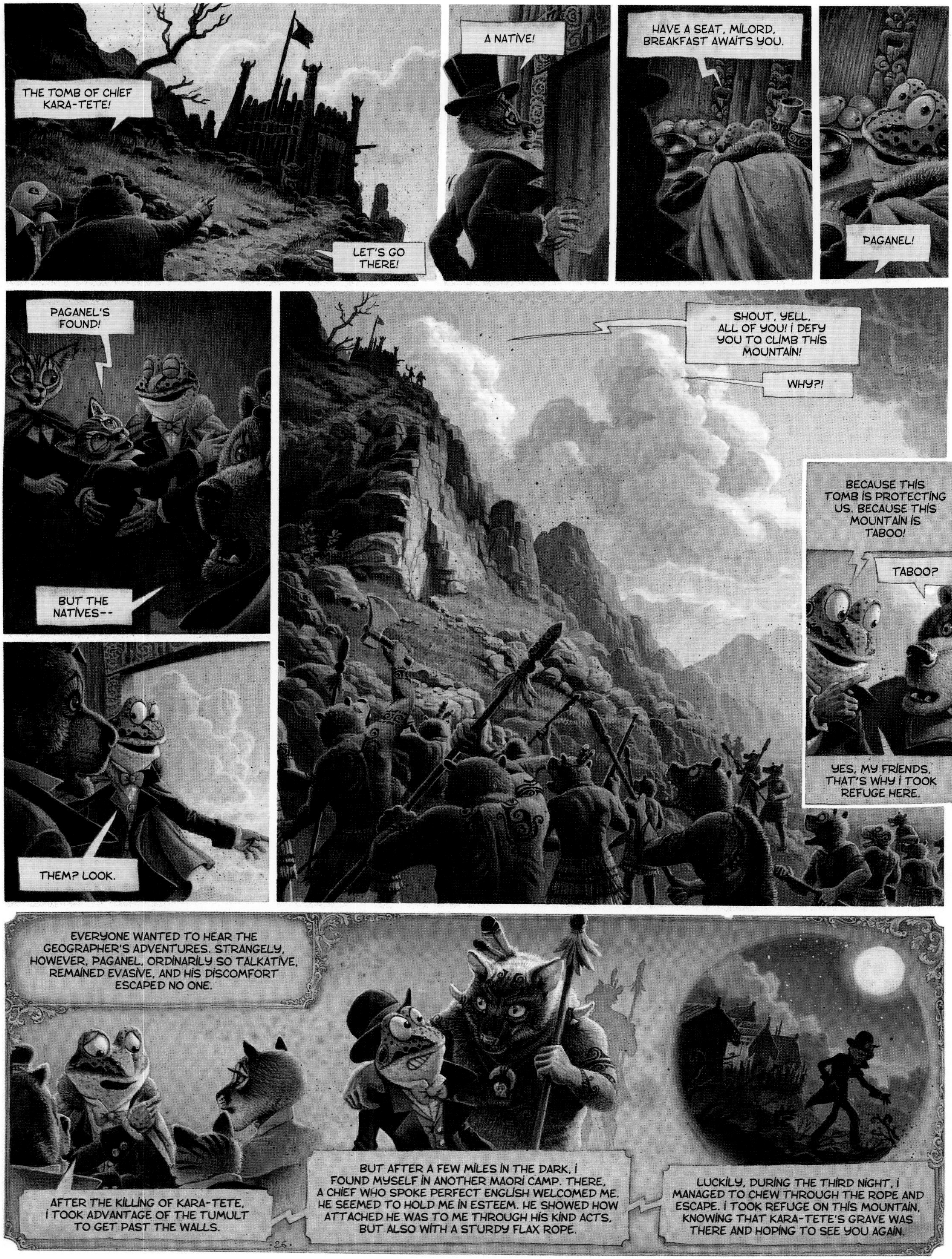
THE TOMB OF CHIEF KARA-TETE!
LET'S GO THERE!
A NATIVE!
HAVE A SEAT, MILORD, BREAKFAST AWAITS YOU.
PAGANEL!
PAGANEL'S FOUND!
BUT THE NATIVES--
THEM? LOOK.
SHOUT, YELL, ALL OF YOU! I DEFY YOU TO CLIMB THIS MOUNTAIN!
WHY?!
BECAUSE THIS TOMB IS PROTECTING US. BECAUSE THIS MOUNTAIN IS TABOO!
TABOO?
YES, MY FRIENDS, THAT'S WHY I TOOK REFUGE HERE.
EVERYONE WANTED TO HEAR THE GEOGRAPHER'S ADVENTURES. STRANGELY, HOWEVER, PAGANEL, ORDINARILY SO TALKATIVE, REMAINED EVASIVE, AND HIS DISCOMFORT ESCAPED NO ONE.
AFTER THE KILLING OF KARA-TETE, I TOOK ADVANTAGE OF THE TUMULT TO GET PAST THE WALLS.
BUT AFTER A FEW MILES IN THE DARK, I FOUND MYSELF IN ANOTHER MAORI CAMP. THERE, A CHIEF WHO SPOKE PERFECT ENGLISH WELCOMED ME. HE SEEMED TO HOLD ME IN ESTEEM. HE SHOWED HOW ATTACHED HE WAS TO ME THROUGH HIS KIND ACTS, BUT ALSO WITH A STURDY FLAX ROPE.
LUCKILY, DURING THE THIRD NIGHT, I MANAGED TO CHEW THROUGH THE ROPE AND ESCAPE. I TOOK REFUGE ON THIS MOUNTAIN, KNOWING THAT KARA-TETE'S GRAVE WAS THERE AND HOPING TO SEE YOU AGAIN.
·26·

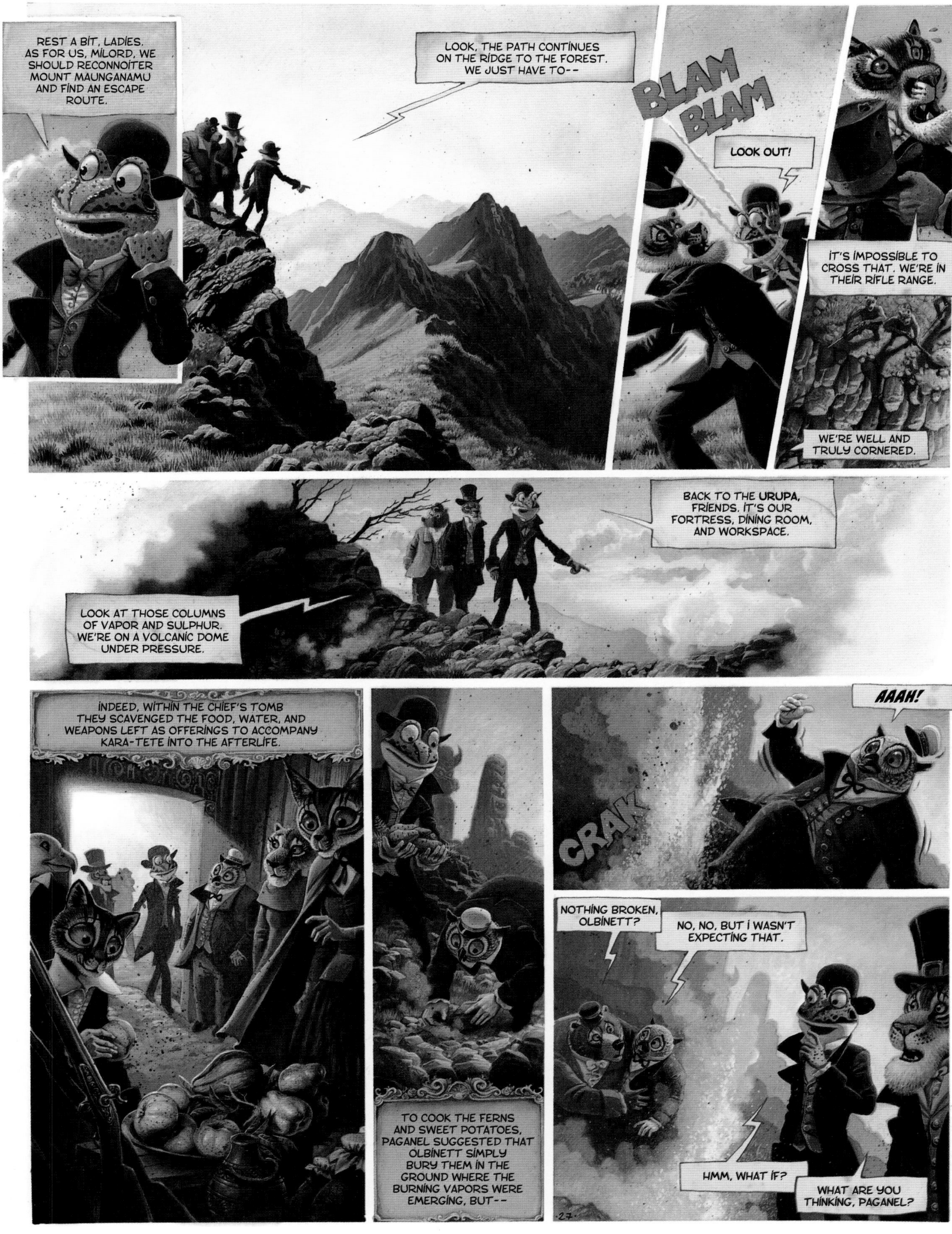
REST A BIT, LADIES. AS FOR US, MILORD, WE SHOULD RECONNOITER MOUNT MAUNGANAMU AND FIND AN ESCAPE ROUTE.
LOOK, THE PATH CONTINUES ON THE RIDGE TO THE FOREST. WE JUST HAVE TO--
BLAM
BLAM
LOOK OUT!
IT'S IMPOSSIBLE TO CROSS THAT. WE'RE IN THEIR RIFLE RANGE.
WE'RE WELL AND TRULY CORNERED.
BACK TO THE URUPA, FRIENDS. IT'S OUR FORTRESS, DINING ROOM, AND WORKSPACE.
LOOK AT THOSE COLUMNS OF VAPOR AND SULPHUR. WE'RE ON A VOLCANIC DOME UNDER PRESSURE.
INDEED, WITHIN THE CHIEF'S TOMB THEY SCAVENGED THE FOOD, WATER, AND WEAPONS LEFT AS OFFERINGS TO ACCOMPANY KARA-TETE INTO THE AFTERLIFE.
TO COOK THE FERNS AND SWEET POTATOES, PAGANEL SUGGESTED THAT OLBINETT SIMPLY BURY THEM IN THE GROUND WHERE THE BURNING VAPORS WERE EMERGING, BUT--
AAAH!
CRAK
NOTHING BROKEN, OLBINETT?
NO, NO, BUT I WASN'T EXPECTING THAT.
HMM, WHAT IF?
WHAT ARE YOU THINKING, PAGANEL?

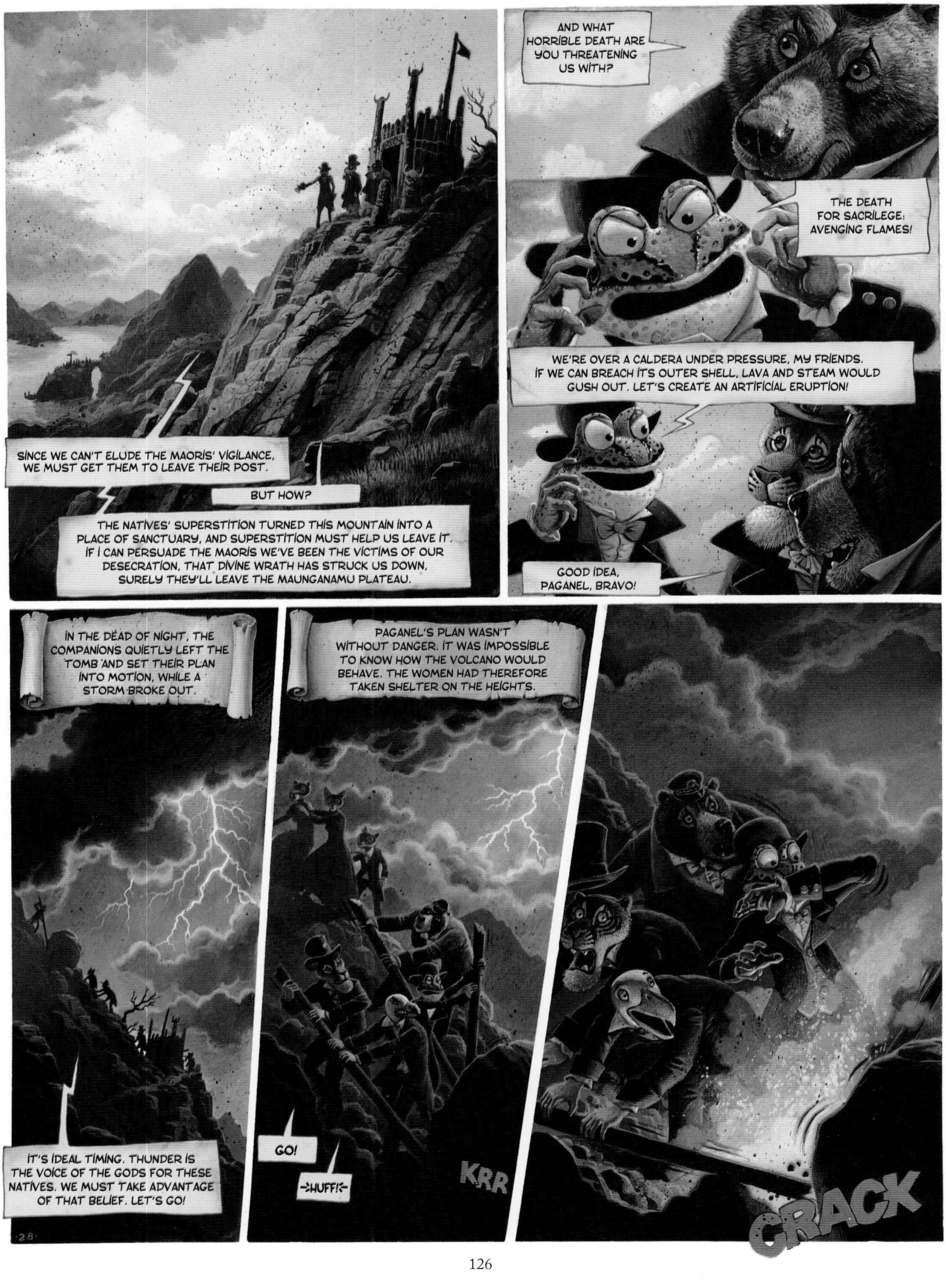

SINCE WE CAN'T ELUDE THE MAORIS' VIGILANCE, WE MUST GET THEM TO LEAVE THEIR POST.
BUT HOW?
THE NATIVES' SUPERSTITION TURNED THIS MOUNTAIN INTO A PLACE OF SANCTUARY, AND SUPERSTITION MUST HELP US LEAVE IT. IF I CAN PERSUADE THE MAORIS WE'VE BEEN THE VICTIMS OF OUR DESECRATION, THAT DIVINE WRATH HAS STRUCK US DOWN, SURELY THEY'LL LEAVE THE MAUNGANAMU PLATEAU.
AND WHAT HORRIBLE DEATH ARE YOU THREATENING US WITH?
THE DEATH FOR SACRILEGE: AVENGING FLAMES!
WE'RE OVER A CALDERA UNDER PRESSURE, MY FRIENDS. IF WE CAN BREACH ITS OUTER SHELL, LAVA AND STEAM WOULD GUSH OUT. LET'S CREATE AN ARTIFICIAL ERUPTION!
GOOD IDEA, PAGANEL, BRAVO!
IN THE DEAD OF NIGHT, THE COMPANIONS QUIETLY LEFT THE TOMB AND SET THEIR PLAN INTO MOTION, WHILE A STORM BROKE OUT.
IT'S IDEAL TIMING. THUNDER IS THE VOICE OF THE GODS FOR THESE NATIVES. WE MUST TAKE ADVANTAGE OF THAT BELIEF. LET'S GO!
·28·
PAGANEL'S PLAN WASN'T WITHOUT DANGER. IT WAS IMPOSSIBLE TO KNOW HOW THE VOLCANO WOULD BEHAVE. THE WOMEN HAD THEREFORE TAKEN SHELTER ON THE HEIGHTS.
GO!
-HUFF!-
KRR
CRACK

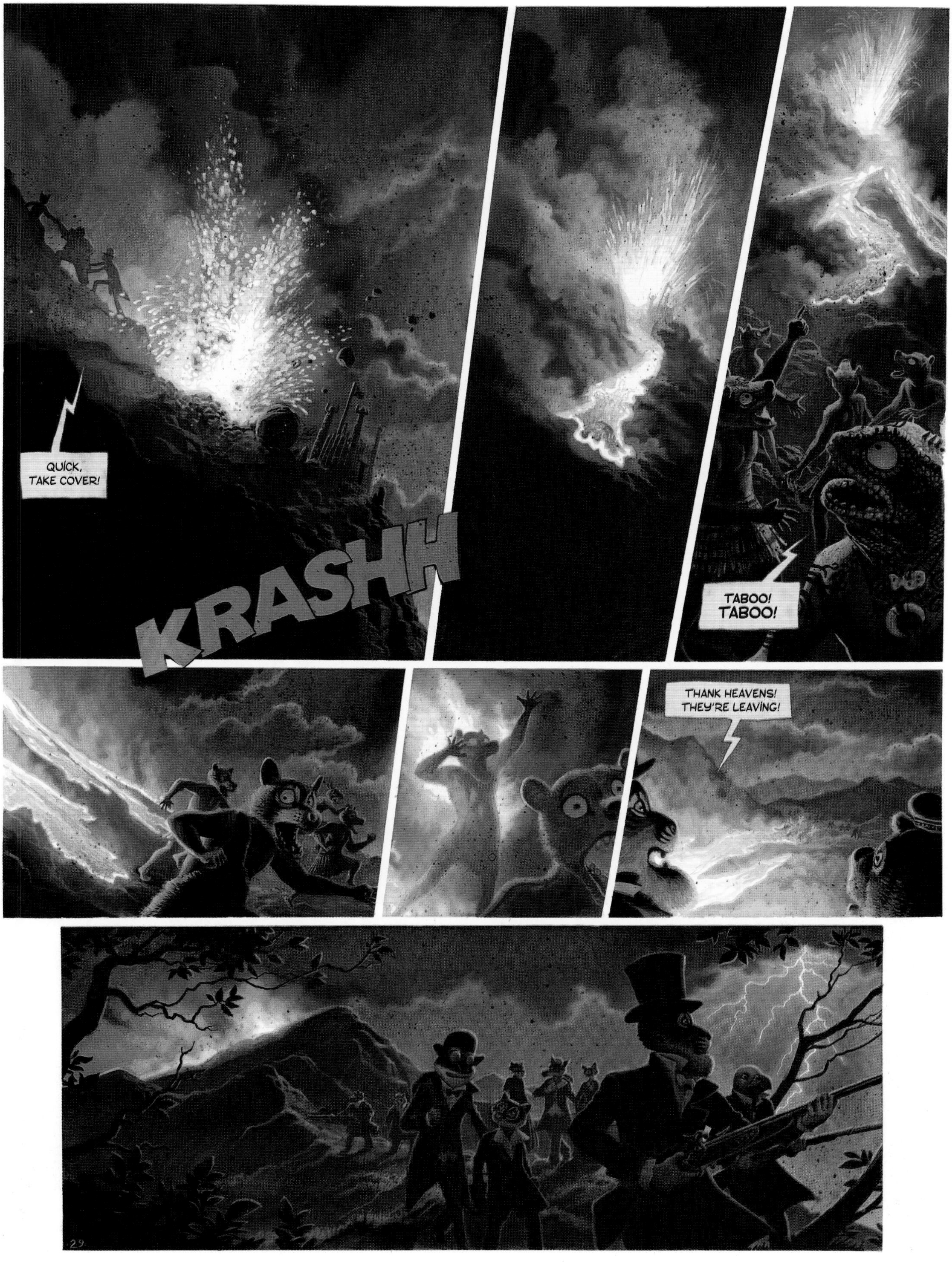
QUICK, TAKE COVER!
KRASHH
TABOO! TABOO!
THANK HEAVENS! THEY'RE LEAVING!

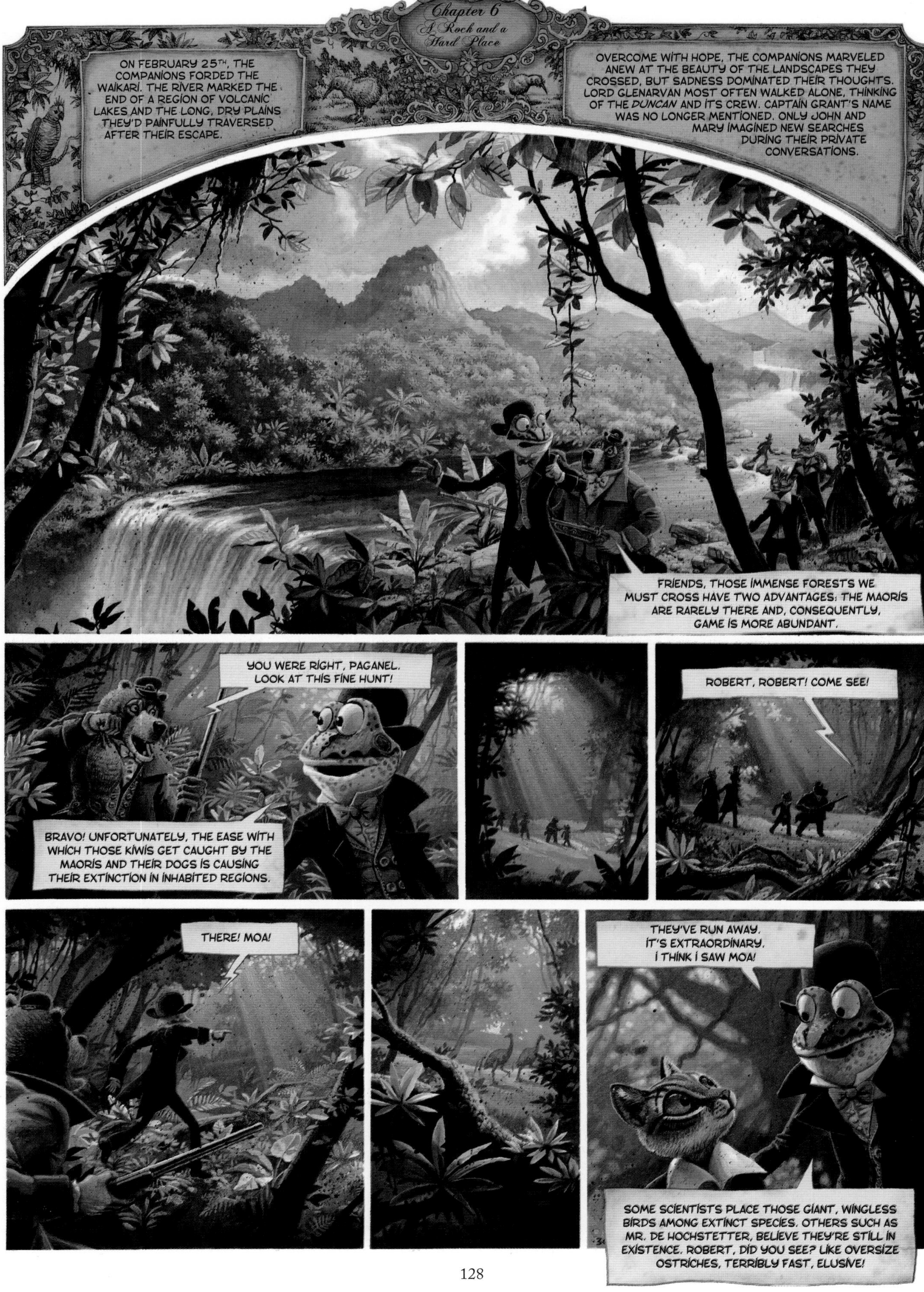
Chapter 6
A Rock and a Hard Place
ON FEBRUARY 25TH, THE COMPANIONS FORDED THE WAIKARI. THE RIVER MARKED THE END OF A REGION OF VOLCANIC LAKES AND THE LONG, DRY PLAINS THEY'D PAINFULLY TRAVERSED AFTER THEIR ESCAPE.
OVERCOME WITH HOPE, THE COMPANIONS MARVELED ANEW AT THE BEAUTY OF THE LANDSCAPES THEY CROSSED, BUT SADNESS DOMINATED THEIR THOUGHTS. LORD GLENARVAN MOST OFTEN WALKED ALONE, THINKING OF THE DUNCAN AND IT'S CREW. CAPTAIN GRANT'S NAME WAS NO LONGER MENTIONED. ONLY JOHN AND MARY IMAGINED NEW SEARCHES DURING THEIR PRIVATE CONVERSATIONS.
FRIENDS, THOSE IMMENSE FORESTS WE MUST CROSS HAVE TWO ADVANTAGES: THE MAORIS ARE RARELY THERE AND, CONSEQUENTLY, GAME IS MORE ABUNDANT.
YOU WERE RIGHT, PAGANEL. LOOK AT THIS FINE HUNT!
BRAVO! UNFORTUNATELY, THE EASE WITH WHICH THOSE KIWIS GET CAUGHT BY THE MAORIS AND THEIR DOGS IS CAUSING THEIR EXTINCTION IN INHABITED REGIONS.
ROBERT, ROBERT! COME SEE!
THERE! MOA!
THEY'VE RUN AWAY. IT'S EXTRAORDINARY. I THINK I SAW MOA!
SOME SCIENTISTS PLACE THOSE GIANT, WINGLESS BIRDS AMONG EXTINCT SPECIES. OTHERS SUCH AS MR. DE HOCHSTETTER, BELIEVE THEY'RE STILL IN EXISTENCE. ROBERT, DID YOU SEE? LIKE OVERSIZE OSTRICHES, TERRIBLY FAST, ELUSIVE!

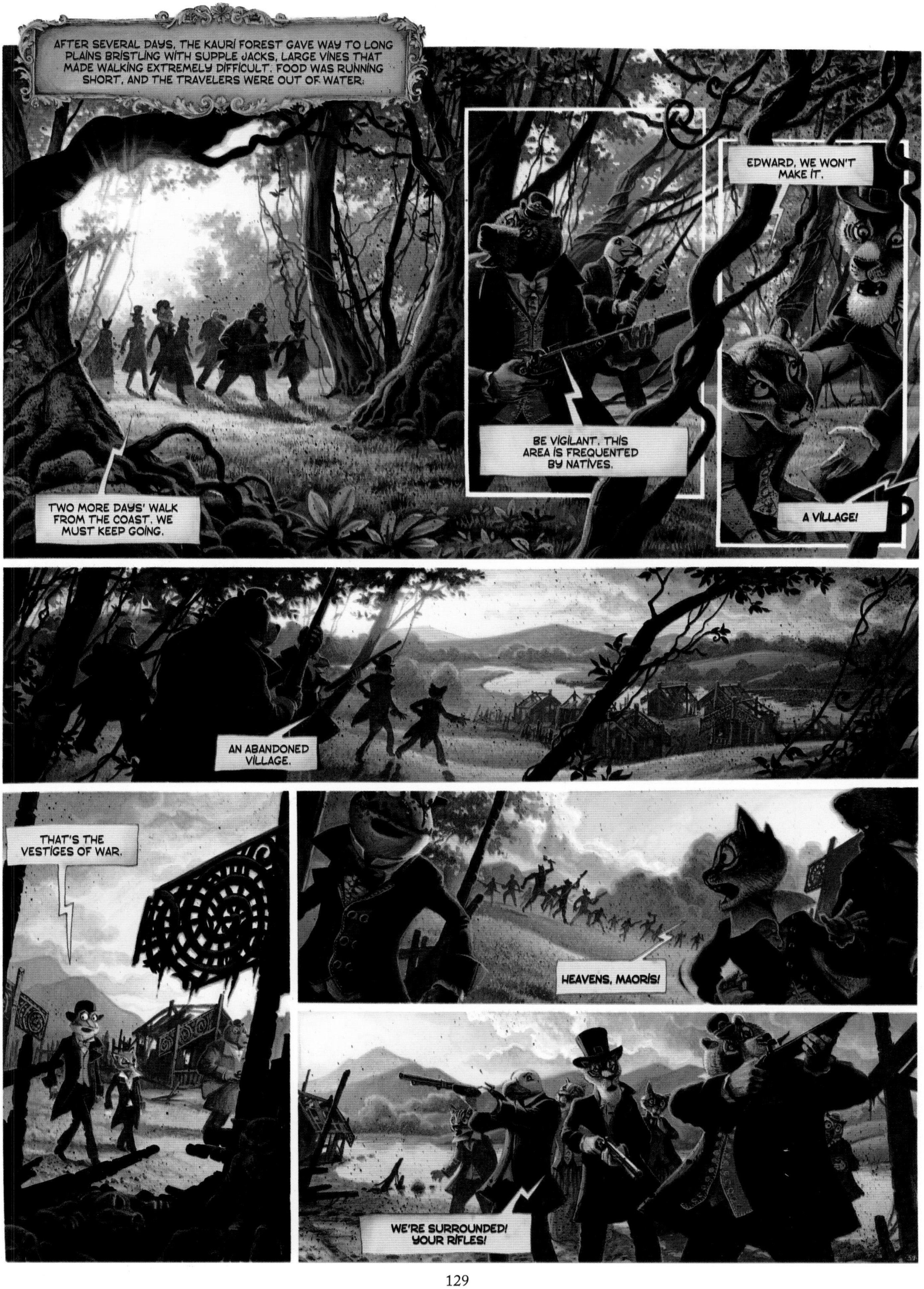
AFTER SEVERAL DAYS, THE KAURI FOREST GAVE WAY TO LONG PLAINS BRISTLING WITH SUPPLE JACKS, LARGE VINES THAT MADE WALKING EXTREMELY DIFFICULT. FOOD WAS RUNNING SHORT, AND THE TRAVELERS WERE OUT OF WATER.
TWO MORE DAYS' WALK FROM THE COAST. WE MUST KEEP GOING.
BE VIGILANT. THIS AREA IS FREQUENTED BY NATIVES.
EDWARD, WE WON'T MAKE IT.
A VILLAGE!
AN ABANDONED VILLAGE.
THAT'S THE VESTIGES OF WAR.
HEAVENS, MAORIS!
WE'RE SURROUNDED! YOUR RIFLES!

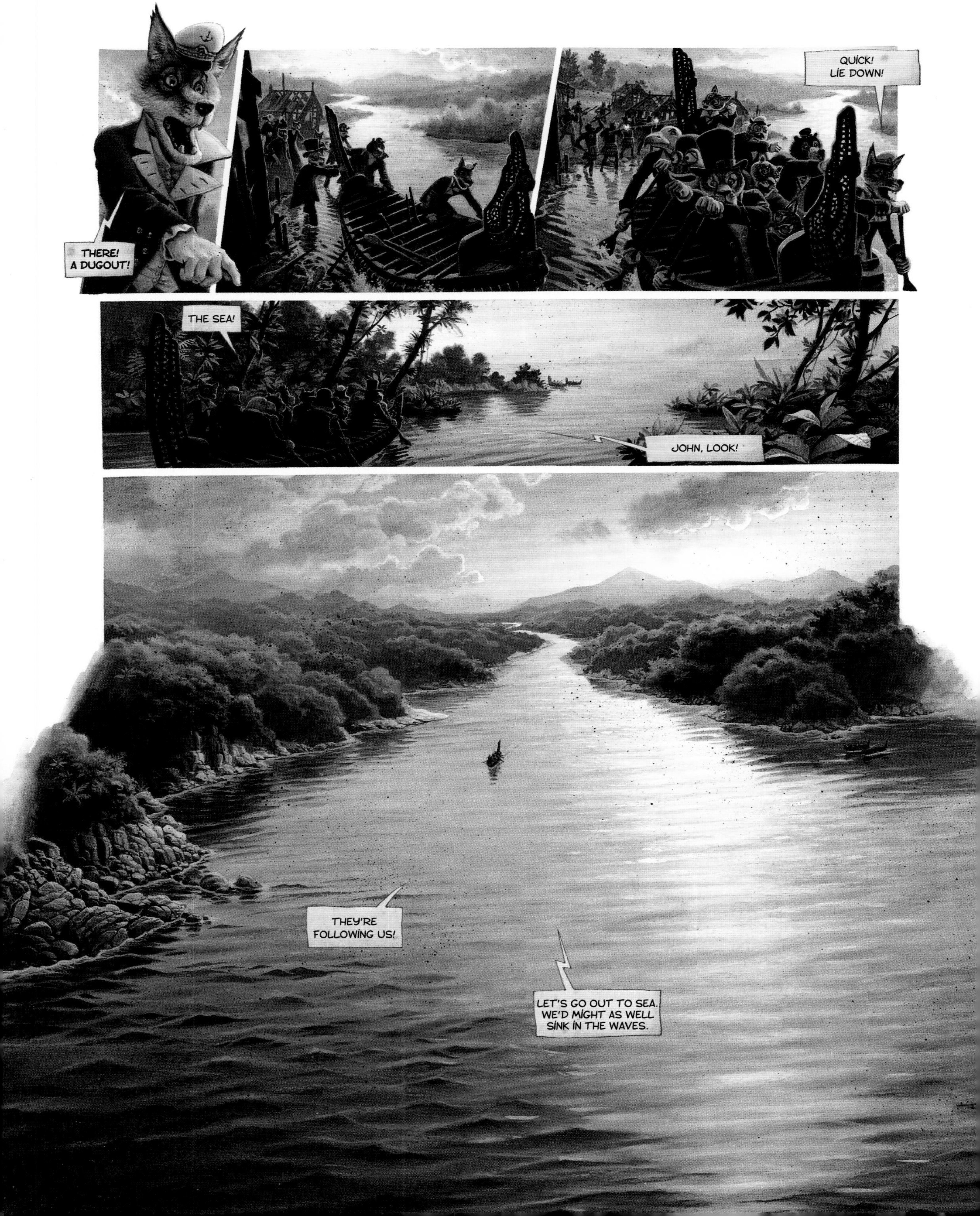
THERE!
A DUGOUT!
QUICK!
LIE DOWN!
THE SEA!
JOHN, LOOK!
THEY'RE
FOLLOWING US!
LET'S GO OUT TO SEA.
WE'D MIGHT AS WELL
SINK IN THE WAVES.

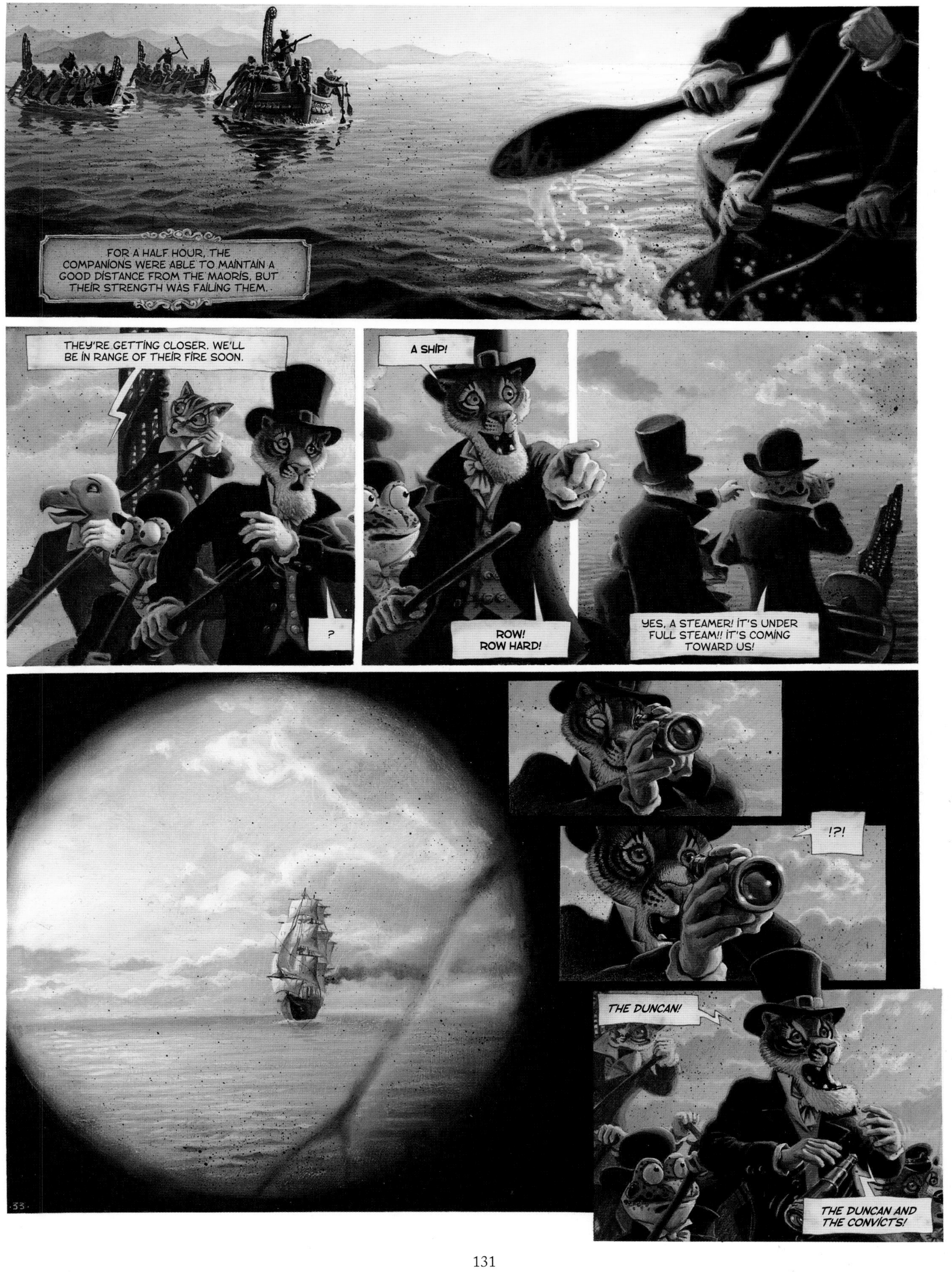

FOR A HALF HOUR, THE COMPANIONS WERE ABLE TO MAINTAIN A GOOD DISTANCE FROM THE MAORIS, BUT THEIR STRENGTH WAS FAILING THEM.
THEY'RE GETTING CLOSER. WE'LL BE IN RANGE OF THEIR FIRE SOON.
?
A SHIP!
ROW! ROW HARD!
YES, A STEAMER! IT'S UNDER FULL STEAM!! IT'S COMING TOWARD US!
!?!
THE DUNCAN!
THE DUNCAN AND THE CONVICTS!
33

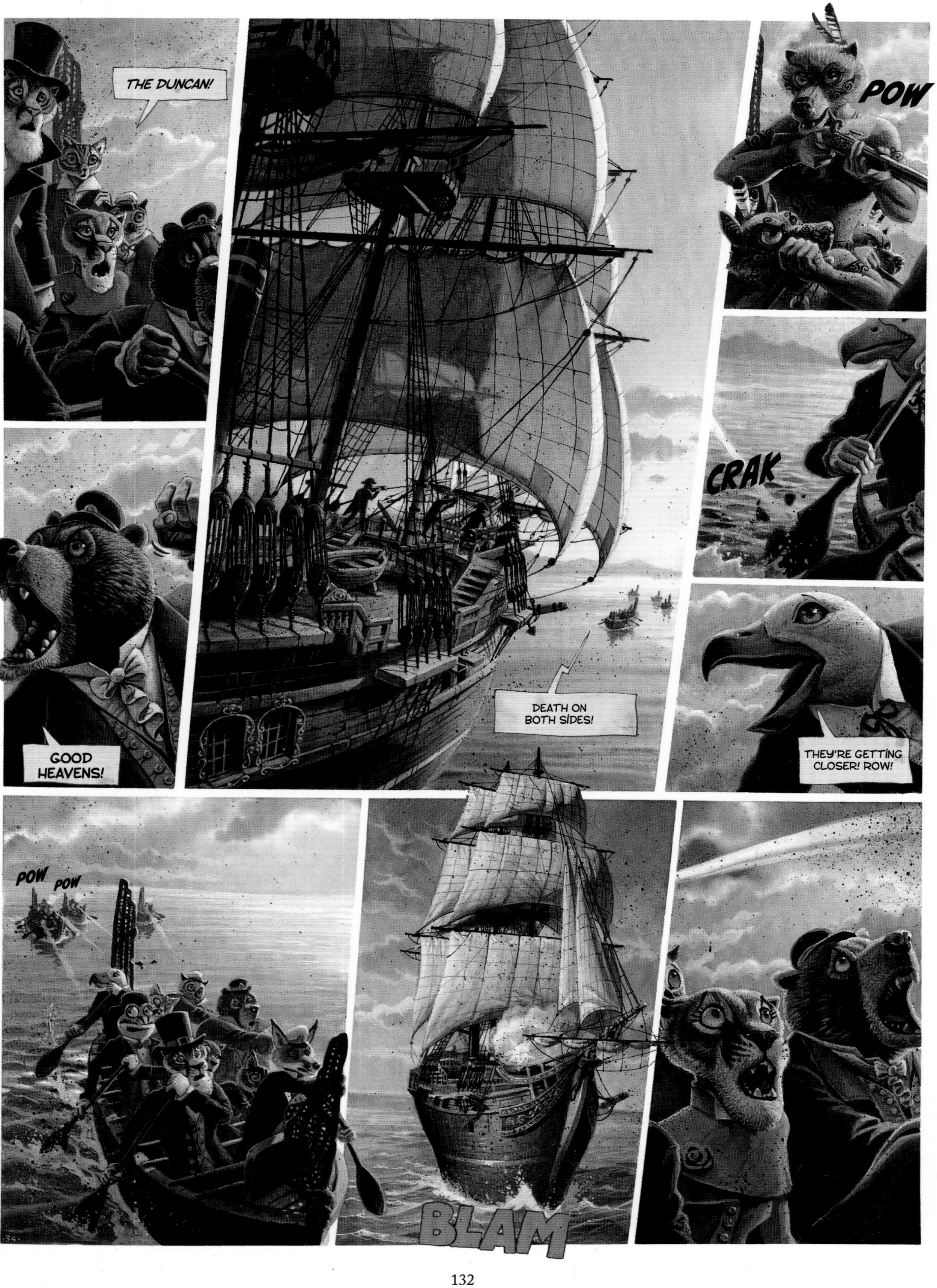
THE DUNCAN!
POW
GOOD HEAVENS!
DEATH ON BOTH SIDES!
CRAK
THEY'RE GETTING CLOSER! ROW!
POW
POW
BLAM

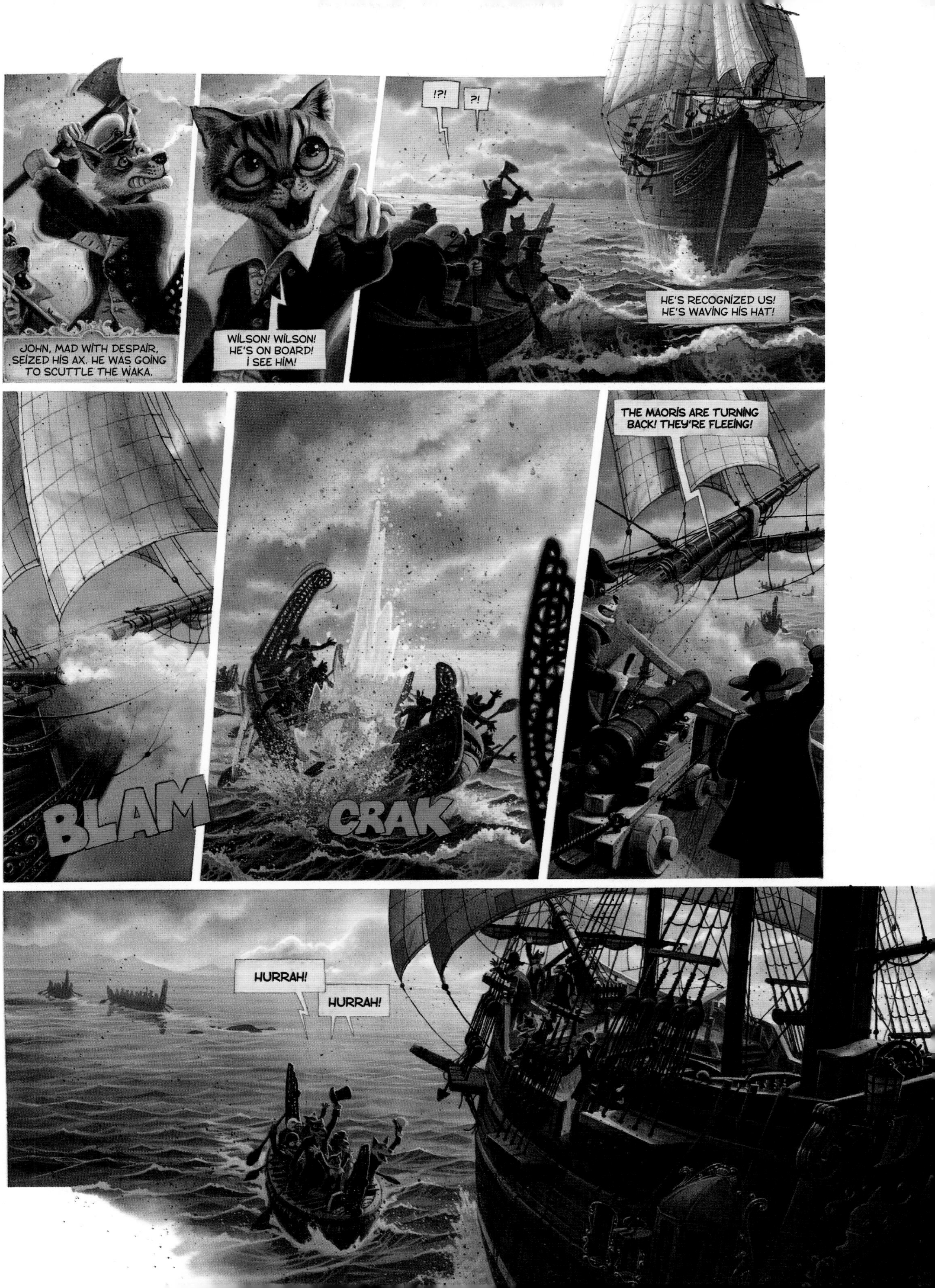
JOHN, MAD WITH DESPAIR, SEIZED HIS AX. HE WAS GOING TO SCUTTLE THE WAKA.
WILSON! WILSON! HE'S ON BOARD! I SEE HIM!
!?!
?!
HE'S RECOGNIZED US! HE'S WAVING HIS HAT!
BLAM
CRAK
THE MAORIS ARE TURNING BACK! THEY'RE FLEEING!
HURRAH!
HURRAH!

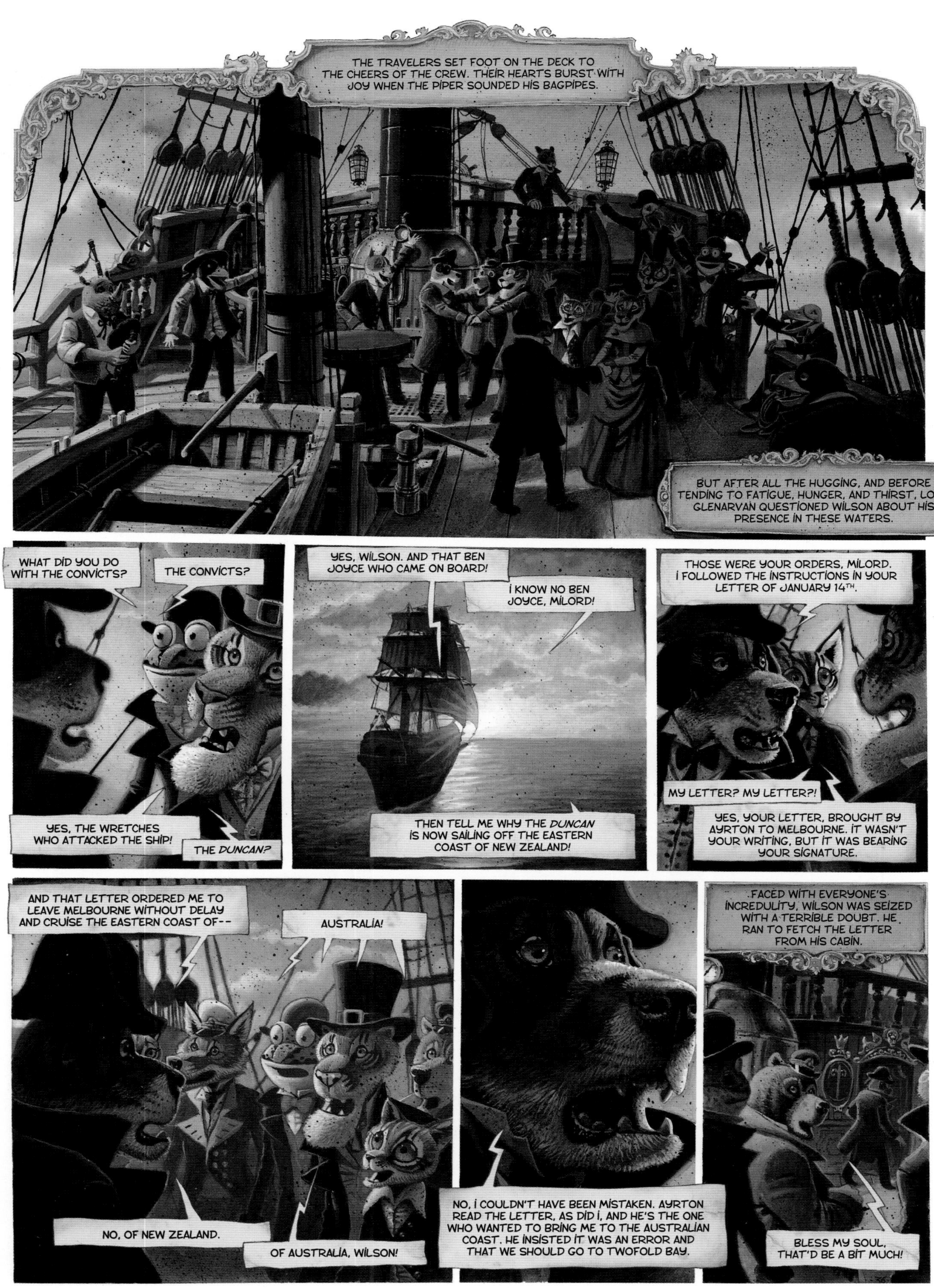
THE TRAVELERS SET FOOT ON THE DECK TO THE CHEERS OF THE CREW. THEIR HEARTS BURST WITH JOY WHEN THE PIPER SOUNDED HIS BAGPIPES.
BUT AFTER ALL THE HUGGING, AND BEFORE TENDING TO FATIGUE, HUNGER, AND THIRST, LORD GLENARVAN QUESTIONED WILSON ABOUT HIS PRESENCE IN THESE WATERS.
WHAT DID YOU DO WITH THE CONVICTS?
THE CONVICTS?
YES, THE WRETCHES WHO ATTACKED THE SHIP!
THE *DUNCAN*?
YES, WILSON. AND THAT BEN JOYCE WHO CAME ON BOARD!
I KNOW NO BEN JOYCE, MILORD!
THEN TELL ME WHY THE *DUNCAN* IS NOW SAILING OFF THE EASTERN COAST OF NEW ZEALAND!
THOSE WERE YOUR ORDERS, MILORD. I FOLLOWED THE INSTRUCTIONS IN YOUR LETTER OF JANUARY 14TH.
MY LETTER? MY LETTER?!
YES, YOUR LETTER, BROUGHT BY AYRTON TO MELBOURNE. IT WASN'T YOUR WRITING, BUT IT WAS BEARING YOUR SIGNATURE.
AND THAT LETTER ORDERED ME TO LEAVE MELBOURNE WITHOUT DELAY AND CRUISE THE EASTERN COAST OF--
AUSTRALIA!
NO, OF NEW ZEALAND.
OF AUSTRALIA, WILSON!
NO, I COULDN'T HAVE BEEN MISTAKEN. AYRTON READ THE LETTER, AS DID I, AND HE'S THE ONE WHO WANTED TO BRING ME TO THE AUSTRALIAN COAST. HE INSISTED IT WAS AN ERROR AND THAT WE SHOULD GO TO TWOFOLD BAY.
FACED WITH EVERYONE'S INCREDULITY, WILSON WAS SEIZED WITH A TERRIBLE DOUBT. HE RAN TO FETCH THE LETTER FROM HIS CABIN.
BLESS MY SOUL, THAT'D BE A BIT MUCH!

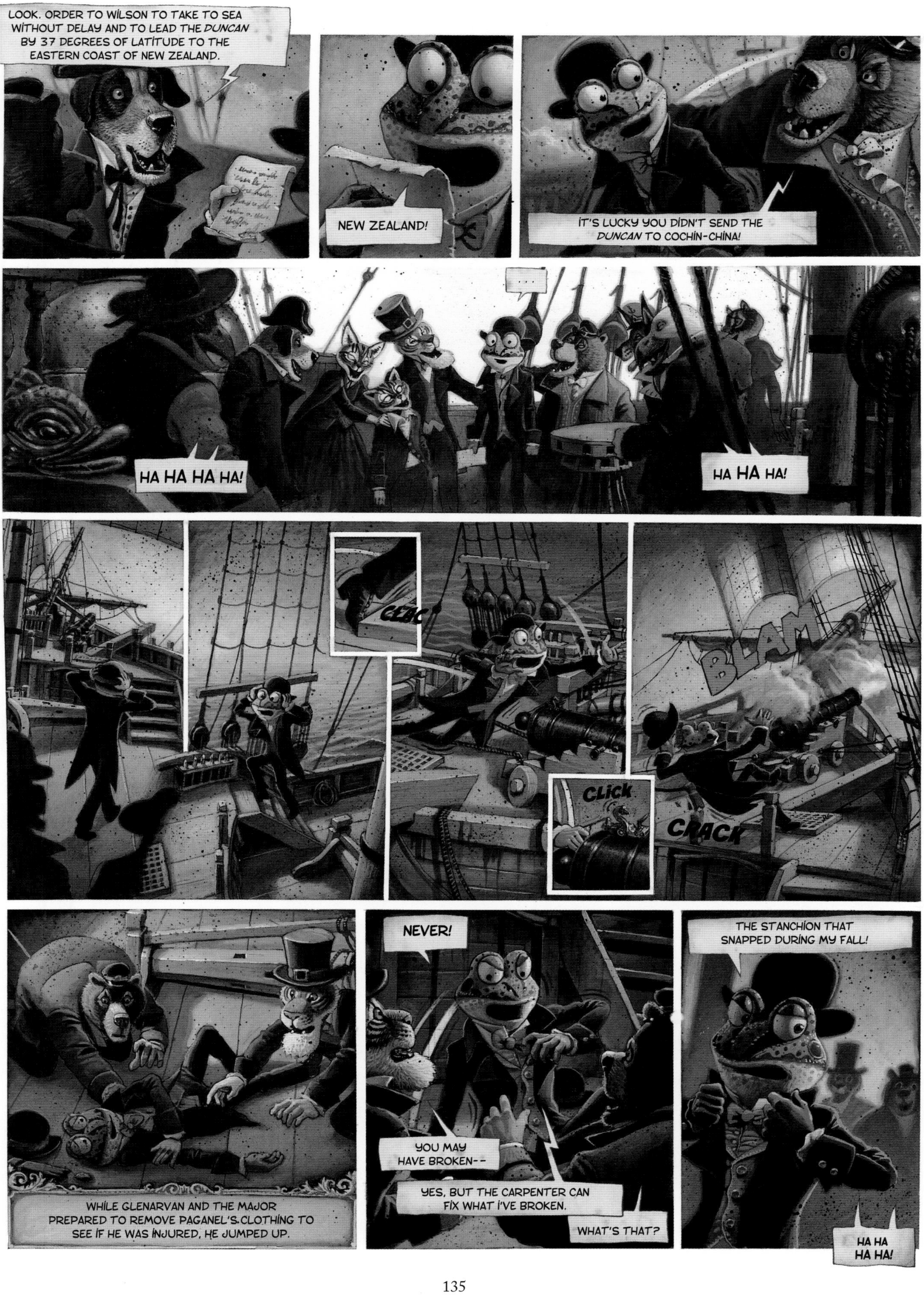

LOOK. ORDER TO WILSON TO TAKE TO SEA WITHOUT DELAY AND TO LEAD THE *DUNCAN* BY 37 DEGREES OF LATITUDE TO THE EASTERN COAST OF NEW ZEALAND.
NEW ZEALAND!
IT'S LUCKY YOU DIDN'T SEND THE *DUNCAN* TO COCHIN-CHINA!
...
HA HA HA HA!
HA HA HA!
CLAC
BLAM
CLICK
CRACK
WHILE GLENARVAN AND THE MAJOR PREPARED TO REMOVE PAGANEL'S CLOTHING TO SEE IF HE WAS INJURED, HE JUMPED UP.
NEVER!
YOU MAY HAVE BROKEN--
YES, BUT THE CARPENTER CAN FIX WHAT I'VE BROKEN.
WHAT'S THAT?
THE STANCHION THAT SNAPPED DURING MY FALL!
HA HA HA HA!

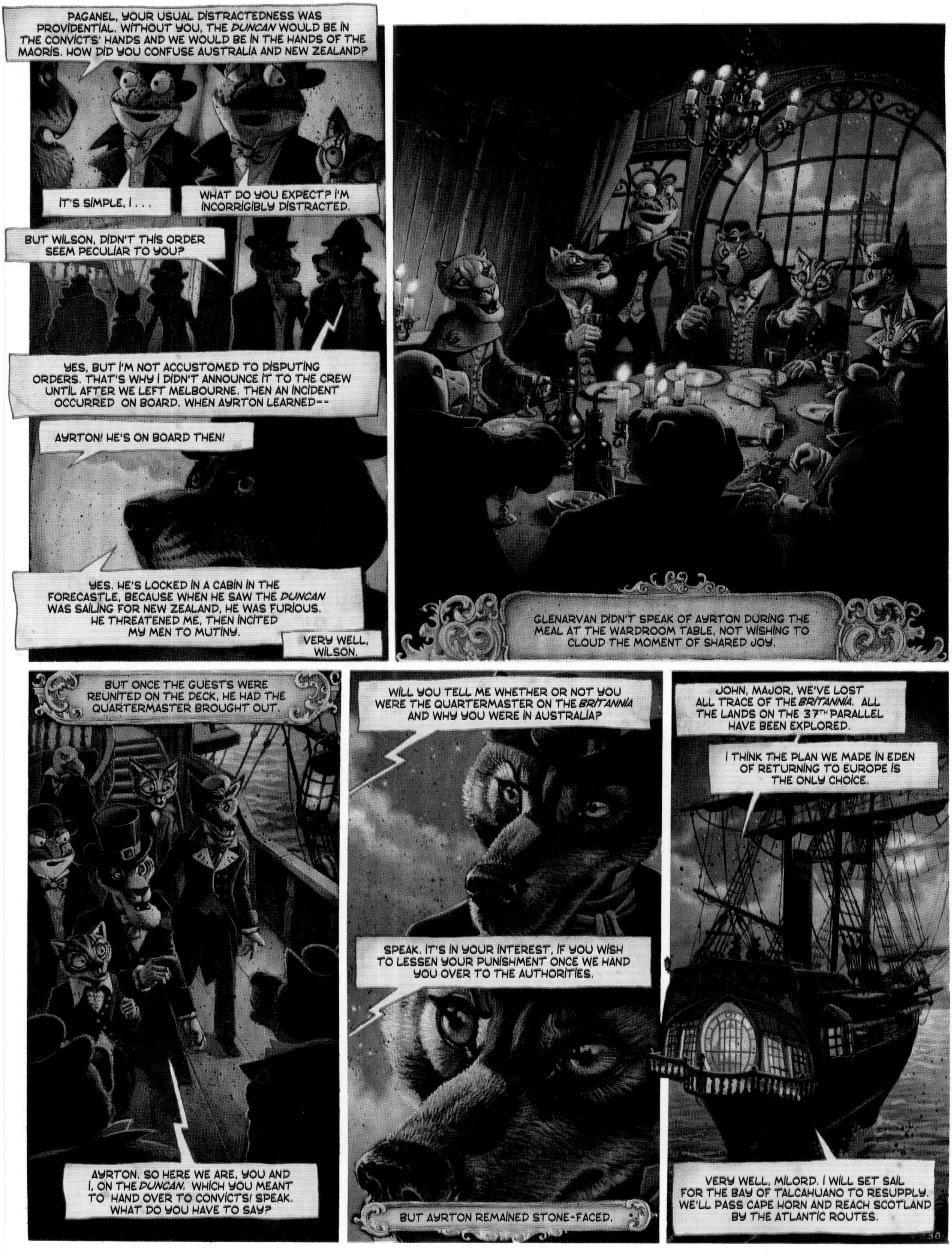
PAGANEL, YOUR USUAL DISTRACTEDNESS WAS PROVIDENTIAL. WITHOUT YOU, THE DUNCAN WOULD BE IN THE CONVICTS' HANDS AND WE WOULD BE IN THE HANDS OF THE MAORIS. HOW DID YOU CONFUSE AUSTRALIA AND NEW ZEALAND?
IT'S SIMPLE, I . . .
WHAT DO YOU EXPECT? I'M INCORRIGIBLY DISTRACTED.
BUT WILSON, DIDN'T THIS ORDER SEEM PECULIAR TO YOU?
YES, BUT I'M NOT ACCUSTOMED TO DISPUTING ORDERS. THAT'S WHY I DIDN'T ANNOUNCE IT TO THE CREW UNTIL AFTER WE LEFT MELBOURNE. THEN AN INCIDENT OCCURRED ON BOARD. WHEN AYRTON LEARNED--
AYRTON! HE'S ON BOARD THEN!
YES. HE'S LOCKED IN A CABIN IN THE FORECASTLE, BECAUSE WHEN HE SAW THE DUNCAN WAS SAILING FOR NEW ZEALAND, HE WAS FURIOUS. HE THREATENED ME, THEN INCITED MY MEN TO MUTINY.
VERY WELL, WILSON.
GLENARVAN DIDN'T SPEAK OF AYRTON DURING THE MEAL AT THE WARDROOM TABLE, NOT WISHING TO CLOUD THE MOMENT OF SHARED JOY.
BUT ONCE THE GUESTS WERE REUNITED ON THE DECK, HE HAD THE QUARTERMASTER BROUGHT OUT.
AYRTON. SO HERE WE ARE, YOU AND I, ON THE DUNCAN. WHICH YOU MEANT TO HAND OVER TO CONVICTS! SPEAK. WHAT DO YOU HAVE TO SAY?
WILL YOU TELL ME WHETHER OR NOT YOU WERE THE QUARTERMASTER ON THE BRITANNIA AND WHY YOU WERE IN AUSTRALIA?
SPEAK. IT'S IN YOUR INTEREST, IF YOU WISH TO LESSEN YOUR PUNISHMENT ONCE WE HAND YOU OVER TO THE AUTHORITIES.
BUT AYRTON REMAINED STONE-FACED.
JOHN, MAJOR, WE'VE LOST ALL TRACE OF THE BRITANNIA. ALL THE LANDS ON THE 37TH PARALLEL HAVE BEEN EXPLORED.
I THINK THE PLAN WE MADE IN EDEN OF RETURNING TO EUROPE IS THE ONLY CHOICE.
VERY WELL, MILORD. I WILL SET SAIL FOR THE BAY OF TALCAHUANO TO RESUPPLY. WE'LL PASS CAPE HORN AND REACH SCOTLAND BY THE ATLANTIC ROUTES.

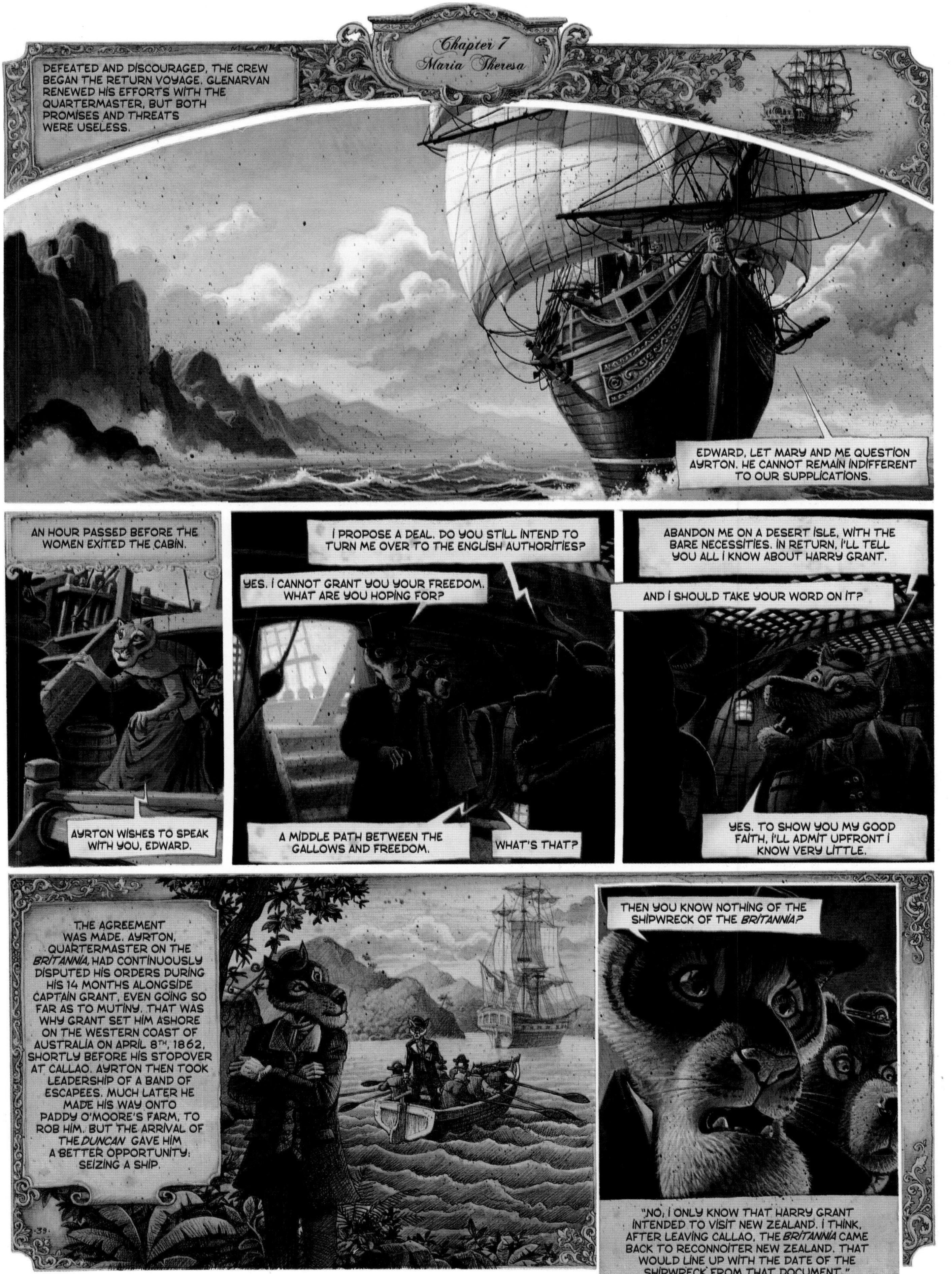
Chapter 7
Maria Theresa
DEFEATED AND DISCOURAGED, THE CREW BEGAN THE RETURN VOYAGE. GLENARVAN RENEWED HIS EFFORTS WITH THE QUARTERMASTER, BUT BOTH PROMISES AND THREATS WERE USELESS.
EDWARD, LET MARY AND ME QUESTION AYRTON. HE CANNOT REMAIN INDIFFERENT TO OUR SUPPLICATIONS.
AN HOUR PASSED BEFORE THE WOMEN EXITED THE CABIN.
AYRTON WISHES TO SPEAK WITH YOU, EDWARD.
I PROPOSE A DEAL. DO YOU STILL INTEND TO TURN ME OVER TO THE ENGLISH AUTHORITIES?
YES. I CANNOT GRANT YOU YOUR FREEDOM. WHAT ARE YOU HOPING FOR?
A MIDDLE PATH BETWEEN THE GALLOWS AND FREEDOM.
WHAT'S THAT?
ABANDON ME ON A DESERT ISLE, WITH THE BARE NECESSITIES. IN RETURN, I'LL TELL YOU ALL I KNOW ABOUT HARRY GRANT.
AND I SHOULD TAKE YOUR WORD ON IT?
YES. TO SHOW YOU MY GOOD FAITH, I'LL ADMIT UPFRONT I KNOW VERY LITTLE.
THE AGREEMENT WAS MADE. AYRTON, QUARTERMASTER ON THE BRITANNIA, HAD CONTINUOUSLY DISPUTED HIS ORDERS DURING HIS 14 MONTHS ALONGSIDE CAPTAIN GRANT, EVEN GOING SO FAR AS TO MUTINY. THAT WAS WHY GRANT SET HIM ASHORE ON THE WESTERN COAST OF AUSTRALIA ON APRIL 8TH, 1862, SHORTLY BEFORE HIS STOPOVER AT CALLAO. AYRTON THEN TOOK LEADERSHIP OF A BAND OF ESCAPEES. MUCH LATER HE MADE HIS WAY ONTO PADDY O'MOORE'S FARM, TO ROB HIM. BUT THE ARRIVAL OF THE DUNCAN GAVE HIM A BETTER OPPORTUNITY: SEIZING A SHIP.
THEN YOU KNOW NOTHING OF THE SHIPWRECK OF THE BRITANNIA?
"NO, I ONLY KNOW THAT HARRY GRANT INTENDED TO VISIT NEW ZEALAND. I THINK, AFTER LEAVING CALLAO, THE BRITANNIA CAME BACK TO RECONNOITER NEW ZEALAND. THAT WOULD LINE UP WITH THE DATE OF THE SHIPWRECK FROM THAT DOCUMENT."
-39-

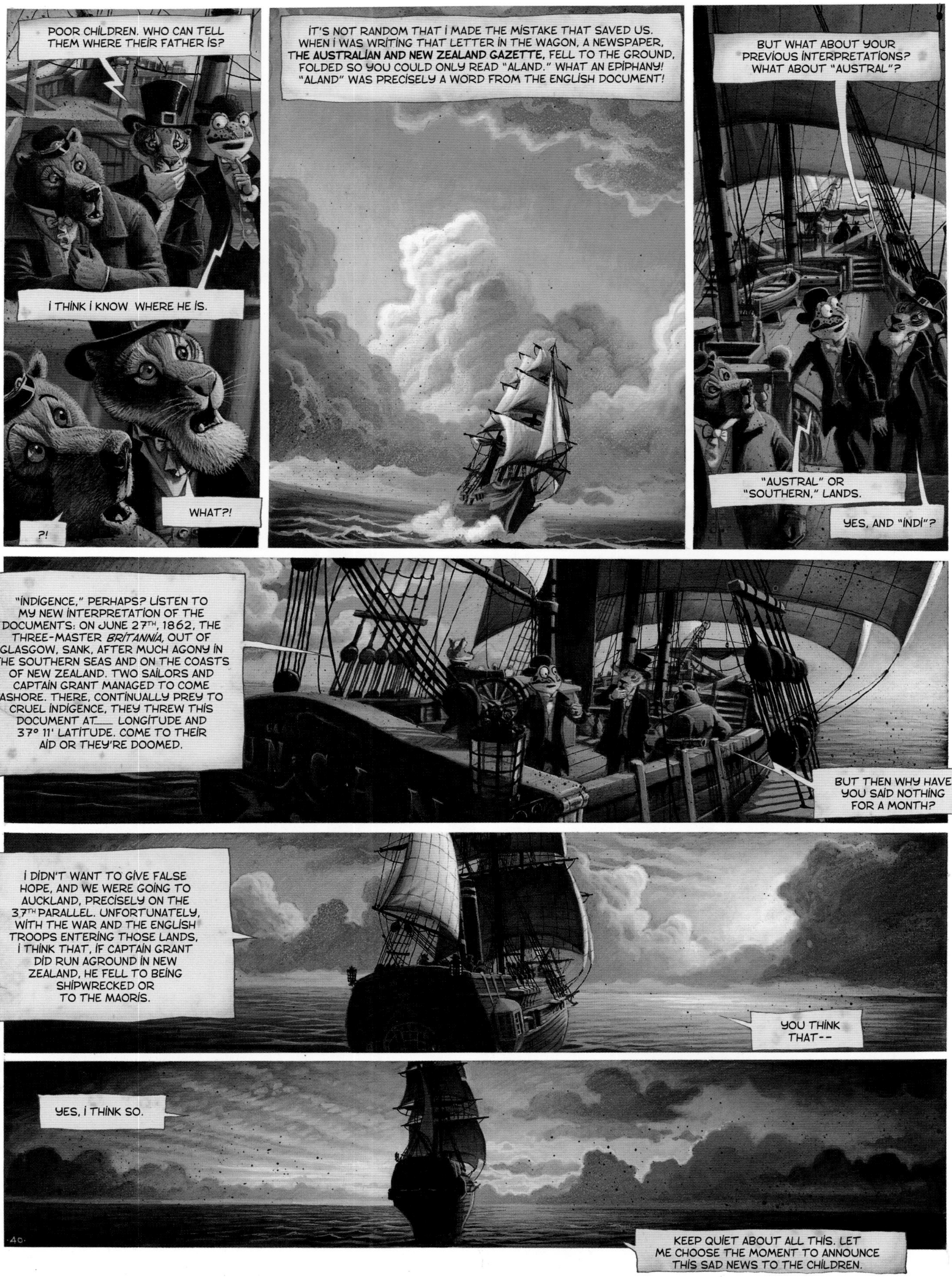
POOR CHILDREN. WHO CAN TELL THEM WHERE THEIR FATHER IS?
I THINK I KNOW WHERE HE IS.
?!
WHAT?!
IT'S NOT RANDOM THAT I MADE THE MISTAKE THAT SAVED US. WHEN I WAS WRITING THAT LETTER IN THE WAGON, A NEWSPAPER, **THE AUSTRALIAN AND NEW ZEALAND GAZETTE,** FELL TO THE GROUND, FOLDED SO YOU COULD ONLY READ "ALAND." WHAT AN EPIPHANY! "ALAND" WAS PRECISELY A WORD FROM THE ENGLISH DOCUMENT!
BUT WHAT ABOUT YOUR PREVIOUS INTERPRETATIONS? WHAT ABOUT "AUSTRAL"?
"AUSTRAL" OR "SOUTHERN," LANDS.
YES, AND "INDI"?
"INDIGENCE," PERHAPS? LISTEN TO MY NEW INTERPRETATION OF THE DOCUMENTS: ON JUNE 27TH, 1862, THE THREE-MASTER *BRITANNIA*, OUT OF GLASGOW, SANK, AFTER MUCH AGONY IN THE SOUTHERN SEAS AND ON THE COASTS OF NEW ZEALAND. TWO SAILORS AND CAPTAIN GRANT MANAGED TO COME ASHORE. THERE, CONTINUALLY PREY TO CRUEL INDIGENCE, THEY THREW THIS DOCUMENT AT___ LONGITUDE AND 37° 11' LATITUDE. COME TO THEIR AID OR THEY'RE DOOMED.
BUT THEN WHY HAVE YOU SAID NOTHING FOR A MONTH?
I DIDN'T WANT TO GIVE FALSE HOPE, AND WE WERE GOING TO AUCKLAND, PRECISELY ON THE 37TH PARALLEL. UNFORTUNATELY, WITH THE WAR AND THE ENGLISH TROOPS ENTERING THOSE LANDS, I THINK THAT, IF CAPTAIN GRANT DID RUN AGROUND IN NEW ZEALAND, HE FELL TO BEING SHIPWRECKED OR TO THE MAORIS.
YOU THINK THAT--
YES, I THINK SO.
KEEP QUIET ABOUT ALL THIS. LET ME CHOOSE THE MOMENT TO ANNOUNCE THIS SAD NEWS TO THE CHILDREN.
·40·

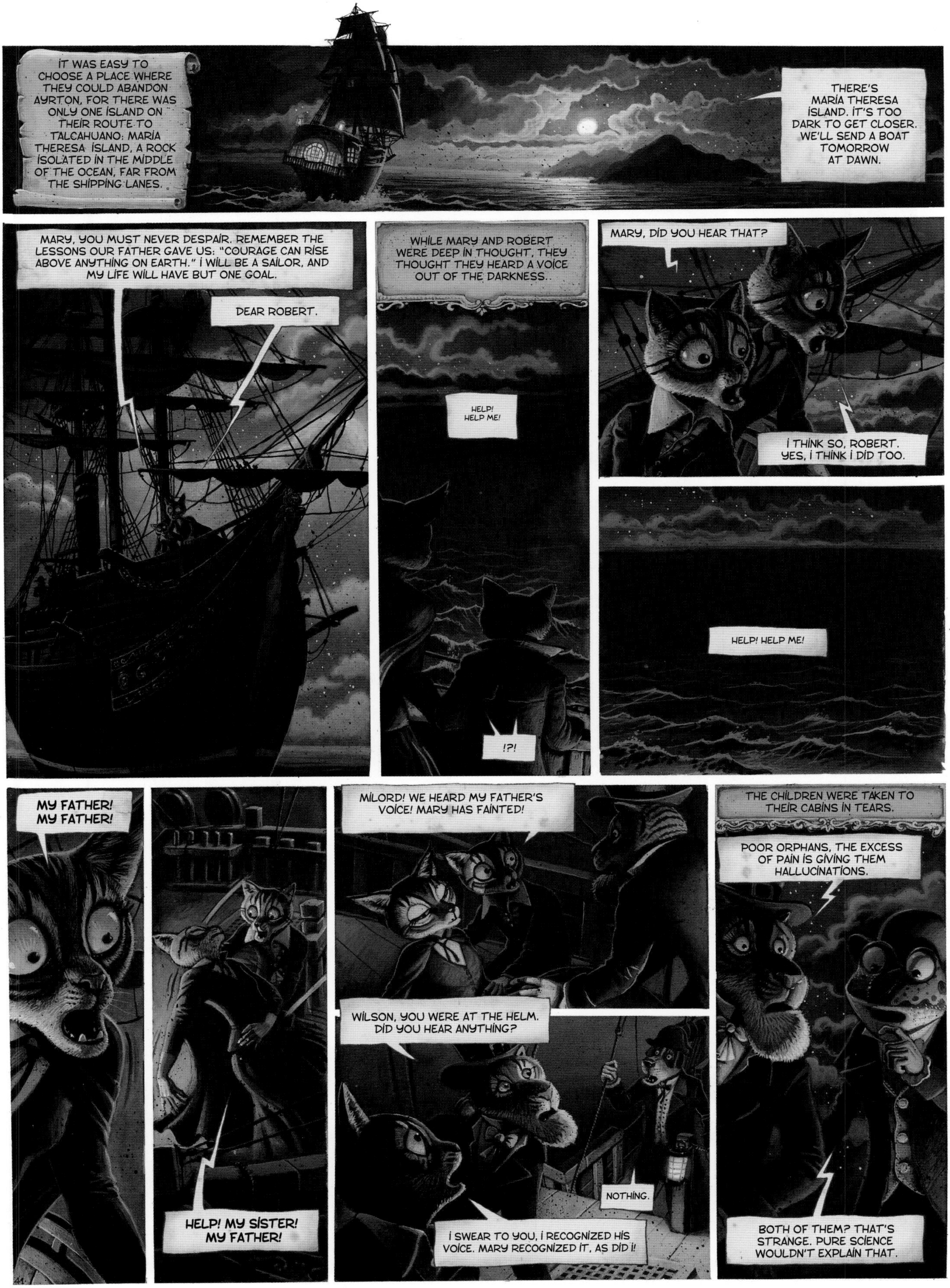
IT WAS EASY TO CHOOSE A PLACE WHERE THEY COULD ABANDON AYRTON, FOR THERE WAS ONLY ONE ISLAND ON THEIR ROUTE TO TALCAHUANO: MARIA THERESA ISLAND, A ROCK ISOLATED IN THE MIDDLE OF THE OCEAN, FAR FROM THE SHIPPING LANES.
THERE'S MARIA THERESA ISLAND. IT'S TOO DARK TO GET CLOSER. WE'LL SEND A BOAT TOMORROW AT DAWN.
MARY, YOU MUST NEVER DESPAIR. REMEMBER THE LESSONS OUR FATHER GAVE US: "COURAGE CAN RISE ABOVE ANYTHING ON EARTH." I WILL BE A SAILOR, AND MY LIFE WILL HAVE BUT ONE GOAL.
DEAR ROBERT.
WHILE MARY AND ROBERT WERE DEEP IN THOUGHT, THEY THOUGHT THEY HEARD A VOICE OUT OF THE DARKNESS.
HELP! HELP ME!
!?!
MARY, DID YOU HEAR THAT?
I THINK SO, ROBERT. YES, I THINK I DID TOO.
HELP! HELP ME!
MY FATHER! MY FATHER!
HELP! MY SISTER! MY FATHER!
MILORD! WE HEARD MY FATHER'S VOICE! MARY HAS FAINTED!
WILSON, YOU WERE AT THE HELM. DID YOU HEAR ANYTHING?
NOTHING.
I SWEAR TO YOU, I RECOGNIZED HIS VOICE. MARY RECOGNIZED IT, AS DID I!
THE CHILDREN WERE TAKEN TO THEIR CABINS IN TEARS.
POOR ORPHANS, THE EXCESS OF PAIN IS GIVING THEM HALLUCINATIONS.
BOTH OF THEM? THAT'S STRANGE. PURE SCIENCE WOULDN'T EXPLAIN THAT.
41

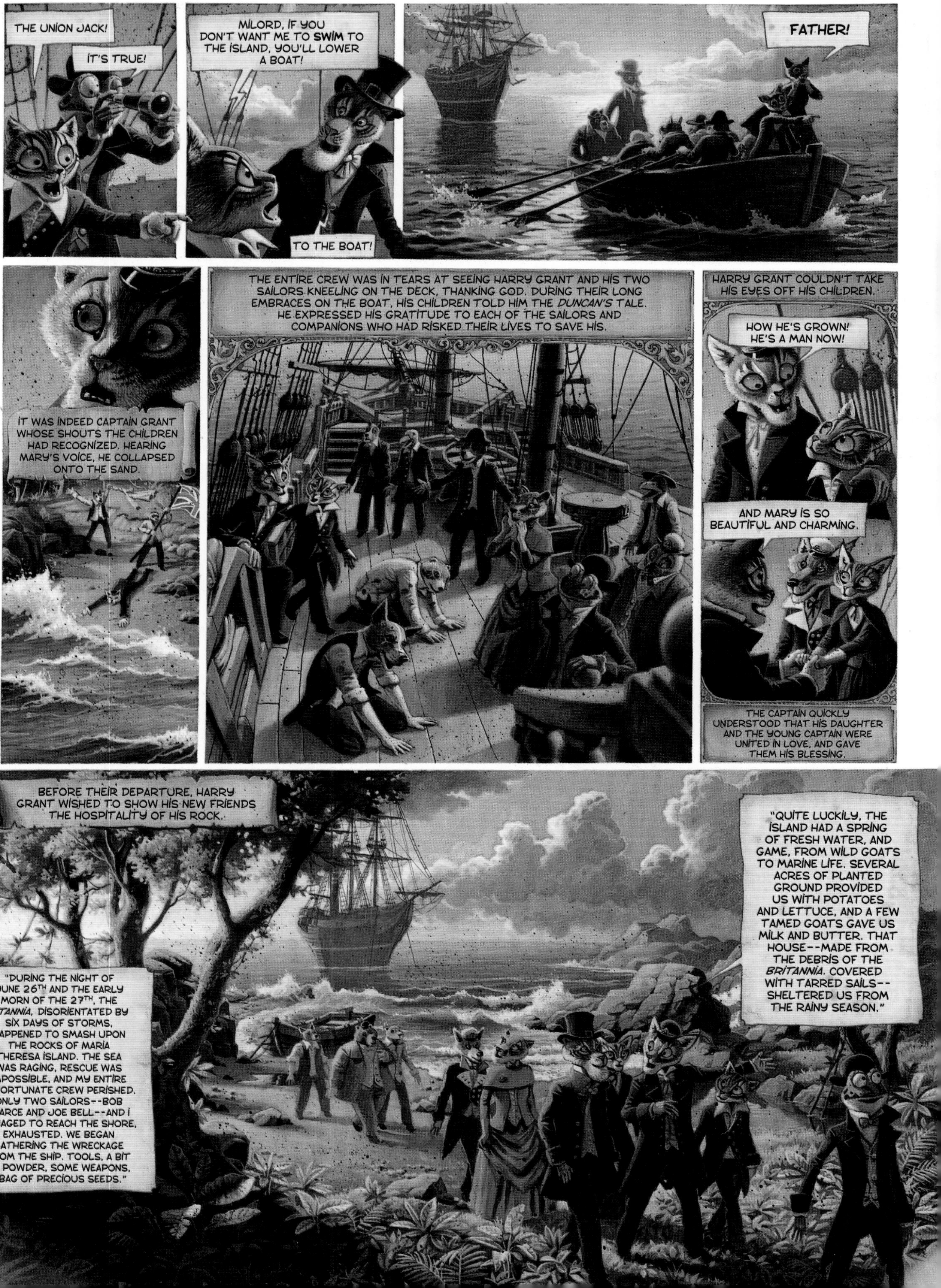
THE UNION JACK!
IT'S TRUE!
MILORD, IF YOU DON'T WANT ME TO **SWIM** TO THE ISLAND, YOU'LL LOWER A BOAT!
TO THE BOAT!
FATHER!
IT WAS INDEED CAPTAIN GRANT WHOSE SHOUTS THE CHILDREN HAD RECOGNIZED. HEARING MARY'S VOICE, HE COLLAPSED ONTO THE SAND.
THE ENTIRE CREW WAS IN TEARS AT SEEING HARRY GRANT AND HIS TWO SAILORS KNEELING ON THE DECK, THANKING GOD. DURING THEIR LONG EMBRACES ON THE BOAT, HIS CHILDREN TOLD HIM THE *DUNCAN'S* TALE. HE EXPRESSED HIS GRATITUDE TO EACH OF THE SAILORS AND COMPANIONS WHO HAD RISKED THEIR LIVES TO SAVE HIS.
HARRY GRANT COULDN'T TAKE HIS EYES OFF HIS CHILDREN.
HOW HE'S GROWN! HE'S A MAN NOW!
AND MARY IS SO BEAUTIFUL AND CHARMING.
THE CAPTAIN QUICKLY UNDERSTOOD THAT HIS DAUGHTER AND THE YOUNG CAPTAIN WERE UNITED IN LOVE, AND GAVE THEM HIS BLESSING.
BEFORE THEIR DEPARTURE, HARRY GRANT WISHED TO SHOW HIS NEW FRIENDS THE HOSPITALITY OF HIS ROCK.
"DURING THE NIGHT OF JUNE 26TH AND THE EARLY MORN OF THE 27TH, THE *BRITANNIA*, DISORIENTATED BY SIX DAYS OF STORMS, HAPPENED TO SMASH UPON THE ROCKS OF MARIA THERESA ISLAND. THE SEA WAS RAGING, RESCUE WAS IMPOSSIBLE, AND MY ENTIRE UNFORTUNATE CREW PERISHED. ONLY TWO SAILORS--BOB LEARCE AND JOE BELL--AND I MANAGED TO REACH THE SHORE, EXHAUSTED. WE BEGAN GATHERING THE WRECKAGE FROM THE SHIP. TOOLS, A BIT OF POWDER, SOME WEAPONS, A BAG OF PRECIOUS SEEDS."
"QUITE LUCKILY, THE ISLAND HAD A SPRING OF FRESH WATER, AND GAME, FROM WILD GOATS TO MARINE LIFE. SEVERAL ACRES OF PLANTED GROUND PROVIDED US WITH POTATOES AND LETTUCE, AND A FEW TAMED GOATS GAVE US MILK AND BUTTER. THAT HOUSE--MADE FROM THE DEBRIS OF THE *BRITANNIA*. COVERED WITH TARRED SAILS--SHELTERED US FROM THE RAINY SEASON."

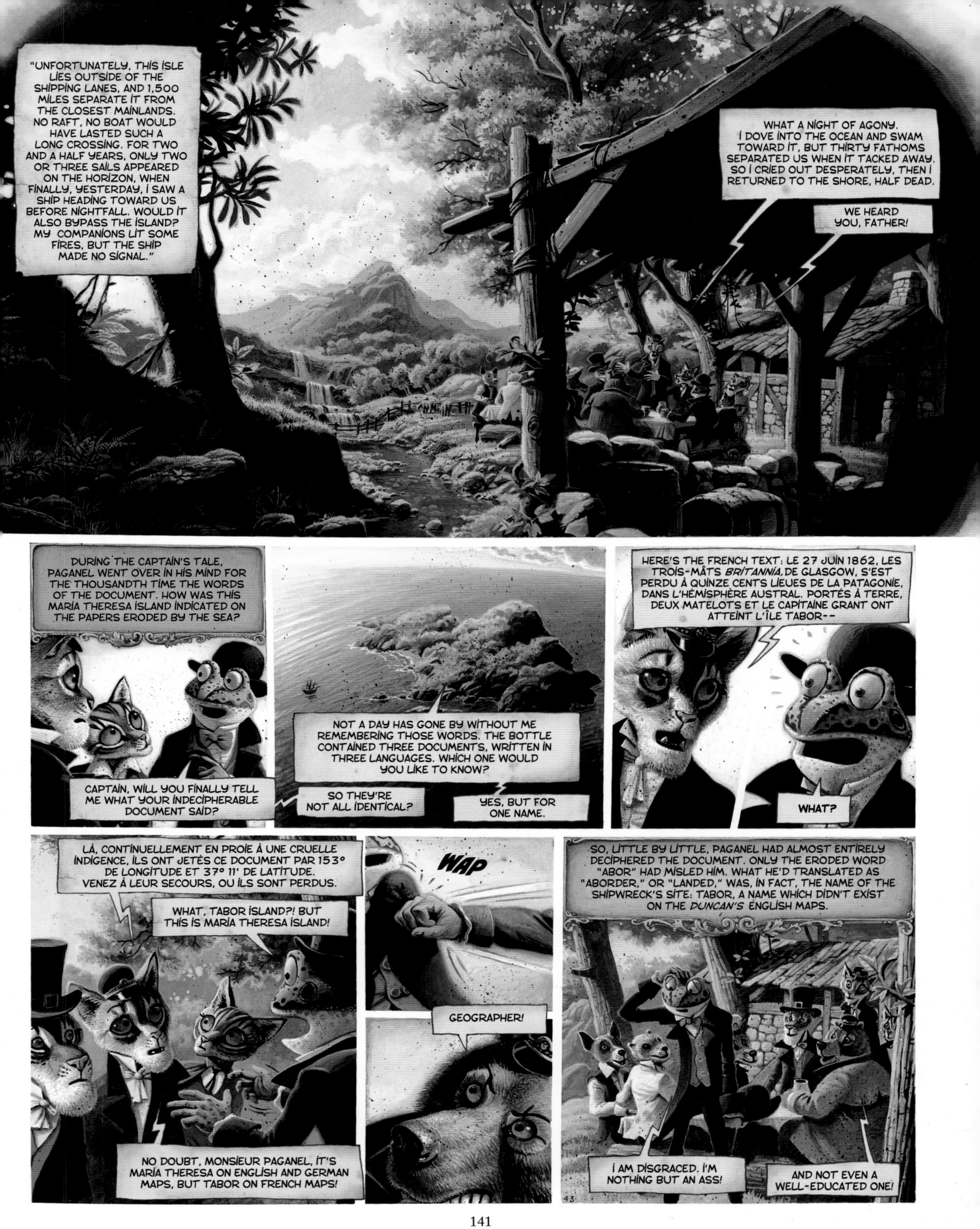
"UNFORTUNATELY, THIS ISLE LIES OUTSIDE OF THE SHIPPING LANES, AND 1,500 MILES SEPARATE IT FROM THE CLOSEST MAINLANDS. NO RAFT, NO BOAT WOULD HAVE LASTED SUCH A LONG CROSSING. FOR TWO AND A HALF YEARS, ONLY TWO OR THREE SAILS APPEARED ON THE HORIZON, WHEN FINALLY, YESTERDAY, I SAW A SHIP HEADING TOWARD US BEFORE NIGHTFALL. WOULD IT ALSO BYPASS THE ISLAND? MY COMPANIONS LIT SOME FIRES, BUT THE SHIP MADE NO SIGNAL."
WHAT A NIGHT OF AGONY. I DOVE INTO THE OCEAN AND SWAM TOWARD IT, BUT THIRTY FATHOMS SEPARATED US WHEN IT TACKED AWAY, SO I CRIED OUT DESPERATELY, THEN I RETURNED TO THE SHORE, HALF DEAD.
WE HEARD YOU, FATHER!
DURING THE CAPTAIN'S TALE, PAGANEL WENT OVER IN HIS MIND FOR THE THOUSANDTH TIME THE WORDS OF THE DOCUMENT. HOW WAS THIS MARIA THERESA ISLAND INDICATED ON THE PAPERS ERODED BY THE SEA?
CAPTAIN, WILL YOU FINALLY TELL ME WHAT YOUR INDECIPHERABLE DOCUMENT SAID?
NOT A DAY HAS GONE BY WITHOUT ME REMEMBERING THOSE WORDS. THE BOTTLE CONTAINED THREE DOCUMENTS, WRITTEN IN THREE LANGUAGES. WHICH ONE WOULD YOU LIKE TO KNOW?
SO THEY'RE NOT ALL IDENTICAL?
YES, BUT FOR ONE NAME.
HERE'S THE FRENCH TEXT: LE 27 JUIN 1862, LES TROIS-MÂTS *BRITANNIA*, DE GLASGOW, S'EST PERDU À QUINZE CENTS LIEUES DE LA PATAGONIE, DANS L'HÉMISPHÈRE AUSTRAL. PORTÉS À TERRE, DEUX MATELOTS ET LE CAPITAINE GRANT ONT ATTEINT L'ÎLE TABOR--
WHAT?
LÀ, CONTINUELLEMENT EN PROIE À UNE CRUELLE INDIGENCE, ILS ONT JETÉS CE DOCUMENT PAR 153° DE LONGITUDE ET 37° 11' DE LATITUDE. VENEZ À LEUR SECOURS, OU ILS SONT PERDUS.
WHAT, TABOR ISLAND?! BUT THIS IS MARIA THERESA ISLAND!
NO DOUBT, MONSIEUR PAGANEL, IT'S MARIA THERESA ON ENGLISH AND GERMAN MAPS, BUT TABOR ON FRENCH MAPS!
WAP
GEOGRAPHER!
SO, LITTLE BY LITTLE, PAGANEL HAD ALMOST ENTIRELY DECIPHERED THE DOCUMENT. ONLY THE ERODED WORD "ABOR" HAD MISLED HIM. WHAT HE'D TRANSLATED AS "ABORDER," OR "LANDED," WAS, IN FACT, THE NAME OF THE SHIPWRECK'S SITE: TABOR, A NAME WHICH DIDN'T EXIST ON THE *DUNCAN'S* ENGLISH MAPS.
I AM DISGRACED. I'M NOTHING BUT AN ASS!
AND NOT EVEN A WELL-EDUCATED ONE!
43

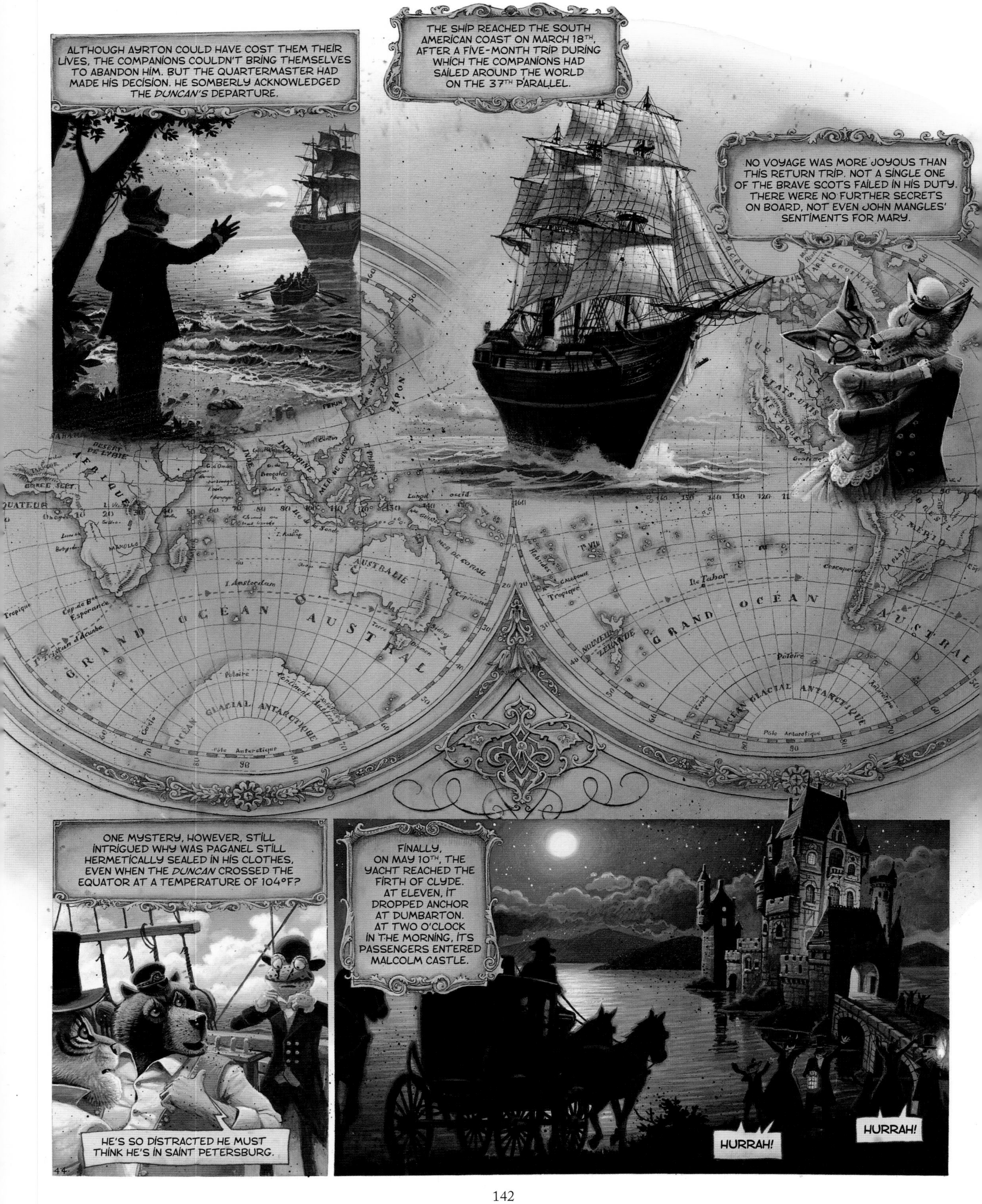

ALTHOUGH AYRTON COULD HAVE COST THEM THEIR LIVES, THE COMPANIONS COULDN'T BRING THEMSELVES TO ABANDON HIM. BUT THE QUARTERMASTER HAD MADE HIS DECISION. HE SOMBERLY ACKNOWLEDGED THE *DUNCAN'S* DEPARTURE.
THE SHIP REACHED THE SOUTH AMERICAN COAST ON MARCH 18TH, AFTER A FIVE-MONTH TRIP DURING WHICH THE COMPANIONS HAD SAILED AROUND THE WORLD ON THE 37TH PARALLEL.
NO VOYAGE WAS MORE JOYOUS THAN THIS RETURN TRIP. NOT A SINGLE ONE OF THE BRAVE SCOTS FAILED IN HIS DUTY. THERE WERE NO FURTHER SECRETS ON BOARD, NOT EVEN JOHN MANGLES' SENTIMENTS FOR MARY.
AUSTRALIE
GRAND OCÉAN AUSTRAL
OCÉAN GLACIAL ANTARCTIQUE
GRAND OCÉAN AUSTRAL
OCÉAN GLACIAL ANTARCTIQUE
ONE MYSTERY, HOWEVER, STILL INTRIGUED WHY WAS PAGANEL STILL HERMETICALLY SEALED IN HIS CLOTHES, EVEN WHEN THE *DUNCAN* CROSSED THE EQUATOR AT A TEMPERATURE OF 104°F?
HE'S SO DISTRACTED HE MUST THINK HE'S IN SAINT PETERSBURG.
44
FINALLY, ON MAY 10TH, THE YACHT REACHED THE FIRTH OF CLYDE. AT ELEVEN, IT DROPPED ANCHOR AT DUMBARTON. AT TWO O'CLOCK IN THE MORNING, ITS PASSENGERS ENTERED MALCOLM CASTLE.
HURRAH!
HURRAH!

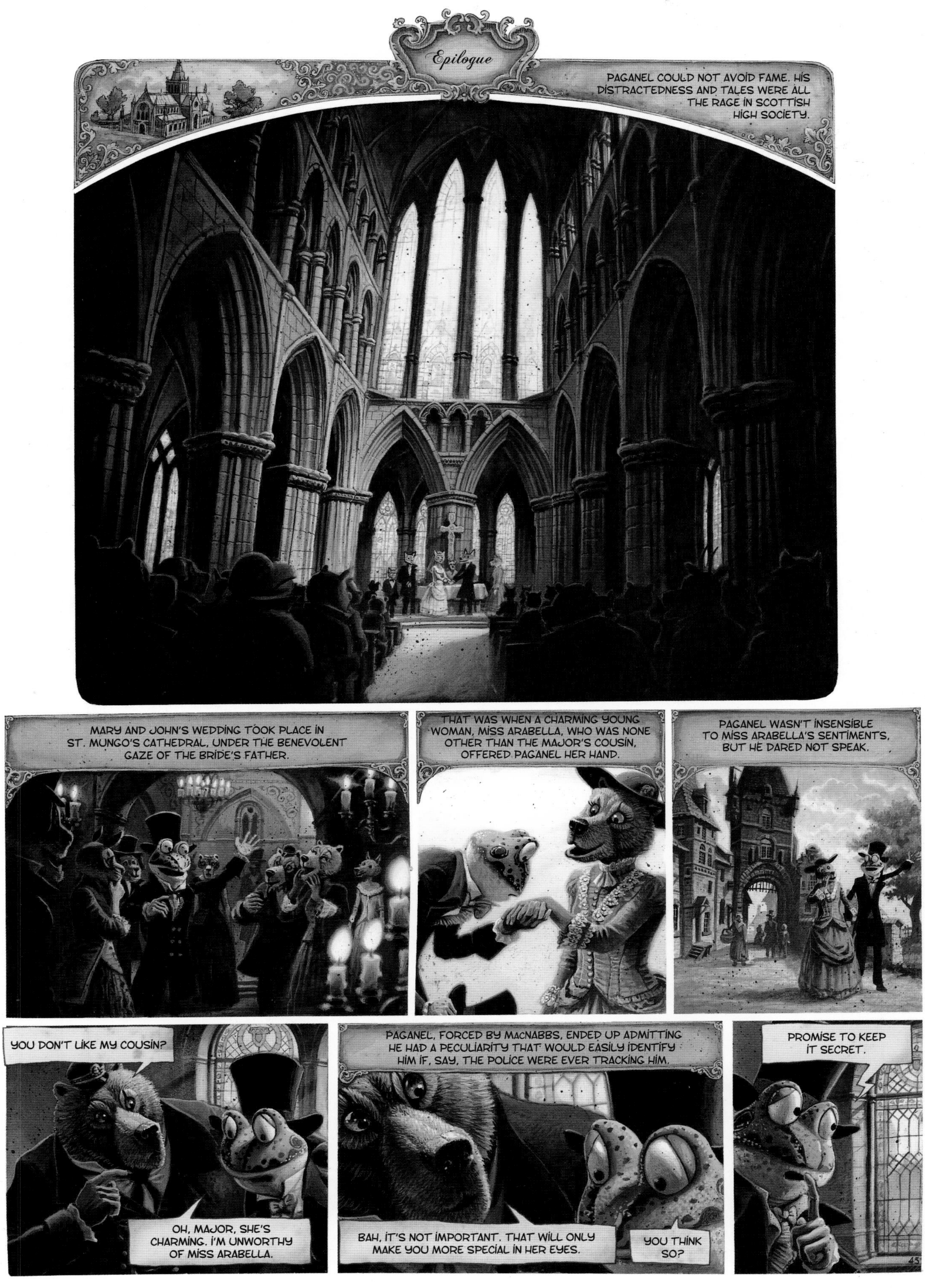
Epilogue
PAGANEL COULD NOT AVOID FAME. HIS DISTRACTEDNESS AND TALES WERE ALL THE RAGE IN SCOTTISH HIGH SOCIETY.
MARY AND JOHN'S WEDDING TOOK PLACE IN ST. MUNGO'S CATHEDRAL, UNDER THE BENEVOLENT GAZE OF THE BRIDE'S FATHER.
THAT WAS WHEN A CHARMING YOUNG WOMAN, MISS ARABELLA, WHO WAS NONE OTHER THAN THE MAJOR'S COUSIN, OFFERED PAGANEL HER HAND.
PAGANEL WASN'T INSENSIBLE TO MISS ARABELLA'S SENTIMENTS, BUT HE DARED NOT SPEAK.
YOU DON'T LIKE MY COUSIN?
OH, MAJOR, SHE'S CHARMING. I'M UNWORTHY OF MISS ARABELLA.
PAGANEL, FORCED BY MACNABBS, ENDED UP ADMITTING HE HAD A PECULIARITY THAT WOULD EASILY IDENTIFY HIM IF, SAY, THE POLICE WERE EVER TRACKING HIM.
BAH, IT'S NOT IMPORTANT. THAT WILL ONLY MAKE YOU MORE SPECIAL IN HER EYES.
YOU THINK SO?
PROMISE TO KEEP IT SECRET.

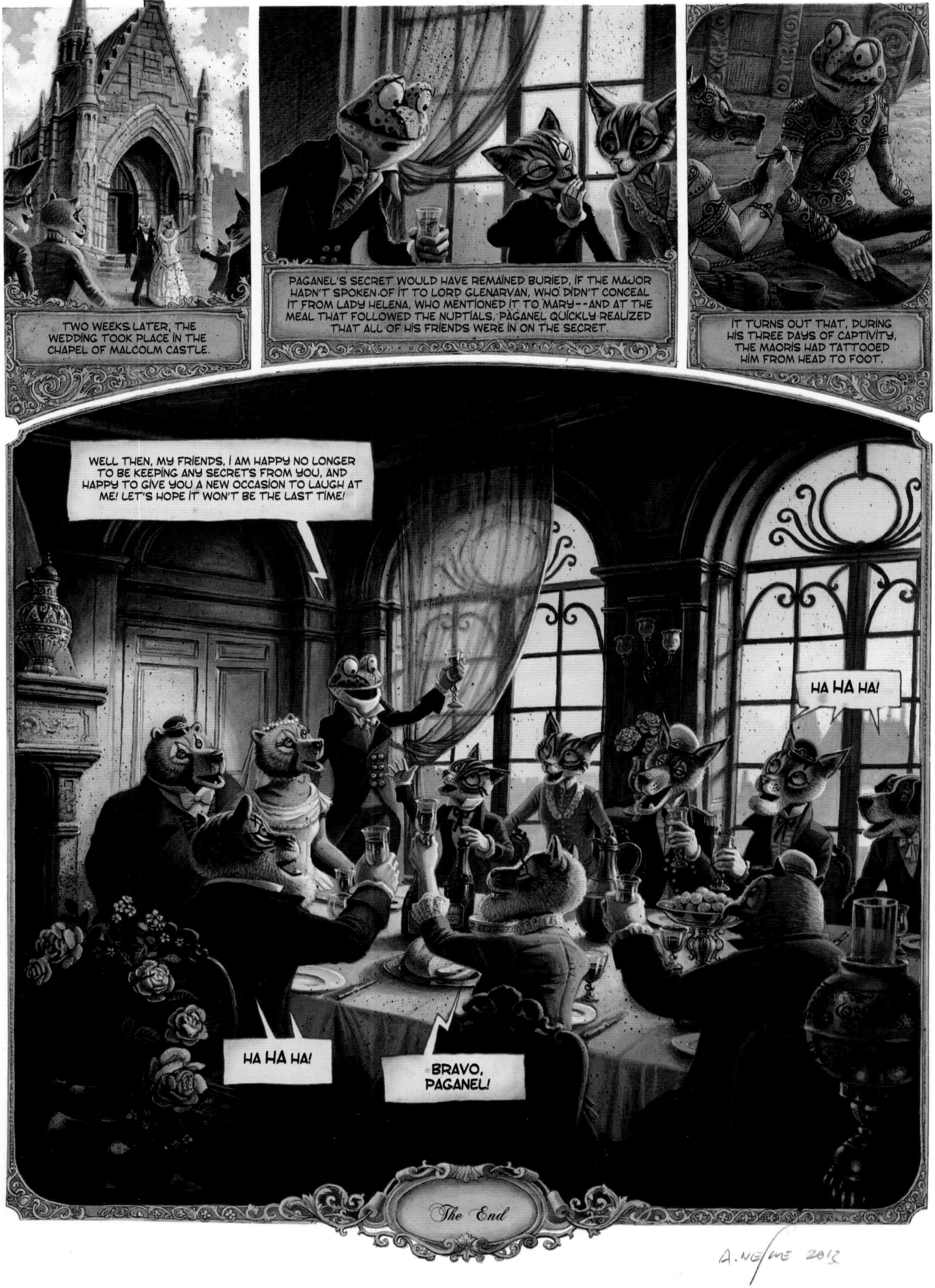
TWO WEEKS LATER, THE WEDDING TOOK PLACE IN THE CHAPEL OF MALCOLM CASTLE.
PAGANEL'S SECRET WOULD HAVE REMAINED BURIED, IF THE MAJOR HADN'T SPOKEN OF IT TO LORD GLENARVAN, WHO DIDN'T CONCEAL IT FROM LADY HELENA, WHO MENTIONED IT TO MARY--AND AT THE MEAL THAT FOLLOWED THE NUPTIALS, PAGANEL QUICKLY REALIZED THAT ALL OF HIS FRIENDS WERE IN ON THE SECRET.
IT TURNS OUT THAT, DURING HIS THREE DAYS OF CAPTIVITY, THE MAORIS HAD TATTOOED HIM FROM HEAD TO FOOT.
WELL THEN, MY FRIENDS, I AM HAPPY NO LONGER TO BE KEEPING ANY SECRETS FROM YOU, AND HAPPY TO GIVE YOU A NEW OCCASION TO LAUGH AT ME! LET'S HOPE IT WON'T BE THE LAST TIME!
HA HA HA!
HA HA HA!
BRAVO, PAGANEL!
The End

A. NESME 2013